Hegel's Concept of Life

Hegel's Concept of Life

Self-Consciousness, Freedom, Logic

KAREN NG

OXFORD
UNIVERSITY PRESS

OXFORD
UNIVERSITY PRESS

Oxford University Press is a department of the University of Oxford. It furthers
the University's objective of excellence in research, scholarship, and education
by publishing worldwide. Oxford is a registered trade mark of Oxford University
Press in the UK and certain other countries.

Published in the United States of America by Oxford University Press
198 Madison Avenue, New York, NY 10016, United States of America.

Library of Congress Cataloging-in-Publication Data
Names: Ng, Karen (Karen K.), author.
Title: Hegel's concept of life : self-consciousness, freedom, logic / Karen Ng.
Description: New York, NY : Oxford University Press, [2020] |
Includes bibliographical references. |
Identifiers: LCCN 2019036521 (print) | LCCN 2019036522 (ebook) |
ISBN 9780190947613 (hardback) | ISBN 9780190947644 (epub) |
ISBN 9780190947620 (online) | ISBN 9780190947637 (updf)
Subjects: LCSH: Hegel, Georg Wilhelm Friedrich, 1770–1831. |
Hegel, Georg Wilhelm Friedrich, 1770–1831. Wissenschaft der Logik. |
Self-consciousness (Awareness) | Life. | Logic, Modern. |
Kant, Immanuel, 1724–1804. Kritik der Urteilskraft.
Classification: LCC B2948 .N494 2020 (print) |
LCC B2948 (ebook) | DDC 193—dc23
LC record available at https://lccn.loc.gov/2019036521
LC ebook record available at https://lccn.loc.gov/2019036522

To my parents, with love

Contents

Acknowledgments

My greatest gratitude goes to Jay Bernstein for his unfailing support and wisdom from the very beginning of this project. Jay read and commented on the entire manuscript and its earlier iteration in the form of a dissertation. I am beyond fortunate to have had him as a teacher, and his example continues to guide my philosophical thinking and practice. I owe a great deal of thanks to Richard Bernstein, whose unforgettable graduate seminar at The New School for Social Research first guided me through a reading of the *Science of Logic*. I also want to express my deepest gratitude to Frederick Neuhouser, whose input and support has been invaluable.

Dean Moyar and Terry Pinkard read the whole manuscript, and I am immensely grateful to them for their insight and comments. Their criticisms no doubt made the book better, but errors are of course my own. Christoph Menke lent critical insight concerning absolute method at an early stage. Andreja Novakovic and Rocío Zambrana discussed many of these ideas with me, as did Thomas Khurana and Dirk Quadflieg. For conversations and other support or assistance, thanks to G. Anthony Bruno, Markus Gabriel, Kristin Gjesdal, Axel Honneth, Daniel James, Jim Kreines, Paul Redding, Kelly Swope, and Clinton Tolley. I want to thank my former colleagues at Siena College, and I owe a deep thanks to my colleagues at Vanderbilt for an always stimulating philosophical environment and for continually supporting my work. I also want to thank Vanderbilt for support during a research leave, when much of the writing for this book was completed. The students in my graduate seminar on German idealism in spring 2016 allowed me to work through many ideas at a crucial stage. I owe them thanks for many important and helpful discussions. I am always grateful for the philosophical engagement and hospitality of Rahel Jaeggi, and I owe gratitude to the Center for Humanities and Social Change in Berlin for a research fellowship in 2018. I am very fortunate to have dear friends who supported me in a number of ways while completing this project, including Jacob Blumenfeld, Brendan Fernandes, Federica Gregoratto, Hilkje Hänel, Donny Hodge, Tom Krell, Francey Russell, Fanny Söderback, and Janna van Grunsven.

Portions of chapter 4 appear in "From Actuality to Concept in Hegel's *Logic*," in *The Oxford Handbook of Hegel*. Thanks to Oxford for permission to reprint these parts. I owe thanks to Lucy Randall at OUP for her expert editorial assistance, and also to Kelly Swope for his work on the index.

This book is dedicated to my parents, whose unconditional love and care have made me who I am. Matt Congdon's spirit, wit, and love sustain life daily, preventing it from becoming a realm of shadows.

Abbreviations

Throughout this study, I provide page references, first to the English and then to the German editions of primary texts, separated by a slash (/). Translations have occasionally been modified without notice. Unless otherwise noted, italics in quoted materials appear in the original. "Concept" (*der Begriff*) and "Idea" (*die Idee*) are capitalized throughout when referring to Hegel's technical use of these two terms. This practice has been adopted only to distinguish between technical and nontechnical uses of these terms, both of which appear frequently in this study.

Hegel

In German, Hegel's texts are cited by volume and page number from *Werke in zwanzig Bänden*, edited by Eva Moldenhauer and Karl Markus Michel (Frankfurt am Main: Suhrkamp Verlag, 1969–1970). References to the three volumes of the *Encyclopaedia* and the *Philosophy of Right* are cited by section number, and where appropriate, followed by a remark (A = *Anmerkung*) or addition (Z = *Zusatz*). I have also consulted and sometimes employed Miller's translations of Hegel's *Phenomenology* (1977) and *Science of Logic* (1969). Otherwise, the following translations have been used:

DS   *The Difference Between Fichte's and Schelling's System of Philosophy*. 1977. Translated by H. S. Harris and Walter Cerf. Albany: SUNY Press.

EL   *The Encyclopaedia Logic, Part I of the Encyclopaedia of the Philosophical Sciences with the Zusätze*. 1991. Translated by T. F. Geraets, W. A. Suchting, and H. S. Harris. Indianapolis, IN: Hackett.

GW   *Faith and Knowledge*. 1977. Translated by Walter Cerf and H. S. Harris. Albany: SUNY Press.

PG   *Hegel's Philosophy of Mind: Translated from the 1830 Edition, together with the Zusätze*. 2007. Translated by W. Wallace and A. V. Miller, revised by M. J. Inwood. Oxford: Oxford University Press.

PhG   *Phenomenology of Spirit*. 2018. Translated by Terry Pinkard. Cambridge: Cambridge University Press (cited by paragraph number [¶]).

PN   *Philosophy of Nature: Part Two of the Encyclopaedia of the Philosophical Sciences (1830)*. 1970. Translated by A. V. Miller. Oxford: Oxford University Press.

PR   *Elements of the Philosophy of Right*. 1991. Translated by H. B. Nisbet, edited by Allen W. Wood. Cambridge: Cambridge University Press.

VGP   *Lectures on the History of Philosophy*, 3 volumes. 1995. Translated by E. S. Haldane and F. H. Simson. Lincoln: University of Nebraska Press (cited by volume and page number).

WL   *Science of Logic*. 2010. Translated by George di Giovanni. Cambridge: Cambridge University Press.

Kant

References to Kant are cited by volume and page number of the *Akademie* edition of *Kants gesammelte Schriften*. I have also made reference to Kant's German texts from *Werke in zwölf Bänden*, edited by Wilhelm Weischedel (Frankfurt: Suhrkamp Verlag, 1968). The *Critique of Pure Reason* is cited by the pagination of the first (A) and second (B) editions in the standard manner. I have consulted and sometimes employed Pluhar's translation of Kant's *Critique of Judgment* (1987). Otherwise, the following English translations have been used:

A/B   *Critique of Pure Reason*. 2003. Translated by Norman Kemp Smith. New York: Palgrave Macmillan.

EE   First Introduction to *Critique of the Power of Judgment*. 2000. Translated by Paul Guyer and Eric Matthews. Cambridge: Cambridge University Press.

JL   *The Jäsche Logic*. 1992. In *Lectures on Logic*, translated and edited by J. Michael Young. Cambridge: Cambridge University Press.

KpV   *Critique of Practical Reason*. 1997. Translated by Mary Gregor. Cambridge: Cambridge University Press.

KU   *Critique of the Power of Judgment*. 2000. Translated by Paul Guyer and Eric Matthews. Cambridge: Cambridge University Press.

MN   *Metaphysical Foundations of Natural Science*. 2004. Translated and edited by Michael Friedman. Cambridge: Cambridge University Press.

TP   *On the Use of Teleological Principles in Philosophy*. 2007. In *Anthropology, History, and Education*, edited by Günther Zöller. Cambridge: Cambridge University Press.

Fichte

In German, Fichte's texts are cited by volume and page number from *Fichtes Sammtilche Werke*, edited by I. H. Fichte (Berlin: W. de Gruyter). The following English translations have been used:

GNR   *Foundations of Natural Right According to the Principles of the Wissenschaftslehre*. 2000. Translated by Michael Baur and edited by Frederick Neuhouser. Cambridge: Cambridge University Press.

GWL   *The Science of Knowledge*. 1982. Translated and edited by Peter Heath and John Lachs. Cambridge: Cambridge University Press.

SL   *System of Ethics According to the Principles of the Wissenschaftslehre*. 2005. Translated and edited by Daniel Breazeale and Günter Zöller. Cambridge: Cambridge University Press.

ZEWL   *Second Introduction to the Science of Knowledge for Readers Who already have a Philosophical System*. 1982. Translated and edited by Peter Heath and John Lachs. Cambridge: Cambridge University Press.

Schelling

In German, Schelling's texts are cited by page number from *Friedrich Wilhelm Joseph Schelling: Historisch-kritische Ausgabe*, edited by Jörg Jantzen, Thomas Buchheim, Wilhelm G. Jacobs, and Siegbert Peetz (Stuttgart: Frommann-Holzboog, 1976–) (HkA) and from *Friedrich Wilhelm Joseph Schellings sämmtliche Werke*, edited by K. F. A. Schelling (Stuttgart: Cotta, 1856–1861) (SW). The following English translations have been used:

EEN   "Introduction to the Outline of a System of the Philosophy of Nature, or, On the Concept of Speculative Physics and the Internal Organization of a System of this Science." 2004. In *First Outline of a System of the Philosophy of Nature*, translated by Keith R. Peterson. Albany: SUNY Press. (HkA volume I, 8)

IPN   *Ideas for a Philosophy of Nature*. 1988. Translated by Errol E. Harris and Peter Heath. Cambridge: Cambridge University Press. (HkA volume I, 13)

SI   *System of Transcendental Idealism*. 1978. Translated by Peter Heath. Charlottesville: University Press of Virginia. (SW volume 3)

PART I
THINKING PURPOSIVENESS
FROM KANT TO HEGEL

1

Introduction

Hegel's Concept of Life

There is a central, recurring rhetorical device that Hegel returns to again and again throughout his philosophical system: that of describing the activity of reason and thought in terms of the dynamic activity and development of organic life. On closer inspection, it is evident that Hegel means for us to take his descriptions quite literally, that he means to suggest not that reason is *like* life but that reason *is* a dynamic, living activity in constant development. To leave no doubt as to its central role in his understanding of reason and thought, Hegel not only includes the category of life in his *Science of Logic*, a move as "scandalous" as it is mysterious, but moreover, its specific placement within that text suggests that it plays a foundational role for his entire philosophical system, forming an essential part of his philosophical method.[1] The aim of this book is to understand the concept of life in Hegel's philosophy and to argue that it plays a constitutive, systematic role in how he conceives of the activities of reason and thought. In particular, I focus on Hegel's presentation of a distinctly philosophical, and ultimately, *logical* concept of life that finds its full expression in the *Science of Logic*, the significance of which reverberates throughout Hegel's entire system. What leads Hegel to return again and again to the concept of life in the presentation of his core philosophical ideas concerning self-consciousness, freedom, and logical form? In what sense is life constitutive of reasoning activities, and what exactly does it contribute to the overall project of a critique of reason? What does it mean to say that life is a philosophical, or even a *logical*, concept, and how does this change the way we conceive of Hegel's idealism? Why is the concept of life an orienting focus of Hegel's philosophy, and how might such an orienting focus be defended?

---

[1] Thompson (2008, 25) refers to Hegel's inclusion of life in his system of logical categories as "scandalous."

Hegel's Concept of Life. Karen Ng, Oxford University Press (2020) © Oxford University Press 2020.
DOI: 10.1093/oso/9780190947613.001.0001

It is now widely acknowledged that Hegel's philosophy combines a distinctive strand of Aristotelian naturalism with core insights from Kant's
transcendental idealism, incorporating concepts of teleology and function
alongside conceptions of self-consciousness and freedom.[2] Far from idiosyncratic, Hegel's orientation in the concept of life can be viewed as part of
a long philosophical tradition in which explaining the distinctive features of
organic activity was an essential and constitutive part of the philosophical
task of explaining ourselves.[3] In the wake of the many questions left open
by Kant's critical project—the sticky issue of the thing-in-itself, Kant's dialectic and the impossibility of reconciling freedom and necessity, the unde-
veloped yet all-important idea of self-consciousness—I argue that Hegel's
most sustained and original contribution to the post-Kantian context was
to suggest that the idealist project cannot be completely and coherently articulated without a systematic accounting of life's essential and constitutive
role in the processes and activities of absolute knowing, that idealism itself
as a philosophical program stands or falls depending on whether or not it
can successfully integrate a concept of life into its core philosophical ideas.
For Hegel, integrating a philosophical concept of life as a constitutive feature of the idealist program provides an answer to the three problems
signaled in the subtitle of this book: the problem of self-consciousness and its
status as an absolute ground of knowledge; the problem of freedom or self-
determination, and how this form of activity is compatible with and actual in
the order of nature; and finally, the problem of logical form, and more specifically, the problem of transcendental logic as inherited from Kant, where
there is an a priori unity, identity, and synthesis between concept and object

---

[2] Recently, Pinkard (2012) has perhaps been the most forceful defender of Hegel as a "disenchanted
Aristotelian naturalist." Wood (1990, 33) referred to Hegel's ethical theory in terms of a "dialectical
or *historicized naturalism*." Hegel's naturalism has been a topic of much discussion, and the tide has
turned from viewing Hegel's rationalism as a commitment to anti-naturalism, from viewing Hegel
as holding a variety of naturalist commitments. Although Hegel's distinctive position is not easy to
square with contemporary understandings of naturalism, see, for example, the discussions by Beiser
(2005), Ikäheimo (2012), Khurana (2013a, 2013b, 2017), Ng (2018a, 2019), Papazoglou (2012),
Peters (2016), Stone (2013), and Testa (2013). For a forceful defense of Hegel and German idealism as
committed to anti-naturalism, and an argument that "liberal" naturalism is an unstable position, see
Gardner (2007, 2011).

[3] On the importance of life for early modern philosophy, see Nachtomy and Smith, who write that
"what we today think of as questions of the life sciences were in fact *constitutive* of what early modern
philosophers themselves thought of as philosophy. This is, or ought to be, beyond any historical
doubt" (2014, 6). On the language of living nature and how it thoroughly permeated the discourse of
the Enlightenment, see Reill (2005) and Gaukroger (2010). On the significance of the life sciences for
Leibniz's philosophy, see Smith (2011). On Kant's theory of cognition as thoroughly "organicist" and
informed by epigenesist conceptions of generation, see Mensch (2013) and Sloan (2002).

such that concepts can be identified as the essential form of an object in general. More specifically, Hegel provides answers to these problems by means of what he calls *the Concept (der Begriff)*, but Hegel's theory of the Concept cannot be coherently presented or defended without reference to the constitutive and positive role played by the concept of life. That a philosophical, and ultimately, logical concept of life provides a solution to these three problems is one of Hegel's most original contributions to the German idealist context, or so I will argue in what follows. Although there is increasing recognition of the importance of the concept of life for Hegel's philosophy,[4] its essential role in Hegel's idealism has generally been underappreciated or not fully understood—problems that I hope to begin to correct over the course of this study.

In order to provide a systematic account of the concept of life, this study will defend three interrelated claims. The first is that the core tenets of Hegel's philosophy, and particularly those that concern his concept of the Concept, center on the *purposiveness theme*, inherited from Kant's *Critique of Judgment* (1790).[5] In the third *Critique*, a text that is considered by many to be the key for the development of post-Kantian

---

[4] Full-length studies that focus on Hegel's concept of life include works by Marcuse (1987), whose classic text argues, from a Heideggerian/Marxian perspective, that the investigation into the historicity of being must be grasped into terms of the historicity and activity of life; Hahn (2007), who argues for the centrality of contradiction in Hegel's theory of the organism, demonstrating the importance of this theory for Hegel's understanding of ethical and aesthetic value; and Sell (2013), who takes a historical, systematic, and largely exegetical approach, demonstrating the Aristotelian, Kantian, and Schellingian roots of Hegel's concept of life, and arguing that the logical Concept must be understood as "living" in a non-naturalistic sense insofar as it displays a subject-object and form-content unity, as well as self-actualizing form. For the purposes of my argument, the most important full-length study is by Khurana (2017), who argues that the genesis, form, and actuality of freedom in Hegel can all be traced to the determination of life. Khurana's account also traces Hegel's understanding of the problem of life to Kant's third *Critique*, in which, Khurana argues, Kant demonstrates that life and autonomy are analogous forms. Insofar as Khurana is interested in Hegel's concept of freedom and his practical philosophy, he focuses primarily on the relation between nature and spirit, and thus, on Hegel's *Philosophy of Nature* and *Philosophy of Mind*. I am very sympathetic to Khurana's account, but my primary focus will be the concept of life in Hegel's *Science of Logic*, and my investigation of other relevant texts ultimately aims at understanding Hegel's *Logic*. Other recent full-length studies in which life and teleology play a central role include those by Yeomans (2012), who argues that Hegel's account of teleology in the *Logic* provides an account of Hegel's philosophy of action and freedom of the will, in opposition to arguments in favor of determinism; and Kreines (2015), who argues that life and teleology play a central role in Hegel's theory of explanation, and thus, his metaphysics. For more general accounts of Hegel's logical concept of life, see also Greene (1980), Düsing (1986b), Sell (2006), Kreines (2008a), Ferrini (2009, 2011), Burmeister (2013), and Rometsch (2013).

[5] Pippin (1989) defends Hegel's idealism as continuing the Kantian apperception or self-consciousness theme, a view that, while valuable in many respects, remains radically incomplete and potentially misleading on a variety of fronts. I say more about Pippin's view later. Concerning the importance of Kant's third *Critique* in contrast with other Kantian texts and concepts, Pippin expresses his skepticism as follows:

philosophy,[6] Kant introduced the problem of nature's purposiveness in connection with an investigation into the powers of judgment, essentially arguing that a principle of nature's purposiveness is the condition for the non-arbitrary operation of judgment in its pursuit of empirical knowledge.[7] As part of his investigation, Kant introduces an idea that I argue is central for the development of Hegel's concept of the Concept—namely, the notion of internal purposiveness manifest in the self-organizing form of an organism or natural purpose (*Naturzweck*). The idea of internal purposiveness is the Kantian ancestor and model for Hegel's concept of the Concept, and Hegel repeatedly attests to its importance, claiming that "reason is *purposive activity*," and more emphatically, that internal purposiveness is "Kant's great service to philosophy" (PhG ¶22/3:26; WL 654/6:440).[8] Although the details of Kant's own account are, to be sure, much disputed, what is indisputable is Hegel's unequivocal endorsement of Kant's conception of internal purposiveness and his insistence that it plays a positive, constitutive role with respect to the activities of reason and thought. Schelling, too, notes that "organic nature furnishes the most visible [*sichtbarsten*] proof of transcendental idealism" (SI 122/490). For reasons we will explore in detail, post-Kantian philosophers took the fate of Kant's idealism to be fundamentally tied to the fate of a concept of life, contending that idealism could be successfully defended *only* if the activities of reason could be determined in their essential connection with the form of activity of life. The purposiveness theme thus not only provides an anchor for understanding Hegel's concept of the Concept, but further, provides an anchor for understanding Hegel's philosophical relation to his contemporaries, and in particular, to Fichte, Hölderlin, and Schelling.

> [A]lthough there is widespread agreement that Kant's position in the *KU* [*Kritik der Urteilskraft*] was at least as influential in the development of later Idealism as his theory of self-consciousness, transcendental deduction, or theory of autonomy, and substantial consensus about the terms and issues that formed the core of that influence, there does not, at least on the surface, appear to be much in the consensus account that is very philosophically interesting. The question, in other words, has pretty much become a wholly historical one, a question simply of the proper formulation of an episode in *Ideengeschichte*, an episode without much contemporary or perennial relevance. (1997, 132)

The fundamental orientation of this study in the purposiveness theme is thus essentially at odds with Pippin's assessment.

---

⁶ See, for example, Förster (2009/2010, 2012) and Richards (2002).

⁷ Zammito (1992) charts three phases in the development of Kant's *Critique of Judgment*: the aesthetic turn, the cognitive turn, and the ethical turn. Although I think it is important to read the third *Critique* as a unified text, my main focus in this study concerns the problem of reflective judgment and the Critique of Teleological Judgment, leaving aside Kant's treatment of aesthetics and ethics.

⁸ On internal purposiveness and Hegel's Concept, see Baum (1990) and deVries (1991).

The core dispute between Kant and Hegel in the context of the purposiveness theme concerns whether or not internal purposiveness or the concept of life has a constitutive status with respect to knowledge, a question to which Kant definitively responds in the negative and to which Hegel definitively responds in the positive. This means that Hegel's unequivocal endorsement of internal purposiveness is, in a sense, already a development of Kant's project beyond the Kantian strictures, and it will be important to assess the degree to which Hegel is able to affirm internal purposiveness on grounds that are internal to Kant's own project. On this core dispute concerning the purposiveness theme, I will argue that Hegel presents the problem in essentially Kantian terms—that with respect to the question of whether or not life can be a constitutive concept, Hegel will initially frame the question in terms of a question *quid juris* and *not* in terms of a question *quid facti*.[9] That is, rather than arguing primarily about whether or not nature is living *in fact*, an empirical question whose answer cannot be definitively provided by Hegel within the contexts in which the concept of life figures as part of a philosophical argument (for example, in his accounts of self-consciousness in the *Phenomenology of Spirit* and *Philosophy of Mind*, and most notably, in the section on the "Idea" in the *Science of Logic*), Hegel will instead ask about the question of the *legitimate* and *lawful* employment of the concept of life, attempting to answer the question: *By what right* can we employ the concept of life in a constitutive, objective manner? Why is the concept of life a necessary condition for reason a priori, and how does it enable the possibility of intelligibility as such, shaping our activity and forms of knowing? In framing the question in this way, Hegel, like Kant, means to show that what initially look like subjective conditions of thinking have objective validity and purport, making the question of whether the concept of life is subjective or objective a nonstarter, since the answer is always, and must be, "both." Insofar as life opens up the possibility of intelligibility as such, it is the objective context in which subjects, objects, and their relationship come to have any meaning at all. To be clear, although Hegel indeed affirms that nature is living *in fact*, the strategy of his philosophical arguments with respect to life as a constitutive concept always revolve around the question of what makes the concept of life necessary a priori for self-consciousness and thought, and not primarily around questions concerning empirical nature or the definition of

---

[9] See A84/B116.

matter.[10] As I will try to show, the significance of the concept of life in Hegel's system primarily concerns the activity and form of the Concept, and the culmination of Hegel's contribution can be most clearly seen in the presentation of a *logical* concept of life in the *Science of Logic*.

In connection with the purposiveness theme, the second claim I defend in this study concerns an interpretation of Hegel's *speculative identity thesis*, a thesis that represents the core of Hegel's philosophical method, and one that I argue is best understood in terms of the necessary relation and opposition between self-consciousness and life. Essentially, Hegel develops Kant's insight that purposiveness is the necessary condition and horizon of judgment into a claim about the constitutive import of life for self-consciousness, where self-consciousness is understood in the post-Kantian context as providing an absolute ground for knowledge. Hegel develops his speculative identity thesis through an engagement with the philosophies of Fichte and Schelling, and in particular, in response to Fichte's concept of the self-positing activity of the absolute I. Against Fichte, both Schelling and Hegel, following the path of Kant's purposiveness theme, argue that Fichte's idealism remains merely subjective and incomplete without an understanding of the essential relation between the self-positing activity of the I and the self-organizing activity of living nature. Hegel's first presentation of this thesis can be found in his *Differenzschrift* (1801), where he employs the Schellingian language of *subjective subject-object* and *objective subject-object* in order to defend the constitutive role of purposiveness in the self-positing activity of the absolute I. Although Hegel is often thought to ultimately abandon this Schellingian influence, my argument is that the speculative identity thesis is consistently sustained throughout Hegel's works, and most importantly, that the speculative identity thesis is present in the method of the *Phenomenology of Spirit* and the *Science of Logic*, which suggests that speculative identity can be understood as the method of Hegel's entire philosophical system. Key to Hegel's understanding of the import of life is not simply the claim that transcendental philosophy needs to be complemented by a philosophy of nature, which, as evidenced by the writings of Schelling and Hegel, is also surely the case. What Hegel grasps early on, via Schelling, but also in a way, better than Schelling, is that the concept of life serves an a priori function

---

[10] For a very different reconstruction of this debate between Kant and Hegel, see Kreines (2015, chap. 3). For my review of Kreines, see Ng (2018b).

in the processes of self-conscious cognition, giving immediate shape to our knowledge of ourselves, our knowledge of other selves, and our knowledge of the world.

In developing Hegel's speculative identity thesis, my claim will be that Hegel presents the ground of knowledge as having a *double constitution*.[11] In outline, what this means is that Hegel presents the key tenets of his philosophy—for our purposes: Concept and Idea—as manifesting a double form: life manifests the immediacy of Concept and Idea, an immediacy that contains the potential for the actualization of self-conscious cognition.[12] Why does Hegel claim that life is the *immediate* Concept (the unity of universality, particularity, and individuality) and the *immediate* Idea (the unity of Concept and objectivity), and what significance does this have for Hegel's understanding of the process and activity of knowing? Although it will take the bulk of this study to answer this question, I will argue that here, too, the *Critique of Judgment* provides the most important background for understanding the significance of Hegel's claim concerning the immediacy of life. Building on the purposiveness theme, Hegel will argue that the power of judgment is an actualization of the unity and activity of life-form, a power that is at once enabled and constrained by the unity and activity of life. The key to Hegel's speculative identity thesis is that life is not a determination that is ultimately overcome or fully sublated by self-conscious cognition, but that the identity and opposition between life and self-consciousness constitute the process and activity of knowing, a dialectical process that he comes to call absolute method.[13]

The third claim defended in this study is that Hegel's Subjective Logic can be interpreted as his version of a "critique of judgment." The strategy of the progression of the chapters in the Subjective Logic is to reveal the degree to which the activities of judgment presuppose and are grounded in the unity and activity of life, and central to Hegel's argument is his understanding of *Gattung*-concepts—something's genus, species, or kind. In Hegel's account of judgment, the genus is an "*objective universality*" that provides the necessary

---

[11] See Ng (2013).

[12] See, for example, PhG ¶¶172–173, 189/3:143, 150; WL 517, 689/6:257, 487; and EL §236. My view is sympathetic with what has recently been called a "transformative" theory of rationality in opposition to "additive" theories, and I briefly discuss Hegel's connection to these issues in chapter 7. See also Khurana (2017, 384–387) for differences between Hegel's understanding of the life/spirit relation and transformative theories. On transformative theories of rationality, see Boyle (2016, 2018) and also Kern and Kietzmann (2017).

[13] On a dialectical approach to the relation between life and spirit, see Menke (2006) and Neuhouser (2013).

context for predication, and in particular, governs the ascription of normative predicates to the subject (WL 575/6:335).[14] I will argue that, in particular,
what Hegel calls the judgment of the Concept—the highest form of judgment and what judgment is in truth—is modeled on Kant's understanding of
teleological judgments, showing the enduring importance of the purposiveness theme. In addition to the influence of the third *Critique*, Hegel's theory
of judgment is further informed by Hölderlin, who understands judgment
(*Urteil*) in terms of the "original division" (*ursprüngliche Teilung*) of subject and object. The culmination of Hegel's development of the purposiveness theme is best discerned in what he calls "the original judgment of life"
(*das ursprüngliche Urteil des Lebens*), and my interpretation of the "Idea" will
largely be concerned with unpacking this important, but largely ignored, formulation (WL 678/6:473). My argument will be that "the original judgment
of life" provides the key to understanding the Idea as the ground of Hegel's
philosophical system, representing the full development of the positive and
constitutive role of purposiveness in connection with the activities of self-
conscious cognition. In reading the Subjective Logic as Hegel's "critique of
judgment," I argue that the Idea puts forward the thesis that life opens up the
space of reasons itself, a claim that represents Hegel's distinctive contribution
to post-Kantian idealist philosophy.[15]

Although my interpretation in what follows is based on a careful consideration of Hegel's texts themselves, it would be helpful to say something about
where my interpretation stands in connection with other available options,
and what advantages the interpretation offered in this study affords. It is impossible to be exhaustive here (which is not my aim), and moreover, what will
not be evident in my brief remarks that follow is how much I have learned
from other interpretations in coming to develop my own. Earlier, I referred
repeatedly to Hegel's project in terms of idealism, and moreover, I suggested
that the importance of the concept of life can be understood in terms of resolving some of the problems of Kant's idealism. However, Hegel has also
been interpreted as a realist.[16] Closely related, though by no means identical,
debates concern non-metaphysical versus metaphysical readings of Hegel,

---

[14] On the importance of *Gattung*-concepts for Hegel's philosophy, see Stern (1990) and Kreines (2015).

[15] On the absolute Idea as the "space of reasons," see Pinkard (2002, 249, 263–265).

[16] See, for example, Stern (1990, 2009) and Westphal (1989, 2003).

as well as deflationary versus inflationary readings.[17] There is also an important sense in which Hegel and the German idealists mean to demonstrate that there is no true distinction between idealism and realism, which only complicates the overall debate.[18] Without resolving these debates, my contention in this study is that Hegel's idealism is best understood as grounded in a concept of life, insofar as life provides the model for the realization of subjective aims and ends as something objective, manifesting, as Hegel claims, the form of a "subject-object." Hegel also writes that "[t]he perpetual action of life is thus absolute idealism," which suggests that the activity and form of life is simply the model for idealism as he understands it (PN §337Z). In understanding Hegel's idealism as oriented by a concept of life, my hope is that this version of idealism avoids the disadvantages of two other prominent versions of Hegel's idealism that have been defended in the literature, which identify different key concepts in Kant as Hegel's main source of influence— namely, Kant's notion of apperception and his notion of the intuitive understanding. I contend that the purposiveness theme preserves the advantages of these two views while avoiding their disadvantages, and moreover, comes with some independent advantages of its own.

The argument that Hegel's idealism develops Kant's apperception thesis has been most forcefully defended in Robert Pippin's reading of Hegel. Pippin draws primarily from Kant's Transcendental Deduction in the first *Critique*, emphasizing the idea of transcendental logic and the theory of self-consciousness in order to suggest that Hegel continues and completes Kant's critical project by successfully eradicating the specter of skepticism that is a result of maintaining a realm of unknowable things-in-themselves.[19] The key

---

[17] Kreines (2006) has helpfully catalogued the relevant figures and debates in metaphysical and non-metaphysical readings of Hegel (focusing on his theoretical philosophy), calling for "hybrid" views.

[18] Stern's (2008) discussion of this issue is most instructive. See also Beiser (2002, 2005). Hegel writes: "Every philosophy is essentially idealism or at least has idealism for its principle, and the question then is only how far this principle is carried out. . . . Consequently the opposition of idealistic and realistic philosophy has no significance" (WL 124/5:172). Allais (2015) argues that Kant's philosophy should likewise be understood as both idealism and realism. She writes:

> Kant's distinction [between appearances and things-in-themselves] is based on epistemological considerations, and has epistemological consequences, but it also involves metaphysical claims about what exists and about the mind-dependence of the aspect of reality of which we can have knowledge. Kant's position is a careful combination of realism and idealism, and of metaphysical and epistemological claims. . . . Kant attempts to accommodate as far as possible both philosophical concerns that lead to idealism and those that lead to realism. (2015, 11)

[19] See Pippin (1989). Pippin's (2019) new book was published as this book was going to press, and in that work, which takes up the problem of logic as metaphysics, the logical concept of life plays a

to Pippin's reading is the B-Deduction in particular, where Kant asserts that *both* intellectual and figurative synthesis (synthesis in a concept and synthesis in the form of intuition) have their source in the original synthetic unity of apperception.[20] This detail becomes the crux of Hegel's objection against Kant that intuitions constitute a separate, nonconceptual contribution to knowledge that limits our discursive form of knowing to appearances; instead, our self-actualizing conceptual activity is absolute and "unbounded."[21] Hegel's idealism thus attempts to make good on Kant's own suggestion that "one and the same synthetic unity"—namely, the synthetic unity of apperception— "is the principle of intuition and of the understanding" (GW 70/2:305). In opposition to an original duality that requires synthesis, Hegel argues that synthetic a priori judgments are only possible through an "original, absolute identity of the heterogeneous" (GW 72/2:307).[22] With this presumably Kantian revision of Kant in place, Hegel's *Logic* can then be read as thought's a priori determination of the categories necessary for determining any possible object (an absolute conceptual scheme), all of which are grounded in a theory of self-determining self-consciousness that Hegel calls the Concept.[23]

The advantages of the apperception view are many: In placing the problems of self-consciousness and freedom at the center of Hegel's philosophy, Pippin's reading not only demonstrated the continuity between Kant and German idealism on these central issues but, moreover, demystified what appeared to be a *dogmatic* form of metaphysics in Hegel's texts.[24] In

---

more central role than it did in previous work. However, the apperception theme remains absolutely central for Pippin's approach to the logic as metaphysics problem. I take up Pippin's (2019) new book in detail in a forthcoming article in the *European Journal of Philosophy*.

[20] See B160n: "Space, represented as *object* . . . contains more than mere form of intuition; it also contains *combination* of the manifold . . . so that the *form of intuition* gives only a manifold, the *formal intuition* gives unity of representation. In the Aesthetic I have treated this unity as belonging merely to sensibility . . . although, as a matter of fact, it presupposes a synthesis which does not belong to the senses but through which all concepts of space and time first become possible." See also Pippin (2005) and Pinkard (2002, 247, 248, 258). Longuenesse (2007) also offers a sophisticated interpretation of the post-Kantian Hegel through a careful reading of the Doctrine of Essence. However, she suggests that such a critical, Kantian reading cannot be maintained once we reach the Subjective Logic, arguing that Hegel's Concept is akin to a form of intuitive understanding.

[21] See McDowell (1996, Lecture II).

[22] I provide a different reading of these famous passages from *Faith and Knowledge* in chapter 7.

[23] The passage cited most often in support of the apperception view reads as follows: "It is one of the profoundest and truest insights to be found in the *Critique of Pure Reason* that the *unity* which constitutes the nature of the *Concept* is recognized as the *original synthetic* unity of *apperception*, as the unity of the *I think*, or of self-consciousness" (WL 584/6:254). Pippin cites this passage repeatedly in his writings on Hegel, but see also Brandom (2002, 216).

[24] See Stern's (2009) discussion of the distinction between *metaphysica specialis* and *metaphysica generalis*. I agree with Stern that *metaphysica generalis*, or ontology, is unavoidable. On the ontological

emphasizing the purposiveness theme, I preserve the importance of self-consciousness and self-determination as organizing foci for Hegel's philosophy, while avoiding two disadvantages of the apperception view. The first is the overemphasis on Kant's Deduction argument, which ultimately leads to an idealism that is merely "subjective" according to the post-Kantians.[25] As we will see, even for Kant, the argument of the Transcendental Analytic did not provide a *complete* theory of judgment but required the additional contribution of the third *Critique*, and in particular, its account of reflective judgment and the principle of purposiveness. I will argue that the problem of purposiveness is already present in a nascent form in the first *Critique*, which further shows that the Deduction argument, on its own, and even if accepted in full, remains incomplete according to Kant himself. Moreover, Fichte's contribution to Hegel's own understanding of self-consciousness cannot be fully grasped without also incorporating Hegel's and Schelling's incisive critique of Fichte's idealism as merely subjective primarily on the basis of the purposiveness issue, where Fichte's failure essentially hinges on his inability to grasp the not-I as life.[26] In short, my suggestion is that the self-consciousness theme itself is fundamentally misunderstood and incomplete without placing it within the context of the purposiveness theme.

This brings us to the second disadvantage of the apperception view: without incorporating the constitutive role of purposiveness and life into Hegel's understanding of self-consciousness, the apperception view is anti-naturalist in a way that distorts Hegel's conception of freedom, and moreover, distorts the essentially Aristotelian orientation of Hegel's key concepts.[27] In the apperception account, Pippin and Brandom, for example, affirm self-consciousness's beginnings in life while stripping life of any positive explanatory force in the theoretical and practical activities of self-determining reason. Spirit fundamentally leaves nature and life behind in the course of its self-determination,

---

import of Hegel's *Logic*, see Houlgate (2006), Hanna (1986), and Harrelson (2013). On the primacy of metaphysics over epistemology in Hegel, see Kreines (2015).

[25] Kreines (2015) argues that Kant's Dialectic argument is the key to Hegel's philosophy. Without denying the Dialectic's importance, I will argue in detail in this study that a reading of the Subjective Logic as a whole (especially in the context of Hegel's understanding of the problem of judgment) suggests that the third *Critique* is the more important source of influence. Moreover, the Dialectic argument is repeated in the third *Critique* in the antinomy between mechanism and teleology. See WL 655/6:442.

[26] I discuss this issue in detail in chapter 3, but see also Pippin's (2000) defense of Fichte against charges of "subjective" idealism, and Redding's (1996, 55) discussion of Fichte's failure.

[27] For a definitive account of the importance of life for Hegel's conception of freedom, see Khurana (2017).

and while life can be seen as a cause of spirit, nothing about life has normative authority *for* spirit.[28] On this account, any distinction we might draw
between life and spirit is fully and autonomously self-legislated, a distinction
ultimately decided upon by spirit itself.[29] Far from having a positive or constitutive function as Hegel insists, spirit's freedom is characterized by its *indifference* to the determination of life.[30] The reading offered in this study will
show this view to be mistaken insofar as Hegel consistently presents life and
self-consciousness as sharing the same logical form, revealing cognition's
powers to be essentially shaped by the form and activity of life. Life is not
the "cause" of spirit, but its first actuality; understanding the Concept's
self-actualization requires that we understand this process as essentially
grounded in life, an argument that is presented most clearly by Hegel in the
conclusion of his *Science of Logic*.

The second Kantian concept that has been adopted as the key source of
influence for Hegel is the idea of the intuitive understanding, and most importantly, Kant's discussion of this idea in sections 76 and 77 of the third
Critique.[31] The intuitive understanding is characterized by two distinctive
features that are of particular interest to Hegel and the German idealists, although it is important to keep in mind Kant's insistence that these features
are *not* available to human beings. First, in contrast with the discursive understanding, there is no distinction between possibility and actuality for an
intuitive intellect. The second feature of the intuitive understanding concerns
the relation between universals and particulars, as well as the kind of universal that is available to cognition. Whereas for human, discursive understanding, judgment proceeds from "the *analytical universal* to the particular
(i.e., from concepts to the empirical intuition that is given)," the intuitive understanding instead "proceeds from the *synthetically universal* (the intuition
of a whole as a whole) to the particular, i.e., from the whole to the parts" (KU
5:407). Moreover, unlike the contingent harmony between concept and intuition in the case of the discursive understanding, Kant claims that for the
intuitive understanding, "there is no *contingency* in the combination of the

---

[28] See Brandom (2007) and Pippin (2002, 2011).
[29] See Brandom's (1979) original version of this thesis. In some of Pippin's formulations, this thesis
comes to sound increasingly decisionist: "'[A]ssuming command' . . . of such determinations is
to take oneself to be, authoritatively, *such a determiner*, 'the decider' in the immortal words of our
former president" (2011, 73).
[30] See Pippin (2011, 85–86) for the language of indifference.
[31] See, for example, Förster (2009/20102012), Sedgwick (2012), Düsing (1986a), Dahlstrom
(1998), Hance (1998), and Wretzel (2018).

parts, in order to make possible a determinate form of the whole." For those who defend the importance of the intuitive understanding, the suggestion is that Hegel essentially affirms what Kant denies, with Hegel developing his theory of the Concept by appropriating the key characteristics of the intuitive understanding. To temper the impression that Hegel has simply affirmed the presence of a creative godlike mind, Förster and Sedgwick, for example, have suggested that Hegel can argue that we have the ability to conceive of part/whole relations and organic unity without prima facie violating what we normally consider to be the limits of human understanding, setting aside the way in which the intuitive understanding challenges the actual/possible distinction.[32] Förster further argues that, via the influence of Goethe, Hegel eventually comes to incorporate conceptions of dialectical transition and development into the idea of an intuitive understanding, resulting in his mature philosophical method.

In defending the purposiveness theme, my view preserves the advantages of the intuitive understanding view, which not only recognizes the undeniable influence of the third *Critique* for post-Kantian philosophy but moreover stresses the importance of organic unity and part/whole relations for Hegel's understanding of the Concept. However, there are two potential disadvantages of the intuitive understanding view that I believe the purposiveness theme avoids. The first is a worry about the external relationship between the intuitive understanding and what it perceives: an intuitive understanding that is able to perceive organic wholes leaves unanswered (or at least, undertheorized) the question concerning the reciprocity and even "identity" between subject and object that is so important for Hegel's account. Although both Förster and Sedgwick recognize the importance of this identity,[33] my suggestion here is only that the idea of

---

[32] Sedgwick (2012, chap. 2) argues that Hegel affirms the intuitive understanding without denying the contribution of intuitions. Förster (2012, 144) argues that Kant draws an important distinction between intellectual intuition and the intuitive understanding that is generally overlooked. In brief, he attributes the erasure of the distinction between the possible and the actual to intellectual intuition, whereas proceeding from the whole to the parts is characteristic of the intuitive understanding. Fichte and Schelling follow the (less successful) path of intellectual intuition in their respective philosophies, whereas Goethe and Hegel follow the more successful path of the intuitive understanding in their respective methods. I take it that the upshot of distinguishing between these two forms of cognition is to prevent the capacities of the intuitive understanding from being associated with a divine, godlike, or omnipotent mind, an idea that could only be dogmatic. Indeed, what Förster calls the method of the intuitive understanding comes to be associated with Goethe's scientific writings and Hegel's method of historical development in the PhG, and Förster tracks Hegel's own development by arguing for his eventual abandonment of the idea of intellectual intuition. On the intuitive understanding as non-creative, see also Pinkard (2002, 259).

[33] See Förster (2012, 281–287) and Sedgwick (2012, 62–67).

an intuitive understanding on its own cannot provide an account of the reciprocity and speculative identity between subject and object, and that in simply attributing the powers of the intuitive understanding to the subject, we cannot resolve the problem of speculative identity as it is understood by Hegel. A second related disadvantage, then, is the following: although the intuitive understanding provides an account of how we might understand the *object* in terms of organic unity, it cannot fully account for the purposiveness of the *subject*, and moreover, how self-consciousness itself is constituted in connection with its grasp of living form (in Hegel's repeated formulation, self-consciousness is the genus *for-itself*).[34] Put most simply, Hegel's claim is that our power to grasp organic unity is not due to any special power of an intuitive understanding at all, but simply due to the fact that we *are* this unity and activity, meaning that grasping the form of internal purposiveness is simply part of the process of understanding ourselves. If our so-called power of intuitive understanding is simply due to the fact that we are essentially living beings and living minds, then this takes the idea of the intuitive understanding so far away from Kant's original account that it no longer makes sense to insist on its primary significance. Importantly, although Hegel indeed never abandons his praise of the intuitive understanding,[35] the concluding argument of the *Science of Logic* does not make reference to an intuitive understanding at all, but relies instead on the idea of internal purposiveness, "Kant's great service to philosophy," that opens up the concept of life and thus the Idea. My main contention, then, is that the purposiveness theme is best able to capture the method of Hegel's idealism as a whole; in particular, my interpretation aims at the overarching goal of providing an account of Hegel's Idea in the conclusion of the *Logic*, which I take to be the key to his entire philosophical system.

I begin in chapter 2 by introducing the purposiveness theme, drawing a connection between Kant's discussion of judgment in the first *Critique* and his analysis of reflective judgment in the third *Critique*. In order to understand Hegel's endorsement and appropriation of this theme, my analysis centers on Hegel's suggestion that purposiveness serves a *positive* function in the project of a critique of reason, a suggestion that guides the

---

[34] See PhG ¶¶172–173/3:143 and WL 688/6:486–487.
[35] See, for example, WL 522–523/6:264–266.

interpretation offered in this study. My investigation of the purposiveness theme in Kant attempts to answer two important questions. First, what exactly is the connection between judgment and purposiveness, and why does Kant claim that the operation of judgment presupposes purposiveness as its principle? What function does purposiveness serve with respect to the power of judgment? Second, what is the primary sense of purposiveness relevant for the operation of judgment: external (modeled on artifact creation) or internal (modeled on organic activity and form)? Considering these two sets of questions reveals that purposiveness offers a model for the unity of concept and object sought after by judgment, a unity that is displayed and exemplified in the unity of internally purposive, rather than externally purposive, form. I investigate the reasoning behind Kant's claim that judging nature according to external purposiveness is a "contradiction," a line of reasoning that reveals the reciprocity and essential relation between internal purposiveness and a distinctly human power of judgment. This reciprocity between internal purposiveness and the human power of judgment sets the stage for the interpretation of Hegel offered in the remainder of the study, forming the background of Hegel's understanding of the relationship between life and self-consciousness.

Chapter 3 begins to consider this relationship through an analysis of Hegel's speculative identity thesis, a thesis that Hegel first develops in connection with the philosophies of Fichte and Schelling in the *Differenzschrift*. The *Differenzschrift* presents, in outline, a philosophical method that Hegel continues to develop in the *Phenomenology* and *Science of Logic*, and chapter 3 focuses on understanding and defending this thesis as it is presented in the *Differenzschrift* and the *Phenomenology*. In my analysis of the *Differenzschrift*, I focus on two central issues: first, the importance of Schelling's contribution in understanding the idea of a "subject-object" and how this carries forward the purposiveness theme; and second, how Hegel's critique of Fichte reveals the importance of the purposiveness issue, especially in connection with Hegel's subsequent development of his own account of self-consciousness in the *Phenomenology*. Far from simply a youthful text written under the heavy influence of Schelling, the *Differenzschrift* presents, in outline, a general approach to idealism that Hegel will follow through on in full, developing a Schellingian line of thought that Schelling himself will ultimately abandon. Turning from the *Differenzschrift* to the *Phenomenology*, I argue that the method of this text continues to develop the speculative identity thesis, which is defended through a discussion of Hegel's understanding of the relation between consciousness and self-consciousness, alongside the all-important concept of negativity. In considering the constitutive import of life for self-consciousness, I argue that Hegel (with the continued aid of Schellingian arguments) presents an argument for the speculative identity thesis that comprises three dimensions: the employment of an important analogy, a transcendental argument, and a refutation of idealism argument. By way of these three argumentative strategies, Hegel provides a response to Kant's skepticism with respect to the constitutive import of life, demonstrating its a priori significance for the determination of self-consciousness.

In the remainder of the study, I turn to an investigation of Hegel's *Science of Logic*, with the aim of understanding Hegel's Subjective Logic in particular as his own version of a "critique of judgment." Chapter 4 takes up Hegel's genesis of the Concept argument (or his "immanent deduction" of the Concept) presented in the concluding section of the Doctrine of Essence on "Actuality." In framing his deduction of the Concept in terms of its genesis, Hegel traces the origins of the Concept primarily to two sources: Spinoza's notion of substance, with the aim of transforming substance into subject; and Aristotle's notion of *enérgeia*, which he understands in terms of purposiveness of form. Hegel aims to show that the unity and activity of the Concept is immanent in actuality, and the goal of the concluding section of the Doctrine of Essence is to provide an account of actuality as activity (*Tätigkeit*) and activity of form (*Formtätigkeit*). To understand the process of actualization in terms of activity, I defend two essential arguments presented by Hegel in this section. The first concerns why actuality is not adequately captured in terms of sheer contingency or blind necessity, and how the concept of activity might be understood as immanent to and implicit in the process of actualization. The second concerns the concept of reciprocity (*Wechselwirkung*) and how the process of actualization can be understood as being a cause and effect of itself, displaying the activity and unity of self-determination. What becomes evident in Hegel's genesis argument is that the deduction of the Concept hinges on the deduction of internally purposive form as constitutive of the process of actualization. In essence, the unity and activity of the Concept is the unity and activity of internal purposiveness, and the three moments of Hegel's Concept—universality, particularity, and individuality—reflect the self-organizing form of what Kant called a natural purpose (*Naturzweck*). Hegel's genesis argument thus sets the stage for the progression of the Subjective Logic, which centers on this conception of unity, and ultimately returns in its conclusion to a discussion of life.

Chapters 5 to 8 form one continuous argument, taking up the sections in the Subjective Logic on "Subjectivity," "Objectivity," and "The Idea." In chapter 5, I present the case for a reading of the Subjective Logic in terms of Hegel's "critique of judgment" by turning to the importance of Hölderlin for understanding Hegel's approach to judgment. Although both Hölderlin and Hegel understand judgment (*Urteil*) on the model of "original division" (*ursprüngliche Teilung*), I argue that unlike Hölderlin, Hegel traces the ground of judgment not to the original unity of "Being" but to what he calls "the original judgment of life" (*das ursprüngliche Urteil des Lebens*). The original judgment of life denotes an original form of activity, an original division and unity, that contains the potential for the actualization for self-conscious cognition. Although a complete account of the idea of "original judgment" will not be presented until chapter 7, in chapter 5 I focus on Hegel's analysis of what he calls the subjective Concept in order to show that organic unity and form provide a standard for the unity and form of Concept, judgment, and syllogism. The key to this argument hinges on Hegel's understanding of *Gattung*-concepts (a genus, species, or kind) as the objective, universal context of judgment. I provide a detailed analysis of the "Judgment" chapter in particular and argue that what Hegel calls the judgment of the Concept (essentially, evaluative judgments) is modeled on Kant's understanding of teleological judgments. In order to understand the significance of judgments of the Concept, chapter 5 also provides an analysis of a structural peculiarity in the section on "Subjectivity" in which Hegel conspicuously does *not* present a corresponding form of syllogism for the judgment of the Concept. On the basis of a careful consideration of the chapters on "Judgment" and "Syllogism," I argue that the rational status of judgments of the Concept are not reducible to their being conclusions of sound syllogisms, and I suggest that judgments of the Concept should also be understood as *reflective judgments*. The puzzle of this missing syllogism will also be discussed in chapter 6, where I analyze Hegel's approach to practical syllogisms in connection with teleology.

Chapter 6 considers the transition to "Objectivity," continuing the investigation into the role of the *Gattung* as an objective universal. In the chapters on "Mechanism," "Chemism," and "Teleology," Hegel establishes the genus not only as an objective context of predication but also as the necessary context of objective existence, determining the degree to which self-determining activity can be realized. I provide a defense of Hegel's employment of the ontological argument in the transition to "Objectivity" and argue that the being or existence that can be inferred from the Concept is being as self-individuating activity. The processes of mechanism, chemism, and external purposiveness all fall short of self-determining activity, and I argue that Hegel employs the language of "striving" and "violence" to articulate a delicate balance between two desiderata: on the one hand, maintaining the importance of the life/non-life distinction from the perspective of the activity of self-determining beings; and on the other, grasping the processes of living activity as continuous with lower-level processes in order to avoid a dualistic or supernaturalist metaphysics. To set the stage for completing my account of "the original judgment of life," I discuss what Hegel calls "objective judgment," and I consider its relation to the practical syllogism. Hegel's analysis reveals that there is an irreducible role for judgment as an act of self-determination and self-constitution, an activity that is immediately manifest in the activity of life.

Chapters 7 and 8 provide a detailed analysis of the section on the "Idea," focusing in particular on the discussion of logical life as "original judgment." My reading of the Idea revolves around two interpretive claims: first, that the Idea has a distinctive status within the context of Hegel's *Logic*, as well as his wider system, serving as the ground of both; second, Hegel claims that the Idea must be understood as "doubled," a claim that I interpret in terms of the ongoing dialectic between life and cognition as absolute method (WL 689/6:487). To understand the doubling of the Idea, I return to a key passage from *Faith and Knowledge*, and I argue that, there, Hegel provides a clue to a different solution to Kant's concept/intuition problem than is usually offered. Although Hegel objects to the idea of there being two *heterogeneous* stems of knowledge, he does not object to the idea that knowledge in general consists of the relation between immediacy and self-conscious mediation. I argue that the doubling of the Idea is Hegel's attempt to replace Kant's doctrine of the two stems of knowledge, where *life* and *cognition* take the place of *intuitions* and *concepts*. To understand how this works, I provide a detailed account of the chapter on "Life," suggesting that it provides an a priori schema that at once enables and constrains the activities of self-conscious cognition. The three processes of logical life—corporeality (*Leiblichkeit*), externality (*Äußerlichkeit*), and the genus (*die Gattung*)—are interpreted as three a priori form-constraints presupposed by the actualization of self-conscious cognition, three processes without which cognition would be "empty," or without actuality (WL 677–678/6:469–470). Chapter 8 completes my interpretation of the *Logic* by taking up the final chapters of that text on

"The Idea of Cognition" and "The Absolute Idea." The logical form of life enables and constrains the activities of theoretical and practical cognition, and I argue that cognition is understood by Hegel to be the result of life's self-division from itself, a result of the Idea "doubled." As self-conscious life, theoretical and practical cognition produce various self-conceptions, which have various limitations and powers. I conclude with a discussion of absolute method as the "unity of the Idea of life with the Idea of cognition," arguing that method is best understood as the ongoing dialectic between life and cognition (EL §236Z).

2

"Kant's Great Service to Philosophy"

Purposiveness and Conceptual Form

> For a thing is generated either by art, or by nature. . . . Art is the prin-
> ciple in a thing other than that which is generated, nature is a prin-
> ciple in the thing itself.
>
> —Aristotle, *Metaphysics*

2.1 The Purposiveness Theme

In the chapter on "Teleology" in the *Science of Logic*, Hegel praises Kant on
account of the concept of internal purposiveness introduced in his *Critique
of Judgment*, and associates this concept directly with his own all-important
notion of the "Idea." Hegel's discussion in this context is noteworthy not only
because it is a rare moment of unequivocal high praise for Kant but, more importantly, because Hegel situates the concept of internal purposiveness with
respect to its positive role in the larger project of a critique of reason. Hegel
writes:

> One of Kant's great services to philosophy consists in drawing the dis-
> tinction between relative or *external* purposiveness and *internal* purpos-
> iveness; in the latter he opened up the concept of *life*, the *Idea*, and by so
> doing has done *positively* for philosophy what the *Critique of Reason* did
> but imperfectly, equivocally, and only *negatively*, namely, raised it above the
> determinations of reflection and the relative world of metaphysics. (WL
> 654/6:440–441)

Internal purposiveness is associated with the *concept of life* and the *Idea*, and
Hegel claims that it serves as the positive counterpart to the negative aims
of the *Critique of Pure Reason*, which sought to delimit the powers of cognition and warn us away from extending our knowledge in illegitimate ways.

Hegel's Concept of Life. Karen Ng, Oxford University Press (2020) © Oxford University Press 2020.
DOI: 10.1093/oso/9780190947613.001.0001

In assigning a positive function to the concept of inner purposiveness, Hegel appears to be suggesting that the negative work of the first *Critique* does not stand alone but, rather, requires a positive account of the concept of life as part of the same philosophical project. Thus, if the first *Critique* laid out the ultimate *limits* of pure reason, then life and inner purposiveness shed light on how reason is *enabled* and *empowered*, providing an account of reason's ultimate ground. How exactly are we to understand the positive function of purposiveness in light of the project of a critique of reason? What positive role does life play with respect to the powers of cognition and judgment? Throughout this study, my aim is to understand and defend the positive function attributed to purposiveness by Hegel, and to argue that it is the key to grasping the central tenets of his thought. The aim of this chapter, then, is to introduce the purposiveness theme as it is presented in Kant's philosophy, focusing on the central problems and elements that are important for understanding Hegel's appropriation of this theme. Accordingly, the overview provided of Kant's own treatment of the topic does not aim at completeness but, instead, will attempt to draw out the ways in which Kant's philosophy makes room for and anticipates the positive function of purposiveness identified by Hegel.

At the start, it can appear that the outlook for identifying a positive function for purposiveness in Kant does not look promising. Officially introduced in the third *Critique* in connection with an expanded account of judgment, the various guises of purposiveness discussed in that text are ultimately all relegated to serving a regulative, negative function, and Kant is clear that purposiveness can never serve as a constitutive, positive concept. Hegel, swinging far in the opposite direction, identifies reason itself with *"purposive activity,"* and associates the sense of purposiveness in question with Aristotle's understanding of nature (PhG ¶22/3:26). This Aristotelian background is key for understanding the distinction between external and internal purposiveness invoked by Kant and praised by Hegel: whereas external purposiveness operates roughly on the model of artifact creation and instrumental action, internal purposiveness operates on the model of organic production and life, echoing Aristotle's understanding of the distinction between art and nature. The contrast between these two different ways of understanding unity and organization according to purposes proves to be central, not only for how Kant and Hegel conceive of nature but, more importantly, for their respective approaches to the operation of reason and thought. *This*, I will argue, is where the prospects for a positive role for purposiveness prove most promising: according to Hegel, what Kant "opens up" with the notion of inner purposiveness is a new way of understanding the relation between concepts and objects in the activity of judgment, one that expands and completes the account provided in the Transcendental Analytic. Thus, despite the ultimate disagreement between Kant and Hegel concerning the status of purposiveness as regulative, Hegel's suggestion that there is room in Kant's philosophy for a positive account of purposiveness is nonetheless warranted. Throughout the chapter, I will suggest that purposiveness plays a much bigger role in Kant's philosophy than is usually acknowledged. Specifically, I argue that the problem of purposiveness is already present in the account of judgment presented in the first *Critique*, and that many of the philosophical issues motivating the third *Critique* can be found in nascent form in the first. Indeed, Hegel's reading of Kant suggests that he views the first and the third *Critiques* as offering one, unified account of judging activity, an account that is indispensable for understanding the orientation of Hegel's idealism as grounded in the relation and opposition between self-consciousness and life.

In order to introduce the purposiveness theme in Kant and lay the groundwork for understanding Hegel's appropriation thereof, I will focus on three central issues that lie at the heart of Hegel's philosophical claim that internal purposiveness and life are constitutive of what he calls the Concept (*der Begriff*). First, purposiveness is understood primarily in connection with the operation of judgment. The principle of purposiveness, which brings unity to the unchecked diversity of nature, enables and empowers judgment in its activities of unifying particulars and universals by ensuring that nature displays a cognizable order that is amenable to judgment and suited for its specific powers. My central claim, both in this chapter and throughout this study, is that purposiveness is an enabling condition of judgment, that the power and potentiality of judgment is grounded in internal purposiveness, and ultimately for Hegel, in a logical concept of life. In the present chapter, my approach to the purposiveness theme centers on Kant's claim that this principle is the "condition of the possibility of the application of logic to nature" (EE 20:212n). More directly, Kant shows that "the principle of purposiveness defines the 'space of judgment,'"[1] or in a contemporary turn of phrase, the space of reasons. Purposiveness opens up the horizon of intelligibility and empowers judgment such that it can operate in a non-arbitrary,

---

[1] Allison 2001, 40.

lawful fashion. What a critique of judgment reveals is that judgment's power is essentially shaped and constituted by internal purposiveness and life, a claim that, as I argue in chapters 5 through 8, is fully developed in Hegel's Subjective Logic.

Second, for both Hegel and Kant, there is a primacy of internal purposiveness over external purposiveness when considered in connection with the operation of judgment. Thus, if purposiveness is the condition of applying logic to nature, the sense of purposiveness at stake here is internal rather than external, and this chapter will explore some of the reasons why this is the case. In order to elaborate on the concept of internal purposiveness, Kant will introduce the idea of a *natural purpose* or *Naturzweck*—in essence, the self-organizing, self-producing form of an organism that displays a distinctive, intrinsic normativity. The unity, form, organization, and activity of natural purposes stands in a special relation to judgment, and poses some problems for how judgment is conceived in the Transcendental Analytic.

Third, the primacy of internal purposiveness over external purposiveness ultimately hinges on an essential connection between the former and a distinctively *human* understanding, an essential connection that will be taken up by Hegel and Schelling in terms of a connection between self-consciousness and life. Although this connection is not ultimately explored by Kant, and its full consideration requires leaving the bounds of Kant's system altogether, what it does suggest is that there is a way of understanding the influence of the third *Critique* on German idealism that does not rely on the complicated fate of the idea of an intuitive understanding.

This chapter will proceed as follows. In section 2.2, I provide a brief overview of the theory of judgment presented in Kant's Transcendental Analytic and argue that there are three problems that are left unresolved by the Analytic, which all demonstrate the need for a principle of purposiveness. Moreover, the Appendix of the Transcendental Dialectic contains a discussion that anticipates the principle of purposiveness in significant ways, further demonstrating the wide-ranging importance of this principle for Kant's philosophy. In section 2.3, I turn to Kant's definition of purposiveness as the *unity of the diverse* or the *necessity and lawfulness of the contingent* (KU 5:180, 404), which provides a solution to the threat posed by the contingency and heterogeneity of nature to judgment's activity as it seeks to unite concepts and objects in a non-arbitrary, lawful fashion. The unity of concept and object sought after by judgment is what Kant calls the purposiveness of form, and he offers two models for understanding this idea: external purposiveness, or the model of artifacts and intentional design; and internal purposiveness, or the model of self-organizing organisms. In section 2.4, I show that Kant identifies a "contradiction" in the concept of external purposiveness that makes it unfit as a principle of judgment, and I argue that internal purposiveness is the preferred model for the purposiveness of form. The concept of a natural purpose (*Naturzweck*) provides the basis for this model and opens up a new way of understanding the lawful relation between concepts and objects. I then take up the antinomy of teleological judgment and argue that Kant's solution to the antinomy reveals the essential connection between internal purposiveness and a distinctly human (rather than intuitive) understanding. Finally, I conclude in section 2.5 by considering an initial worry pertaining to Hegel's appropriation of the concept of internal purposiveness as constitutive—namely, that Hegel subscribes to hylozoism. Addressing this concern allows me to clarify the status of the purposiveness theme.

2.2 Purposiveness in the First *Critique* Theory of Judgment

The central problem of the Transcendental Analytic is to investigate the totality of the concepts of the understanding in their a priori employment, to show the legitimacy of their a priori application to objects in general, and to expound precisely how, or under what conditions, such application— namely, judgment—is possible. Book one of the Analytic, the Analytic of Concepts, is an in-depth "*dissection of the faculty of the understanding,*" which is named as the birthplace of concepts and as the faculty of rules that are the necessary conditions for experience in general (A65–66/B90). Book two, the Analytic of Principles, provides a canon for judgment by providing a priori principles that guide the application of a priori concepts to appearances. In essence, the Analytic consists of a complete catalogue and exposition of the exclusively a priori rules that govern the operations of thought, outlining the universal and necessary conditions without which experience would not be possible.

In what has become a focal point of contention for understanding Hegel as a post-Kantian, Kant famously argues that we have two stems of knowledge: intuitions, which arise out of our receptive capacity to receive sense impressions; and concepts, which arise out of and are produced by the spontaneity of thought. Although both intuitions and concepts are required for knowledge (indeed, they are inseparable in actual experience since concepts without intuitions are empty and intuitions without concepts are blind), they can be analytically separated for the purposes of investigating their respective capacities and must be carefully distinguished if we are to properly understand their respective contributions.[2] Both concepts and intuitions have a pure and material aspect: the material aspect of intuition is simply sensation, and the forms of intuition are space and time (as established in the Transcendental Aesthetic); likewise, empirical concepts are generated a posteriori and arise from reflection upon objects of experience, whereas pure concepts are strictly a priori and constitute the form of the thought of an object in general (A50–51/B74–75). This distinction between pure and empirical concepts, and the problems posed by empirical concepts in particular, will be of great importance when we consider the role of the principle of purposiveness in Kant's theory of judgment as it develops from the first to the third *Critique*. In the Analytic, however, Kant is concerned only with our pure, a priori concepts and the a priori principles necessary for their application. Given Kant's concept/intuition dualism, the key question of the Analytic will be how synthesis and unity can arise, given that knowledge is constituted by two heterogeneous parts; and in the two versions of the Deduction, he argues that although we must consider synthesis at different levels (in the A-Deduction, in intuition, in imagination, and in a concept or transcendental apperception; in the B-Deduction, figurative synthesis or transcendental synthesis of imagination, and intellectual synthesis or the transcendental unity of apperception), ultimately *all synthesis and unity of experience* can be attributed to a spontaneous act of the understanding, self-consciousness, or the original synthetic unity of apperception, the "I think" that accompanies all my representations (B131ff).

Concepts in general are defined by Kant as follows:

[A] concept is always, as regards its *form*, something *universal* which serves as a *rule*. (A106; my emphasis)

Whereas all intuitions as sensible, rest on affections, concepts rest on *functions*. By "function" I mean the *unity of the act of bringing various*

---

[2] There is now a growing literature on Kantian nonconceptualism challenging the widely accepted post-Kantian reading of Kant in which concepts and intuitions are always and in principle inseparable in actual experience. In many of these discussions, McDowell's Hegelian reading of Kant is usually cited as the key representative of conceptualism that defenders of nonconceptualism aim to defeat. See, for example, the discussions in Allais (2009), Hanna (2008), and Schulting (2016). I discuss the role of immediacy in cognition for Hegel in chapter 7.

representations under one common representation. Concepts are based on the *spontaneity of thought,* sensible intuitions on the receptivity of impressions. (A68/B93; my emphasis)

[A] concept . . . is nothing but the *consciousness of this unity of synthesis.* (A103; my emphasis)

There are five central features of Kant's understanding of concepts that are important to note here, features that provide important background for Hegel's understanding of "the Concept" and its mode of operation. First, a concept always refers to the determination of *form* rather than content; more specifically, we might say that the form-giving power of concepts is what enables them to determine the manifold of content in question. However, the form of a concept in the Analytic is understood in a distinctively transcendental sense, and it hinges on the important distinction between general and transcendental logic. Logic for Kant is "the science of the rules of the understanding in general" (A52/B76). In general logic, thought abstracts from *all* content of knowledge, from all objects of the understanding and their differences—for example, pure versus empirical intuitions. General logic deals only with "the mere form of thought," and consists of the strictly a priori rules that constitute the canon of the understanding in its empirical or transcendental employment, considering only the relation of concepts to other concepts and *not* concepts to objects (A54/B78).[3] Transcendental logic, which is a distinctively Kantian contribution and the one that Hegel's *Logic* is said to transform, does not abstract from the entire content of knowledge but considers "the rules of the pure thought *of an object*" (A55/B80; my emphasis); that is, it considers concepts only as they relate a priori to objects. Concepts of transcendental logic constitute the form of thought of an object in general, making up the minimal necessary conditions of possibility for all experience and knowledge. In the Analytic, Kant is concerned strictly with transcendental logic, and the categories are the a priori concepts that constitute the necessary forms of thought required for the experience of an object in general. Whatever else may be said concerning Hegel's approach to logic, its indebtedness to Kant's conception of transcendental logic is undeniable,

---

[3] "General logic, as we have shown, abstracts from all content of knowledge—that is, from all relation of knowledge to the object—and considers only the logical form in the relation of any knowledge to other knowledge; that is, it treats of the form of thought in general" (A55/B79).

and transcendental logic is, minimally, the point of departure for any under-standing of Hegel's *Science of Logic*.[4]

Second, the form of concepts has the character of *universality*. Closely connected with universality for Kant is necessity, and anything that warrants the denomination of a priori always has both these characteristics. However, whereas pure concepts are both universal and necessary, empirical concepts are contingent, though still universal in a more limited sense. The univer-sality of a priori concepts is strict and allows of no exceptions (they are *necessary* conditions), while the universality of empirical concepts is al-ways relative and contingent because it is derived from experience, holding only in "most cases," and insofar as an exception has yet to be found.[5] The contingency of empirical concepts is ineliminable, in part due to the con-tingency of particulars themselves, and in part due to the contingency of the harmony between an empirical concept and its content. Although this problem of contingency at the empirical level is not technically a problem for the Transcendental Analytic, we will see in a moment that Kant's theory of judgment and his understanding of the relation between universals and particulars turns out to be "radically incomplete" until he is able to find a way to secure a certain lawfulness of the contingent in the empirical realm.[6]

The third aspect of the Kantian concept is often remarked to be a novelty of the Copernican Turn that marks its distinctive progress from rationalist, empiricist, and other pre-Kantian ways of thinking about concepts. Kant claims that a concept is something universal that serves as a *rule*, meaning that concepts govern like rules and are not ideas, essences, abstractions, or mental images but, rather, are rules that the understanding gives to itself, which allow us to experience the world as rule-governed.[7] Indeed, "eve-rything in nature, both in the lifeless and in the living world, takes place

---

[4] On Hegel on Kant's transcendental logic, see WL 40–41/5:59–60.

[5]

> [E]xperience never confers on its judgments true or strict, but only assumed and compar-ative universality, through induction. We can properly only say, therefore, that, so far as we have hitherto observed, there is no exception to this or that rule. If, then, a judgment is thought with strict universality, that is, in such a manner that no exception is allowed as possible, it is not derived from experience but is valid absolutely a priori. Empirical universality is only an arbitrary extension of a validity holding in most cases to one which holds in all, for instance, in the proposition, "all bodies are heavy."

When, on the other hand, strict universality is essential to a judgment, this indicates a special source of knowledge, namely a faculty of a priori knowledge. Necessity and strict universality are thus sure criteria of a priori knowledge, and are inseparable from one another" (A2/B3–4).

[6] Allison 2001, 20.

[7] On concepts as rules in Kant, see Pippin (1979, 1976).

according to rules," and moreover, we ourselves, as knowers equipped with concepts and categories, are "lawgiver[s] of nature" (JL 9:11; A126). Inherent in the concept of a rule is that it must have *normative authority*: a rule without normative authority is not a rule, but a mere guideline, suggestion, or recommendation. Thus, concepts as rules, and as conditions for the possibility of experience, also have normative authority, and they govern experience with the strict necessity of laws.

The two final aspects of the Kantian concept must be thought closely together: *spontaneity* and *unity*. Kant refers to concepts as functions, and functions are defined as unity of the act of bringing various representations under one common representation, an act of spontaneity that brings unity to the manifold of sensations, as well as unity among concepts themselves. In defining concepts as functions of unification, Kant binds his theory of concepts with his theory of judgment, claiming that "the only use which the understanding can make of these concepts is to judge by means of them" (A68/B93). Both concepts and judgments are "functions of unity among our representations," expressing the spontaneity of the understanding to collect what is many into one (A69/B93–94). In fact, Kant suggests that we can reduce all acts of the understanding to judgment, to an act of unification, and in addition to being a faculty of rules, the understanding is also a faculty of judgment. Concepts then, are further defined as "predicates of possible judgments [that] relate to some representation of a not *yet* determined object" (A69/B94). By claiming that concepts are predicates of possible judgments, Kant is able to derive a set of a priori concepts—the categories—from the logical functions of judgments, a crucial yet notoriously controversial step in the argument of the Transcendental Analytic.[8] The key here is that both concepts and judgments are acts of unity and synthesis, and Kant is able to derive his set of a priori categories from the logical functions of judgments because "the same function which gives unity to the various representations *in a judgment* also gives unity to the mere synthesis of various representations *in an intuition*; and this unity, in its most general expression, we entitle the pure concept of the understanding" (A79/B104–105). The synthetic unity characteristic of concepts and judgments both find their origin in a spontaneous act of the

---

[8] The cogency and importance of Kant's metaphysical deduction has been much discussed; see, for example, Strawson (1996, 30–31) and Longuenesse (1998). On Hegel's criticism of the metaphysical deduction, see, for example, WL 541/6:289.

understanding, and it is through the unifying function of the understanding that thought is able to determine its objects.

Concepts thus constitute the universal form of objects, operating as rules for the determination of their unity, and originate from the spontaneous activity of the understanding. I highlight these five features of Kant's theory of concepts because, despite some important modifications, all of which will stem from his appropriation of the purposiveness theme, Hegel's concept of the Concept will also be defined by these features, likewise fulfilling all five functions. Given the quick overview of Kant's theory of concepts from the first *Critique*, how exactly does purposiveness fit into this story? I will suggest that there are three interrelated problems left unresolved by the Analytic that all demonstrate the need for a principle of purposiveness, which is not officially introduced until the third *Critique*: first, the problem of underdetermination; second, the problem of concept acquisition; and third, the problem of systematicity. We can view these three problems as the questions to which purposiveness serves as the answer, an answer that both completes Kant's own account of the operation of the power of judgment, and signals the positive function of purposiveness that Hegel remarks upon in the Subjective Logic.

We can begin to understand the need for a concept of purposiveness along with a critique of our capacity for judgment by turning to a distinction drawn by Henry Allison between transcendental and empirical chaos, or the threat of disorder and utter contingency in experience at the transcendental and empirical levels, respectively.[9] The transcendental apparatus of the Aesthetic and Analytic blocks transcendental chaos by guaranteeing an a priori lawfulness of the contingent at a very general but nonetheless very important level. The decree of the Copernican Turn states that objects *must* conform to our concepts; in the Analytic, this means that objects of experience must conform to the minimal form and order provided by the a priori concepts of the understanding—namely, the categories. Most paradigmatically, this entails that experience must conform to the law of causality based on a mechanical model as laid out in the Second Analogy. Transcendental chaos is ruled out by securing the legitimacy, authority, and necessity of the original unity of apperception in the two versions of the Transcendental Deduction: insofar

---

[9] See Allison (2001, 38). My account here is highly indebted to Allison's and follows him in important respects. See also Zuckert (2007, chap. 1, esp. 25) on the threat posed by diversity and contingency.

as it must be possible for self-consciousness or the "I think" to accompany all my representations, these representations must thereby be subject to the conceptual ordering of the categories.[10] Self-consciousness as the spontaneous ground of synthetic unity is what fends off the threat of transcendental chaos, providing a general order to the manifold and ensuring that *all* objects appear in conformity with the a priori laws of the understanding.

However, nothing in the Analytic blocks the threat of empirical chaos, or disorder and contingency in nature at the empirical level. This threat poses a problem insofar as the success of the Copernican Turn requires that objects conform not only to our a priori concepts, but to our empirical ones as well. The necessity and normativity involved in the conformity to empirical concepts is, however, of a different kind from what is involved in the former. At the transcendental level where appearances must conform with the a priori forms of intuition alongside the categories, all under the conditions of the unity of apperception, the necessity and normativity involved is *absolute* and *strict*. Transcendental chaos would involve a different space or time, events without causes, or objects with no intensive magnitudes; for Kant, these possibilities are epistemologically inconceivable in a strong sense, which is what allows for the strict, a priori necessity of the transcendental apparatus of the Aesthetic and Analytic. Empirical chaos registers a slightly different problem, in which "the uniformity that nature necessarily exhibits in virtue of its conformity to the transcendental laws imposed by the very nature of the understanding *does not translate into an empirically accessible uniformity, understood as one which could support induction and analogy.*"[11] In other words, empirical chaos is the concern that we cannot expect to find, broadly speaking, regularities in nature. Empirical chaos would mean that we could not expect similar objects to have similar properties, involve similar processes, or behave in similar ways under similar conditions; in fact, we would have no sense at all of repeatability in nature. An empirically chaotic nature would entirely thwart all talk of types, species, genera, or natural kinds, and despite conformity with transcendental laws, nature itself would nonetheless amount to a "crude chaotic aggregate," preventing the effective employment of inductive or analogical reasoning. Although empirical chaos poses a significant threat to our power of judgment, it is a somewhat weaker

---

[10] As Kant writes, "for otherwise something would be represented in me which could not be thought at all, and that is equivalent to saying that the representation would be impossible, or at least would be nothing to me" (B131–132).

[11] Allison 2001, 38; my emphasis.

threat than that of transcendental chaos, insofar as empirical chaos and order can admit of flexibility and degree without undermining judgment in a way that transcendental chaos and order cannot. As we will see, purposiveness as the answer to the threat of empirical chaos will also imply a weaker and different sense of necessity and normativity, one that is not strict (broad regularities and unity of form in nature can admit of exceptions, anomalies, fuzzy boundaries, and borderline cases, not to mention evolutionary change), but one that is nonetheless sufficiently robust to guide the power of judgment.[12] Although the threat of empirical chaos does not in any way undermine the work Kant has done in the Transcendental Analytic, I tend to agree with Allison that the theory of concepts and judgment contained therein remains radically incomplete insofar as empirical chaos remains a possibility. Near the end of the B-Deduction, Kant reminds his reader that the categories can in no way fend off empirical chaos by making reference to the problem of empirical laws, or what he calls here "special laws":

> [A]ll possible perceptions, and therefore everything that can come to empirical consciousness, that is, all appearances of nature, must, so far as their connection is concerned, be subject to the categories. Nature, considered merely as nature in general, is dependent upon these categories as the original ground of its necessary conformity to law (*natura formaliter spectata*). Pure understanding is not, however, in a position, through mere categories, to prescribe to appearances any *a priori* laws other than those which are involved in a *nature in general*, that is, in the conformity to law of all appearances in space and time. Special laws, as concerning those appearances which are empirically determined, cannot in their specific character be *derived* from the categories, although they are one and all subject to them. To obtain any knowledge whatsoever of these special laws, we must resort to experience.... (B164–165)

The key to this passage lies in the distinction Kant draws between nature in general, or nature viewed from a formal perspective (*natura formaliter spectata*), and nature as the sum of all appearances, or nature viewed from a material perspective (*natura materialiter spectata*).[13] The Analytic is

---

[12] I owe this point of clarification to Jay Bernstein, who has helped me immensely in thinking through this problem.
[13] See B163–164.

primarily concerned with the formal perspective of nature in general and how nature in this formal sense can and in fact *must* appear under the ordering of the laws of the understanding. But being in conformity with the law of all appearances in space and time, although fending off the threat of transcendental chaos, nonetheless leaves experience rather formless and underdetermined. As Kant suggests, empirically determined appearances, or nature viewed from a material perspective (which is how we experience nature for the most part), requires further ordering by "special laws"—empirical laws and concepts—that, although subject to the categories, can only be acquired by turning to experience itself, where induction and analogy play a central role in cognitive processes. When we resort to experience, however, the tools we have for dealing with transcendental chaos prove insufficient for fending off empirical chaos. The categories and principles of the understanding "are not of themselves sufficient to account for the possibility of acquiring empirical concepts," and even worse, they cannot "guarantee the existence of a cognizable order at the empirical level."[14] In short, the Analytic underdetermines experience to such a high degree that as soon as we leave the confines of considering "formal" nature, which appears more and more to be purely an exercise of abstract analysis (we never experience nature as "nature in general"), we are faced with the task of providing order and unity to an empirical manifold that may be entirely resistant to our powers of cognition. The a priori categories and principles of the understanding overgeneralize and underdetermine to such a degree that judgment finds itself helpless when faced with empirical, material nature. As Allison writes: "How, for example, could one apply the concept of causality to a given occurrence unless it were already conceived as an event of a certain kind, for example, the freezing of water?"[15] Thus, although Kant is suggesting that we must resort to experience to acquire special laws, it appears that absent *any* empirical concepts and laws, the a priori categories themselves cannot be applied to particular cases in a way that constitutes knowledge.[16]

[14] Allison 2001, 24, 37. Allison also discusses this issue as a failure to sufficiently account for what Kant calls judgments of experience (2001, 31–32, 37). Elsewhere, he writes that the categories and principles of the Analytic do not "suffice to ground any particular causal law or even to guarantee that such laws are there to be found" (Allison 2000, 80). See also Neiman (1994, 49), who writes that the operations of the understanding are "routine, automatic, and mechanical," and only offers a very basic synthetic unity that leaves much of experience undetermined and unexplained; and Friedman (1991, 76). Kant discusses underdetermination at KU 5:179–181.

[15] Allison 2001, 24.

[16] On the problems surrounding Kant's delimitation of a priori and empirical concepts, see Schrader (1957/1958). Zuckert (2007, 27) argues that there are three specific types of empirical knowledge "that are not determined or guaranteed by the categorial principles": first, the empirical

Two points are worth noting here with respect to the underdetermination of the categories and the threat of empirical chaos. The first is that the transcendental unity of apperception—the all-important thesis of the Deductions that self-consciousness is the ultimate and spontaneous source of unity in experience—does *not* suffice to address how it is that we can make determinate judgments regarding empirical, material nature. Self-consciousness guarantees the unity of nature in general for experience at a transcendental level, but on its own and without further resources, it cannot secure the possibility of empirical concepts that are required for the experience of nature at the empirical level. This is important to keep in mind, both with respect to the introduction of the principle of purposiveness in the third *Critique* and with respect to understanding Hegel's appropriation of Kant in his own theory of concepts and self-consciousness. Although Hegel will undoubtedly take on important aspects of Kant's apperception thesis, what the problem of underdetermination minimally suggests is that a theory of self-consciousness and its a priori concepts does not on its own suffice to account for the possibility or actuality of knowledge.[17] Even for Kant, what will be required is, second, an account of the lawfulness of the contingent at the empirical level, what he calls *the purposiveness of nature*, to ward off empirical chaos and guarantee the possibility of acquiring empirical concepts that allow us to experience empirical nature as rule-governed. Purposiveness comes to pick up the slack of the categories, so to speak, by ensuring that there is a cognizable order at the empirical level where the categories can operate alongside the requisite empirical concepts to produce knowledge of empirical nature. We can begin to see that although self-consciousness and its a priori categories are the formal conditions of possibility for experience in general, it is equally the case that purposiveness will be required as a condition for the determinacy and applicability of self-consciousness's categories and principles.

Still facing the threat of empirical chaos and closely related to the problem of underdetermination is the problem of empirical concept acquisition. In the passage from B164–165 quoted earlier, the description of acquiring empirical concepts sounds somewhat circular: experience of empirical nature is

---

conceptualizability of nature; second, the systematic ordering of natural kinds and laws; and third, the existence and knowability of necessary empirical laws.

[17] This poses serious problems for Pippin's understanding of the "apperception theme" from Kant to Hegel, or at least reveals the apperception theme to be an incomplete account of the relation between these two thinkers.

governed by empirical laws that cannot be derived from the categories, and we must resort to the same experience in order to acquire empirical laws.[18] Since the categories on their own do not provide sufficient order to experience to guarantee that empirical laws are there to be found, it appears that Kant is presupposing the very empirical concepts needed for experience without having explained their condition of possibility. The difficulty and import of providing a plausible account of how empirical concepts are acquired is further exacerbated by the fact that it no longer seems as if categories can be coherently actualized in judgment in the absence of *any* empirical concepts and laws.[19] Kant's oft-cited account of concept acquisition in §6 of the *Jäsche Logic*, which presumably provides an answer to this question, is also famously full of problems. There, Kant argues that the logical operations of comparison, reflection, and abstraction are the conditions for the "generation of every concept whatsoever" (JL 9:94). In order to acquire the concept of a tree, for example, I first compare a spruce, a willow, and a linden in order to discern the differences between them (the leaves, branches, and trunk are of different shapes and sizes). Then, I reflect on their similarities, noting that despite these differences, they in fact all have leaves, branches, and a trunk. Finally, I abstract from the relevant qualities in order to arrive at the concept, "tree."

The details and difficulties of Kant's account have been much discussed, so here I will only sum up three problems with this account that have been frequently noted.[20] First, it does not seem plausible that the three acts are enacted separately, and one after another; rather, if they are the processes involved in acquiring concepts at all, they must be seen as three aspects of one overarching

---

[18] Allison writes: "Since, in contrast to empiricists such as Hume, [Kant] identified experience with empirical knowledge rather than merely the reception of the raw material for such knowledge (impressions), Kant was committed to the view that experience presupposes the possession and use of concepts. And this naturally gives rise to the question of the genesis of those concepts that are required for the very experience through which empirical concepts are supposedly formed" (2001, 23). In addition to circularity, another objection to Kant's account of concept acquisition is that it gives rise to an infinite regress (Allison 2001, 26–27). On concept formation, see also Ginsborg (2006b, esp. 38–41; 1997b) and Longuenesse (1998, chaps. 5 and 6).

[19] For reasons of space, I have omitted a discussion of the schematism here. However, Allison, taking up Longuenesse's treatment of the role of schemata in concept formation, comes to the conclusion that the problems of circularity and regress remain (see 2001, 26), and that the need for a "principle to which judgment must appeal in its logical reflection directed toward the acquisition of empirical concepts for use in judgment" is unavoidable (28). In chapter 7 (sections 7.1.1 and 7.2), I discuss the connection between Hegel's logical determination of life and Kant's schematism.

[20] See, for example, the work of Longuenesse (1998, 115–127), Allison (2001, 21–24), and Ginsborg (2006b, 38–40). Zuckert (2007, 50–52) defends Kant's account of concept acquisition in the *Jäsche Logic*.

activity. Second, the problem of circularity remains, insofar as knowing which relevant properties to compare and which to abstract from presupposes that I must already have some concept of a tree available. Finally, it appears that acquiring the concept of a tree further presupposes that I have a whole host of other concepts (leaves, branches, trunk), resulting in an infinite regress. Acquiring the concept of a tree depends upon having the concept of a leaf, which in turn depends upon having the concept of growth, and so on ad infinitum. As with the problem of underdetermination, the account of empirical concept acquisition turns out to be implausible and incomplete without the introduction of a principle of purposiveness that can guide the logical operations involved in the formation of concepts—most notably, the logical operation of *reflection*— by guaranteeing that empirical nature displays a sufficient degree of order in relation to our cognitive capacities.

Within the context of the first *Critique*, the closest Kant comes to formulating something akin to the principle of purposiveness can be found in the Appendix of the Transcendental Dialectic where he takes up the problem of reason's systematic unity. In the opening of the Analytic, Kant had already suggested that the totality of the knowledge of the pure understanding must exhibit "*interconnection in a system*," constituting a "system, comprehended and determined by one idea" (A65/B89–90). Knowledge that did not form a systematic whole—in short, knowledge that remained a disconnected aggregate—would not qualify as *science* (*Wissenschaft*) in the sense favored by Kant and, later, by the German idealists.[21] We can understand the systematic unity of science as an attempt to fend off chaos at the level of our concepts and categories: reason seeks to bring unity and order to the concepts of the understanding, unifying the manifold of concepts under higher and higher principles with the goal of unification under one unifying idea. Kant writes in the Appendix:

> If we consider in its whole range the knowledge obtained for us by the understanding, we find that what is peculiarly distinctive of reason in its attitude to this body of knowledge, is that it prescribes and seeks to achieve its *systematization*, that is, to exhibit the connection of its parts in conformity with a single principle. This unity of reason always presupposes an idea, namely, that of the form of a whole of knowledge—a whole which is prior to

---

[21] On the Analytic not providing the conditions for science, see Neiman (1994, 52). On the unity of science and its connection to purposiveness, see Guyer (2001) and EE 20:208–209.

the determinate knowledge of the parts and which contains the conditions that determine *a priori* for every part its position and relation to other parts. This idea accordingly postulates a complete unity in the knowledge obtained by the understanding, by which this knowledge is to be not a mere contingent aggregate, but a system connected according to necessary laws. (A645/B673)

Reason seeks to organize the knowledge of the understanding as an organic whole, such that the relation between concepts themselves is not merely contingent but also unified according to necessary laws just like the manifold of experience. Although this demand of reason might seem somewhat excessive, what Kant has in mind is something rather familiar: just as we assume that individual things, despite their differences, can be united into species and kinds, we assume that different species, despite their differences, can be united into a genus, and genera into a family, and so on and so forth, until the highest possible unity is reached (A651–652/B679–680).[22] As Kant suggests, we "recognize a relationship of the different branches, as all springing from the same stem" (A660/B688). We can think of the need for systematization in close connection with the problems of underdetermination and empirical concept formation: systematic unity is the logical counterpart to the unity of the diverse at the empirical level required to fend off the threat of empirical chaos that undermines cognition's efforts to determine nature according to empirical concepts. If we assume that empirically determined nature is not chaotic, then it follows that our concepts that provide order and form to empirical nature must not be chaotic, either. Indeed, Kant specifies the demand for systematic unity with three further principles that are clearly connected with the purposiveness of nature at the empirical level: the principle of homogeneity in the manifold of experience (that particulars display a sufficient degree of homogeneity such that unity under species and higher genera is possible),[23] the principle of specification (that there is diversity and

---

[22] There is much debate within the philosophy of biology concerning the status of these classifications. My reading of Kant and Hegel is compatible with a variety of approaches, and it is not my aim to associate them directly with specific, contemporary views. For an account of such classifications as ontologically unfounded, see Dupré (1995). For an excellent overview of contemporary debates concerning the problem of natural kinds, see Campbell, O'Rourke, and Slater (2011).

[23] Already in the Schematism, Kant wrote that "[i]n all subsumptions of an object under a concept the representation of the object must be *homogeneous* with the concept. . . . This, in fact, is what is meant by the expression 'an object is contained under a concept'" (A137/B176). To further stress the importance of the principle of homogeneity, Kant writes that "in the absence of homogeneity, no empirical concepts, and therefore no experience, would be possible" (A654/B682).

specificity in unity under lower species and subspecies), and the principle of affinity (that there is continuity between all our concepts). Systematic unity thus completes the attempt to bring order and unity to the objects of experience by bringing order and unity to reason itself.

Kant is insistent, however, that the systematic unity of our knowledge is merely an *idea* of reason: it is "only a *projected* unity," a hypothetical employment of reason—because the idea of such a unity remains problematic (A646/B674)—that is merely regulative in directing the understanding and *not* constitutive of objects themselves (A647/B675). We treat our body of knowledge *as if* it were orderable into an increasingly systematic and inclusive unity as a heuristic guide for our cognitive powers in acquiring and organizing our concepts, but we do not determine objectively that our knowledge is in fact systematizable in this way. As the Appendix progresses, however, the status of systematic unity becomes increasingly unclear. At first, Kant begins by discussing the need for systematization as a *logical* principle, whose function is to "assist the understanding by means of ideas," guiding the understanding as a merely regulative principle (A648/B676). The function of this logical principle is distinguished from a *transcendental* principle, which would instead prescribe systematic unity to objects a priori and constitute them in a necessary, objective manner. But as Kant continues to elaborate on the logical principle of systematic unity, he begins to question how such a principle could be legitimately employed without the presupposition of a transcendental principle "whereby such a systematic unity is a priori assumed to be necessarily inherent in the objects" (A650–651/B678–679). Interestingly, Kant poses the question in terms of authority: by what warrant could reason employ such a logical principle of unity in its organization of the understanding's concepts, if nature itself turned out to be entirely heterogeneous, a "crude chaotic aggregate," rendering reason's aim for unity entirely incompatible with the actual constitution of nature?[24] To avoid the possibility that reason has set itself a goal entirely at odds with nature, Kant then claims that the principle of unity is in fact a "necessary law" and "objectively valid," since without the presupposition of a systematic unity of nature, there would be "no reason at all, and without reason no coherent employment of

---

[24] Kant continues: "For with what right can reason, in its logical employment, call upon us to treat the multiplicity of powers exhibited in nature as simply a disguised unity, and to derive this unity, so far as may be possible, from a fundamental power—how can reason do this, if it be free to admit as likewise possible that all powers may be heterogeneous, and that such systematic unity of derivation may not be in conformity with nature? Reason would then run counter to its own vocation, proposing as its aim an idea quite inconsistent with the constitution of nature" (A651/B679).

the understanding, and in the absence of this no sufficient criterion of empirical truth" (A651/B679).

Kant goes on further to suggest that whether or not it has been previously acknowledged, such a *transcendental* presupposition is in fact "hidden" in the principles of philosophers, for without it, the very concepts of genera and species, and "any other universal concept," would be incoherent and impossible to formulate (A651/B679, A654/B682). This is a rather strong and suggestive claim: Kant is arguing here, already in the first *Critique*, that reason requires a transcendental principle of the systematic unity of nature in order for the understanding to acquire and employ concepts, that "no understanding at all would obtain" *without* such a transcendental principle (A654/B682). Despite these strong claims, the status of the principle of unity, along with the principles of homogeneity, specification, and affinity, nonetheless remain ambiguous insofar as Kant continues to discuss these principles as both logical and transcendental in the Appendix.[25] To add further confusion, he also continues to maintain that they are mere ideas of reason and allow only of regulative employment. Without covering over the ambiguities, or attempting to force an easy resolution upon them, I want to suggest that whether the principle is determined as logical or transcendental, what is important here is Kant's formulation of systematic unity, homogeneity, specification, and affinity as the *a priori, necessary, and objectively valid conditions of any employment of the understanding and of empirical truth.* Thus, even by the standards of the first *Critique*, Kant has identified the need for a set of principles, all akin to the principle of purposiveness, to address the problems of underdetermination and concept acquisition left unresolved by the Analytic, and without which experience of nature at the empirical level, along with the possibility of acquiring "special laws," would not be possible. Formulated in this way, there is a clear continuity between the principle of systematic unity in the Appendix and the principle of purposiveness, particularly as it is described in the first and second introductions of the third *Critique*.[26]

---

[25] Rolf-Peter Horstmann (1989, esp. 165–168) argues that the principle of unity in the Appendix is in fact a *logical* principle and, hence, incompatible with the transcendental principle of purposiveness later described in the third *Critique*. Against Horstmann, Allison (2000, 81) argues that this principle in the Appendix must be seen as a "genuinely *transcendental* principle." I tend to agree with Allison on this issue, but I also think that Kant's use of terminology is particularly messy here, suggesting some genuine indecision.

[26] On the similarities and differences between the Appendix and the account of purposiveness in KU, see Zuckert (2007, 26–42, esp. 31–32).

Finally, it is worth noting that Kant's description of the hypothetical employment of reason in the Appendix can be viewed as prefiguring somewhat the activity of reflective judgment in the third *Critique*. The key difference of course between these two operations is that the former refers to reason's activity as guided by a regulative idea, whereas the latter is an activity of judgment guided by a new transcendental principle, but the similarity between them—in that both ascend from a particular to an indeterminate universal—is quite apparent from Kant's descriptions. In the Appendix, Kant compares the apodeictic use of reason with its hypothetical use by claiming that in the former, the universal is certain and "only *judgment* [*Urteilskraft*] is required to execute the process of subsumption, and the particular is thereby determined in a necessary manner" (A646/B674). In the latter case of reason in its hypothetical use, the universal is problematic, a mere idea, and we are only certain of the particular. Guided by "ideas as problematic concepts," reason can only "*approximate* the rule to universality" (A647/B675). Kant is thus explicit concerning the connection between the apodeictic use of reason and determinative judgment which is already defined in the first *Critique* as the subsumption of a particular under a pre-given concept or universal, but here he also anticipates the activity of reflective judgment which ascends from a given particular to an indeterminate universal in describing the hypothetical use of reason.[27] The connection is of some importance because at the very least, it signals to us not only that there is something incomplete about

[27] There is much debate about the continuities and discontinuities of these issues between the first and third *Critiques*. As noted, Allison argues for continuity between systematic unity as a properly transcendental principle in the Appendix and the transcendental principle of purposiveness in the third *Critique*. On the issue of the hypothetical use of reason and reflective judgment, he acknowledges the similarity between them in addressing the movement from particulars to indeterminate universals, but also stresses the differences between the accounts and insists that properly speaking, the first *Critique* of course contains no a priori principle of judgment and no *explicit* delimitation of the distinction between determinative and reflective judgment (see Allison 2001, 14–20; 2000, 83–84). However, Allison is also sympathetic with Longuenesse's argument for the continuity between determinative and reflective judgment, and with the idea that reflective judgment is a theme that is present in Kant's system well before the third *Critique*. The innovation of the third *Critique*, according to Longuenesse, is not the idea of reflective judgment generally, but the idea of a "*merely* reflective judgment," such as the ones we make when we judge something to be beautiful. However, she defends this thesis by focusing on the Analytic (and the Amphiboly in particular) rather than the Appendix (see Longuenesse 1998, 163–166). Neiman (1994, 48–62) is also sympathetic to the idea of a strong continuity between the first and third *Critiques*, particularly on the issues of underdetermination and the necessity of a regulative principle to guarantee the possibility of empirically determined nature as well as science. Horstmann (1989) argues for the incompatibility between the first and third *Critique* on these issues, as does Makkreel (1991, 49–51). Finally, Zuckert (2007, 43–44) acknowledges the important continuities between the Appendix and third *Critique* accounts, while also arguing that the third *Critique* emphasizes the need for a new type of principle of the unity of the diverse that is not present in the Appendix account..

a merely determinative, subsumptive account of judgment[28] but, further, what might be required to answer the problem of how we acquire empirical concepts by resorting to experience.

None of this is meant to suggest that the introduction of reflective judgment and its a priori principle of purposiveness in the third *Critique* do not represent radical innovations from the point of the view of the first, or that there are not significant differences between the various discussions of judgment, reason, regulative ideas, and transcendental principles in the first and third *Critiques*. My contention is only that the problems which motivate the third *Critique*, particularly as articulated by Kant in the introductions to the *Critique of Judgment*, are already present in the first, and hence, that Hegel's suggestion regarding the positive function of purposiveness serving as a necessary supplement to the negative project of the first *Critique* is not only well founded as a reading of Kant but also a sentiment arguably shared by Kant himself. In the third *Critique*, it will become clear that purposiveness not only resolves the problem of empirical knowledge for Kant but, further, that it provides the condition for a much broader conception of experience that includes meaningful engagements with aesthetic and organic objects.[29] In the next section, I turn directly to Kant's formulation of the principle of purposiveness as presented in the *Critique of Judgment*, which provides a solution to the problem of empirical chaos already opened up by the first *Critique*.

2.3 "Applying Logic to Nature": The Principle of Purposiveness

In the *Critique of Judgment*, Kant employs the notion of purposiveness in three related ways: first, as a newly proposed transcendental principle of nature's purposiveness for the operation of reflective judgment (and arguably for judgment more broadly speaking);[30] second, in reference to the subjective purposiveness of our cognitive powers, which is accompanied by the

---

[28] Allison writes that "an account of judgment solely in terms of determination is inherently incomplete, requiring as its complement the activity that Kant terms 'reflection'" (2001, 18).

[29] One could argue that purposiveness also provides the condition for a full grasp of morality and history, although it is well beyond the aim of this book to defend that claim.

[30] Kant claims in §76 of KU that without purposiveness, we could not even make determining judgments, that the purposiveness of nature is "necessarily valid for our *human power of judgment* as if it were an objective principle" (KU 5:404).

feeling of pleasure in reference to beautiful objects; and third, in reference to the objective, material purposiveness of organic products, which appear to be self-organizing and exhibit in their unity a reciprocal determination between causes and effects.[31] In this section, I will address purposiveness in the first sense and begin to spell out in more detail Kant's own view concerning the positive function of purposiveness for his theory of concepts and judgment. In the next section (2.4), I will address purposiveness in the third sense in reference to organic products, arguing that internal purposiveness is the primary sense of purposiveness that opens up the horizon of intelligibility and judgment.[32]

Two years prior to the publication of the third *Critique*, Kant had claimed that the employment of teleological principles always "concern[s] the method of thinking," already suggesting that reflection upon purposes and ends concerns our concepts, categories, and principles, rather than the nature of things or objects considered independently of our modes of thought (TP 8:160). Indeed, Allison suggests that "the principle of purposiveness defines the 'space of judgment,'"[33] and Kant himself claims in the first introduction that purposiveness is the "condition of the possibility of the application of logic to nature" (EE 20:212n). Although reasoning on the basis of purposes is, in the Western philosophical tradition, most commonly associated with Aristotle, the emphasis on logic and the method of thinking is an important Kantian innovation that places teleological notions within the context of the Copernican Turn, in which the determination of objects cannot be considered in isolation from the concepts employed by cognition in its operations of knowledge.[34] That purposiveness for Kant concerns logic and the method of thinking needs to be highlighted in particular, since my argument in later chapters will be that Hegel's appropriation of the purposiveness theme is oriented in the same way, with Hegel eventually turning to develop a distinctly logical concept of life in connection with his philosophical method. Still addressing the same problems of underdetermination, empirical concept acquisition, and systematicity, Kant now turns directly to

---

[31] Zuckert (2007, 64) takes the latter two types of judgments to be "exhibitions" of reflective judgment generally.

[32] For reasons of thematic unity and space, I will not be addressing purposiveness in the second sense in connection with aesthetic judgments.

[33] Allison 2001, 40.

[34] See Horstmann (2013) on the epistemic significance of purposiveness and its connection to the objective validity of judgments. In chapter 6, I take up Hegel's suggestion that purpose, as the concrete universal, is the basis of objective judgment (see WL 656/6:443–444).

our power of judgment, our capacity "to think the particular as contained under the universal,"[35] and claims that reflective judgment, which ascends from particulars to universals, especially in those cases where no available universal suffices to determine the particular before us, requires its own transcendental principle in order to operate at all (KU 5:179).

The introduction of reflective judgment signals a significant shift in orientation from the Appendix account, in which reason and its regulative ideas were assigned the task of ensuring that nature in its material manifold could be assumed to have a cognizable order. Unlike reason, which operates at the level of ideas in order to provide an overarching unity, and whose sole object is the understanding and its effective operation,[36] judgment is concerned directly with our experience of concrete, empirical particulars and the possibility of their determinability. The emphasis here should be placed on the idea of particulars: insofar as judgment thinks the *particular* as contained under a universal, Kant is now not only concerned with the systematic unity of reason but also with the ground-level business of what it means to "resort to experience" in all its contingency, where the assistance of the categories proves idle.[37] And indeed, despite this shift in the assignment of duties, Kant continues to reiterate the same problem we saw earlier—namely, that the a priori laws of the pure understanding "concern only the possibility of a nature as such," that there is a diversity in nature that is "left undetermined by these laws," and that this infinite diversity would leave us groping around in a "crude chaotic aggregate without the slightest trace of a system" (KU 5:179; EE 20: 209).

Kant's solution in the form of the principle of purposiveness is defined as the *unity of the diverse* or the *necessity and lawfulness of the contingent* (KU 5:180, 404). What he has in mind concerns the harmony or fit between our cognitive powers and nature—that is, the appropriateness of our cognitive

---

[35] Compare this with the first *Critique* definition: "all judgments are functions of unity among our representations" (A69/B93). Ginsborg (2006b, 35–36) suggests that Kant's definition of judgment as thinking the particular as contained under the universal refers to two senses of universality (universality in terms of the generality of concepts that allow us to identify common features of individual objects, and universality in terms of universal validity for a plurality of subjects), and argues that the second sense is primary.

[36] See A643–A644/B671–B672.

[37] See also EE 20:213: "But for those concepts which must first of all be found for given empirical intuitions, and which presuppose a particular law of nature, in accordance with which alone *particular* experience is possible, the power of judgment requires a special and at the same time transcendental principle for its reflection, and one cannot refer it in turn to already known empirical concepts and transform reflection into a mere comparison with empirical forms for which one already has concepts."

capacities and concepts to be directed toward knowing nature, and the appropriateness of nature's forms to be amenable to our knowledge. In framing the problem in terms of cognitive fit—between knowing and world, subject and object, concepts and nature—the scope of this principle and the potential range of its positive functioning come to look rather wide, appearing not only to define the space of judgment, as Allison suggests, but also providing the ground-level enabling condition under which judgment can think the particular as contained under the universal in the first place. As an antidote to the "disturbing" threat of boundless heterogeneity, diversity, and contingency of nature that would prevent us from successfully forming empirical judgments (EE 20:209), Kant specifies the task of the principle of purposiveness as follows:

> The principle of reflection on given objects of nature is that for all things in nature empirically determinate *concepts* can be found, which is to say the same as that in all of its products one can always presuppose a form that is possible for general laws cognizable by us. For if we could not presuppose this and did not ground our treatment of empirical representations on this principle, then all reflection would become arbitrary [*Geratewohl*] and blind, and hence would be undertaken without any well-grounded expectation of its agreement with nature. (EE 20:211–212)[38]

The scope of this claim is so wide, and the capacity it provides to judgment so powerful, that it should surely give us pause: everything in nature is in principle conceivable according to concepts, and nothing in nature is in principle beyond the reach of judgment's powers. Moreover, the principle of purposiveness prevents judgment from being arbitrary, haphazard, and blind: without this principle, the agreement of our judgments with nature (the agreement of concepts and objects) would be ungrounded and contingent. It is in a footnote to this passage that Kant claims purposiveness as a condition for applying logic to nature, that logic itself could not be binding on experience without the assumption of nature's purposiveness. The scope of purposiveness seems to be matched only by the scope of the threat judgment faces, a threat so immense that it could render all reflection arbitrary and without ground. This transcendental principle of *"the logical use of the power of judgment"* provides the basis for a *"logical system,"* which allows us

---

[38] See also EE 20:202–203; and KU 5:180–181.

to assume that "nature in its boundless multiplicity has hit upon a division of itself into genera and species" that makes possible not only the formation of empirical concepts but also the possibility of conceptual ascent (EE 20:213–214).[39] The purposiveness of nature thus provides the horizon for the meaningful experience of particulars, the horizon of conceptualizability and determinability, and serves as the solution to the problem of empirical chaos left open by the first *Critique*. In short, purposiveness opens up the very possibility of judgment.

Before turning to two conceptual puzzles in connection with the notion of purposiveness, an important and familiar Kantian qualification should be noted. Although there is no doubt as to the a priority and transcendentality of this principle, Kant designates a strange kind of authority to purposiveness insofar as it serves not to constitute the object but only to regulate our own subjective activity of reflective judgment. The principle of purposiveness is still *regulative* with respect to our cognition: it does not tell us that nature actually *is* purposive, but only tells us that we must judge nature *as if* it were organized in this way. Purposiveness only tells us how we ought to judge, and Kant contrasts what he calls the heautonomy of judgment with autonomy: whereas the former legislates a law to itself and only has subjective validity, the latter legislates objectively (gives laws to nature in the case of the understanding, and to the realm of freedom in the case of reason). Unlike the categories, the principle of purposiveness cannot determine or constitute an object but refers solely to the subject who *must* judge in this way, who in fact always already does so, even if only covertly or implicitly, if reflection is to yield determinate, empirical knowledge. For Kant, purposiveness thus remains a subjective, a priori, transcendental principle without constitutive power, a claim that Hegel and Schelling will take great pains to reject.[40] Contra Kant, Hegel will suggest that purpose, properly understood, is the Concept in its concrete, objective existence, a claim I will take up in detail in part II of this study.

---

[39] "The special principle of the power of judgment is thus: *Nature specifies its general laws into empirical ones, in accordance with the form of a logical system, in behalf of the power of judgment*" (EE 20:216).

[40] See, for example, WL 656/6:443–444: "The Concept, as end [*Zweck*], is of course an *objective judgment*.... But the end relation is not for that reason a *reflective* judging that considers external objects only according to a unity, *as though* an intelligence had given this unity *for the convenience of our cognitive faculty*; on the contrary it is the absolute truth that judges *objectively* and determines external objectivity absolutely."

Although purposiveness comes to play a central role in Kant's account of how we judge particulars, it also raises a number of problems, and there are two in particular that I want to address. In defining judgment's principle as the unity of the diverse and the lawfulness of the contingent, what purposiveness describes is a *relation* between concepts and objects, or in Kant's broader terms, the relatability of logic and nature. Purposiveness attempts to guarantee that the fit between concepts and the particulars that fall under them is not merely a contingent accident but also obtains some kind of necessity and has the status of a law. The unity in question thus cannot be aggregative but must constitute a lawful, internal organization of an object and tell us something essential about its being and/or functioning. Kant spells out the purposive relation between concept and object as follows:

> insofar as the concept of an object also contains the ground for the object's actuality, the concept is called the thing's *purpose* and a thing's conformity with that character of things which is possible only through purposes is called the *purposiveness* of its form. (KU 5:180)

> a purpose is the object of a concept insofar as we regard this concept as the object's cause (the real ground of its possibility); and the causality that a *concept* has with regard to its *object* is purposiveness (*forma finalis*). (KU 5:220)

We speak of purposes and purposiveness when the relation between concept and object is one in which a concept is taken to be the cause of an object. The notion of cause is specified by Kant here as the ground of an object's *actuality* or the *real ground of its possibility*—for now I simply want to highlight this understanding of "cause" in the definition of purposiveness and note that it is of utmost importance for Hegel's concept of the Concept, and more specifically, for his concept of actuality (*Wirklichkeit*) and self-actualization, which will be taken up in detail in chapter 4. Two problems can be gleaned from Kant's definition. The first is that purposiveness describes a relation between concept and object that is explicitly denied to the concepts of the understanding in the first *Critique*. There, concepts denoted merely the *formal* possibility of objects, and sensation was required to determine the actuality of an object.[41] Kant is emphatic, even in the third *Critique*, that when

---

[41] See A218/B265, A225/B272.

the understanding thinks something according to its concept, that thing is merely possible, whereas it is only when the understanding is aware of something as given in intuition that the thing is actual.[42] In a purposive relation, concepts are sufficient for determining the actuality or *real* possibility of objects, suggesting that what Kant means by "concept" here is somewhat different from his standard account. In a purposive relation, a concept has the power to determine the actuality of an object. How is this possible? The answer is that the model for the purposive relation described by Kant is clearly that of intentional artifice or design: a concept is taken to be the cause of an object when its designer conceives of the concept in advance, creating the object in conformity with the preconceived concept. Thus, objects that are created according to preconceived concepts, like artifacts, display a purposiveness of form by being both the actualization of a concept in an *object* (for example, a Rubik's Cube), and by indicating the purposive activity of a designer *subject* who brought the concept to its actualization (for example, Ernö Rubik). In the case of designed objects, not only is the relation between concept and object necessary but also the concept determines the unity and functioning of the object in a lawlike manner.

Rather than resolving the problem, however, the artifact/designer model of purposiveness simply raises a further one: given that Kant's principle concerns the purposiveness of *nature*, the analogy with artifacts becomes rather unhelpful and unconvincing insofar as one has to posit a designer-God as the ultimate architect of nature. Despite a certain appeal of the design model, which enables us to establish the necessary relation between concept and object that is the desideratum of our knowledge of nature, treating nature *as if* it were an artifact not only runs counter to our sense that there is a crucial difference between artificial (created) and natural objects but, further, Kant's own philosophy suggests that such a designer-God can never be known by us at all. At best, there can be something like a moral proof or postulation of God for pure practical reason, and indeed, this is how the *Critique of Judgment* ends. This would appear to be a rather unsatisfactory conclusion to what looks like the central problem facing Kant's theory of judgment: Kant cannot be suggesting that our daily, routine activity of forming empirical judgments and acquiring empirical concepts requires that we judge nature *as if* it were an artifact designed by a God we cannot know. This makes the burden of proof for his theory of judgment so incredibly high, and the

---

[42] KU 5:402.

theory itself so unwieldy, that we would be wise to simply reject it wholesale. The artifact model thus comes to look inherently unfit as an explanation of the purposiveness of nature, and we have yet to find an appropriate model for the concept-object relation that would ensure that judgment's operations are not arbitrary and blind.

I will argue that the way out of this problem—understanding the purposiveness of nature as the necessary horizon of determinability for judgment *without* resorting to the artifact model—can be found by way of the concept of *internal* purposiveness. To be clear, I am not suggesting that this is the path taken by Kant; as we shall see, although Kant considers this path seriously and with great insight, and even comes close to drawing such a conclusion, purposiveness remains an undoubtedly regulative concept within the confines of the critical project. I will argue, however, that although Kant distinguishes between different senses of purposiveness, it is inner purposiveness that should be taken as primary, and further, that it is the appropriate concept-object model sought after by Kant in finding a solution to the problem of reflective judgment. In addition to the manifold problems involved with positing an intentional artificer of nature, the larger conceptual problem is that the artifact model can only bring us as far as *external* purposiveness, a means-ends relation that is inappropriate for explaining nature even by Kant's own standards. Thus, although inner purposiveness is never granted constitutive status for Kant, his own, preferred model according to intentional design fails by his own account, and it is this line of thought that leads Hegel to affirm inner purposiveness as, in fact, Kant's better argument.

2.4 Internal Purposiveness and *Naturzwecke*

In the Critique of Teleological Judgment (CTJ), Kant specifies the idea of nature's purposiveness beyond a principle of the unity of the diverse by turning directly to what is called the real, objective, and material purposiveness of nature. Rather than simply considering judgment's need for a principle of unity and lawfulness, objective purposiveness considers the unity and lawfulness present in nature's forms themselves, most evidently displayed in the organization and activity of living organisms. Although the account of objective purposiveness takes us beyond purposiveness as a subjective principle, my argument will be that there is a primacy of internal purposiveness over external purposiveness implied in Kant's discussion, a primacy that reveals the essential connection between purposiveness as objectively displayed in the form of an organism and purposiveness as a necessary condition for the activity of judgment.[43] Specifically, I contend that Kant's resolution to the antinomy of teleological judgment suggests that there is a reciprocity between internal purposiveness and a distinctly human understanding, which sets the stage for the interpretation of Hegel defended in the remainder of this study.

Kant distills the idea of objective, material purposiveness of nature by drawing two distinctions in the opening sections of the CTJ. The first is between an objective purposiveness that is merely formal and intellectual and one that is properly material and real. Using the example of geometric figures, Kant argues that although such figures are objectively purposive—"useful for solving many problems by a single principle, and each of them presumably in an infinite variety of ways" (KU 5:362)—this purposiveness is formal because the possibility of such figures does not depend on the formulation of any determinate purpose: the possibility of circles, triangles, and hexagons do not depend upon any specific use that we might put them to, and they can be conceived by the understanding without the formulation of any purpose whatsoever. In the case of real or material purposiveness—for example, a garden composed of an aggregate of trees, flower beds, and walks (KU 5:364)—we cannot conceive the possibility of the object without the concept of a purpose, which means that material purposiveness necessitates teleological thinking and teleological judgments.

The second distinction Kant draws is that between an objective purposiveness that is merely relative or external and one that is internal—the key distinction cited by Hegel as Kant's great service to philosophy. External purposiveness "is called either usefulness (for human beings) or benefit (for any other creature)," and we make judgments as to the relative purposiveness of objects whenever they are taken simply as means (KU 5:367). We can see many examples of relative or external purposiveness in nature: sandy soil is beneficial for spruces, and hence, sand is relatively purposive when considered in connection with the existence and thriving of spruces; grass is beneficial, necessary in fact, for the existence of cattle, sheep, and horses; these animals in turn are beneficial for human civilization (KU 5:367–369). It is clear that artifacts also fall under this general description of external

---

[43] On the basis of a passage from EE 20:218, Ginsborg (2006a, 465) also argues that there is a connection between purposiveness as a subjective principle of judgment and purposiveness as objectively ascribed to organisms.

purposiveness, insofar as they are created as "means that other causes employ purposively" (KU 5:367). We build houses as the means for achieving the purpose of dwelling (or renting), and we make hammers as the means for achieving the purpose of hammering; in short, external purposiveness displays relations of utility. In order to articulate the meaning of internal purposiveness, a case in which *"everything is an end and reciprocally also a means"* (KU 5:376), Kant turns to the concept of a natural purpose or end (*Naturzweck*), describing it as follows:

> But in order to judge something that one cognizes as a product of nature as being at the same time an end, hence a *natural end* [Naturzweck], something more [than the comparison with a product of art[44]] is required if there is not simply to be a contradiction here. I would say provisionally that a thing exists as a natural end *if it is cause and effect of itself.* (KU 5:370–371)

Kant is claiming that we need something more than a comparison with artifacts if there is not to be a contradiction in his attempt to spell out a notion of objective, material purposiveness—what exactly is the contradiction here? I want to suggest that what Kant is calling a contradiction is the claim, entertained throughout the third *Critique*, that the purposiveness of nature can be understood on the model of artifact production and design. This is a contradiction because even in our everyday use of the term "natural," what we mean is precisely something *not* designed, created, or conceived with intention. Conceiving of nature as a product of art means that nature is not natural (it is, instead, artificial), which at first glance, looks like a contradiction in terms. Thus, despite the fact that Kant himself has employed the comparison with artifacts, what he is stating here is that, strictly speaking, comparing nature with artifacts has to be a contradiction in terms, that treating nature as a product of art is not to explain the purposiveness distinctive of nature at all. This is what the distinction between internal and external purposiveness is meant to draw out: when we conceive of nature as a product of art, we are at most viewing it as embedded in relations of external purposiveness, as mere means toward ends external to the products themselves. Picking up on this contradiction identified by Kant, Hegel's chapter on "Teleology" in the

---

[44] In the previous paragraph, Kant is discussing the experience of someone who comes across a hexagon drawn in the sand. This person arrives at the conclusion that the hexagon must be the result of a rational cause, and thus, that the purposiveness of the figure can only be considered a product of art (KU 5:370).

Science of Logic likewise criticizes all forms of teleology that depend upon "an *extramundane* intelligence" or an "*absolute* will," which "suffers [in] that it only goes as far as *external purposiveness*" (WL 652–653/6:438–440).[45] Kant also notes: "*external* purposiveness of natural things offers no sufficient justification for using them at the same time as ends of nature, as grounds for the explanation of their existence" (KU 5:377). Thus, although Kant generally describes the principle of purposiveness in terms of judging nature *as if* it were art, along the lines of a designer/artifact model,[46] he is now claiming in the CTJ that judging nature according to the principle of external purposiveness, where nature is viewed "as a means that other causes employ purposively," is both "reckless and arbitrary [*ein sehr gewagtes und willkürliches Urteil*]" (KU 5:367, 369). The suggestion that judging nature according to external purposiveness is reckless and arbitrary is key, since earlier, Kant had claimed that the entire point of the principle of purposiveness was to *prevent* judgment from becoming arbitrary and blind (EE 20:212). In addition to being a contradiction, external purposiveness now looks to be inherently unfit for its intended role of guiding the activity of judgment as it seeks a necessary, lawful unity of concept and object in its investigations of empirical nature. To avoid judgments such as god made snow so that we could travel by sleigh, or (a favorite example of Hegel's) cork trees so that we might have bottle stoppers,[47] what is required instead is a model for understanding purposiveness that is not structured around ideas of intentionality or design. The only plausible, non-contradictory way to conceive of the purposiveness of nature, then, is to conceive of a reciprocal relation between causes and effects, or means and ends, internal to an object, a form of self-organization distinctly characteristic of living organisms.

Using a tree as an example, Kant elaborates on what it means for something to be the cause and effect of itself in three different ways: first, at the level of the species, a natural purpose is the cause and effect of itself insofar as a tree will produce another tree of its own kind; second, at the level of the individual, a natural purpose is the cause and effect of itself insofar as a tree maintains, generates, and develops itself by assimilating materials from its environment; third, a natural purpose is the cause and effect of itself in the

---

[45] "The more the teleological principle was linked with the concept of an *extramundane* intelligence and to that extent was favored by piety, the more it seemed to depart from the true investigation of nature, which aims at cognizing the properties of nature not as extraneous, but as *immanent determinatenesses* and accepts only such cognition as a valid *comprehension*" (WL 652/6:438).

[46] See KU 5:193 and EE 20:215–218.

[47] See PN §245Z.

mutual dependence and reciprocal causality between its parts, for each part of the tree is at once a cause and effect of every other part of the tree (KU 5:371–372). In §65, Kant continues to elaborate on the internal purposiveness of *Naturzwecke* by specifying a reciprocal relation between whole and parts such that parts are dependent upon the whole and the whole dependent on its parts: "in such a product of nature each part is conceived as if it exists only *through* all the others, thus as if existing *for the sake of the others* and *on account of* the whole . . . (consequently each produces the others reciprocally)" (KU 5:373–374). Kant calls this the *self-organization* of the natural product and uses an example of a watch to further elucidate his point: although we can certainly understand the function of a watch according to part/whole relations, the parts of the watch do not produce one another, nor do they produce the watch as a whole; a watch cannot produce further watches but requires an intelligent designer; if parts of a watch are missing or broken, the watch cannot repair itself—all of which natural purposes can do (KU 5:374). Kant then differentiates between machines, which have mere "*motive* force," and self-organizing beings, which have "*formative* force" [bildende *Kraft*].[48]

There are two features of Kant's presentation of the unity and form of *Naturzwecke* that are especially important for understanding how this contributes to a theory of judgment and concepts beyond the account of the first *Critique*. First, Kant's presentation of the unity and form of natural purposes allows us to reconsider the original definition of the purposiveness of form—a relation of causality between concept and object—without resorting to notions of design. In section IV of the published introduction and §10 of the Critique of Aesthetic Judgment, Kant had stated that the purposiveness of form was characterized by a concept-object relation in which a concept contains the ground for an object's actuality, and that it is only in such cases that we refer to the concept or object as a purpose or end.[49] Purposiveness of form refers to the power or "causality" of a concept with regard to its object, and this relationship defined for Kant the unity of diversity and lawfulness of the contingent that provided the horizon of determinability for judgment. The unity and form of a natural purpose displays this power of causality *without* invoking design: the whole—a "synthetic universal":[50]

---

[48] See also KU 5:419. On the influence of Kant on Blumenbach, see Larson (1979) and Lenoir (1980; 1982). For critiques of Lenoir, see Richards (2000); and Zammito (2012).

[49] See the discussion in section 2.3 of Kant's definition of purposiveness form at KU 5:180 and 5:220.

[50] KU 5:407.

the unity and form of a single organism, the unity and form of a species or genus—comes to stand in for a concept, and the reciprocal dependency of whole and parts allows us to conceive of a necessary, lawful relation between concept and object that meets the requirements for purposive form. This form of self-organization and the power of the whole to shape the actuality of the object suggest an entirely different understanding of concepts, a different understanding of conceptual form, in which the latter are neither formal nor empty but, instead, internally self-actualizing and concrete. As I will argue at length in the remainder of this study, the internal organization of a natural purpose becomes the basis for Hegel's concept of the "Concept," allowing him to transform each of the five interrelated functions associated with Kant's concept of the concept discussed in section 2.2 (form, universality, rule/normativity, spontaneity/activity, and unity).

Once the purposiveness of form is redefined in accordance with internal rather than external purposiveness, a second feature of Kant's discussion further expands the theory of concepts and judgment provided in the first *Critique*—namely, a different understanding of necessity and normativity. Earlier, I claimed that whereas the solution to transcendental chaos involved establishing absolute and strict conformity with a priori concepts, purposiveness as the solution to empirical chaos involves a weaker sense of necessity and normativity, one that allows for degrees of nonconformity (exceptions, anomalies, fuzzy boundaries, borderline cases, evolutionary change) without thereby undermining either the power of reflective judgment in its search for unity and order in nature, or the power of the whole in providing unity and form to the object in question.[51] For Kant, the self-organization of a natural purpose expresses a distinctive *internal normativity and necessity* that recalls Aristotle's claim that nature is a "principle in the thing itself."[52] Kant explains the necessity and normativity in question as follows:

A teleological judgment compares the concept of a product of nature as it is with one of what it *ought to be* [*was es* sein soll]. Here the judging of its

---

[51] As Michael Thompson (2008) has argued, the "degree" of conformity and nonconformity between concept and object here is not tracked statistically—that is, the purposiveness of form is not a claim about the power of a whole or synthetic universal to determine the actuality of a particular object in "most cases." See also the discussion in Chaouli (2017, 238–239).

[52] Aristotle, *Metaphysics* XII.3.1070a8. Across nearly all his writings, Kant will also define life as an inner principle or inner capacity of spontaneous activity and self-movement. For example, in the *Metaphysical Foundations of Natural Science*, Kant writes: "*Life* is the faculty of a *substance* to determine itself to act from an *internal principle*" (MN 4:544).

possibility is grounded in a concept (of the end) that precedes it *a priori*. There is no difficulty in representing the possibility of products of art in such a way. But to think of a product of nature that there is something that it *ought to be* and then to judge whether it really is so already presupposes a principle that could not be drawn from experience (which teaches only what things are). (EE 20:240)

Here, Kant is already indicating that the concept of internal purposiveness in question, insofar as it has power over what a product of nature is and ought to be, is something a priori. Although he does not develop this thought further, Hegel, too, will ultimately claim that the logical concept of life is an a priori concept insofar as it provides the necessary basis governing the actuality of all cognition, expressing a normative power to shape both what cognition is and what it ought to be.[53] Regarding the previous passage, the example Kant uses to elaborate on the ought-character of natural purposes is to compare our judgment of a stone and our judgment of an eye: whereas the stone can be judged as useful for many purposes (building, throwing, sitting, sculpting), we judge that an eye was *meant* for seeing (seeing is the purpose of eyes), that eyes that can't see, or see imperfectly, are defective in some way. Hannah Ginsborg has argued that for Kant, this is a distinctive sense of natural normativity that is neither a cognitive ought of theoretical reason, nor a moral ought of practical reason, nor even the weaker ought of practical rationality that we might attribute to a hypothetical creator.[54] Rather, although it is a "thin" sense of normativity, "there is nothing mysterious about it," and we frequently invoke this sense of normativity when we speak of particulars in relation to their natural kind or species.[55] Just as the concept of normativity changes in light of the background of inner purposiveness, so does the concept of necessity: necessity in the relevant sense here does not mean true in all possible worlds (eyes are meant for seeing, or evolved to see, only in our actual world), nor does it require the elimination of all contingency (understanding that eyes are meant for seeing is compatible with all sorts of contingencies involved in their evolution and ongoing functioning);

---

[53] Bernstein (2001, 301) discusses life as a "material a priori." This would fit Kant's own description of a natural purpose, which he illustrates through the tree example: the unity and form of the tree (the concept as purpose) precedes and shapes its functioning, determining whether it functions well or badly, but this unity and form is only ever materially manifest in actual trees, and has no self-sufficient existence independent of the actual lives of trees.

[54] See Ginsborg (1997a; 2001; 2006a).

[55] Ginsborg 1997a, 356; see also Ginsborg 2014.

rather, necessity is indexed to a purposive whole that supplies substantial unity and form while accommodating nonconformity, deficiencies, and un-realized potentialities.[56] For now, we can note once more that nothing about this internal self-organization requires the positing of intentional design: just as individual parts (or organs) are purposive with respect to the whole and are dependent on the whole for their actuality and functioning, organic individuals are purposive with respect to their kind or species and are like-wise dependent on their species for their actuality and functioning. Insofar as Kant himself views external purposiveness as inadequate and contradictory as a model for the purposiveness of nature, the preferred model of purposive-ness considered in connection with judgment must fall to *internal* purpos-iveness, or the unity, lawfulness, and self-organization of natural purposes.

There are two final puzzles that I want to address before turning briefly to Hegel's transformation of inner purposiveness as an organizing principle of his own philosophical system. Both of them reveal Kant's enduring ambiv-alence concerning the concept of inner purposiveness and the depth of his commitment to the thought that this idea has a merely regulative status. As we will see in the chapters that follow, Hegel spends much of his own argu-mentative efforts trying to defeat this claim in various ways, which at the very least reveals the extent to which he felt the force of Kant's opposition. Turning to the first puzzle, although Kant is clear that the organization of natural purposes cannot be sufficiently grasped on the model of artifacts, he struggles to find an appropriate "analogue" and claims that perhaps we can come closer to "this inscrutable property if one calls it an *analogue of life*" (KU 5:374). This proposal is immediately rejected, however, since for Kant, "all matter, as such, is lifeless," and committing to this analogy would mean committing to hylozoism (the belief that all matter is living or ensouled), which would be nothing less than "the death of all natural philosophy" (MN 4:544).[57] Notice the strangeness of Kant's claim here: we cannot treat organisms as living things, and organism and life are sufficiently distinct that we cannot even treat them as loosely analogous. Although one might have thought that in talking of inner purposiveness and natural purposes Kant was already talking about life all along, the analogue claim makes it clear that this is not the case. Strictly speaking, for Kant, life "is the faculty of a being to act in accordance

---

[56] I discuss Hegel's treatment of modality and necessity in chapter 4 and his treatment of "judgments of necessity" in chapter 5.
[57] See also KU 5:394.

with the law of the faculty of desire [*Begehrungsvermögen*]," where the faculty of desire is the capacity of a being "to be through its representations the cause of the actuality of these representations" (KpV 5:9n).[58] Kant's tree example therefore does not fit into this definition of life, and only organisms with the capacity to act according to representations of their desires would count as life according to this definition.[59] Having rejected the analogy with life, Kant claims that there is in fact nothing that is analogous to the internally purposive causality displayed by natural purposes, and in a last attempt, he tentatively suggests that we could perhaps draw a "remote" analogy with our own capacity to act according to purposes. The inconceivability of analogues here between organism, life, and human purposiveness remains an impasse, one that post-Kantian thinkers will attempt to resolve with great interest.

The second puzzle concerns the discussion of the intuitive understanding in §§76 and 77. In §70, Kant presents the antinomy of teleological judgment, which as noted by Hegel, can be viewed as a more specified version of the third antinomy from the first *Critique*.[60] The antinomy is between mechanistic principles, on the one hand, and teleological principles, on the other: either all material things are judged to be possible on the basis of mechanical principles alone, or some material things cannot be judged as possible on the basis of mechanistic principles alone and, instead, require teleological ones (KU 5:387). Implied in the first claim is that there is no causality according to purposes (including our own), and hence, no freedom. Implied in the second claim is that causality according to purposes (including our own) is indeed possible, and hence, that freedom is possible. Officially, the antinomy is resolved by claiming that there is no antinomy at all, that there is only the "appearance" of an antinomy: when both are treated as regulative principles for reflective judgment, they do not conflict, for as long as neither

---

[58] On Kant's use of this term, see the Kant-Lexicon entry on "life" in Ng (forthcoming). See also Zammito (2006, 762–763) and Chaouli (2017, 258–259) on Kant's distinction between organism and life.

[59] Although Hegel will not operate with Kant's distinction between organism and life, nearly all of the central discussions of life in his philosophy associate life in the relevant sense with desire and self-consciousness. Importantly, in the chapter on "Life" in the *Logic*, the form of activity in question clearly belongs to an animal that acts in accordance with desires, that feels pain and inner contradiction, involving "enough psychology to accommodate representations and enough physiology to enable representations to direct the organism in its actions" (Chaouli 2017, 259). The life in question in the *Logic* (and also in the *Phenomenology*) pertains generally to animals and not plants, which suggests that Hegel is attuned to the distinction between organism/natural purpose and life that Kant is operating with, even if he does not follow it to the letter. It is interesting to note, however, that scientists are increasingly attributing psychological predicates to plants, which further challenges the strict distinction between organism and life that Kant is trying to draw here.

[60] See WL 655/6:442.

are constitutive of an object, there is no contradiction in following mechanical principles as far as we can, and at the same time, employing teleological ones when mechanical ones prove insufficient. A conflict only arises when we claim both forms of causality as constitutive of objects.[61] Despite his attempts to deflate the antinomy as mere appearance, however, it is clear that at least as stated, the two maxims presented are indeed contradictory (all things are mechanically explicable/some things are mechanically inexplicable), and that shifting from a constitutive to a regulative perspective (or from an ontological to an epistemological one)[62] does not suffice to resolve the opposition at hand. One way of understanding the weakness of Kant's position is to consider the exact difference between a regulative and constitutive principle in the specific context of reflective judgment that we are being asked to entertain: we are being told that, as an epistemic requirement of our capacity to judge particulars, we must treat certain objects of nature (and even nature as a whole) *as if* they were possible according to purposes, but that we must never claim, ontologically, that such objects (and nature as such) are in fact possible according to purposes. In practice, however, the difference between the *as if* and the *in fact* is very difficult to determine, for it seems that if I commit myself to studying nature according to mechanistic principles, I am likewise committed to the thought that nature is mechanically constituted such that mechanical explanations are satisfactory; if I commit myself to studying nature according to teleological principles, I am likewise committed to the thought that nature is purposively constituted such that teleological explanations are satisfactory.[63] In short, even regulative principles "seem to involve some kind of ontological commitment," and the insistence that such principles are merely regulative comes to look more and more empty.[64] The slippery distinction between regulative and constitutive principles thus cannot settle the dispute.

The resolution to Kant's antinomy is presented in two stages. First, Kant introduces the infamous notion of the intuitive understanding by way of contrast to the human understanding, and he presents it as a negative point

---

[61] Allison (1991) argues that there is a genuine antinomy even when mechanism and teleology are treated as regulative principles, citing Hegel (as many scholars do) as having pointed this out in the *Science of Logic*. He also suggests that Kant's reference to mechanism in the third *Critique* should be understood as distinct from Kant's account of mechanism in the first and second *Critiques*. On Kant's understanding of mechanism, see Ginsborg (2004) and McLaughlin (1990; 2014).

[62] See Allison (1991, 30).

[63] This is also pointed out by Allison (1991, 30–32) and Ginsborg (2006a, 459).

[64] Allison 1991, 31.

of reference in order to better delimit our own capacities and powers. For an intuitive understanding, there is no distinction between actuality and possibility (no distinction between being and thought), and further, such an understanding has the capacity to intuit the whole as a synthetic universal without there being contingency in the combination of the parts.[65] However, the positing of the intuitive understanding is meant to provide the context for bringing what is distinctive about the *human* understanding more clearly into view. Thus, the second step of Kant's argument consists in returning us to the peculiarities of our human understanding, and reminding us that the entire problem of nature's intrinsic purposiveness is one that only arises for, and corresponds specifically to, "our *human power of judgment*": if there were no meaningful distinction for us between concepts and sensible intuition, if we could immediately intuit the necessary and strict unity between universals and particulars, wholes and parts, without any interruptions of contingency, then there would never have been a threat of empirical chaos, and hence, the need for a principle of purposiveness in the first place (KU 5:404).[66] Even if one tempers the notion of the intuitive understanding and emphasizes, as Eckart Förster does, that the intuitive understanding should *only* be associated with the capacity to intuit the whole as a synthetic universal without there being contingency in the combination of the parts, and not with any divine causative power, this capacity is still unnecessary for grasping the purposiveness of nature, as well as unrealistic for the human understanding or any other living mind.[67] Earlier, I argued that that the relevant sense of normativity and necessity associated with the purposiveness of form *does not require the elimination of all contingency*. Rather, the normativity and necessity indexed to an internally purposive whole expresses a unity of form that can accommodate the necessity of contingency.[68] Thus, even the more restricted notion of the intuitive understanding is unnecessary for grasping the unity of a natural purpose. Instead, Kant resolves the antinomy by stating that for our own human understanding, mechanism must be "subordinated" to teleology, "which, in accordance with the transcendental principle of the purposiveness of nature, can be readily be done" (KU 5:414). He reiterates that "*given the constitution of our understanding*, we must always subordinate all such

---

[65] Förster (2012) argues that these two dimensions should be kept distinct, with the former pertaining to intellectual intuition and the latter pertaining to the intuitive understanding.

[66] Zuckert (2007, chap. 4) also reads the resolution of Kant's antinomy by emphasizing the distinctive character of our human intellects.

[67] See Förster (2012, 144–145).

[68] I discuss Hegel's treatment of the necessity of contingency in chapter 4.

mechanical grounds to a teleological principle" (KU 5:415; my emphasis). Thus, to resolve the antinomy, Kant does not attempt to reconcile mechanism and teleology, nor does the resolution of the antinomy depend upon positing the possibility of an understanding decidedly distinct from our own; rather, according to the principle of purposiveness, mechanistic principles must be subordinated to teleological ones, which suggests that there is a priority of teleology over mechanism *from the perspective of judgment's power*. The subordination of mechanism to teleology takes place, Kant claims, as soon as we acknowledge something as a natural purpose, for here mechanical principles will necessarily be "inadequate" (KU 5:415).

In resolving the antinomy in this way, Kant also allows us to return to his earlier quest of finding an appropriate analogue for the self-organization of natural purposes. In affirming the correlation between the need to employ teleological principles and the specific character of our human understanding, the "remote" analogy between the inner purposiveness of natural purposes and our own purposiveness begins to look less remote: there is an essential connection between inner purposiveness and the human understanding, a reciprocity between life and mind, that is suggested by Kant's resolution to the antinomy, but it is one that he does not explore. As should now be clear, this reciprocity is one that Hegel will explore in great detail, beginning from his earliest publications to his mature philosophy, and especially in his notorious and all-important *Science of Logic*.

2.5 Purposiveness and Hegel's Concept

In exploring Hegel's claim that internal purposiveness plays a positive role in the project of the critique of reason, I emphasized three lines of argument in Kant's consideration of the topic that are important for the interpretation of Hegel defended in the remainder of this study. First, purposiveness for Kant serves the function of an enabling, empowering condition for judgment, preventing judgment from becoming arbitrary in its acts of unification joining concepts and objects. In short, the critique of the power of judgment reveals its power to be grounded in the principle of purposiveness, a ground without which judgment would be arbitrary, haphazard, and blind. I argued that purposiveness thus plays a much bigger role in Kant's philosophy than is usually acknowledged, is already present in nascent form in the first *Critique*, and that Kant's theory of judgment remains radically incomplete without a consideration of this theme. Second, in considering the details of the principle of purposiveness, what we discovered is that despite frequent formulations in which purposiveness is presented on the model of intentional design and artifacts, this characterization of nature is, on Kant's own accounting, a contradiction, and moreover, a contradiction that prevents the principle of purposiveness from serving its purported function of blocking arbitrariness in judgment. The shortcomings of the artifact model reveal that internal purposiveness has primacy over external purposiveness in connection with judgment, and specifically, that the self-organizing unity of natural purposes provides the appropriate model for the necessary, lawful relation between concept and object—the purposiveness of form—sought after by Kant. Third and finally, I argued that the solution to Kant's antinomy of teleological judgment revealed that the primacy of internal purposiveness, and more broadly, the subordination of mechanism to teleology, is essentially connected with the human power of judgment. Whereas the primacy of internal purposiveness must be thought in its essential connection to the human understanding, the intuitive understanding, long considered to be of utmost importance for Hegel and German idealism, reveals itself to be both unnecessary for grasping the purposiveness of form and unrealistic as a characterization of living minds. In exploring purposiveness as an enabling and empowering condition of judgment, Kant opens up the idea that there is a constitutive reciprocity between internal purposiveness and the power of thinking, a constitutive reciprocity that leads us beyond the confines of the Kantian system. These three lines of argument set the stage for understanding Hegel's appropriation of the purposiveness theme, laying the groundwork for the claim that life is constitutive of self-consciousness and the Concept.

In order to conclude our present discussion and in anticipation of the interpretation of Hegel offered in the rest of this book, I want to briefly address an initial concern that can be raised against Hegel's unequivocal affirmation of inner purposiveness as playing a constitutive and positive role in his philosophy, given the account of this concept presented in this chapter. In affirming inner purposiveness as constitutive, a worry arises that Hegel thereby commits himself to the hylozoism—the doctrine that all matter is imbued with life—that Kant took great pains to avoid. In not respecting the Kantian strictures, Hegel (not unlike his erstwhile friend, Schelling) implausibly comes to view all of nature as one big giant organism (a world-soul in Schellingian terms) and spiritualizes matter to such a degree that we end up with an extravagant form of idealism, resulting in an unjustifiably metaphysical philosophy that is both counter to the natural science of his own time (and ours) and philosophically indefensible. Hegel's organicism is thus a liability of his philosophy, rather than a merit, and we would be better off siding with Kant, at least on this score.

Although it is clear that Hegel did indeed hold some version of a romantic conception of nature, much recent scholarship has shown that its proponents were not only highly conversant with the sciences of their time, but moreover, were quite influential for the development of subsequent sciences in the nineteenth century, particularly pertaining to biology and even evolutionary theory.[69] At the very least, this suggests that an offhand dismissal of romantic philosophy and science is neither conceptually nor historically warranted. Regarding Hegel himself, scholars have also shown that he was highly knowledgeable of the sciences of his day, despite falling on the wrong side of some major scientific questions, in particular regarding evolution.[70] But it is not my aim to defend Hegel's *Naturphilosophie* here.[71] Rather, I will argue in the chapters to follow that the key to Hegel's appropriation of inner purposiveness is not to be found in a theory of matter or a philosophy of nature but, rather, in a theory of conceptual form and activity[72] and, ultimately, a science of logic that eschews making substantial claims about the construction of matter at all. Far from committing himself to hylozoism, Hegel is in fact, throughout his career, highly critical of employing notions of force and living force as explanatory paradigms. Further, Hegel does *not* view nature as one big giant organism; rather, in a modernized Aristotelian vein and consistent with a contemporary scientific division of labor, Hegel distinguishes carefully between physical/mechanical processes, chemical processes, and biological/organic processes, demonstrating a subtle understanding of their connections and disconnections, their identity and their differences. It is his theory of the Concept that is driven by the idea of inner purposiveness, rather than his theory of matter. What interests Hegel is the connection between living form and conceptual form, living activity and conceptual activity; in short, what interests Hegel is the horizon of meaning and intelligibility that emerges in the identity and non-identity between life and self-consciousness,

---

[69] On this, see Reill (2005), Richards (2002), and Lenoir (1982).

[70] For an argument that this error was a contingency and that Hegel's philosophy is in fact entirely amenable to evolutionary theory, see Findlay (1958) and Harris (1998).

[71] For such defenses, see the work of Cohen and Wartofsky (1984), Horstmann and Petry (1986), Petry (1987, 1993), Houlgate (1998), Stone (2005), Pinkard (2005), and Rand (2007).

[72] See the discussion in deVries (1991, 54, 63).

and the real possibilities of freedom and knowledge this relation affords. The worry about hylozoism is thus a nonstarter: not only is Hegel not committed to hylozoism in his conception of nature, but further, this objection misunderstands the positive role of inner purposiveness for Hegel's approach to a theory of conceptual form. In defending the importance of life for judgment, what does not follow, then, are the following sorts of claims: that everything in nature is alive, that we judge *everything* according to teleological concepts, and that judgment cannot distinguish between mechanical and teleological processes. Instead, Hegel's transformation of Kant's purposiveness theme illuminates life as the objective context that opens up the possibility of rendering things intelligible, one that fundamentally shapes the activities of self-consciousness and thought.

3

Hegel's Speculative Identity Thesis

The animal is immediately identical with its life-activity. It does not distinguish itself from it. It is *its life-activity*. Man [*sic*] makes his life-activity itself the object of his will and of his consciousness. He has conscious life-activity. It is not a determination with which he directly merges. Conscious life-activity directly distinguishes man from animal life-activity. It is just because of this that he is a species-being. Or it is only because he is a species being that he is a conscious being, i.e., that his own life is an object for him. Only because of that is his activity free activity.

—Marx, *Economic and Philosophic Manuscripts of 1844*

A mended sock is better than a torn one; not so with self-consciousness.

—Hegel, *Aphorisms from the Wastebook*

3.1 The Importance of Hegel's *Differenzschrift*

In demonstrating the reciprocity between judgment and purposiveness, what the *Critique of Judgment* shows is the need to reconsider the idealist project in light of the constitutive import of life.[1] Although Kant clearly saw the importance of purposiveness, both for the systematic unity of reason and for the operation and power of judgment, Kant never brings these insights to bear on the idea that is arguably at the heart of his transcendental idealism—namely, the unity and spontaneity of self-consciousness. In some respects, this is not entirely surprising; as Dieter Henrich contends, Kant has no theory of self-consciousness, and although "the *Critique of Pure Reason* . . . [is] a theory *based* on self-consciousness, [it] nowhere treats self-consciousness as its subject."[2] It is thus no surprise that post-Kantian philosophers immediately

---

[1] This chapter reconsiders some themes taken up in an earlier essay of mine (Ng 2013).
[2] Henrich 2003, 249–250.

Hegel's Concept of Life. Karen Ng, Oxford University Press (2020) © Oxford University Press 2020.
DOI: 10.1093/oso/9780190947613.001.0001

turned to this question as the heart of the matter, acknowledging that transcendental idealism and its possible developments stand or fall with the fate of a theory of self-consciousness.

In considering the problem of self-consciousness, Henrich also contends that drawing the connection between life and mind, especially as it concerns their respective self-referential characters, is long-standing within the history of Western philosophy. Establishing a connection between the self-referential character of self-moving, self-preserving life and the self-referential character of mental acts was prevalent in ancient Greek thought, but these attempts at connection came to a halt in modern philosophy, beginning with Descartes. According to Henrich, modern philosophers such as Descartes, Leibniz, and Locke "severed the links between the metaphysical problem of the self-reference of the mind and the metaphysical problem of what life or a substance is," leading ultimately to "the autonomy of the philosophy of mind."[3] This diagnosis of the fate of the connection between self-consciousness and life is reflected in Henrich's reading of Hegel's development, in which Hegel's early, romantically inflected interest in the concept of life (and love) is eclipsed by a more sober, strictly logical notion of autonomous negation that receives its fullest treatment in the *Science of Logic*.[4] According to Henrich, negation fulfills two fundamental requirements—adopted by Hegel via the influence of Hölderlin—that are necessary for an absolute or ultimate principle of philosophy: first, complete, original self-reference; and second, separation, division, and opposition.[5] Whereas in the earlier phases of Hegel's development, these two requirements are fulfilled by love and life, Hegel's mature and definitive philosophical system fulfills these two requirements by employing the conception of autonomous negation, thus following the trajectory of modern philosophy in severing the connection between life and mind toward the autonomy of the philosophy of mind.

The aim of this chapter is to contest this understanding of Hegel's development. I argue that Hegel, far from severing the connection between self-consciousness and life, inserts their essential relation into his philosophical method, a method that can already be discerned in his first published text, known as the *Differenzschrift* (1801), and is sustained into

---

[3] Henrich 2003, 248, 249.
[4] See Henrich (2003, 299–331). See also Bowman's (2013, 48–54) discussion of Henrich's autonomous negation.
[5] See Henrich (2003, 314). Henrich (2003, 176–177, 187) also suggests that original self-reference and opposition are the two fundamental principles for Fichte's conception of mind.

his mature works, most notably, the *Phenomenology of Spirit* (1807) via the concept of negativity, and in the *Science of Logic* (1812–1816) via the notions of Concept and Idea.[6] As noted by H. S. Harris, "[t]he abiding significance of the *Difference* essay emerges when we recognize that it is the first chapter of a 'discourse on method' which Hegel carried on for the rest of his life."[7] My goal in this chapter is to think through the implications of this claim in order to set the stage for my interpretation of the *Logic* in part II. Specifically, I will argue in chapter 8 that Hegel's absolute method in the conclusion of his *Science of Logic* consists in a dialectic of life and cognition, an account of philosophical method that finds its beginnings in the *Differenzschrift*.

In defending the importance of the *Differenzschrift*, I will suggest that Hegel's Schellingian critique of Fichte presented therein, via the idea of speculative identity, provides an important clue for understanding how Hegel appropriates the purposiveness theme for his own philosophy. In the *Differenzschrift*, one of the earliest presentations of his "speculative" thinking, Hegel makes clear that what is at stake in understanding the relation between subjective and objective elements that we can call absolute is the relation between self-consciousness and life. The language of life and the organic that is omnipresent in the *Differenzschrift* should thus, decidedly, *not* be interpreted as romantic flourish or youthful impressionability; rather, I will argue that it is one of the most important presentations of Hegel's thesis that life and inner purposiveness play a constitutive role in what it means for knowing to be absolute, self-determining, and free. To be clear, I will not be presenting Hegel as a straightforward Schellingian. Indeed, as has been frequently noted,[8] Hegel's departure from Schelling can already be glimpsed in this early work, and my aim is not simply to assimilate Hegelian and Schellingian ideas. Here, I simply want to emphasize that there is a Schellingian line of thought concerning the constitutive import of life and inner purposiveness that Hegel adopts and, importantly, never again rejects, which is evident in this early text via the idea of speculative identity, one that is key for understanding his mature philosophical method. This Schellingian contribution is often overlooked in favor of the Fichtean one or is considered an awkward stage

---

[6] Henrich (2003, 311) places the *Differenzschrift* as the "third" position of Hegel's philosophical development and appears to suggest that even at this stage, life and love are already inadequate expressions of an absolute principle of philosophy.

[7] Harris 1977, 15.

[8] See, for example, the work of Pippin (1989, 60–63), Redding (1996, chap. 3), and Harris (1977).

in Hegel's development, and it is these assumptions that I want to contest.[9] Instead, and continuing to develop the purposiveness theme introduced in chapter 2, I show that Hegel entirely agrees with Schelling that "organic nature furnishes the most visible [*sichtbarsten*] proof of transcendental idealism" (SI 122/490).

Speculative identity thus represents Hegel's argumentative strategy for transforming Kant's claim concerning the reciprocity between judgment and purposiveness into his own thesis concerning the reciprocity between self-consciousness and life. Hegel's development of the purposiveness theme will need to provide a rejoinder to the impasse discussed in the previous chapter concerning Kant's insistence on the merely regulative status of purposiveness, and must provide a positive account of its constitutive status. I begin in section 3.2 by presenting an outline of the speculative identity thesis as understood by Hegel and Schelling, focusing in particular on Hegel's Schellingian terminology from the *Differenzschrift*, the "subjective subject-object" and the "objective subject-object." In addition to demonstrating how speculative identity carries forward the purposiveness theme, I present four central claims contained within the speculative identity thesis that will be developed in more detail in the remainder of the chapter but also in the remainder of this study. Section 3.3 takes up Hegel's critique of Fichte presented in the *Differenzschrift*. Although Hegel will adopt large portions of Fichte's theory of self-consciousness, I argue that the critique of Fichte's idealism as "subjective" hinges on Fichte's inability to conceive of nature as internally purposive and living. The critique of Fichte is key for understanding Hegel's own conception of self-consciousness, in which life plays a central and constitutive role. In section 3.4, I take up the speculative identity thesis in light of Hegel's *Phenomenology of Spirit*, showing how it represents a development of Hegel's method. Focusing on the notion of "negativity," and the relation between consciousness and self-consciousness, I suggest that Hegel, again with the help of Schelling, offers three argumentative strategies for the claim that life is constitutive of self-consciousness, and thereby, of experience and knowledge. I conclude in section 3.5 by briefly anticipating some of the ways that the speculative identity thesis will be carried forward in the *Science of Logic*.

---

[9] Pippin goes as far as naming a "Schelling problem" (1989, 61).

3.2 Speculative Identity in Outline: Objective and Subjective "Subject-Objects"

In brief, speculative identity refers to the relation between subjective and objective elements that is at stake in any attempt to understand the nature of knowledge. Elaborating on the exact nature of subjectivity, objectivity, and their distinction and relationship will of course get quite complicated, but it is important to keep in mind that despite his use of this unusual terminology, Hegel's overarching goal remains quite straightforward. We can begin to unpack the idea of the speculative, speculative identity, and speculative thought by identifying two of its central features, one negative and one positive. Negatively, Hegel contrasts speculative thinking with reflection, on the one hand, and "common sense" (*der gesunde Menschenverstand*), on the other. Hegel's discussion of these terms can be quite difficult to pin down: "reflection" is a term borrowed from Schelling's *System of Transcendental Idealism* (1800), but Hegel's use of it does not always map directly onto Schelling's.[10] Reflection is a philosophical approach characteristic of many early modern thinkers, as well as Hegel's contemporaries—from the empiricisms of Locke and Hume; to Descartes, Leibniz, and Kant; and even to some post-Kantians like Reinhold, Schulze, and Fichte (the notable omission here is, of course, Spinoza, whose relation to Hegel will be discussed in chapter 4). A term that attempts to cover so much ground is bound to be imprecise (and arguably ungenerous to its opponents), but we can settle on two problems that Hegel views as endemic to philosophies of reflection—namely, dualism and formalism. In one form or another, all of these thinkers construct their philosophies based on an assumed dualism and opposition between, roughly, mind and world (subject and object), and the distinct causal orders that each represents. This fixed opposition is never given independent justification and, moreover, results in a situation where these dualisms lead to skeptical or dogmatic conclusions concerning the possibility of their nonetheless necessary reconciliation, where the impossibility of reconciliation would amount to the impossibility of knowledge. A short sampling of solutions for possible reconciliation include god, habit and custom, pre-established harmony, and various accounts of a priori synthesis enacted by the unity of self-consciousness. Formalism and different types of abstract thinking then arguably follow as a

---

[10] See SI 94–133/454–504. On Hegel and Schelling, see also Cerf (1977, xvii), Pippin (1989, 66–67), and Siep (2014, 21–28).

result of dualism: because the gulf between mind and world, or subject and object, results in heterogeneous causal orders, the capacities, ideas, thoughts, concepts, categories, and representations of mind are inherently limited in their ability insofar as they are fundamentally abstracted from the content of the world. Hegel eventually calls this the instrument view of cognition, where mind as an instrument or tool (*Werkzeug*) is both distinct from the self (a tool at the self's disposal) and comes to filter, distort, reshape, or be a mere copy of that which it purports to know.[11] What Hegel calls "common sense" begins with the same dualistic presumptions of reflection but is further shaped by the fundamental opposition between the finite and the infinite, the human and the divine.[12] In its insistence on the absolute opposition between the finite and human, and the absolute and the divine, common sense resorts to feeling and faith as sources of assurance and consolation. The thought of Jacobi is paradigmatic of this type of approach,[13] but Hegel may also be more or less obliquely referring to Kant, Fichte, Schleiermacher, and even Hamann. Although Hegel's complaints against reflection and common sense are sweeping, his diagnosis also cuts quite deep and manages to capture many of the characteristic problems and tendencies of his philosophical predecessors and contemporaries, not to mention his successors.

Hegel's objections to the philosophy of reflection can be made more precise if we turn to its culmination in Kant's distinction between understanding (*Verstand*) and reason (*Vernunft*), where reflection is associated with the mistaken assumption that *Verstand* should be taken as the standpoint of the absolute. In relation to Kant's philosophy, Hegel's main objection to the operations of *Verstand* is that it gets stuck in the "positing of opposites" in which opposition appears in the form of antinomies that come to represent the limitations of finite understanding (DS 94, 109/2:26, 41). In what is a common post-Kantian refrain, Hegel contends that Kant had in fact failed to understand his own best insight: whereas the understanding holds fast to fixed, irreconcilable oppositions and operates relative to their terms (paradigmatically, concept and intuition; but also infinite and finite, "spirit and matter, soul and body, faith and intellect, freedom and necessity, etc."), the aim of reason and its "sole interest" according to Kant "is to sublate [*aufzuheben*]

---

[11] On the instrument view of cognition, see the introduction to the PhG and EL §10.

[12] The translators' note in the English edition of the *Differenzschrift* (DS 98, note 20) on the term *der gesunde Menschenverstand* is helpful here. In addition to sharing a meaning with what is called common sense in English, the German term stresses two further things: human as opposed to divine understanding, and *Verstand* as opposed to *Vernunft*.

[13] See GW 97–152/2:333–393.

such rigid antitheses," which suggests that Kant in fact provides a solution to his own antinomial thinking while at the same time stripping such a solution of all power in the determination of knowledge (DS 90/2:21). Positively, then, Hegel associates speculative thinking with what Kant calls *reason*, stating baldly that "[t]he principle of speculation is the identity of subject and object" (DS 80/2:10). On the surface of things, such a formulaic and abstract pronouncement does not look to be all that helpful; after all, *some* kind of identity between subject and object is the desideratum of nearly *all* theories of knowledge, including the theories that Hegel associates with reflection. What, then, is distinctive about Hegel's positive thesis of speculative identity, and how does it resolve the problems of dualism and formalism just discussed?

My argument will be that Hegel's positive thesis concerning speculative identity integrates two features of Kant's philosophy via Schelling: first, the well known claim that self-consciousness or the I is the ultimate source of the unity of knowledge and experience; and second, central features of the purposiveness theme introduced in the previous chapter—most notably, the idea that the unity and self-organization displayed by life is an enabling condition of cognition. Subject-object identity, then, is understood by Hegel and Schelling in terms of the fundamental insight from Kant's third *Critique*— namely, that there is a reciprocal and constitutive connection between the unity of self-conscious judgment on the one hand, and the unity of internal purposiveness or life on the other. Indeed, this is how Schelling introduces the concept of transcendental philosophy in his 1800 *System*, where he writes: "[a]ll knowledge is founded upon the coincidence of an objective with a subjective," where the objective is associated with nature understood as containing the potential within itself for the production of self-conscious life, and the subjective is understood as self-conscious intelligence, or *das Ich*, which has the power to determine a realm of objectivity (SI 5/339). Hegel echoes Schelling's understanding of the relation between subjective and objective elements, writing: "For absolute identity to be the principle of an entire system it is necessary that *both* subject and object be posited as subject-object" (DS 155/2:94). Key for understanding Hegel's positive account of speculative identity is his description of the subject side or self-consciousness as the *subjective subject-object* (SSO), and the object side or nature as the *objective subject-object* (OSO). Although this is perhaps not the most elegant way of putting things, it captures something important about the independent terms, as well as their necessary interrelation. We can immediately note that the two terms share a similar structure in that both are subject-objects. What exactly does Hegel mean by a "subject-object"?

Like many of Hegel's terms in the *Differenzschrift*, the term "subject-object" can be traced back to Schelling's identity philosophy, and here specifically, to his philosophy of nature. In the "Introduction to the Outline of a System of the Philosophy of Nature" (1799), Schelling explains the concept of nature as follows:

> *Nature* as a mere *product* (*natura naturata*) we call nature as *object* (with this alone all empiricism deals). *Nature as productivity* (*natura naturans*) we call *nature as subject* (with this alone all theory deals). (EEN 202/41)

> We can say of nature as object that it *is*, not of nature as subject; for this is being or productivity itself. (EEN 203/42)

> Nature must originally be an object to itself; this change of the *pure subject* into an *object to itself* is unthinkable without an original diremption [*ursprüngliche Entzweyung*] in nature itself. (EEN 205/44)

> [A]ll *persistence* also only exists in nature as *object*; in nature as *subject* there is only infinite activity [*unendliche Thätigkeit*]. (EEN 205/45)

> [Nature] must therefore be at once infinite and finite; it must be only seemingly finite, but in infinite *development*. (EEN 206/46)

In these passages, Schelling claims that we can take a twofold view on nature: nature as thing, product, persistence, and finite object; and nature as productivity, activity, spontaneity, and infinite subject. A subject-object, or something with the structure of a subject-object, exists as a self-relation that persists by means of its own activity, a characterization that recalls Kant's definition of a natural purpose as a "cause and effect of itself," internally organized such that everything is reciprocally means and ends at once. As an object to itself, living nature not only produces itself as an object but also takes an interest in its own persistence and objectivity. The self-relation suggested by the interest in one's own objectivity (which is largely unconscious in nature)[14]

---

[14] For Hegel and Schelling, their consistent assumption is that nature is unconscious. The position defended here does not depend on that being the case, however; the best knowledge that we currently

requires the positing of a self or subject, a locus of activity and causal power, a self-generating productivity that Schelling calls "infinite *development*." Without needing to accept Schelling's more ambitious thesis regarding a world-soul,[15] the characterization of living nature as both subject and object speaks to the structural reflexivity of living nature as self-directing, self-organizing, and self-producing, which can be identified without subscribing to any form of hylozoism or animism. To say that something is a subject-object rather than a mere object is to acknowledge something's interest in its own persistence, an interest that is made most manifest through the resistance something shows to being reduced to a mere object.[16] Schelling further claims that there is an "original diremption in nature," that "nature must not be identity, but duplicity," and more emphatically, that it is "original duplicity" (EEN 205, 204/44). If we treated nature as a mere object, we would miss something essential about its reflexive structure and the necessary interest that living things take in their own persistence, which serves as an organizing principle of their activities; if, however, in viewing the spontaneity and productivity of nature we treated nature as pure subject, we would be guilty of anthropomorphizing nature, projecting our own faulty notion of intentionality onto natural processes. The term "subject-object" captures the dual point of view appropriate for the characterization of living beings in their reciprocal activity and passivity. The "original diremption" of nature thus also refers to the struggle of living things against their own inevitable progression into decline and death. For individual living things, life can be viewed as a struggle against finitude, the struggle of the subject-object against reduction to mere objectivity, one that inevitably fails; it is only from the perspective of a universal species, or nature as a whole, that nature can be viewed as infinite activity and development, as infinite subjectivity.[17] In the *Differenzschrift*, Hegel suggests that this "necessary diremption [*notwendige Entzweiung*]," alongside identity, is a necessary feature of life (DS 91/2:21). In section 3.4, I will argue that this idea of necessary diremption is an early

---

have concerning a large number of animal species suggests that this is not the case, with a growing (though not complete) scientific consensus.

[15] See IPN 35/87; and Schelling (2010).

[16] There is a clear connection here to Spinoza's conception of *conatus* and striving. See Spinoza, *Ethics* III P6–9.

[17] That the species or the "whole" represents universality and true infinity does not mean, of course, that either are *eternal*. Hegel's concepts of concrete universality and true infinity concern a structural claim about a type of self-relation, rather than a claim about eternal essences and existence.

statement of what will eventually be articulated by Hegel under the heading of *negativity*. In part II, I will argue that this original diremption plays a central role in the Subjective Logic under the heading of the "original judgment of life," a claim that results in what Hegel calls the "doubling" of the Idea.[18] For now, it is clear that *speculative* identity, unlike ordinary senses of the term "identity," is a relation in which opposition, separation, duplicity, and *Entzweiung* remain ever present. Hegel writes: "Hence, the absolute itself is the identity of identity and non-identity; being opposed and being one are both together in it" (DS 156/2:96).

In referring to both sides of speculative identity with the term "subject-object," Hegel, in a Schellingian vein, means to make explicit both the necessary connection and the essential opposition between self-consciousness and the inner purposiveness of life. The SSO represents a living self-consciousness or self-conscious life, one that is self-developing in the manner of living things and one for whom awareness of life-form (the structure of the subject-object) is constitutive of its awareness of self.[19] This claim is suggested in the *Differenzschrift*, where it is still formulated in accord with Schelling's identity philosophy, but it will be fully developed in the *Phenomenology* and the *Science of Logic* in a uniquely Hegelian direction, one that stresses the importance of life-*form* for the self-constitution of rational form. For now we can simply make note of the fact that in referring to self-consciousness as the SSO, the structural inner purposiveness of the subject-object is internal to the idea of self-consciousness and permeates its entire mode of self-relation. We might say that a *subjective* subject-object is a form of inner purposiveness that is *for-itself*—that is, that self-consciousness at once grasps and constitutes its own living self-relation as the ground of all its knowings and doings. The influence of Fichte's notion of the *Tathandlung* is important for understanding the subjective dimension of this activity, and I will take this up in more detail in section 3.3. The OSO represents unconscious or nonconscious life, what Kant had called in the third *Critique* the objective purposiveness of nature. Although Hegel adopts the Schellingian terminology, it is important to note that Schelling's own views on objective purposiveness, particularly as they concern self-consciousness and questions of judgment, were themselves

---

[18] See WL 678/6:473, 689/6:487.

[19] Schelling writes in the 1800 *System*: "A concept of this sort, is that of an object that is at once opposed to, and the same as, itself. But the only such object is one *that is at once cause and effect of itself*, producer and product, subject and object.—The concept of an original identity in duality, and *vice versa*, is thus to be found only in the concept of a *subject-object*, and only in self-consciousness does such a concept originally manifest itself" (SI 30/373).

inspired by the third *Critique* and largely follow its lead on two central issues.[20] The first is the very definition of objective purposiveness, or what is
referred to in the *Differenzschrift* as the OSO. In his introduction to *Ideas for
a Philosophy of Nature*, Schelling describes organic nature and its internal organization in terms that are nearly identical to Kant's:

> The organic, however, produces *itself*, arises *out of itself*; every single plant
> is the product only of an individual *of its own kind* [Art], and so every
> single organism endlessly produces and reproduces only *its own species*
> [Gattung]. . . it is cause and effect of itself. No single part could *arise* ex-
> cept in this whole, and this whole itself consists only in the *interaction*
> [Wechselwirkung] of the parts. In every other object the parts are *arbi-
> trary*. . . . Only in organized beings are they *real*; they exist without my par-
> ticipation because there is an *objective* relationship between them and the
> whole. Thus a *concept* [Begriff] lies at the base of every organization, for
> where there is a necessary relation of the whole to the part and of the part
> to the whole, there is *concept*. But this concept dwells in the *organization
> itself*, and can by no means be separated from it; it *organizes itself*, and is
> not simply, say, a work of art whose concept is to be found *outside* it in the
> understanding of the artist. Not only its form but its *existence* is purposive
> [*zweckmäßig*]. (IPN 30–31/81–82)

This passage is a helpful and concise summary of Kant's central claims concerning inner purposiveness in the third *Critique*: that a natural purpose is
the cause and effect of itself; that the reciprocal relation between the parts
of an organism constitute a self-organizing whole; that in the purposive relation a concept is the ground or cause of the object; that the lawfulness and
purposiveness of living things is internal rather than external—that is, that
means and ends are reciprocally self-relating in the object and not externally
orchestrated by a designer or artisan, that it is internally purposive without
a purpose.[21] Alluding to the resolution of the antinomy of teleological judgment where Kant had suggested that mechanism *must* be subordinated to
teleology, Schelling claims that when faced with objective purposiveness, we

---

[20] Beiser (2002, 509ff; 2003, chap. 9) also argues that *Naturphilosophie* must be thought in connection with Kantian problems rather than in direct opposition to the well known Kantian strictures.

[21] Schelling stresses the implausibility of external purposiveness and the designer-god argument in
IPN 33–34/85–86. See Zuckert (2007, 80–81) for a discussion of the purposiveness of nature as purposiveness without a purpose.

are "in no way *free*" and "absolutely constrained" to "confess that the unity with which you think is not merely *logical* (in your thoughts) but *real* (actually outside you)" (IPN 33, 32/84). Schelling is thus suggesting that the logical unity of thought is manifest in the real, actual unity of living nature, that there is an essential connection between conceptual form and the purposiveness of form. As we will see in later chapters, it is Hegel, and *not* Schelling, who will develop this thought to its full potential in the *Logic*.

Nonetheless, in drawing a connection between conceptual and purposive form, Schelling clearly follows Kant on a second central issue: objective purposiveness is always and only determined in relation to a mind or judging subject, meaning that there is a necessary relation between the objective purposiveness of nature and the purposiveness of the judging subject. He writes: "[O]rganization as such is conceivable only in relation to a *mind* [Geist] . . . purposiveness is conceivable only in relation to a judging intellect" (IPN 32/83). To put it in the terms of the *Differenzschrift*: an OSO is conceivable only in relation to an SSO, and the SSO is constituted essentially by its awareness of the subject-object mode of relation. This is another way of thinking about the reciprocity between purposiveness and judgment that we considered in the previous chapter, but now with a clearer view as to what it means for inner purposiveness to be *constitutive* of the self-conscious subject. In essence, then, Hegel's speculative identity thesis—the identity and non-identity of SSO and OSO—attempts to present the relation and opposition between self-consciousness and life as the absolute foundation of an entire system of philosophy, clearly carrying forward the purposiveness theme in a direction that emphasizes the reciprocity between the unity and activity of mind and the unity and activity of life.

Although the *Differenzschrift* presents an early and important outline of the speculative identity thesis, from here, the Schellingian story, as well as Hegel's recounting of it, starts to look increasingly inconclusive. In the *Ideas*, Schelling appears to fluctuate between two positions: first, a Kantian position on the regulative status of purposiveness that insists on its necessity for judgment while denying that it is constitutive of knowledge;[22] and second, a suggestive but underdeveloped claim concerning the immediacy of our knowledge of life in relation to the constitution of self-consciousness. It is

---

[22] "It is therefore a necessary maxim of reflective reason, to presuppose everywhere in nature a connection by end and means. And although we do not transform this maxim into a constitutive law, we still follow it so steadfastly and so naively that we assume that nature will, as it were, voluntarily come to meet our endeavor to discover absolute purposiveness in her" (IPN 41/94).

this second, all-important claim that remains highly obscured in these early texts, but I want to suggest that despite its underdeveloped character in the *Differenzschrift*, it is of utmost importance because it inspires Hegel's mature account of self-consciousness in the *Phenomenology* and *Philosophy of Mind*, and it comes to play a foundational role in key arguments from the *Science of Logic*. In section 3.4, I will provide a defense of the Hegelian version of this fundamental claim regarding life and self-consciousness presented in the *Phenomenology*, but for now I want to spell out a rough outline of the Schellingian/Hegelian speculative identity thesis that can be gathered from these early texts, a rough outline that will be further developed in the remainder of the chapter, as well as in the remainder of this study. These four claims constitute the core of Hegel's appropriation of the purposiveness theme, a theme whose full development culminates in the account of method presented in the section on the "Idea" in the *Logic*.

S1. Being and life

Both Hegel and Schelling begin by adopting a version of the Aristotelian claim concerning the identity of being and living for things that live—namely, that *for that which is alive, to be is to live*.[23] This prevents an equivocation concerning the term "being" or existence: there is a fundamental difference in the meaning of being when we speak of things that are alive and when we speak of things that are not alive. One crucial difference is that living things have an intrinsic interest in their continued existence and well-being, or as Schelling suggests, living things are "subject-objects." Another is the teleological structure of life-activity, or the unity and form of what Kant calls inner purposiveness. In presenting the speculative identity of subject and object in terms of the essential connection between self-consciousness and life, Hegel and Schelling are suggesting that the subject/object problem, which defines the problem of knowing as such, cannot be resolved until we understand how life fundamentally shapes the subject and its modes of knowing, and moreover, understand that the realm of objectivity should be understood not in terms of the immediacy of sheer being but in terms of the immediacy of life.

---

[23] For Aristotle's version of the claim, see *De Anima* 415b12ff. Aristotle writes: "for in everything the essence is identical with the ground of its being, and here in the case of living things, their being is to live, and of their being and their living the soul in them is the cause or source."

To be clear, this does *not* mean that all being is life; rather, life is what immediately opens up the possibility of being *as intelligible*, of being as a realm of objectivity knowable by a subject. The difference between being as life and being as non-life is categorical and irreducible *from the point of view of things that live*, and fundamentally shapes their comportment towards themselves and the world.[24]

S2. I think, I live/I act, I live

Both Hegel and Schelling return to a basic Cartesian claim concerning self-consciousness as an enacted, posited foundation—importantly transformed via Fichte's first principle discussed in section 3.3—and restate it in light of the claim of S1, such that "I think, I exist" becomes "I think, I live," due to the identity of being and living for things that are alive.[25] Self-consciousness or *das Ich* is therefore fundamentally constituted by its awareness of life, or again, awareness of self and awareness of life are fundamentally bound together. To prevent intellectualizing the "I think" such that it is understood exclusively in theoretical terms, we will see through an engagement with Fichte that the I must essentially be understood as a self-positing *act*, an act in which theoretical and practical aims are unified. Famously, Hegel defines self-consciousness as "desire in general," which further develops Fichtean themes.

S2(a). Refutation of idealism

Both Hegel and Schelling (again via Fichte) will present arguments that prevent S2 from amounting to a solipsistic claim. Both will try to show that there must be awareness of life outside me (Schelling calls this "affection" by the organism), and that there are practical demands placed upon me by other living self-consciousnesses through which my own self-awareness and self-certainty are constituted.[26] Undoubedtly, the most famous account of the

---

[24] Michael Thompson (2008) presents a version of the categorical irreducibility of life argument.

[25] See esp. the passage quoted later from IPN 38–39/91–92.

[26] On "affection," Schelling writes: "The organism is the condition under which alone the intelligence can distinguish itself, as substance or subject of the succession, from the succession itself. . . . [T]he affection of the [organism] therefore precedes the presentation [*Vorstellung*] in consciousness, and must appear, not as conditioned thereby, but rather as the condition thereof" (SI 127/497). I discuss this passage in section 3.4.2. On the practical demands placed upon the I by other

constitution of self-consciousness in relation to life and the struggle for rec-ognition is found in Chapter IV of Hegel's *Phenomenology*. For Hegel, the connection between self-consciousness and life opens up a claim about the relation between self-consciousness and its species, which he famously calls spirit or *Geist*.

S3. The immediacy and activity of life

For both Schelling and Hegel, life has the character of immediacy, and its relation to self-consciousness is likewise characterized as an immediate re-lationship. Although the quality of the immediacy of life has various guises, this immediacy is generally associated with an immediate form of activity. Whereas Fichte and Schelling associate the immediacy of life with "intui-tion" and "affection," Hegel associates the immediacy of life with the form of inner purposiveness as such, emphasizing its concretely universal character, referring to life already as the immediate shape of both Concept and Idea. Although Hegel is usually thought to be generally opposed to all forms of im-mediacy, the immediacy of life is not an immediacy that can be finally over-come or even fully "sublated" in the process and actualization of knowing. This is due to its structural role in Hegel's philosophical method, which makes the immediacy of life different from other guises of immediacy that show up in other contexts of discussion. In what follows we will begin to see some of the ways in which life is understood as immediate, but the full significance of the immediacy of life will not be evident until the discussion of the *Science of Logic* in part II. For now, we can simply note that Hegel himself affirms that there is a crucial place for immediacy that cannot be eliminated: "*there is* nothing, nothing in heaven or in nature or mind or anywhere else which does not equally contain both immediacy and mediation, so that these two determinations reveal themselves to be *unseparated* and inseparable and the opposition between them to be a nullity" (WL 46/5:66).[27]

---

self-consciousnesses, Schelling writes: "But if this idea arises only *in me*, how can I be persuaded that anything corresponds to it outside me? It is also obvious that I am persuaded of a life and self-existence outside me only *practically*. I must in practice be *compelled* to acknowledge beings outside me, who are like me . . . who resemble me in external shape and appearance" (IPN 39/92). See also SI 160–174/538–557; and GNR 3–84/III: 1–91.

[27] See also EL §12Z: "The relationship of *immediacy* and *mediation within consciousness* will have to be discussed explicitly and in detail below. At this point, it suffices to point out that, although

S4. Life and the space of reasons

What the life/self-consciousness relation establishes is the basic form and boundaries of what we might call "the space of reasons," or in a more Hegelian vein, the "realm of freedom" (*das Reich der Freiheit*).[28] We have already noted that Hegel associates speculative thinking with what Kant calls reason. In the *Phenomenology*, Hegel will argue that the relation between self-consciousness and life shapes the process of experience and knowing; in the *Logic*, Hegel will present the relation between life and cognition as an "absolute method," one where life as a form of activity at once enables and constrains the activities of cognition and the determination of all truth. In the *Differenzschrift*, and in Schelling's texts from the same period, this thesis is suggested by references to absolute identity, but for the most part, it remains largely implied and underdeveloped. Further, Schelling ultimately abandons this line of thought after the period of identity philosophy, and it is Hegel who develops the full extent of this thesis in his *Science of Logic*.[29]

Schelling sums up claims S1–4 as follows:

> [I]f there is in me life and soul . . . I can become aware of either only through *immediate* experience. That I *am* (think, will, etc.) is something that I must know, if I know anything at all. Thus I understand how an idea [*Vorstellung*] of my own being and life arises in me, because if I understand anything whatsoever, I must understand this. Also, because I am immediately aware of my own being, the inference to a soul in me even if the conclusion should be false, at least rests on one indubitable premise, that I *am, live, imagine* [vorstelle], *will*. But how do I now come to transfer *being, life*, etc., to things *outside* me? For just as soon as this happens, my immediate knowledge is converted into *mediate*. But now I maintain that there can be only an *immediate* knowledge of being and life, and that what *is* and *lives* only is and lives insofar as it first and foremost exists *for itself*, is aware of its life through being alive. . . . For life can as little be represented outside life as consciousness outside consciousness. (IPN 38–39/91–92)

both moments *appear* to be distinct, *neither of them* may be absent and they form an *inseparable* combination."

---

[28] See WL 513/6:251: "In the *Concept*, therefore, the realm of *freedom* is disclosed."
[29] With respect to the *Logic*, S4 will be taken up in part II of this study.

Here is Hegel's highly obscure summation of the same claims in the *Differenzschrift*:

> [T]he subject can become objective to itself because it is originally objective, that is, because the object itself is subject-object, or the object can become subjective because originally it is just subject-object. Both subject and object are subject-object. This is just what their true identity consists in, and so does the true opposition they are capable of. (DS 159/2:99)

> For absolute identity to be the principle of an entire system it is necessary that *both* subject and object be posited as subject-object. . . . [The] subjective subject-object needs an objective subject-object to complete it, so that the absolute presents itself in each of the two subject-objects, and finds itself perfected only in both together as the highest synthesis that nullifies both insofar as they are opposed. As their point of absolute indifference, the absolute encloses both, gives birth to both and is born of both. (DS 155/2:94)

In the remainder of the chapter, I will begin to develop these four claims in more detail, and the speculative identity thesis will provide the framework for the interpretation of the *Science of Logic* in part II of this study. What should become evident is that Hegel not only never abandons the specific configuration of speculative identity presented in the *Differenzschrift* but, further, that the identity and non-identity between life and self-consciousness becomes the methodological orientation and foundation of his entire philosophical system. All this continues to be in line with the purposiveness theme introduced in chapter 2, attempting to make good on the Kantian insight that purposiveness constitutes the horizon of judgment and is the condition under which logic can be applied to nature. In order to understand the speculative identity thesis in more detail, we now need to incorporate an important missing piece of the puzzle—namely, Fichte's conception of self-consciousness and Hegel's appropriation and critique thereof. Hegel's critical engagement with Fichte will begin to shed light on the claims just outlined and will prepare the way for our discussion of the *Phenomenology* in section 3.4.

3.3 Self-Consciousness and Fichte's Incomplete Synthesis

3.3.1 Hegel's *Fichtekritik*

A large section of Hegel's 1801 *Differenzschrift* is dedicated to criticizing Fichte, primarily on account of his purely subjective idealism. This is in line with Schelling's complaint in *Ideas for a Philosophy of Nature* that Fichte restricts subject-object identity to a "special feature" of subjective conscious-ness, or the subjective subject-object (IPN 54/110). On the surface of things, Hegel's objection to Fichte looks simple enough: although Fichte intends to present the self-positing subject—what he calls I=I, the self as both sub-ject and object—as the absolute foundation of all theoretical and practical knowing, the outcome of his philosophical science is a doctrine of infinite striving whereby subject-object synthesis is aimed at but never achieved. The central argument in the *Differenzschrift* is that the three fundamental principles presented as the foundation of Fichte's system in the 1794/1795 *Grundlage der gesammten Wissenschaftslehre* do not add up to subject-object identity at all but leave us with absolute, irreconcilable opposition, an "end-less sequence of finitudes," and a "self-destructive demand" to strive toward a synthesis that is in principle impossible (DS 131, 134/2:67, 70).[30] As I will argue here, the questions of life and objective purposiveness loom large in Hegel's critique and are key for understanding his eventual appropriation of Fichtean ideas.

---

[30] Most of my account of Fichte here draws from the 1794/1795 *Wissenschaftslehre* because this is the text that Hegel draws most from. However, Hegel, in the first sentence of the section on Fichte in the *Differenzschrift* writes that "[t]he foundation of *Fichte's system* is intellectual intuition, pure thinking of itself, pure self-consciousness, I=I, I am" (D119/2:52). This is puzzling, because the term "intellectual intuition" is absent from the 1794/1795 text, and intellectual intuition is not explicitly stated to be the foundation of Fichte's system until the Second Introduction of 1797. Most scholars agree that the introductions from 1797 belong to a different period of Fichte's development in Jena, and that it is important to keep them separate from the 1794/1795 system (see, e.g., Neuhouser 1990, 34–35). Concerning the term "intellectual intuition" in particular, I will follow Breazeale who defends the view that the idea of intellectual intuition is present in the 1794/1795 text even if the term itself is absent (see Breazeale 2013, 199). Further, since it is not evident that Hegel distinguished care-fully between these texts, or even between the various terms contained in the passage quoted here, I will also draw from the 1797 introductions alongside my account of Hegel's treatment of Fichte's three principles from 1794/1795. Although Fichte employs many different terms in his Jena period in an attempt to articulate the absolute I as a foundational principle of philosophy, for Hegel's purposes, it is clear that what is at stake in these endeavors is an attempt to provide a critical, idealist account of absolute self-consciousness as the foundation for a system of philosophy, and this will be the orienta-tion of my account of Fichte that follows. In his discussion of the practical side of Fichte's philosophy, Hegel draws additionally from the *System of Ethics* and the *Foundations of Natural Right*.

We can very briefly sketch the outlines of Fichte's three principles as follows. The first principle is doubtless the most famous and original of Fichte's doctrines: the doctrine of intellectual intuition, or the self-positing I. Although self-consciousness as a theme, and even as foundational for experience and knowledge, is a claim that is present in much of modern philosophy from Descartes to Kant, Henrich contends that Fichte's is, properly speaking, the first theory that takes self-consciousness as its primary subject matter and tries to work through the details of its functioning.[31] The first principle establishes I=I as the absolute foundation of all possible knowing. I=I is an absolute and immediate act of intellectual intuition in which the I posits itself as existing and as existing *for itself* at once. The language of positing, or *sezten*, means to set or to put in place: the I that posits itself is an act of self-constitution that not only posits the I as necessarily existing for itself but, further, is an absolute act that sets in place an entire schema of subject-object opposition such that things can be *for* the I at all.[32] To emphasize the contrast between the self-positing I as free, self-determining activity and the assertion of consciousness as a mere fact, Fichte describes the former as a *Tathandlung* (a "fact-act" or "deed-act"), to emphasize its distinction from a mere *Tatsache* (a fact, but also literally, a "deed-thing").[33] In essence, we can say that the *Tathandlung* enacts the I as an activity that is for itself, one that serves as the condition for the determination of any possible fact. The key throughout Fichte's account is to distinguish, categorically and emphatically, the self-reverting activity of the I from any kind of thing, fact, or mere being. The language of intellectual intuition suggests that the relation between the I as subject (self-positing activity) and the I as object (existing for itself) is immediate: I am, I exist is immediately implied and contained in the act of self-positing. The self-positing I is absolute because it is spontaneous and unconditioned by anything outside of itself, and can only be denied on pain of a performative contradiction—the act of denying one's own existence and

---

[31] See Henrich (2003, 249–250; 1983).

[32] I am following Wayne Martin here, who writes: "the cognitive acts or capacities that make conscious representation possible must include not only the familiar sensory capacities but also certain fundamental cognitive acts whereby I generate for myself the schema of subject-object opposition. Part of the point of describing these as acts of "positing" (the German is *setzen*, cognate of the English verb "to set") is to emphasize that this schema cannot itself be drawn from experience but serves rather as a general condition thereof" (Martin 1997, 93). Nearly every account of Fichte has something to say about the language of *setzen*. See, for example, the accounts of Henrich (2003, 233–235) and Neuhouser (1990, chap. 3).

[33] On the history of these terms and their philosophical significance, see Franks (1997).

the denial of self-positing are themselves acts of self-positing, ones that are simply unaware of the presuppositions of such denials.

In one and the same act of self-positing, Fichte's second and third principles are also set into place: empirical consciousness or the finite I in opposition to a world, and the principle of division that relates the first principle to the second through mutual limitation. The second principle is also called the principle of opposition (*Entgegensetzung*), wherein the absolute I=I sets itself in opposition to a not-I. Fichte's thought here is that in order for the absolute self-positing of the I to be something determinate, its self-positing must at once be an act of "oppositing," counterpositing, or the positing of that to which it stands opposed.[34] Positing an I that exists for-itself includes the positing of that which is not-I, otherwise I=I remains entirely indeterminate in that nothing stands opposed to it. The I=not-I is empirical or finite consciousness (what Hegel usually refers to simply as "consciousness") that sets itself in opposition to a world, which is only possible on account of the absolute self-positing activity of the absolute I. The third principle must follow if the first and second are not to cancel each other out: synthesis must take place between I=I as absolutely unconditioned and I=not-I as finite and conditioned, or else the foundation of Fichte's system is simply another antinomy.[35] The possibility of mutual limitation between the absolute and empirical I is established through the principle of divisibility. Mutual limitation without mutual cancelation or destruction is only possible if both I and not-I are divisible. If I and not-I were not divisible, their mutual limitation would result in a negation of the whole rather than a part, so it is divisibility which ensures that mutual limitation results in determinateness and reciprocal determination (*Wechselbestimmung*) rather than mutual destruction (or: determinate negation rather than antinomy).[36]

Throughout this entire process, Fichte is also already beginning to establish the basic categories of self-consciousness in tandem with the establishing of its fundamental principles—for example, the categories of reality, negation, limit, and determination. This method of deriving the basic categories

---

[34] Fichte is clearly subscribing to a version of the "all determination is negation" thesis.

[35] In Hegel's words, "[Fichte's] task is now to suspend [*aufzuheben*] the apparent opposition of transcendental and empirical consciousness; and in general terms, this is done by deducing the latter from the former" (DS 120/2:53). And later, "Philosophy must describe the totality of empirical consciousness as the objective totality of self-consciousness" (DS 122/2:55).

[36] Note here that for Fichte, the problem of synthesis in judgment is essentially connected with division and divisibility, a thought that is key for Hegel's own understanding of judgment. See chapters 5 and 7, this volume, for a discussion of Hegel's account of judgment as original division (*Urteil* as *ursprüngliche Teilung*).

of cognition in a proto-dialectical fashion from the principle of absolute self-consciousness is meant both as a correction to Kant's metaphysical deduction and is a clear anticipation of Hegel's own dialectical method, although Hegel will depart from the emphasis on first principles that is central for the methods of both Fichte and Schelling.[37] From the three fundamental principles, Fichte's system then divides into a consideration of the foundations of theoretical and practical knowing, which are both founded upon the infinite activity of the self-positing I. Whereas theoretical knowing is primarily concerned with the possibility of the not-I determining the I (the world determining the mind, developed through the category of reciprocal determination and the productive power of imagination), practical knowing is concerned with the possibility of the I determining the not-I (the mind or will determining the world), which is presented through the striving doctrine. What begins as a theory of self-consciousness positing itself as an absolute foundation ends with a conception of the I as an act of infinite striving toward a synthesis—with itself as absolute and with a world that conforms to the will—that is in principle impossible for finite human beings. Fichte writes:

> The result of our inquiry so far is therefore as follows: *in relation to a possible object*, the pure-self-reverting activity of the I is a *striving* [Streben]; and as shown earlier, *an infinite striving* at that. This boundless striving, carried to infinity, is the *condition of the possibility of any object whatsoever:* no striving, no object. (GWL 231/I: 261–262)

The *Tathandlung* of the I=I presented in the beginning of Fichte's system as its foundation turns out to be an act of infinite striving toward self-identity, rather than its unconditional self-positing. This leads to Hegel's pronouncement that "I *equals* I turns into I *ought* to be equal to I. The result of the system does not return to its beginning" (DS 132/2:68).[38] The key to understanding how the striving doctrine in fact underwrites Fichte's entire system lies in the idea of the primacy of the practical. Fichte writes: "reason cannot even be theoretical, if it is not practical; that there can be no intelligence in human beings, if they do not possess a practical capacity. . . without a striving, no

---

[37] On Fichte's dialectical method, see Martin (1997, chap. 5).
[38] Fichte essentially affirms this. He writes, "It is that of the I as intellectual intuition, from which the Science of Knowledge sets out, and of the I as idea, with which it ends" (ZEWL 83/I: 515).

object at all is possible" (GWL 233/I: 264). The infinite striving of the practical I turns out to be the condition under which theoretical knowing or empirical consciousness has an object at all, which suggests that what ultimately underwrites subject-object identity is not the intellectual intuition of the absolute I=I but, rather, the infinite striving of finite consciousness toward a self-identity that it can in principle never achieve.[39] Fichte's affirmation of the primacy of the practical suggests that the I as infinite striving is indeed the proper foundation of his entire philosophical system, a foundation that, for Hegel, amounts to "a self-destructive demand, since it postulates a union [of subject and object] which still must not happen" (DS 134/2:70).[40]

In essence, the three fundamental principles attempt to present a theory of self-consciousness that explains what it means for self-consciousness to be the ground and foundation of all determinate acts of knowing. Starting from the idea of the self-positing I, Fichte is able to present an entire schema of subject-object identity and relation founded upon absolute self-consciousness, securing what he views to be a truly critical foundation for a continuation of Kant's transcendental project.[41] The influence and originality of Fichte's account of self-consciousness is undeniable, and as evidenced in the 1800 *System*, large portions of Fichte's theory are taken as a starting point for Schelling's philosophy of this period.[42] Hegel's own theory of self-consciousness is also highly indebted to Fichte's account, and the language of positing and its cognates (*setzen, voraussetzen, Gesetztsein*—to posit, to presuppose, posited being) play a central role in the *Logic*, particularly in the Doctrine of Essence, where Hegel once again takes up the problem of reflection. Schelling's departure from Fichte, and Hegel's accounting of this departure, hinges on claiming that Fichte's idealism remains merely subjective,

[39] There is debate concerning whether Fichte should be understood as arguing for the primacy of the practical, or the unity of theoretical and practical knowing. Martin interprets the primacy of the practical in terms of an explanatory primacy: "For Fichte, striving or drive cannot be understood as a result of our cognitive appropriation of the object; it must be taken as an explanatorily more primitive relation" (Martin 1997, 127). Breazeale (2013, chap. 14) argues for the equiprimordiality of theoretical and practical reason.

[40] There are surely dimensions of Hegel's criticism of Fichte that have Fichtean rejoinders, the key one being that what Hegel has presented is less a critique of Fichte than an adequate description of exactly what Fichte meant to argue. The best attempt to defend Fichte's infinite striving doctrine against Hegel's criticisms that I am aware of is Martin's (2007).

[41] See chapter 7, this volume, for a discussion of life as a schema.

[42] The 1800 *System* begins with deduction of the principle of transcendental philosophy that is nearly identical to Fichte's in both form and content. Schelling's 1801 *Presentation of My System of Philosophy* continues to employ Fichtean (and Spinozist) methodologies, as well as Fichtean terms and content, despite Schelling's intentions in 1801 to distinguish his (one true) system of philosophy from Fichte's overly subjective version of idealism.

not only on account of the striving doctrine in which subject-object identity remains an ought-to-be but, moreover, on account of the fact that Fichte lacks an adequate conception of nature that would allow for synthesis between the subjective and the objective in a manner appropriate to absolute knowing. Although Hegel's critique of Kantian and Fichtean ought-claims is well known and has been widely discussed, what is usually overlooked in approaching Hegel's critique of Fichte is Hegel's insistence that Fichte lacks an appropriate conception of nature and life that could actualize subject-object identity in a way that would not be a "synthesis by way of domination [*Beherrschens*]" or a "relation of subservience [*Verhältnis der Botmäßigkeit*]," which would not amount to a genuine synthesis of subject and object at all (DS 138/2:75).[43] Hegel is suggesting that Fichte's synthesis is not only incomplete on account of the striving doctrine but, further, that the incomplete synthesis enacted by the Fichtean subject is one that takes place by way of domination of the object, insofar as Fichte lacks an account of an objective subject-object as a necessary counterpart to his subjective subject-object. To translate: Fichte lacks an appropriate conception of the objective purposiveness of nature that renders his account of self-consciousness incomplete; the result is "domination" of the object by the subject insofar as synthesis now looks to be an imposition of the subject, posited or put in place exclusively by the subject with little input from the object (the most we hear about the object is that it is a "check," "impetus," or *Anstoß* on our activity).[44] As Hegel himself suggests, the problem of Fichte's merely subjective idealism "is most strikingly apparent in the *relation of the I to nature*" (DS 135/2:72). What I now want to suggest is that the problem of nature's objective purposiveness,

---

[43] Hegel importantly retains this language of non-domination when speaking of concepts in the preface to the second edition of the *Science of Logic*, dated a week before his death. He writes: "Or again, to speak of *things*, we call the *nature* or *essence* of things their concept, and this is only for thought; but still less shall we say of the concepts of things that we dominate them [*daß wir sie beherrschen*], or that the determinations of thought [*Denkbestimmungen*] of which they are the complex are at our service; on the contrary, it is our thinking that must accommodate itself to them [*nach ihnen beschränken*] and our arbitrariness or freedom [*Willkür oder Freiheit*] ought not to want to mold them to suit itself" (WL 16/5:25).

[44] For a comprehensive and systematic accounting of the role of the *Anstoß* in Fichte, see Breazeale (2013, chap. 7). Hegel writes: "in Fichte's reconstruction of identity one [side] dominates and the other is dominated [*in dieser Rekonstruktion der Identität hingegen ist das eine das Herrschende, das andere das Beherrschte*]; the subjective is not equal to the objective. They stand in a relation of causality instead; one of them goes into servitude [*Botmäßigkeit*]" (DS 138/2:75). Redding (1996, 55) argues that Fichte's failure to produce an objective subject-object amounts to a failure of "conceiving of an 'embodied-mind' from an external, third person point of view. That is, within the categories of Fichte's deduction there is no way to treat human beings in an *epistemologically hermeneutic way*, that is, to conceptualize them in such a way that one can recognize them as intentional subjects with points of view, and not as mere things."

which has been overlooked in favor of the ought-critique, is the key to understanding Hegel's critique of Fichte.

3.3.2   Dead Nature and Life in Fichte's I

In the latter half of Hegel's discussion of Fichte in the *Differenzschrift*, there
is a constant refrain that one of the most objectionable results of Fichte's
striving doctrine, apart from its internal incoherence, is that it renders nature
lifeless and dead. Hegel writes:

> It follows that both in the theoretical and in the practical respect *nature* is
> something essentially determined and dead. (DS 139/2:76)

> From this highest standpoint [of reflection] nature has the character of ab-
> solute objectivity, that is, of death. (DS 140/2:77)

> The standpoint which posited nature as living, disappears. . . . [R]eason is
> nothing but the dead and death-dealing rule of formal unity. . . (DS 142/
> 2:79)

> [T]he essence of nature is atomistic lifelessness. (DS 142/2:80)[45]

The accusation of lifelessness can appear to be at once metaphorical and
opaque, and despite the fact that this accusation is prevalent throughout
Hegel's texts, it is not always entirely clear what the force of Hegel's objection amounts to. The clearest way to approach Hegel's objection is to begin
by considering the theoretical and practical standpoints from which nature
might be considered. From the theoretical standpoint, Hegel contends that
"nature is self-limitation intuited [*die angeschaute Selbstbeschränkung*] . . . it
is the objective side of self-limitation . . . and its fundamental character is oppositedness [*Entgegengesetztsein*]" (DS 139/2:76). If nature's

---

[45] Hegel also writes concerning Fichte's conception of right: "This concept of limitation constitutes
a realm of freedom where every truly free reciprocal relation of life, every relation that is infinite and
unlimited for itself, that is to say, beautiful, is nullified; for the living being is rent into concept and
matter and nature goes into servitude" (DS 144/2:82). And of Fichte's concept of the state: "But that
state as conceived by the intellect [*Verstandesstaat*] is not an organization at all, but a machine; and
the people is not the organic body of a communal and rich life, but an atomistic, life-impoverished
multitude" (DS 149/2:87).

Grundcharakter is oppositedness and limitation, self-consciousness for its part remains defined and constituted by its fundamental opposition to nature such that nature appears as an absolute limitation for theoretical self-consciousness. Essentially, defining nature in terms of opposition and limitation means that theoretical consciousness is, in turn, defined by these same terms, in spite of the fact that Fichte clearly means to demonstrate that the I is self-determining rather than determined. Now, Fichte is clearly aware of this problem, and nowhere appears to deny it; in fact, Part II of the 1794/1795 *Wissenschaftslehre*, dedicated to a discussion of theoretical knowledge, is largely an attempt to work through the problem of mutual opposition and limitation such that the opposed terms do not cancel each other out but, rather, result in synthesis and reciprocal determination in a way that leaves the self-determination of the I intact. Hegel seems to be suggesting that conceiving of nature essentially in terms of oppositedness—at once a "check" on and "impetus" for our activity—leaves theoretical consciousness with two options: either the activity of consciousness is simply determined and caused by the object, or consciousness overcomes this determination by the object by "dominating" it, where domination refers to merely negating an external limitation or opposition, rather than genuine synthesis or even genuine reciprocal determination. The thought is that in setting up the relation to nature in terms of external limitation and opposition, Fichte is then unable to move beyond this opposition in a way that could reveal theoretical consciousness to be truly self-determining. In short, nature as determined and dead renders consciousness determined in its fixed opposition to it: either nature determines consciousness causally or consciousness overcomes the causal determination of nature by means of domination.

Fichte would probably respond to this by saying that, indeed, theoretical consciousness on its own cannot resolve this problem, and that "investigation of this point lies beyond the bounds of theory," requiring an account of practical activity and its primacy (GWL 164/I: 178). From the practical standpoint, what appears to be at stake is not external nature but our own existence as natural beings or our inner nature. Here, Hegel extends his critique not only to the account of the practical I presented in the 1794/1795 *Wissenschaftslehre* but also to the further development of the practical domain that includes Fichte's *Grundlage des Naturrechts* and the *Sittenlehre*. The nature at issue here concerns the system of natural drives and feelings that play the role of limitation and opposition in relation to the practical I. Concerning the natural drives, Hegel's refrain is that they are subservient to and dominated by the drive toward freedom, where the character of fixed opposition is again decisive in undermining freedom's striving as having the character of self-determination. Striving is infinite, and its goal of synthesis and reconciliation is impossible, owing to the necessary opposition posed by the natural drives, which express the nature of limitation and boundedness, "fixed and determined independently of freedom" (SL 105/IV: 109). This suggests that far from being a solution to the problem, the practical finds itself in the same situation as the theoretical: insofar as nature is conceived as fixed opposition and limitation in relation to the I's activity, the I finds itself determined rather than self-determining, at most dominating inner and outer nature without ever achieving true synthesis. Hegel writes:

> The practical faculty of the I can no more achieve absolute self-intuition than its theoretical faculty could. Both alike are conditioned by an *Anstoß* which, as a brute fact [*Faktum*], cannot be derived from the I; the deduction of it amounts to a demonstration that it is the condition of the theoretical and practical faculty. The antinomy remains an antinomy and is expressed in striving. (DS 133/2:69–70)[46]

We can sum up Hegel's critique as follows: when nature is conceived as dead opposition, self-consciousness in turn cannot determine itself as self-determining, which is the primary aim of Fichte's entire philosophy. The terms "domination" and "subservience" are meant to signal the opposite of freedom and self-determination, and Hegel will continue in later texts to use terms such as domination and violence to describe external relationships in which fixed opposition cannot be overcome, most notably in his discussion of lordship and bondage, and also in the discussion of mechanical relationships in the *Logic*. If freedom and self-determination are relations of being at home with oneself in one's other, as Hegel suggests, one cannot be free if the other in question (here, nature) is conceived exclusively in terms of limitation and opposition. We can consider Hegel's objection in connection with Kant's worry about judgment's powers in the face of nature's contingency: just as a contingent or merely externally purposive nature leaves

---

[46] Criticizing Kant and Fichte together, Hegel essentially raises the same objection in the *Phenomenology*: "The pure reason of this idealism, in order to reach this *other* which is *essential* to it . . . is involved in a direct contradiction; it asserts essence to be a duality of opposed factors, the *unity of the apperception* and equally a *thing*; whether the thing is called an *alien Anstoß*, or an *empirical* being, or *sensibility*, or the *thing in itself*, it still remains in its concept the same, namely, something alien to that unity of apperception" (PhG ¶238/3:184–185).

judgment's powers reckless and arbitrary, unable to establish an internal and necessary relation between concept and object, nature as fixed opposition leaves self-consciousness forced between being determined by nature or dominating it. Both amount to unfreedom and arbitrariness, a "relation of causality [*Kausalitätsverhältnis*]" rather than a relation of freedom (DS 138/ 2:75).[47] Hegel's contention is that Fichte's incomplete synthesis is primarily due to his inability to conceive of nature as life—as internally purposive, as an objective subject-object.

Before turning to Hegel's treatment of self-consciousness and life in the *Phenomenology*, I want to see how far the engagement with Fichte brings us with respect to claims S1–3 detailed earlier. Despite Hegel's criticism that the dead nature of Fichte's theory undermines his attempts to provide a robust account of the I's self-determination, there are many clues in Fichte's discussions which suggest that he in fact saw the importance of life for his deduction of self-consciousness.[48] Two discussions should be noted in particular that are important for Hegel's account. The first concerns Fichte's understanding of the self-positing activity of the I. In refashioning the Cartesian foundation of the indubitable I think, I am, what Fichte repeatedly emphasizes is the *performative* nature of this foundation—that it is a foundation brought into existence only by its being enacted.[49] Thus, the key, categorical distinction that Fichte takes great pains to articulate is the distinction between act and fact, between activity and thinghood. If there is one, overarching claim that Fichte means to get across, it is that self-consciousness is not a fact, not a thing, not an inert object, but an activity: "The act [*Handeln*] in question is simply the concept of the I, and the concept of the I is the concept of this act; both are exactly the same" (ZEWL 35/I: 460). Although the exact character of this self-reverting activity can sometimes appear opaque, it is clear that Fichte associates this activity with the "source of life [*Quelle des Lebens*]" (ZEWL 38/I: 463), and he describes his foundation as follows:

[47] Note that Fichte would agree with Hegel concerning the unfreedom of the "relation of causality." He writes that "the relationship between free beings is interaction through freedom, and not causality through mechanically operative force" (ZEWL 78/I: 509).

[48] In a turn of phrase that captures a key thought for Kant, the German idealists, and the early German romantics, Fichte claims that life is an "analogue of *freedom* in nature" (Fichte 1971, 244). See also the discussions in Khurana (2013a).

[49] See ZEWL 38/I: 463: "*intellectual intuition* . . . is the immediate consciousness that I act, and what I enact: it is that whereby I know something because I do it." To be clear, I am of course not suggesting that Fichte is a Cartesian; in fact, it is widely acknowledged that he begins in a manner similar to Descartes only to then demonstrate, quite decisively, an anti-Cartesian point. On Fichte's anti-Cartesianism, see Wood (2006; 2016, 49–50).

[I]t is a special consciousness, viz. an immediate consciousness or intuition, albeit not a sensory intuition relating to a material existence [*materielles Bestehen*], but an intuition of sheer activity [*blossen Thätigkeit*], not static but dynamic; *not a matter of being* [Seyn], *but of life*. (ZEWL 40/I: 465; my emphasis)[50]

Here Fichte is claiming that the immediate consciousness or intuition of activity, in which the I posits and constitutes its being-for-self, is essentially a consciousness or intuition of life. The terms, "I," "activity," and "life," are tightly interwoven in Fichte's account, and it is important to get some clarity on his exact point. In a somewhat counterintuitive vein, Fichte separates life from material existence or subsistence, and even being in general. The reason that life is contrasted with existence and being is that Fichte means to associate, and even identify, *activity* with life. That is, existence and being lie on the side of facts and things, which is precisely what the I as activity is *not*. The tight connection between the notion of activity and the notion of life necessarily separates life from mere existence and allows Fichte to lend some minimal content to his all-important yet highly opaque notion of self-positing activity. The sheer activity, or *Tätigkeit*, in question is the activity of life, and the immediate intuition of this activity is the self-constituting act of the I. Although the activity of life will itself need to be articulated in further detail, Fichte's suggestion here is that the notion of activity must be thought of as essentially connected with the problem of life, that the activity in question cannot be understood without making explicit its essential connection to life.

The second discussion that is of particular importance for Hegel's account is Fichte's understanding of the practical I. In Part III of the 1794/1795 *Wissenschaftslehre*, the importance of life is more explicitly articulated, and Fichte writes of the self-positing I that "it must have the principle of life and consciousness solely within itself" (GWL 241/I: 274).[51] As the key for his doctrine of infinite striving, the practical I can be thought of as a fundamentally "divided" self, a division that is articulated by Fichte through an account of

---

[50] See also ZEWL 30/I: 454: "The Science of Knowledge is a very different matter. Its chosen topic of consideration is not a lifeless concept . . . but a living and active thing which engenders insights from and through itself, and which the philosopher merely contemplates. His role in the affair goes no further than to translate this living force into purposeful activity."

[51] See also GWL 270/I: 308; and GWL 245/I: 279: "According to the account just put forward, the principle of life and consciousness, the ground of its possibility—is admittedly contained in the I."

drives and feelings.[52] Fichte's discussion in Part III is extremely difficult and complex, but for our purposes what is important is his use of two distinctions in his understanding of the practical I. The first is the distinction between life and the lifeless. Fichte begins his account of the practical by discussing the relation or equilibrium between striving and counterstriving (the practical instantiation of the relation between the I and the not-I), which are given more determinate shape by being posited as drive and feeling, respectively.[53] To understand this relationship, Fichte asks us to imagine for a moment that the I is a lifeless thing in the shape of an elastic sphere A, which is compressed by another body B with the same properties. In the mutual force they exert upon one another, A will expand as soon as the compression by B is retracted, and vice versa. Although this example is meant to be illustrative of the relation and possible equilibrium between drive and feeling, Fichte qualifies the example, writing that by contrast, "drive is an *inner* force [my emphasis], determining itself to causality. The lifeless body has no causality whatever, save *outside* itself. . . . [T]he lifeless can contain no drive" (GWL 258, 269/I: 293, 307). The difference between elastic spheres A and B and the relation between drive and feeling contained within the I consist in the idea of there being a "*feeling* of force," which is the "principle of all life" (GWL 260/I: 296; my emphasis).[54] The idea of a "feeling" of force requires a shift in perspective from the lifeless to life, for although the elastic spheres allow us to understand the idea of mutual force, one can only speak of a "feeling" of force from the internal perspective of something that feels, from the perspective of something for whom feeling inheres. It is thus in the context of his deduction of feeling and its posited determination that Fichte writes, "the living is divided from the dead," suggesting that the feeling of force through which the practical I is posited is fundamentally the principle of life.

The second distinction that is central to Fichte's account of the practical I is the distinction between life, on the one hand, and intelligence, consciousness, and reflection, on the other. It is through the latter that drive and the feeling of force can attain to the status of free and rational action, something that "we achieve . . . by absolute freedom, not through a *transition*, but by means of a *leap*" (GWL 262/I: 298).[55] The leap from the feeling of force to moral

---

[52] On this, see Breazeale (2013, chap. 6). Breazeale (167–170) also argues that feeling plays the role of the *Anstoß* for the practical I.

[53] See GWL 253–256/I: 287–291.

[54] "Kraftgefühl ist das Princip alles Lebens" (GWL 260/I: 296).

[55] Fichte also writes, "From this absolute spontaneity alone there arises the consciousness of the I" (GWL 262/I: 298).

feeling or the feeling of duty takes us far beyond the scope of this discussion, but what is important for our purposes is simply that Fichte employs the distinction between consciousness and life in the continual development of his account of the striving and counterstriving of the practical I. That is, Fichte builds his account of practical striving on the basis of, first, a distinction between the living the non-living and, second, a distinction between life and consciousness of life. This is what it means for the I to contain the principle of life and consciousness within itself, and the articulation of the division within the I in these terms will be extremely important in Hegel's development of the speculative identity thesis. Thus, despite Hegel's criticisms, Fichte in fact has important resources in his system that acknowledge the constitutive importance of life—resources from which Hegel will happily draw.

To conclude our discussion of Schelling, Fichte, and Hegel's *Differenzschrift*, we can see that Fichte in fact gets us quite far with respect to claims S1–3. With respect to S1, the identity of being and living for things that live, it appears that the key Fichtean distinction between activity and facticity cannot be clearly articulated without the distinction between life and non-life. This distinction is categorical and irreducible, not from the perspective of material existence, but from the perspective of an idealism that tries to establish subject-object identity on the basis of self-consciousness or the I. Regarding S3, the claim concerning the immediacy and activity of life, Fichte's discussion of intellectual intuition as the intuition of the activity of life, and his account of the practical I that is constituted by the feeling of force (the principle of life), surely suggest that the grasp of life is immediate, that the grasp of life takes place as an immediate intuition. This point is also essentially connected to S2—I think, I live, now more clearly cast in terms of I act, I live. Here again, Fichte's identification of activity with life in his account of intellectual intuition and the I's self-positing, alongside the determination of the primacy of the practical, is decisive, and Chapter IV of Hegel's *Phenomenology* should be understood with this Fichtean background in mind. But for now, when Fichte states that "the self-positing I and the existing I are perfectly identical, one and the same," it is evident that the *existing* I (*das seyende Ich*) must be understood as the *living* I (GWL 99/I: 98).[56] More specifically, the being or existence at issue for that which can posit its

---

[56] "[D]as sich setzende Ich, und das seyende Ich sind völlig gleich, Ein und ebendasselbe" (GWL 99/I: 98).

own self-activity, for that which can feel the force of its own self-limitation, is nothing but life.

3.4 Speculative Identity in Hegel's *Phenomenology of Spirit*

3.4.1 Method and the Relation between Consciousness and Self-Consciousness

If the *Differenzschrift* is the "first chapter" of Hegel's discourse on method presented through the idea of speculative identity, the *Phenomenology of Spirit* speaks quite explicitly about the problem of philosophical method, forming an essential stage for arriving at the standpoint of the *Science of Logic*. Although Hegel is consistent in stating that the problem of method belongs properly to logic,[57] he states that in "the *Phenomenology of Spirit* I have presented an example of this method with respect to a concrete object, namely *consciousness*" (WL 33/5:49). Hegel further claims that the *Phenomenology* provides a deduction of the concept of philosophical science (*Wissenschaft*) that is presupposed by the *Logic*, and that as far as understanding the relation between these two texts, the *Phenomenology* is the "first part" of the latter and the *Logic* is the "sequel" to the former (WL 29, 11/5:43, 18). All of this justifies our turning to the *Phenomenology* in order to demonstrate how Hegel develops his speculative identity thesis, setting the stage for the official and mature presentation of his philosophical method in the *Logic*.

How are we to understand the *Phenomenology* as presenting an example of Hegel's method, especially if that method is understood in terms of speculative identity? Two short passages from Hegel's preface are instructive:

> It might seem necessary to state at the outset the principal points concerning the *method* of this movement, that is, the method of Science [*Wissenschaft*]. . . . its genuine exposition belongs to logic, or is instead even logic itself, for the method is nothing but the structure of the whole in its pure essentiality [*der Bau des Ganzen in seiner reinen Wesenheit*]. (PhG ¶48/3:47)

---

[57] See PhG ¶48/3:47.

On the one hand, this nature of scientific method is inseparable from the content, and on the other hand, it determines its rhythm by way of itself, and it has,
as has already been noted, its genuine exposition in speculative philosophy.
(PhG ¶57/3:55)

Here, and in a manner that is consistent throughout his works, Hegel emphatically rejects thinking about method in terms of an external form that is
applied to some particular content. Instead, what method identifies is the essential structure or form of the entire investigation, one that is shaped essentially by the development of its specific content. Hegel's favorite example of
the wrong approach to philosophical method is the attempt to employ what
he views as broadly mathematical methods to philosophical topics—most
notably, Spinoza's attempt to provide an account of substance by means of the
geometric method.[58] In trying to follow Spinoza in this approach, at least at
certain junctures of their work, Schelling and Fichte, too, according to Hegel,
are guilty on this score. To put Hegel's point in the simplest terms, we can say
that the method has to be appropriate for its object, but since we cannot know
what is appropriate for the object prior to a full investigation of it, the very approach of laying out one's method in advance will not be available in the usual
way. This problem is what leads Hegel to what is usually known as his dialectical
approach, one that affirms a certain circularity in philosophical investigations
as necessary, and one that shies away from approaching philosophy in terms
of first principles. To use one of Hegel's more vivid examples, we can't learn to
swim before we get into the water, so it is only after we go through the process of
learning (and failing to learn, often to the point of drowning) that we can grasp
the method as a result.[59]

Given that Hegel's investigation in the *Phenomenology* is the "science
of the *experience of consciousness*," I will argue that we can approach the
problem of method by looking at the relation between consciousness and
self-consciousness as the essential structure of the whole text (PhG ¶88/

---

[58] In the Transcendental Doctrine of Method, Kant also stresses that mathematical methods and
approaches should not be imported to philosophical investigations. He writes: "Mathematics is thoroughly grounded on definitions, axioms, and demonstrations. I will content myself with showing
that none of these elements, in the sense in which the mathematician takes them, can be achieved or
imitated by philosophy; and that by means of this method the mathematician can build nothing in
philosophy except houses of cards" (A727/B755).

[59] "But to want to have cognition *before* we have any is as absurd as the wise resolve of Scholasticus
to learn to *swim before he ventured into the water*" (EL §10Z).

3:80).[60] The relation between consciousness and self-consciousness as the continual process through which self-consciousness develops knowledge of itself simply *is* the method of the *Phenomenology*, and this is attested to by Hegel's discussion in both the introduction and the concluding chapter on absolute knowing (*das absolute Wissen*).[61] In both contexts Hegel discusses the process of knowing in a highly abstract way, but we can start with a relatively straightforward explanation of this process framed in idealist terms:

> Consciousness *distinguishes* something from itself while at the same time it *relates* itself to it. Or, as it is expressed: There is something *for consciousness*, and the determinate aspect of this *relating*, or the *being* of something *for a consciousness*, is *knowing*. (PhG ¶82/3:76)[62]

We come to know an object by distinguishing ourselves from it and relating to it; the object is not-I, but in order to know it, I must also stand in some relation to the object—otherwise, the object could not be something *for* me. We can read this as Hegel's gloss on Kant's famous "I think" claim, and as an elaboration of the crux of Fichte's three principles: knowing consists in determining the different ways in which something can be *for a consciousness*, which hinges on understanding the full extent of the activity of distinguishing and relating as an ongoing process. In using the two terms "distinguishing" and "relating," Hegel can in turn talk about two aspects of the object, or two ways of taking an object: first, as something external to, separate from, and independent from me, the object as it is *in itself*; and second, as something essentially related to and *for consciousness*, the object as it is in accord with our concepts and ways of knowing. In the first mode, consciousness stands opposed to its object in an immediate way and maintains a clear distinction between itself and the object: the object is *not*-I, something alien, something other, something still as yet unknown or not fully known, something implicit.[63] In the second mode, consciousness, in relating itself to the object, at

---

[60] As is well known, "science of the experience of consciousness" was another early title for the *Phenomenology* and was included in some early editions (see Pinkard 2000, 203).

[61] In the chapter on "Absolute Knowing," Hegel writes: "Spirit is in itself the movement [*die Bewegung*] which is cognition—the transformation of that former *in-itself* into *for-itself*, of *substance* into *subject*, of the object of *consciousness* into the object of *self-consciousness*, i.e., into an object that is just as much sublated, that is, into the *Concept*. The movement is the circle that returns into itself, the circle that presupposes its beginning and reaches it only at the end" (PhG ¶802/3:585).

[62] This crucial passage is a paraphrase of Reinhold's (1985, 70) principle of consciousness: "In consciousness a representation is distinguished from what is represented and from what does the representing and is set in relation to them both."

[63] Miller translates *an sich*, or in-itself, as implicit.

once becomes aware that the object is something *for itself*, that being aware of something being *for* it is at once to be aware of itself as something that knows, as something that distinguishes itself from and relates itself to objects. In this second, *mediated* relation to the object, the object is no longer something merely immediate, alien, or unknown but also something grasped by consciousness according to its concept of itself. Thus, what emerges in this process of distinguishing and relating is not just the object as it is known by consciousness but, more importantly, *self*-consciousness. That is, the very activity of coming to know an object, the activity of distinguishing and relating, presupposes an awareness of the self who distinguishes and relates.[64] In the transformation that takes place between taking an object as *in-itself* and taking it as something *for-consciousness*, there is a transformation in consciousness such that consciousness of an object becomes self-consciousness. What Hegel calls knowing here is the process of being continually thrown back upon ourselves in our ongoing attempts to know the object—knowledge of the object and knowledge of the self thus go hand in hand.

We can note an important feature of this gloss on the central idealist thesis that consciousness presupposes self-consciousness—namely, Hegel's contention that the actuality of knowing and knowledge must be grasped as an ongoing process in continual motion, a process of development that is dynamic, full of life, and even beset with contradiction. Hegel writes: "*Inasmuch as the new true object arises from it*, this *dialectical* movement which consciousness exercises on itself and which affects both its knowledge and its object, is precisely what is called *experience [Erfahrung]*" (PhG ¶86/3:78). The new object is the object taken in the second sense just discussed—namely, the object as grasped and known by self-consciousness. Hegel emphasizes that the movement and transformation at stake concern not only the object but also the consciousness who knows, that what is called *experience* in the context of the "science of the experience of consciousness" is the process through which self-consciousness, in distinction from and in relation to its objects, is continually enriched and transformed. We can elaborate on this concept of experience in two ways. In concrete terms, what experience denotes is *Bildung*, the education or cultural formation of self-consciousness actualized in historical shapes as it attains knowledge of itself as self-determining and free.

---

[64] It is important not to read Hegel's language of the two objects too literally. The point is not that there are literally two objects but that the activity of knowing an object and the corresponding self-awareness this produces is a dynamic process in which a change takes place in both the object and the self.

In more formal or abstract terms, this experience is essentially shaped by the identity and non-identity of consciousness with its object (or subject and object) and the identity and non-identity of consciousness with its concept of itself. This diremption and dividedness (*Entzweiung*), or to use the term more prominent in the *Phenomenology*, this *negativity*, is essential to and, in a way, presupposed by the idea that experience is a process in continual motion and development. To understand how the term "negativity" is used in the *Phenomenology* to denote the thesis of speculative identity, now developed according to distinctively Hegelian concepts and methods, we can turn to Hegel's own definition:

> The disparity [*Ungleichheit*] which exists in consciousness between the I and the substance which is its object is the distinction between them, the *negative* in general. It can be regarded as the *defect* of both, though it is their soul, or that which moves them [*das Bewegende*]. That is why some of the ancients conceived the *void* as that which moves, for they rightly saw the *negative* as that which moves, though they did not yet grasp that the negative is the self. Now, although this negative appears at first as a disparity between the I and its object, it is just as much the disparity of the substance with itself. (PhG ¶37/3:39)

The negative is that which moves and it moves by means of the disparity between subject and object. But at the end of the passage, Hegel clarifies that this characterization is not quite sufficient, and suggests that there are in fact *two* disparities or *Ungleichheiten* at stake if we are to truly understand the negative as that which moves: first, the disparity between I and its object or a disparity within the self; and second, the disparity of the substance with itself, or a disparity within the object. The negative, which can be viewed as a defect or limitation, but should more importantly be viewed as the soul or life of the process of knowing, thus requires that the I is self-divided as a *subjective subject-object*, and that the object is self-divided as an *objective subject-object*. Hegel's understanding of negativity in the *Phenomenology* thus carries forward the speculative identity thesis of the *Differenzschrift*, or so I will argue. In order to clarify this point, we will have to elaborate on the exact role of life in Hegel's discussion of the transition from consciousness to self-consciousness that takes place in the first part of Chapter IV of the *Phenomenology*. I will argue that in referring to the negative as a double disparity, Hegel is in fact claiming that the dialectical movement of experience through which consciousness is reconciled with self-consciousness is essentially structured by the thesis of speculative identity.

3.4.2 Life, Self-Consciousness, Negativity: The Argumentative Strategies

How does life become the crux for understanding the relation between consciousness and self-consciousness such that experience itself is structured by negativity? In the first three chapters of the *Phenomenology* on "consciousness," Hegel discusses various ways of remaining with the first mode of taking the object as immediately distinguished from consciousness *in-itself*: as the immediate "this" of sense-certainty; as the thing with properties of perception; and as an object of forces and laws corresponding to the understanding, or *Verstand*. In the process of coming to know the object, convinced that the object *in-itself* is the bearer of truth, consciousness in each case is thrown back upon itself and is forced to acknowledge its active role in the process of knowing, particularly as it concerns the unity of the object. Thus, the first three chapters represent illustrations—drawing on unnamed examples from modern empiricism and Kant—of why knowledge of objects presupposes that we have some account of the self that brings form and unity to the object; in short, the first three chapters make the case for the necessity of taking the idealist turn, illustrating the method presented in the introduction.

In order to understand how life enters into this story, we can return briefly to the contributions from Fichte and Schelling. We can start with the Fichtean contribution since it is more well known.[65] In presenting self-consciousness as absolute, self-positing activity, Fichte essentially distinguishes self-consciousness in the relevant sense as different in kind from the consciousness of objects. This is important, for if self-consciousness were simply an instance of consciousness of an object, where the object X in this case just happens to be myself, then we are both (i) presupposing what we are trying to explain—that is, consciousness of an object; and (ii) creating an infinite regress of consciousness whereby consciousness of an object presupposes self-consciousness, but self-consciousness simply represents another instance of consciousness of an object, thereby continually pushing back the condition of self-consciousness

---

[65] On the Fichtean contribution, see Pippin (1989, chap. 3) and Henrich (1983).

ad infinitum. Much has been written about this Fichtean contribution, and indeed, it is absolutely essential for understanding Hegel's transition to self-consciousness in which he begins by stating that "self-consciousness is *desire* in general [Begierde *überhaupt*]" (PhG ¶167/3:139). In claiming that self-consciousness is desire, Hegel follows Fichte on two important counts: first, in arguing that self-consciousness, again in the relevant sense, must be different in kind from our usual representation of objects; and second, that as *activity*, self-consciousness is primarily a striving, practical activity constituted by drives and the feeling of force, or what Fichte called the "principle of life." However, in conceiving of self-consciousness as desire, where *Begierde* is a primitive type of animal appetite with additional connotations of sexual desire and lust,[66] Hegel also moves away from Fichte's account of intellectual intuition, whereby self-consciousness's self-constitution takes place by means of an immediate, absolute act. Instead of an absolute foundation "shot from a pistol," as it were, desire is simply the first stage of self-consciousness's long journey of development and self-realization. Although desire will develop into more sophisticated, rationally mediated forms of self-consciousness, culminating in the free will, self-consciousness will also never cease to be desire, nor will its experience be such that it ceases to be structured by desire as an orienting force. If for Fichte the claim was "no striving, no object," then for Hegel it is "no desire, no experience." Finally, desire is *unlike* infinite striving in that desire *can be satisfied*. The key to the satisfaction of self-consciousness as desire lies in finding and constituting the right kinds of objects, and it is this journey that the *Phenomenology* recounts as a path of doubt and despair (PhG ¶78/3:72).

If Fichte provides us with some background for understanding the claim that self-consciousness is desire in general, Schelling provides us with the background for understanding Hegel's developmental approach to self-consciousness that recounts the history of its various "shapes," or *Gestalten*. Hegel's method in the *Phenomenology* is novel not only because it takes a developmental approach to self-consciousness but, more importantly, because it presents the development of self-consciousness *in tandem with an account of the development of self-consciousness's objects*. This method is clearly influenced by Schelling's 1800 *System* in which each concept of the

---

[66] In their respective discussions of self-consciousness as desire, Pippin refers to the desire in question as "orectic" (2011, 12), whereas Brandom (2007) prefers the term "erotic."

I corresponds to a specific concept of an object, and directly carries forward the thesis of speculative identity.[67] The key claim from the 1800 *System*
that Hegel adopts as his own in the transition from consciousness to self-
consciousness is one that we have already seen in the *Differenzschrift*—namely,
that the appropriate object corresponding to the I as self-consciousness is,
first and foremost, the organic object or life. Before trying to unpack that
thought, we can turn to Hegel's and Schelling's descriptions of this essential
relation between self-consciousness and its living object.

Here is Hegel in the *Phenomenology*:

> But *for us*, or *in itself*, the object which for self-consciousness is the nega-
> tive element has, on its side, returned into itself, just as on the other side
> consciousness has done. Through this reflection into itself the object has
> become *life*. What self-consciousness distinguishes from itself *as existing*,
> also has in it, in so far as it is posited as existing, not merely the character
> of sense-certainty and perception, but it is being that is reflected into itself,
> and the object of immediate desire is a *living thing* [*ein* Lebendiges]. (PhG
> ¶168/3:139)

Schelling in the 1800 *System*:

> The organism is the condition under which alone the intelligence can
> distinguish itself, as substance or subject of the succession, from the suc-
> cession itself, or under which alone this succession can be something in-
> dependent of the intelligence. That it now appears to us as though there
> were a transition from the organism into the intelligence, whereby an affec-
> tion of the former brings about a presentation [*Vorstellung*] in the latter, is
> a mere illusion, because we can indeed know nothing of the representation
> before it becomes an object to us through the organism: the affection of the
> organism therefore precedes the presentation in consciousness, and must
> thus appear, not as conditioned thereby, but rather as the condition thereof.
> (SI 127/497)

---

[67] Here is Schelling recounting the relevant moments from his own deduction that lead up to the
organic object: "Since we now stand at the summit of all production, namely at the organic, we are
accorded a retrospect over the whole series. We can now distinguish in nature three orders of intuition: The simple, that of stuff, which is posited therein through sensation; the second, that of matter,
which is posited through productive intuition; and lastly the third, which is characterized by organization" (SI 126/496).

And Hegel again, in the third part of the *Encyclopaedia*, the *Philosophy of Mind*:

> [C]onsciousness in the form of understanding . . . finds its solution in so far as there the object is reduced or elevated to the *appearance* of an *existing interior* that is for itself [*eines für sich* seienden Inneren]. Such an appearance is the *living thing* [das Lebendige]. In the contemplation of this, self-consciousness is ignited; for in the living thing the *object* turns into the *subjective*; there consciousness discovers its own self as the *essential* of the object, it reflects itself out of the object into itself, becomes an object to itself. (PG §418Z)

Two things should be kept in mind as we try to understand these puzzling passages: first, that whatever Hegel and Schelling are claiming here with respect to the relation between self-consciousness and its living object, the claim should not be interpreted in strictly empirical terms; and second, that these passages are direct responses to problems raised by Hegel's critique of Fichte, which argued that Fichte lacked the appropriate concept of an object to properly account for the activity of self-consciousness as self-determining in its form. I will suggest that we can understand these passages as putting forward an argument made up of three interconnected dimensions: the employment and renewal of a prominent analogy, a transcendental argument, and a refutation of idealism argument. While no single dimension, on its own, will prove to be entirely sufficient, each one will lend support where others fall short.

The first, most straightforward way of understanding Hegel's and Schelling's point here is to read them as suggesting that there is an instructive analogy to be drawn between the activity and self-relation of living things, and the activity and self-relation of self-consciousness. This analogy was already evident from the employment of the term "subject-object" to describe both the subjective and the objective dimensions of speculative identity in Hegel's *Differenzschrift*. In these passages, this point is clarified and reiterated: first, the organism's returning to itself or "reflection into itself" is mirrored in self-consciousness; second, the organism's inwardness, as something in which inwardness obtains, and as something that can be *for-itself*, is mirrored in self-consciousness; finally, the subject-object structure of the organism, its self-division as subject-object and its ability to turn the objective into something subjective, is likewise mirrored in self-consciousness. In each case, the living thing is a first actuality and mirror of the central features of self-consciousness that we aim to establish: self-reference and self-relatedness; inwardness as a condition of it being something that can be *for-itself* and that things can be *for*; self-dividedness, *Entzweiung*, and negativity; and finally, the ability to transform the object into something subjective, substance into subject, where that subjectivity or mine-ness has the character of objectivity. The employment of this analogy—one prominent among the post-Kantian idealists and early romantics, and one recently renewed in enactivist theories of mind that draw on biology, psychology, neuroscience, and evolutionary theories of cognition[68]—is a first step toward understanding why Schelling claims that "organic nature furnishes the most visible proof of transcendental idealism" (SI 122/490). That the structure and activity of self-consciousness are reflected in the organism furnishes some minimal yet decisive support for idealism's overarching goal of subject-object identity, and a reason to infer that subject-object identity is not simply possible but also actual, and actual as a process of ongoing, living, self-actualization.[69]

On its own, however, drawing this analogy will not be sufficient, for the analogy neither accounts for the differences in what is being compared nor explains the exact *relation* that is being established between self-consciousness and life.[70] This latter omission is particularly important, since Hegel states that the living thing is an object *of desire*, that self-consciousness is *ignited* by the living thing, and in Schelling's version, even that the *affection* of the organism is a condition for the presentation (*Vorstellung*) in consciousness. In the *Science of Logic*, Hegel writes of the logical concept of life that it is a *presupposition* of self-conscious cognition (WL 676/6:470). This brings us to the transcendental argument, which argues that life is a necessary condition of self-consciousness, not as a matter of empirical, causal, or natural necessity, but as a matter of a priori necessity.[71] What Hegel and Schelling

---

[68] The most sustained treatment of the analogy between mind and life can be found in Thompson (2007).

[69] Chapters 1 and 2 of Khurana's (2017) *Das Leben der Freiheit* contain the most sustained treatment of the analogy argument in Kant, which Khurana presents as an analogy between living self-organization and autonomy.

[70] Further, as mentioned in footnote 48, this chapter, Fichte affirms the analogy argument, so establishing an analogy between self-consciousness and life will not be enough to differentiate Hegel and Schelling from Fichte.

[71] In attributing a transcendental argument to Hegel and Schelling here, I do not mean to suggest that theirs, and Hegel's in particular, will operate exactly like Kant's. As I will argue, the transcendental

are suggesting, then, is that the actuality and activity of self-consciousness presupposes the actuality and activity of living things as its enabling condition. Although this is a complicated claim, the most direct way of understanding their approach is to recall again Hegel's objection to Fichte, which argued that Fichte's I remained conditioned and limited by a not-I, or *Anstoß*, that resulted in absolute opposition. In repeatedly objecting to Fichte's "dead nature" and "relation of domination," we can now see with more clarity that Hegel's complaint is not primarily that the I is conditioned by a not-I but, rather, that Fichte has the wrong concept of the not-I, the wrong concept of an object as the appropriate correspondent to self-consciousness. As Hegel writes, the I cannot achieve "absolute self-intuition" when it is conditioned by an *Anstoß*; rather, the I achieves self-consciousness, self-intuition, and self-feeling only in relation to life.

Let us look at Hegel's passages first before turning to Schelling's. Hegel will give us a general sense of the transcendental argument, whereas Schelling's is stated more explicitly as a refutation of idealism. In the *Phenomenology*, what immediately precedes the appearance of desire and its living object is consciousness in the form of the understanding, or *Verstand*, faced with an object conceived as an expression of force. What the understanding first discovers in the object of force is a distinction between the outer and the inner of an object, a distinction between how the object *appears* and what the object is *in-itself*. In the chapter on "Force and the Understanding," this distinction is presented ultimately as one between a sensible, changeable world of appearances and a supersensible, unchanging world of laws. But for our purposes, what is important is that the distinction between *appearances* and the *inner truth/essence/in-itself-ness* of things generates the needed ambiguity and disparity in the object that drives consciousness toward self-consciousness. Recall Hegel's distinction in the introduction between *in-itself* and *for-consciousness* that articulated the negativity driving the process of experience:

> Consciousness knows *something*, and this object is the essence, or the *in-itself*. However, the object is also the *in-itself* for consciousness. As a result, the ambiguity [*Zweideutigkeit*] of this truth comes on the scene. We see that

---

argument needs an important qualification. Nonetheless, since Hegel and Schelling are both arguing about the conditions and necessary presuppositions of self-consciousness, the use of transcendental arguments seems appropriate.

> consciousness now has two objects: One is the first *in-itself*, and the second
> is the *being-for-it of this in-itself*. (PhG ¶86/3:78–79)

What is articulated in the introduction as two objects is presented in "Force
and the Understanding" as two worlds: the world of appearances (*being-for-consciousness*) and the supersensible world (*being-in-itself*). The key for
Hegel, however is to show that the language of two worlds and two objects
should not be taken literally, and that it is a mistake to approach this ambiguity or disparity in terms of an absolute dualism where the gulf between the
two objects or two worlds is unbridgeable: what something is *in-itself* and
what it is *for-consciousness*, essence and appearance, inner and outer, must
be grasped by consciousness as one and the same. In grasping these two
moments as one and the same, consciousness becomes self-consciousness.
Once consciousness grasps the unity of these distinct moments, Hegel
describes the object of consciousness no longer in terms of forces and laws,
but as infinity (*Unendlichkeit*) and life, described as follows:

> difference as *inner* difference, or difference *in its own self*, or difference as
> *infinity*. (PhG ¶160/3:131)

> This simple infinity, or the absolute Concept, may be called the simple es-
> sence of life, the soul of the world. . . . the *relating to itself* is rather an act
> of *dividing* [das Entzweien]; or, in other words, that very self-sameness
> [*Sichselbstgleichheit*] is an inner difference. (PhG ¶162/3:132)

Once consciousness grasps the disparity in the object as an inner difference,
as self-divided and self-relating at once, the object of consciousness–cum–
self-consciousness is infinity, or the living object. Although Hegel will describe life in much further detail in paragraphs 169–172, the key at the end
of the chapter on "Force and the Understanding" is the emphasis on the inwardness of the object—what Hegel calls in the *Philosophy of Mind*: "the *appearance* of an *existing interior* that is for itself." In paragraph 162, infinity is
repeatedly described as unity, self-identity, self-sameness, and self-relation
that contains inner difference and division ("*Das* Sichselbstgleiche entzweit
sich"), echoing the *Differenzschrift*'s characterization of necessary *Entzweiung*
and identity as essential features of life. The appearance of infinity reflects
back upon consciousness, and Hegel writes: "The understanding's *explanation* is primarily only the description of what self-consciousness is" (PhG

¶163/3:133). The living object is thus the object that provides consciousness with the resources to adequately grasp itself as self-consciousness, allowing consciousness to understand and explain its own inwardness, self-relation, self-dividedness, and activity. In short, to grasp the processual unity of *in-itself* and *for-itself* is to grasp the unity and inner division of life. Reflected back upon the self, that self-relation and self-dividedness is what Hegel calls desire, or self-consciousness divided from itself as it reaches out into the world of living things in order to find satisfaction and self-identity. Hegel is thus claiming that as a matter of transcendental, a priori necessity, the appropriate not-I that opposes itself to the I, such that the I can be determined to be self-determining, is not an *Anstoß*, but life. Life is the only object that expresses the unity and division—a unity and negativity of form—adequate to the unity and division characteristic of the activity of the I. In grasping the unity and activity of life, self-consciousness immediately grasps and constitutes itself, setting into place, as Fichte argued, a schema of subject-object identity and opposition. Summing up their reciprocal relationship, Hegel writes: "this unity is, as we have seen, just as much its repulsion from itself; and this concept *divides* itself [entzweit *sich*] into the opposition between self-consciousness and life" (PhG ¶168/3:139).

This begins to shed some light on the dense passages in the beginning of Chapter IV, where Hegel discusses "the determination of life as it has arisen from the Concept" (PhG ¶169/3:140). In the initial development of the living object as infinity, Hegel focused on inwardness and unity in self-division, demonstrating the unity of the moments of *in-itself* and *for-itself* as infinite self-relation. In the subsequent discussions of the broader context of living things and processes, Hegel focuses on developing a concept of life as a genus- or species-process (*Gattungsprozeß*) that articulates *being-for-self* and *being-for-another* as an ongoing integrated activity. That is, the inner division and self-relation at the micro level of a singular living thing is developed into the independence of individual members and their processual dissolution into unity at the macro level of the activity of the species. The subsequent development of the concept of life as the universal form of activity of the species, where the species likewise manifests internal self-division and the unity of a "self-developing whole," becomes the key in paragraphs 172 and 173, in which Hegel confirms that self-consciousness can have the "pure 'I'" as an object only insofar as it is the "genus for itself" (PhG ¶171, 173/3:142, 143). Although the discussion in these paragraphs is highly opaque, even by Hegelian standards,

Hegel's general description of the processual activity of the species as a whole echoes many of the features identified by Kant as characteristic of *Naturzwecke*. What Hegel needs to establish at this stage is a new concept of an object adequate to self-consciousness's grasp of its own self, a concept of an object that manifests the unity of form not unlike that of the unity of a natural purpose. Most important, life as genus articulates not only the idea of a *whole* but also the idea of concrete, objective universality that is central for many of the key arguments in the *Logic*. In the *Phenomenology*, however, the aim is to develop a concept of life that is adequate for the introduction of the concept of spirit, or *Geist*, where I and We are reciprocally means and ends in the ongoing life of the species.

In articulating the processual movement of life in terms of the necessary relation between *being-for-self* and *being-for-another*, Hegel is setting up the necessary conditions for his famous discussion of the lord and bondsman as the struggle of self-consciousness as it tries to negotiate the necessary relation between independence and dependence (*Selbständigkeit* and *Unselbständigkeit*) in recognizing and being recognized by others. Thus, in his discussions of life at both the micro and macro levels, what Hegel means to establish are the necessary conditions for self-consciousness's grasp of its own activity, initially as self-relation and self-division, and in its further development, as the process of the species that plays out for *Geist* through struggles for recognition. We can see that although Hegel draws inspiration from Fichte's notion of the *summons* (*Aufforderung*) in his understanding of the relation of recognition, his critique of Fichte continues to be decisive: even when Fichte ultimately and correctly suggests that the appropriate not-I that allows the I to determine itself as self-determining must be another I (in Hegel's words: "a self-consciousness exists *for a self-consciousness*"), a necessary condition that renders our turning to this relationship as legitimate and coherent, is a grasp of the concept of the genus or species. Without some minimal grasp of the concept of the species, in which members are essentially united and differentiated through activities defined by their relation to the whole, the notion of recognition or summons lacks sufficient grounding, in that one will not be able to demonstrate the a priori necessity of turning to another self-consciousness, as opposed to some other conception of the not-I. It is the concept of the life of the species that allows us to turn, *necessarily*, to another self-consciousness, rather than to some other concept of an object to which self-consciousness can relate.[72] The fully articulated concept of life, which is presented by Hegel as the entire process of the species, is thus a necessary condition for the concept of self-consciousness, and for the concept of spirit, or *Geist*. Here is the crucial passage from Hegel:

> It is the *simple genus* [einfache Gattung], which in the movement of life itself does not *exist for itself as this simple*. Rather, in this *result*, life points towards something other than itself, namely towards consciousness, for which life exists as this unity, or as genus. But this other life for which the *genus* as such exists, and which is the genus for itself, namely, *self-consciousness*, initially exists . . . as the *pure I*. (PhG ¶¶172–173/3:143)

This statement is crucial for two reasons. First, it reiterates a claim we saw in both Kant and Schelling that life and inner purposiveness—here, the unity of the genus—is to be treated in its essential relation to self-consciousness. The concept of life is a condition for self-consciousness's self-constitution and self-positing, but life is only a concept *for* self-consciousness; living things that are not self-conscious do not have a *concept* of life in the sense being articulated here (though they may have a *feeling* or *intuition* of life). There is, then, a reciprocity between self-consciousness and life, but their identity and non-identity are intractable, ongoing, and necessary as a condition for self-conscious experience. Second, it puts forward the position that self-consciousness should be understood as the genus that is *for-itself*—namely, as life that knows itself as a universal genus, as life that can grasp, constitute, and determine itself as spirit. Lest we think that spirit therefore overcomes or even fully sublates life, Hegel stresses the following at the end of the life and death struggle between self-consciousnesses in which each risks life—with very limited success—for the sake of freedom:

> In this experience, self-consciousness learns that life is as essential to it as pure self-consciousness. (PhG ¶189/3:150)

---

[72] Fichte essentially agrees on this point, although he does not spell this out in terms of self-consciousness and life. Fichte writes that "*if there are to be human beings at all, there must be more than one. . . . it is a truth that can be rigorously demonstrated from the concept of the human being*. As soon as one fully determines this concept, one is driven from the thought of an individual human being to the assumption of a second one, in order to be able to explain the first. Thus the concept of the human being is not the concept of an individual—for an individual human being is unthinkable— but rather the concept of a species" (GNR 37–38/III: 39).

Life is *as essential* as pure self-consciousness because the former is a necessary condition for the latter, because without the former, the latter cannot be conceived, determined, or articulated. This statement goes a long way in beginning to account for the conclusion of Hegel's *Logic*, in which life and self-conscious cognition are again enlisted as providing a method not just for the contents of the *Logic* but also for Hegel's system as a whole. For now, in presenting Hegel's method in the *Phenomenology* as a transcendental claim about the constitutive import of life, a path is open to us for interpreting life as a *logical* concept, as a concept with categorial significance for determining the shape of experience.

Let us try to reconstruct Hegel's argument step by step:

T1. Consciousness distinguishes itself from and relates itself to objects. (PhG ¶82/3:76)

T2. Consciousness's distinguishing and relating generates a disparity or ambiguity in the object: the object as it is *in-itself*, and the object as *for consciousness*. (PhG ¶¶37, 86/3:39, 78–79)

T3. In grasping the unity of this disparity, or the identity of this non-identity, consciousness attains self-consciousness. (PhG ¶¶86, 162–166/3:78, 132–139)

T4. The only object that displays the unity of this disparity, the object of experience as something that is *in-and-for-itself* (self-dividing yet self-relating, displaying a unity and distinction of inner and outer), is infinity, or life. (PhG ¶¶162, 169–172/3:132, 139–143)

T5. To understand the unity and inner distinction between *in-itself* and *for-itself* is to understand the living object. (PhG ¶¶162, 169–172/3:132, 139–143)

T6. The grasp of the living object is a necessary condition for self-consciousness. (PhG ¶¶168, 172–173, 189/3:139, 142–143, 150)

T7. The grasp of life as a genus-process is a necessary condition for spirit or *Geist*, where *Geist* is understood in terms of relations of recognition. (PhG ¶¶172–173, 186–189/3:142–143, 147–150)

This, I want to suggest, is the argument put forward by Hegel that allows him to carry forward the thesis of speculative identity, found already in outline, in the *Differenzschrift*:

T8. The ambiguity, disparity, and negativity between life and non-life, and life and self-consciousness, is the motor and structure—the method—of the experience of consciousness through which self-consciousness is continually actualized as a process of development.

Before turning to some potential worries one could raise with respect to Hegel's argument, I want to point first to two important advantages that this argumentative strategy affords, even if the argument itself will eventually be subject to certain important qualifications. First, in presenting the need for a concept of life in terms of a transcendental argument, Hegel tries to address Kant's skepticism with respect to inner purposiveness directly; recall that despite its overarching importance, the concept of inner purposiveness was relegated in the third *Critique* to having a merely regulative status for the power of judgment. In beginning with premises that Kant would accept—namely, the spontaneity of self-consciousness as the source of the unity of experience and a distinction between appearances and things-in-themselves—Hegel tries to tackle Kant's question *quid juris: By what right* do we employ the concept of life, or the principle of purposiveness, in our activities of judgment? Hegel's answer (heavily informed by Fichte and Schelling) is that we are justified in employing this concept because we cannot conceive self-consciousness without it, because the possibility of understanding the relation between *in-itself* and *for-consciousness* hinges on our being able to grasp a concept of life. Hegel transforms Kant's Copernican Revolution not by presenting life as a category among others in a metaphysical deduction but, rather, by arguing for its constitutive character, inserting it into our concept of self-consciousness and reconceiving the structure of experience according to the internal relation between self-consciousness and life. The unity of the objects of experience afforded by the unity of self-consciousness is thus thoroughly underwritten by the concept of life as a matter of a priori necessity, which allows Hegel to argue, contra Kant, that inner purposiveness indeed has a constitutive status.

A second advantage of Hegel's transcendental strategy is that it in turn strengthens the employment of the analogy between self-consciousness and life, which despite some potential shortcomings, nonetheless plays such a prominent and underappreciated role in post-Kantian idealism. The analogy between life and self-consciousness—which consists in sharing structural features such as interiority and being-for-self, reflexivity and self-reference, self-organization and autonomy, self-production and self-determination—is constantly reiterated by the idealists not just for the sake of finding the right metaphors but also for working toward the goal of demonstrating the constitutive import of life for self-consciousness, and ultimately, for the categorical framework with which we come to determine our objects of knowledge. The analogy is supported by the transcendental argument, which aims to demonstrate the internal relationship between the terms being compared, which in turn reveals the analogy to be of genuine explanatory import, and not merely an external and contingent comparison.

This leads us to some potential worries. In the argument presented here, a lot hinges on the claim in T4 that the object which displays the unity and disparity of being *in-and-for-itself* is infinity or life. The most pressing rejoinder here is that there are in fact no such objects as described in T4, even if it is the case that it is necessary for us to *conceive* of life in order to articulate the concept of self-consciousness. This reveals the limits of transcendental arguments to address the *actuality* of their objects, rather than their mere possibility, for one could accept the full extent of the argument laid out and yet continue to insist that there are no *actual* living objects to which the concept of life refers. Addressing this worry will lead us to qualify the kind of transcendental argument being attributed to Hegel, as well as to clarify some further aspects concerning the distinctiveness of Hegel's phenomenological method. But to stay with transcendental arguments for just a moment longer, we can first look briefly at Schelling's attempt to address this issue in what can be interpreted as his version of the refutation of idealism.

In the passage cited earlier from the *System of Transcendental Idealism* (1800), quoted alongside the two passages from Hegel's *Phenomenology* and *Philosophy of Mind*, Schelling is trying to establish that the organism is the condition for the "presentation [*Vorstellung*] in consciousness." To clarify that our relation to the organism qua condition is not simply one of another representation, Schelling refers to this condition as an "affection [*Affektion*]" of the organism, an affection that precedes any representation in consciousness as its enabling condition. The term "affection" denotes a kind of receptivity in being affected by an object, but it also denotes a certain immediacy: affection is not yet conceptual understanding, and to be affected by something is not, in the first instance, to have a fully conceptually mediated relation to that by which we are affected. As if to make very clear his intent to defend an argument similar to the one found in Kant's "Refutation of Idealism," Schelling also poses the problem in terms of the consciousness of determination in time, referring to the "succession of presentations" and consciousness's ability to distinguish itself from the succession in an act of self-consciousness or intellectual intuition. Like Kant, Schelling's claim is that the existence and intuition of things outside me— here, not just things in general but specifically the organism—is a condition for my inner intuition of myself as distinct from the "succession of presentations." Here is another passage from Schelling in which this argument is stated quite directly:

> But now the intelligence was to intuit, not merely the succession of its presentations [*Vorstellungen*] as such, but itself, and itself as active [*thätig*] in the succession. If it is to become an object to itself as active in the succession (externally, of course, for the intelligence is now merely outwardly intuitant), it must intuit the succession as sustained by an inner principle of activity [*Thätigkeit*]. But now the internal succession, outwardly intuited, is motion [*Bewegung*]. Hence the intelligence will be able to intuit itself only in an object that has an internal principle of motion within itself. But an object such as this is said to be alive. Hence the intelligence must intuit itself, not merely *qua* organization as such, but as living organization. (SI 124/ 493)[73]

In order to intuit myself as *active* in the succession of presentations, and not just as a passive viewer or recipient of a movie-like succession of presentations of which I play no part in shaping, Schelling is suggesting that I must *actually intuit* this activity in external objects. This suggests that the a priori necessity of life is not just conceptual but also in fact requires that there actually *exist* living objects in the world and that I can be affected by them in the appropriate way. The *immediacy* that is attributed to life in both Hegel and Schelling is also captured here and can now be interpreted in two senses: first, life is immediate in a general conceptual sense because of its a

---

[73] Here is Kant's version of the refutation of idealism claim: "I am conscious of my existence as determined in time. All time-determination presupposes something *persistent* in perception. This persistent thing, however, cannot be something in me, since my own existence in time can first be determined only through this persistent thing. Thus the perception of this persistent thing is possible only through a *thing* outside me and not through the mere *representation* of a thing outside me. Consequently, the determination of my existence in time is possible only by means of the existence of actual things that I perceive outside myself" (B275–276).

priori necessity for self-consciousness's self-positing (as Hegel puts it, self-conscious cognition *presupposes* life); second, life is immediate because we are affected by living objects such that the distinction between the living and the non-living strikes us immediately, and in a way that is neither exhausted by further conceptual mediation nor fully up to our control. As the term "affection" suggests, there is a certain passivity here in our intuition of this inner principle of activity, and the immediacy of the distinction between life and non-life for things that are alive is put forward here as a kind of phenomenological necessity, an immediacy without which I could not intuit myself as active in the further mediation of the succession of presentations in experience.[74] The refutation of idealism argument thus provides further defenses against Kant's skepticism with respect to life, deepening the sense in which life must be viewed as constitutive—not just transcendentally, but actually—for self-conscious experience.

With this Schellingian contribution in view, we can now qualify the sense in which Hegel's transcendental argument is to be understood. The transcendental argument is also quite explicitly a phenomenological one, one that is presented by Hegel *via negativa* by way of the ongoing failure of correspondence between concepts and objects. This makes clear Hegel's acknowledgment of two important points: first, that Hegel accepts Schelling's refutation of idealism argument whereby the a priori necessity and immediacy of life must be presented in experience; but also, second, in order to avoid a dogmatic and naively optimistic immediatism about the "affection" by the organism (a kind of myth of the given with respect to life), Hegel must present the actual experience of consciousness as one in which our recognition and acknowledgment of life is momentary at best, constantly obscured, and continually fails.[75] Indeed, as soon as self-consciousness as desire and its living object appear on the scene, self-consciousness acts to *negate* life, first in the object outside itself (eating the object, killing the other), and second, in its own self by risking its life and denying life's significance for the actualization

---

[74] The best statement of this thesis is found in Jay Bernstein's *Adorno: Disenchantment and Ethics*, and I am highly indebted to Bernstein for clarifying this line of thought. Bernstein (2001, 303) writes: "In this instance, 'is living' is a *material* a priori predicate. What makes it material is that its a priori power is not detachable from the exemplary instances through which it is experientially announced. It is an an priori distinction that imposes itself on us. Or, as we might now be tempted to say: it is *the* a priori distinction that is here imposed on us, for in controlling the direction of 'all our reactions' it is equally announcing or introducing into our reactions the very idea of normative appropriateness (toward the object), of our having attitudes that are normative."

[75] Another important departure from Schelling is Hegel's characterization of life as Concept (PhG ¶162/3:132), which anticipates the logical account of life defended in the *Logic*.

of its freedom. Hegel tries to show the futility of our ongoing attempts to simply negate life, which results variously in repeated dissatisfaction, turning ourselves and others into mere things, relations of domination and subjugation, and most important, false and one-sided conceptions of freedom. While the phenomenological argument cannot guarantee the strong a priori necessity of life in the strict transcendental sense, what it can show is the learning process through which consciousness attains self-consciousness by way of its continual engagement with, and its negation and acknowledgement of, its essential relation to life. Rather than reading this as weakening the transcendental argument, however, we can view it as strengthening its force, bringing together theoretical and practical considerations that emerge in considering the actual, experiential development of self-consciousness and spirit. The transcendental and phenomenological arguments thus mutually reinforce one another: the phenomenological account of spirit's development lends content and actuality to the transcendental account, and the transcendental account lends necessary structure and form to the phenomenology of spirit such that its shapes amount to more than just a contingent, disconnected gallery of pictures.

To conclude our present discussion, I want to briefly take up two final worries concerning the interpretation of Hegel presented thus far. The first concerns Hegel's consistent position with regard to the contingency and irrationality of nature, even when one is considering organic, living nature. Thus, despite the constitutive importance of the concept of life for Hegel's understanding of self-consciousness, he also argues that the universality and organization that can be observed in organic nature is, at best, weak and "superficial," admitting of endless exceptions and contingencies, certainly not displaying the kind of necessity that seems requisite for the argument spelled out here.[76] Hegel writes that in nature there is "indifferent contingency and indeterminable irregularity. In the sphere of nature contingency and determination from without has its right. . . . This is the *impotence* [Ohnmacht] of nature" (PN §250).[77] How do we square these claims with what I am

---

[76] See PhG ¶¶245, 255, 262/3:188, 197, 202. The discussion in "observing reason" is quite characteristic. Here, Hegel discusses the weak universality and contingency of nature, which is reflected in our categorizations into genera and species where there are endless exceptions and blurry boundaries, while at the same time affirming the *Zweckbegriff* as expressing the true essence of organisms, reiterating its essential relation to self-consciousness (see esp. ¶¶256–258/3:198–200). See also ¶295/3:224: "[T]o observation reason exists as *life as such*. However, life as such in its differentiation has no rational sequence and demarcation and is not a system of shapes grounded in itself."

[77] See also WL 536/6:282: "This is the impotence of nature, that it cannot adhere to and exhibit the strictness of the Concept and runs wild in this blind conceptless multiplicity. We can *wonder* at

attributing to Hegel as his speculative identity thesis? Here it is important to emphasize that the concept of life that is most relevant for our discussion does not concern how we conceive of nature but, rather, how we conceive of self-consciousness and its activity of knowing. As I suggested in chapter 2, the innovation of Hegel's approach to the concept of life is best found *not* in his philosophy of nature but in his understanding of conceptual activity and conceptual form. Thus, the relative irrationality and contingency of nature can stand alongside the *logical* concept of life without any contradiction, for what Hegel is interested in is not empirical nature in its irreducible contingency but, instead, the *essential form and structure* of life-activity that is expressed in the concept of an internal purpose or end (*Zweckbegriff*), in the internal self-division and self-relation of organic self-production. Hegel can therefore affirm both the constitutive import of inner purposiveness and the contingency of nature at once: while nature in its existence and differentiations attains to a weak universality at best, what is *not* contingent is that life as conceived here is a necessary condition for self-consciousness. Speculative identity thus does not require that nature is carved at the joints, nor does it require that Hegel subscribe to a strong essentialism about natural kinds.[78] Nature remains contingent, but what is not contingent is that the life/non-life distinction, and the specific kind of activity and form that is ascribed to life in this distinction, is necessary a priori for the constitution of self-conscious experience.

The second worry can be phrased as follows: even if life is constitutive in the sense argued here, isn't the *ultimate* object that constitutes self-consciousness *not* life but, rather, another self-consciousness? Thus, after all is said and done, Hegel will still insist that the relevant self-negating object that appropriately mirrors self-consciousness is another self-consciousness rather than life, which suggests that life is superseded or sublated after all. The development of *Geist* is the story of its moving away from natural life and leaving it behind, so the living object, like forces and laws, like the thing and properties, and like the immediate "this" of sense-certainty, also gets left behind, and subsequently plays no role in Hegel's understanding of the relation between self-consciousnesses that takes place under the

nature's manifold genera and species and the endless diversity of her formations, for *wonderment* is *without Concept* and its object the irrational."

---

[78] For a defense of Hegel as a natural kinds essentialist, see Knappik (2016). See also the discussion of natural kinds in Kreines (2008b).

heading of recognition. To address this worry, the first step is to affirm that, indeed, the *ultimate* object that constitutes self-consciousness is another self-consciousness, in a relation that, as Hegel says, already expresses what is meant by *Geist* (PhG ¶177/3:145). However, if as I have argued, life is in fact a necessary a priori condition for our grasp of self-consciousness, then we must carry forward this a priori condition as we further consider self-consciousness in its necessary relation to other self-consciousnesses. This is why Hegel not only writes that "life is as essential as pure self-consciousness" in the wake of the life and death struggle, but he further emphasizes in his staging of the recognition thesis that as the genus that is *for-itself*, self-consciousness is "a living self-consciousness" (or, a subjective subject-object, a living mind) (PhG ¶176/3:144). When Hegel writes that self-consciousness is "living," this should again not be taken in a strictly empirical sense, which would appear to be stating the obvious; rather, we can apply the same transcendental and phenomenological arguments employed earlier in understanding the relation between self-consciousnesses. If we say that another self-consciousness is a necessary condition for self-consciousness from a transcendental standpoint, what we need to carry forward in this claim are the previous a priori conditions that have already been established as necessary for getting to this point: first, a distinction between life and non-life; and second, as part of our grasp of the concept of life, a notion of genus or species. These conditions already give substantial shape to the idea of self-consciousness existing *for* a self-consciousness: both self-consciousnesses and their relationship are defined, at least in part, by the distinction between life and non-life, or now, life and death; and further, both self-consciousnesses are defined as being members of the same species, whose activities and identities can at least potentially be defined according to the unity or "universal medium" of the species (PhG ¶¶ 169, 171/3:140–142). Although both the distinction between life and death and the concept of the species will undergo subsequent transformations in their meaning and content as spirit undergoes development, qua transcendental conditions, these terms will also retain their original meanings and content as defined initially in relation to *mere* life. Put another way, the immediacy of life qua a priori condition is retained such that neither the life/non-life distinction nor the concept of the species can simply be redefined by fiat. Both have an essential form that constrains the actualization of self-consciousness while also providing the ground for any possible self-actualization. This last point will be put forward most forcefully in the *Science of Logic* and will be discussed at length in chapter 7.

From the phenomenological standpoint, we can see how life is carried forward for Hegel in two steps. First, according to the refutation of idealism argument, there must in fact *be* other living self-consciousnesses, and I must be able to be immediately affected by them in the appropriate way such that I can intuit their activity as reflected in myself.[79] With the concept of species already in place, Hegel can now claim, further, that the relation between a self-consciousness faced by another self-consciousness is mutual and reciprocal, that each is for the other what the other is for itself. Second, in his phenomenological description of this encounter, Hegel again begins by stating that what the other self-consciousness is for me, that what I intuit in the other in the first instance by way of immediate affection, is life. He writes:

> What comes on the scene here is an individual confronting an individual. In the way that they *immediately* make their appearance, they exist for each other in the way ordinary objects do. They are *self-sufficient* shapes absorbed within the *being* of *life* —for the existing object has here been determined to be life. (PhG ¶186/3:148)

In this passage, Hegel is carrying forward Schelling's "affection" thesis but with respect to self-consciousness: although what is ultimately being established here is the reciprocal relation between two self-consciousnesses, a necessary part of what is immediately recognized or acknowledged in the other is its life, its living activity and form. One consequence of this is that I would not be able to recognize the other *as* a self-consciousness if I did not also at the same time recognize its aliveness. However, recognition of aliveness is also not enough, since the goal is to recognize the other as a self-consciousness, *not* simply as life. What follows is very well known: in order to mutually prove to the other that I am a self-consciousness and not mere life, the individuals engage in a life-and-death struggle in an attempt to prove that they are *not* mere life, that life is *not* essential to their self-determination. However, the sheer negation of life here proves futile, and

---

[79] Hegel writes: "For self-consciousness, there is another self-consciousness; self-consciousness is *outside of itself*. This has a twofold meaning. *First*, it has lost itself, for it is to be found as an *other* essence. *Second*, it has thereby sublated that other, for it also does not see the other as the essence but rather sees *itself* in the *other*" (PhG ¶179/3:146).

Hegel writes that in this engagement, "they only indifferently leave each other free-standing, like things" (PhG ¶188/3:150). That engaging with one another like *things* is not sufficient for attaining self-consciousness follows from what has already been established earlier in Chapter IV—namely, that the living object is a necessary condition for self-consciousness. It is in this context that Hegel proclaims that "life is as essential as pure self-consciousness," which suggests that phenomenologically, what I must intuit in the other is both life *and* self-consciousness at once, that what it means for self-consciousness to be *for* a self-consciousness is the mutual recognition of this double constitution. Hegel's phenomenological account of the encounter between self-consciousnesses is thus constructed entirely around the relation to life: what each first recognizes in the other is life; to prove that they are self-consciousnesses and not mere life, they try to negate life in themselves and in the other; the futility of negating life leads to the lesson that what self-consciousness recognizes in itself and in the other is both self-consciousness and life at once. As with before, however, because Hegel wants to avoid dogmatism and naiveté about the immediacy of this recognition, what ensues is a more sophisticated attempt to negate life in myself and in the other: the master attempts to assert her self-sufficiency and independence from mere life by subjugating the slave to carry out the labor of life, trying again, in a mediated way, to reduce the other to a mere tool or thing. But as Hegel will show again and again, life is as essential as pure self-consciousness, and it is the negativity of this double constitution that continues to drive forward the experience of consciousness on its journey of self-actualization.

3.5 Transition: Speculative Identity in the *Science of Logic*

I have argued in this chapter that the thesis of speculative identity, presented in outline in the *Differenzschrift* and developed in the *Phenomenology of Spirit*, should be viewed as Hegel's distinctive approach to an idealist philosophical method. Specifically, I demonstrated that the identity and non-identity of the *subjective subject-object* and the *objective subject-object*, interpreted as expressing the internal, structural, and essential reciprocity between self-consciousness and life, should be understood as the foundation and method of Hegel's idealism. Incorporating the Schellingian contribution and the critique of Fichte presented in Hegel's *Differenzschrift*, the science of the experience of consciousness in the *Phenomenology* was interpreted as defending the constitutive import of life against Kant's skepticism by way of both transcendental and phenomenological strategies. Hegel's theory of self-consciousness, and his understanding of the development and self-actualization of spirit, are thus thoroughly underwritten by speculative identity, presenting, as he says, an "example" of his philosophical method.

In addition to providing such an example, the *Phenomenology* sets the stage for the *Science of Logic*, providing a deduction for the very idea of "science." How, then, can we understand the transition from phenomenology to logic, from an account of experience to an account of the categories or "thought-determinations" (*Denkbestimmungen*) of logical cognition, given the thesis of speculative identity that has been presented in this chapter? Three brief remarks will help us prepare the transition to our discussion of Hegel's *Logic* in part II.

First, in the presentation of the transcendental argument, what we saw was that the concept of life at stake in that context was already a logical, non-empirical concept of life, with the status of something a priori. This provides some precedence and background for Hegel's official treatment of life as a logical category in the conclusion of his *Logic*, and suggests that life may serve a similar or parallel function for our understanding of logical cognition. It is evident from Hegel's text that he treats thinking and its self-generated system of thought-determinations as living in at least two senses: first, thinking itself is treated as a living activity in constant development, driven by inner division and contradiction; second, the system of categories themselves form a self-developing organic whole, where each individual category attains to its full significance only in its relation to the entire system. Thus, at a very general level, and from the very outset, thought thinking itself is modeled on internally purposive activity, set in contrast to the "dead bones" and "dead forms" of prior approaches to logic (WL 12, 27/5:19, 41). Hegel further claims that the only way to "quicken" the dead bones of logic is through method, that "*method* . . . alone can make [logic] fit to be pure science" (WL 32/5:48). The method of speculative identity will thus continue to play an important role in Hegel's treatment of pure thought and its categories, providing a framework by which we understand the role of life in the project of the *Logic* as a whole.

Second, if the *Phenomenology* provides us with a deduction to the standpoint of science, then that standpoint is the standpoint of the Concept (*der Begriff*) or conceptual thinking (*begreifende Denken*). In articulating this standpoint in the introduction of the *Logic*, Hegel recalls his critique of reflection and *Verstand*, and now situates his objection specifically in terms of the separation between form and content. What Hegel opposes is the assumption by ordinary common sense that thoughts are *mere* thoughts, that thinking is empty and abstract by its very nature. Rather, speculative logic or science treats thinking as both form and content at once, and the term "thought-determinations" is meant to call attention to the concreteness and determinacy generated by thought itself, solely on account of its own activity or productivity. Hegel describes the standpoint of the Concept attained in absolute knowing and presupposed by the general concept of logic as follows:

> Pure science thus presupposes the liberation from the opposition of consciousness. It contains *thought insofar as this thought is equally the thing as it is in itself* [die Sache an sich selbst]; or the *thing in itself* insofar as this *is equally pure thought*. As *science*, truth is pure self-consciousness as it develops itself and has the shape of the self, so that *that which exists in and for itself is the conscious Concept and the Concept as such is that which exists in and for itself*. (WL 29/5:43)

Here Hegel reiterates the importance of the distinction and relation expressed by that which is *in and for itself*, but specifically in connection with logic as pure science. First, the relation between in and for itself is expressed now as the relation between *die Sache an sich selbst* and thought, where what is *in-itself* is the thing, fact, or matter itself and what is *for-itself* is the *Sache* as grasped and determined by thought. Second, Hegel writes that for logic, what we are concerned with is the *pure* shape of self-consciousness, or logical (and not phenomenological) self-consciousness, which he calls the Concept. In a section of the introduction entitled "General Division [*Einteilung*] of Logic," Hegel spells out the division of the text into an Objective Logic and a Subjective Logic, where this division is now associated with the "*judgment* [Urteil]" or division of the Concept itself (WL 38/5:56). This idea of division, evoked now by the terms *Einteilung* and *Urteil*, recalls the importance of the term *Entzweiung* from our earlier discussion. In the context of logic, the division into Objective and Subjective Logic is framed in terms of judgment or "original division" (*ursprüngliche Teilung*), but even in the logical context, Hegel will eventually determine this idea as "the original *judgment* of life [*das*

ursprüngliche Urteil *des Lebens*]" (WL 678/6:473).[80] At the level of the introduction, Hegel's pronouncements do not get beyond allusion and wordplay,
but what is clear is that Hegel means to carry forward the thesis of speculative identity, and that he will attempt to translate the *Entzweiung* and negativity originally associated with life into the logical terms of Concept and
judgment.

Finally, the all-important Hegelian notions of Concept and Idea are
both explicitly defined with respect to speculative identity. As we will discuss in detail in part II, Hegel consistently presents both notions as doubly
constituted: in their immediacy, they take the form of life, and as mediated,
conscious, and *for-itself*, they take the form of self-conscious cognition. What
this means for a science of logic will be explored in the rest of the book, but
what is undeniable is that the thesis of speculative identity will remain at the
heart of Hegel's philosophical method and continue to play a defining role in
the mature presentation of Hegel's idealist project.

---

[80] See also WL 552/6:304: "Judgment is the self-diremption of the Concept . . . the *original division*
[ursprüngliche Teilung] of what is originally one; the German word for judgment, *Urteil*, thus refers
to what judgment is in and for itself."

PART II

THE PURPOSIVENESS
OF THINKING IN HEGEL'S *LOGIC*

4

Actuality and the Genesis of the Concept

4.1 What Is the Genesis of the Concept?

Hegel's use of the term "Concept" is unlike our usual use of the term, and it is often quite jarring, even for longtime readers of Hegel, to talk of *the* Concept, instead of concepts that we might have of *x* or *y*.[1] In order to provide some context for Hegel's use of the term, I want to return briefly to two central passages from Kant's third *Critique* where he defines purpose and purposiveness, but now with a particular focus on Kant's use of the term "concept." Kant writes:

> [I]nsofar as the concept of an object also contains the ground for the object's actuality, the concept is called the thing's *purpose* and a thing's conformity with that character of things which is possible only through purposes is called the *purposiveness* of its form. (KU 5:180)

> [A] purpose is the object of a concept insofar as we regard this concept as the object's cause (the real ground of its possibility); and the causality that a *concept* has with regard to its *object* is purposiveness (*forma finalis*). (KU 5:220)

In these passages, Kant describes purposiveness of form in terms of a particular causal power of the concept: the power of a concept to be "the ground for the object's actuality," and the power of a concept to be the cause of an object as "the real ground of its possibility." Purposiveness of form is attributed to concepts insofar as they exhibit the power to ground the actuality and possibility of an object, where there is an emphasis on *real* possibility, rather than merely formal or logical possibility. A concept, in the sense described here, has the power to determine what is actual, the power to determine actuality

---

[1] Portions of this chapter are drawn from my contribution (Ng 2017) to the *Oxford Handbook of Hegel*. I have previously discussed the concept of actuality in Hegel in an earlier article (Ng 2009).

Hegel's Concept of Life. Karen Ng, Oxford University Press (2020) © Oxford University Press 2020.
DOI: 10.1093/oso/9780190947613.001.0001

through the purposiveness of its form. I will propose that these passages from Kant provide us with a clear definition of what Hegel means by *the* Concept, and that the genesis of the Concept, presented most directly in the concluding section of the Doctrine of Essence entitled "Actuality," should be understood as Hegel's systematic, philosophical defense of the purposiveness of form as constitutive of the Concept. In short, what Hegel calls the genesis of the Concept, or the "immanent deduction" of the Concept, is his attempt to provide, in the logical context, a series of arguments for the constitutive character of inner purposiveness for any account of self-conscious conceptual activity whereby determinations of thinking have the power to determine actuality.[2] If, according to the infamous *Doppelsatz*, there is a speculative identity of the rational and the actual, then what the treatment of actuality in the logical context reveals is that Hegel's *Doppelsatz*, which captures in a slogan the heart of Hegel's idealism, cannot be fully grasped without an understanding of purposiveness's essential role in the determination of that identity. Hegel's affirmation of purposiveness's role in conceptual activity and power is evidenced by many statements from various contexts. He writes: "purpose [*Zweck*] is the Concept itself in its concrete existence" (WL 652/6:438); "reason is purposive activity [*zweckmäßige Tun*]" (PhG ¶22/3:26); and finally, "the forms of the Concept are *the living spirit of what is actual*; and what is true of the actual is only *true in virtue of these forms, through them* and *in them*" (EL §162Z).[3] Hegel's concept of the Concept thus continues to develop and transform Kant's purposiveness thesis by introducing a distinctive notion of actuality (*Wirklichkeit*), which receives its fullest treatment in the transition from Objective to Subjective Logic.

In order to elucidate the role that purposiveness of form plays in Hegel's deduction, this chapter will take up a detailed discussion of the section on "Actuality" that brings about the transition from the Doctrine of Essence to the Doctrine of the Concept, a section comprising three chapters: "The Absolute," "Actuality," and "The Absolute Relation." Key to my interpretation is Hegel's aim in these chapters to understand actuality in terms of "activity of form," or *Formtätigkeit*, and thereby to provide an argument for the genesis of the Concept. Activity of form can be understood essentially as Hegel's own term for the purposiveness of form, one that he develops through an

---

[2] Hegel refers to the immanent deduction of the Concept at WL 514/6:252. On the genesis of the Concept, see WL 509, 512, 514, 530/6:246, 251, 252, 274.

[3] See also the discussion in EL §6 of the self-producing or self-engendering character of actuality and rationality.

engagement with Spinoza's conception of substance, Aristotle's conception of actuality, and most importantly, the category of reciprocity (*Wechselwirkung*) in which causes and effects are in reciprocal interaction. Although the varied contents of the section on "Actuality" can often seem disconnected and obscure, they are unified in their aim of effecting the immanent transformation from substance to subject, from necessity to freedom and self-determination, an immanent transformation that takes place by means of an investigation into the concept of actuality, asking how the process of actualization can be conceived of in terms of self-actualization.[4] In understanding activity of form in terms of purposiveness, Hegel argues that the genesis of the Concept arises from and is an actualization of purposive activity, once again demonstrating the reciprocity and speculative identity between life and the self-conscious Concept.

This chapter will proceed as follows. I begin in section 4.2 by offering an overview of the notion of actuality and activity of form, and very briefly consider how Hegel employs the notion of actuality in the context of his understanding of nature, spirit, and logic. This gives us a sense of the overarching importance of the concept of actuality throughout Hegel's system, and establishes that Hegel's understanding of actuality is essentially informed by a conception of purposive activity, one that is heavily influenced by Aristotle's notion of *ènérgeia*. With this background in mind, I turn in section 4.3 to Hegel's engagement with Spinoza in the chapter entitled "The Absolute," demonstrating the motivation for beginning his genesis-argument with the concept of substance and revealing two important ways that Hegel's approach departs from Spinoza. Hegel's critique of substance leads him to turn to a priority of modes over substance, and I discuss the chapter on modality and the process of actualization in section 4.4. The "Actuality" chapter revolves around three essential issues: first, the distinction between contingent existence and actuality; second, a thesis about the priority of actuality, which again, is adopted from Aristotle; and third, Hegel's aim to show that the process of actualization, if we are to understand that process *beyond* the terms of sheer contingency and necessity, requires a concept of purposive activity and self-actualization. To develop that concept of purposive activity, I turn in section 4.5 to the chapter entitled "The Absolute Relation," where Hegel presents the category of reciprocity, arguing that it "sublates" the determination of mechanism. Expressing the relation in which something is

---

[4] See Zambrana's (2015, chaps. 3 and 5) discussion of the actualization theme in Hegel's *Logic*.

the cause and effect of itself, reciprocity is the final stage of Hegel's genesis-argument and completes his deduction of the Concept. I conclude in section 4.6 with some remarks concerning the reciprocity between life and Concept, and argue that like Hegel's earlier account of self-consciousness, the Concept must be understood as doubly constituted.

4.2 Actuality and "Activity of Form" (*Formtätigkeit*): Nature, Spirit, Logic

In order to set up our discussion of the section on "Actuality" in the *Science of Logic*, it is important to appreciate the sheer ubiquity of this concept throughout Hegel's system. Very broadly speaking, actuality is Hegel's appropriation of Aristotle's notion of *ènérgeia*.[5] What leads Hegel to return again and again throughout his system to the notion of actuality is his interest in articulating a determinate conception of *activity*, or more specifically, an *activity of form* (*Formtätigkeit*) in which pairs such as form and matter, inner and outer, or essence and existence, are not presented as fundamentally opposed.[6] When something is actual in Hegel's technical sense, it exhibits an internal, reciprocal relation between form and content, or concept and reality, which indicates self-determining, internally purposive activity at some level and to some degree; most importantly, the identification of something as actual indicates the presence of rational form. Actuality denotes internally purposive activity but also, potentially, the *products* of this activity; thus, Hegel will refer variously to thought-determinations, knowledge, artworks, constitutions, and institutions of ethical life as actual, insofar as they in turn reflect the self-determining form characteristic of its producers. In exhibiting the essential form of self-determination, actuality is further distinguished from mere existence: whereas what merely exists has the essential form of

---

[5] See Ferrarin (2001, 2006). For a discussion of actuality in connection with other related terms (reality, objectivity, actuosity), see Lécrivain (2000).

[6] The terms "activity of form" or "form-activity" (*Tätigkeit der Form, Tun der Form, Formtätigkeit*) are used by Hegel in various contexts. See the discussion of form and matter in the "Ground" chapter, WL 393–395/6:90–93; the discussion of the hypothetical syllogism, WL 622/3:397; the discussion of the relation of substantiality, EL §§150–151; and the discussion of the realization of purpose as Concept, EL §212. In *Hegel's Critique of Metaphysics*, Longuenesse (2007, 151–162) also argues that the outcome of Hegel's discussion of actuality in the *Science of Logic* is a concept of activity (*Tätigkeit*). Although I am largely sympathetic with her account, my approach to actuality here will differ from hers in that my main argument is that Hegel's concept of activity is essentially tied to his concept of life, which must be understood as an appropriation of Kant's notion of the purposiveness of form.

contingency and exhibits, at best, an external relation between form and content, what is actual displays a necessary connection between form and content that makes it grounded and rational. Here is Hegel explaining actuality in Aristotle in his *Lectures on the History of Philosophy*:

> There are two leading forms, which Aristotle characterizes as that of potentiality (*dúnamis*) and that of actuality (*enérgeia*); the latter is still more closely characterized as entelechy (*entelecheia*), which has the end (*tò télos*) in itself, and is the realization of this end. . . . To Aristotle, the main fact about Substance is that it is not matter merely . . . matter itself is only potentiality, and not actuality—which belongs to form—matter cannot truly exist without the activity of form. With Aristotle *dúnamis* does not therefore mean force (for force is really an imperfect aspect of form), but rather capacity which is not even undetermined possibility; *enérgeia* is, on the other hand, pure efficaciousness out of itself [*die reine Wirksamkeit aus sich selbst*]. (VGP 2:138–139/19:154)[7]

In this passage, Hegel associates actuality with the realization of an internal purpose or end (*Zweck*), which he illustrates by describing the relation and distinction between form and matter. Following Aristotle, Hegel identifies matter with potentiality and form with actuality and activity. Absent the activity of form, matter, Hegel suggests, cannot truly be something determinate; in a sense, the notion of *pure* matter is an abstraction, for matter is always already shaped by some activity of form. We can think of *Formtätigkeit* in two ways. First, activity of form brings shape and determinacy to *objects*. Matter must have form in order to be something determinate, and this form can be the result of something external to the object (a result of external causes, forces, or powers) or it can result from an object's own activity (a child that grows into an adult).[8] In the latter case, this points to a second way of understanding activity of form—namely, as an activity that potentially shapes and determines a *subject* of activity. Activity of form is potentially formative of a self, displaying a locus of self-activity and a form of *self*-determination alongside the determination of objects. *Formtätigkeit* is therefore what makes a

---

[7] On Hegel on Aristotle's notion of *enérgeia*, see also EL §142Z. See García's (2016) excellent discussion on the differences between Hegel and Schelling's interpretation of actuality in Aristotle. García argues that, against Hegel, Schelling interprets actuality in distinction from entelechy.

[8] These are, of course, not mutually exclusive processes, but I take them to be analytically distinct ways of understanding formation.

thing (an object or a subject) *actual*, what brings form to matter, what makes the indeterminate determinate, rendering sheer immediacy into posited being (*Gesetztsein*). To talk of form is thus to talk of the process and activity of *formation*; if form constitutes what is actual, then understanding actuality requires that we understand the process and activity of actualization, the full realization of which is the activity of self-actualization. Hegel's Aristotelian approach to actuality leads him to tie the problems of form and activity together such that neither can be grasped without reference to the other. The notion of activity of form is the means by which Hegel transforms Kant's thesis about the purposiveness of form into his own distinctive concept of the Concept.

With this idea of activity of form in mind, we can elaborate on and qualify Hegel's *Doppelsatz* as follows: in identifying the rational and the actual, it is in fact more accurate to identify actuality with formative activity that constitutes an end in itself. Of course, rational activity remains exemplary of this type of activity, but it should be noted that Hegel's characterization of activity of form is in fact much broader than what would ordinarily be construed as rational. We can consider for a moment how Hegel takes up the issue of *Formtätigkeit* from three distinct but related perspectives, which make up the keystones of his philosophical system. First, from the perspective of *nature*, what exemplifies the unity of form and matter characteristic of the actual is the activity and productivity of living nature, and in particular, of animal organisms. In the *Philosophy of Nature*, Hegel discusses the totality of the earth as an implicit process of formation (*Bildungsprozeß*), which is fully realized only in animal activity, for the animal is nothing but the product of "its own self-process" (PN §339Z). Reminding us that Kant had defined the animal as an end-in-itself, Hegel follows suit by describing the animal as a *Selbstzweck*, insofar as the animal produces itself from out of its own activity: whereas the earth merely *endures* (*dauert*), undergoing transformations due to external forces, the animal produces and reproduces itself and its species through its own formative activity. In the productivity of organisms, form and matter, inner and outer, are not opposed but, rather, exist in a necessary, internal relation of self-production. Hegel writes: "Whenever inner and outer, cause and effect, end and means, subjectivity and objectivity, etc., are one and the same, there is life" (PN §337Z). The idea of activity and "pure efficaciousness out of itself" thus finds immediate expression in the self-production of living beings.

Second, from the perspective of *spirit*, Hegel defines *Geist* itself as "*manifestation*" and "absolute *actuality*" (PM §383). In referring to spirit as absolute actuality, Hegel means to present the individual and collective activity of human agents as an expression of freedom. Spirit's activity of self-production can be understood as a process of *Bildung*, as the social and historical activity of cultural formation through which increasing universal consciousness of freedom is realized. On the side of subjective spirit, Hegel's conception of the soul as actuality is explicitly drawn from Aristotle and is articulated as the activity of form whereby the unity of soul and body is continually produced. As soul develops into consciousness and mind, culminating in what Hegel calls the "actual free will," the activity of subjective spirit is actualized into objective spirit, an actuality that takes the form of the objective side of freedom (PG §§481–482). In the domain of objective spirit, the practices, customs, laws, and institutions that are the products of free willing are actual to the degree that they in turn function as the conditions for the further realization of free activity. This self-referring, reciprocal activity of subjective and objective spirit is the general shape of spirit as absolute actuality; as Hegel suggests, spirit as manifestation "does not reveal *something*; its determinacy and content is this very revelation," its determinacy and content is nothing but its own activity of form (PG §383). In the context of spirit, actuality as formative activity that constitutes an end in itself is presented as free and rational activity on the part of human agents in their social and historical development.

Finally, from the perspective of *logic*, which is the main focus of the discussion that follows, actuality represents the unity of essence and appearance, bringing us from the Doctrine of Essence to the Doctrine of the Concept. In the *Logic*, Hegel also describes actuality simply as manifestation and self-expression, where this is intended to describe the essential relation that obtains between essence and appearance in the determination of anything we would call actual.[9] In the chapter immediately preceding the section on "Actuality," titled "The Essential Relation," Hegel takes up three pairs of concepts that allow him to explore the unity and relation of form: the relation

---

[9] See WL 464/6:185: "What something is, therefore, it is wholly in its externality [*Äußerlichkeit*]....
[I]ts externality is, therefore, the expression [*Äußerung*] of what it is in itself; and since its content and form are thus utterly identical, it is, in and for itself, nothing *but this: to express itself*. It is the revealing [*das Offenbaren*] of its essence, and this essence, accordingly, consists simply in being that which reveals itself." And EL §142: "Actuality is the unity, become immediate, of essence and existence, or of what is inner and what is outer. The expression of the actual is the actual itself, so that it remains something essential in this expression and is only something essential in so far as it is in immediate external existence [*Existenz*].... [I]ts existence [*Dasein*] is only the *manifestation of itself.*"

of whole and part, the relation of force and its expression, and the relation of inner and outer. In each case, Hegel argues for the unity and essential relationship between the terms of each pair and, further, presents each pair as an increasingly determinate expression of the relation between essence and appearance. The unity of inner and outer, as the final result of this relation, is described by Hegel as "absolute form," a "*form relation*," "*identity of form*," and "*absolute actuality*" (WL 461, 465/6:182, 186).[10] All these denominations attest to Hegel's goal, in the final stage of his deduction of the Concept, to present the determination of actuality as an activity of form, at once as an activity of thought-form and an activity of form of the actual. The deduction of the activity of form is thus necessary for the deduction of the Concept, and the logical determination of actuality will present a defense of this idea in three stages: first, through a critique of Spinoza's metaphysics of substance; second, through an account of modality that argues for the priority of actuality over possibility, demonstrating the need for thinking of actuality in terms of purposive self-actualization; and finally, through a critique of a mechanistic approach to causality, resulting in the category of reciprocity in which inner purposiveness of form is revealed as constitutive of the freedom and power of the Concept.

4.3 The Absolute: Hegel's Critique of Substance

4.3.1 Spinoza

Hegel presents his genesis or deduction of the Concept primarily in terms of an immanent critique of Spinoza, but we can begin by noting that Hegel's praise of Spinoza is surely as significant as his criticism. Concerning this all-important predecessor of German idealism, Hegel writes: "thought must begin by placing itself at the standpoint of Spinozism; to be a follower of Spinoza is the essential commencement of all philosophy" (VGP 3:269/20:165).[11] In the context of Hegel's deduction, it appears that Spinoza is the

---

[10] The discussion of force and its expression alongside the discussion of inner and outer recalls the discussion in the *Phenomenology* in the transition from consciousness to self-consciousness discussed in section 3.4.2.

[11] See also VGP 20:163–164: "Spinoza ist Hauptpunkt der modernen Philosophie: entweder Spinozismus oder keine Philosophie." The undeniable influence of Spinoza and the *Pantheismusstreit* on post-Kantian thought is very well established (see esp. Beiser 1987; Franks 2005; Förster and Melamed 2015).

philosopher to beat: "The only possible refutation of Spinozism can only consist, therefore, in first acknowledging its standpoint as essential and necessary and then raising it to a higher standpoint *on the strength of its own resources*" (WL 512/6:250). What makes Spinoza's system so significant for Hegel such that the Concept *must* be deduced from its resources? Why Spinoza, and is this really the best strategy for Hegel at this crucial moment in the transition to the Doctrine of the Concept?

To answer the question of "why Spinoza?" we can return briefly to the notion of speculative identity and consider the extent to which Spinoza's philosophy reflects Hegel's understanding of this idea. The central philosophical concept that defines Spinoza's system is the notion of infinite, self-causing, necessary, absolute substance, which constitutes the essence and existence of all reality. What has long been viewed as the most scandalous feature of Spinoza's thought is that he identifies infinite, self-causing substance with "God or Nature" (*Deus sive Natura*), a phrase that conveys the equivalence or identity of the terms in question. In defining substance in these terms, Spinoza is suggesting that God is immanent in nature rather than transcendent of it and, further, that to speak of the activity and causality of God is at once to speak of the activity and causality of nature. Considered admittedly from a high altitude, we can already see why the idea of substance as *Deus sive Natura* would be so attractive and compelling for thinkers like Hegel and Schelling: in constructing a philosophical system based on the identity of God and nature as absolute actuality, Spinoza provides a model for thinkers who likewise want to determine the identity of reason and nature as absolute, unifying the activity and causality of nature with the activity and causality of freedom. Whereas Spinoza argues for God's immanence within nature, Hegel and Schelling, as we have seen, aim to demonstrate that the infinite activity of reason and freedom is immanent in nature and, more specifically, immanent in the activity characteristic of life. Infinite, self-causing substance defined as *Deus sive Natura* thus appears as a natural starting point for Hegel's genesis argument; in simply defining substance, Spinoza has already brought together a set of philosophical ideas that are all key for Hegel's understanding of absolute, speculative thought, including infinity, self-determination, necessity, the identity of essence and existence, actuality, and the identity of spirit and nature. The key dispute between Hegel and Spinoza is not so much about the descriptors of substance as it is about the determination of *substance*, rather than *Concept* and ultimately *Idea*, as that which is absolute. Hegel's immanent deduction of the Concept from substance can thus also be read as his immanent transformation of *Deus sive Natura* into his distinctive understanding of speculative identity, where "God or nature" will be recast in terms of Concept and life. Spinoza's philosophy represents the closest attempt in modern philosophy at something akin to a speculative identity thesis, and we can understand the "immanence" of Hegel's immanent deduction as follows: the Concept is immanent to substance insofar as substance as actuality is understood as the activity of form characteristic of both freedom and life. As Hegel writes: "The Concept has substance for its immediate presupposition; what substance is *in itself* is *manifested* in the Concept" (WL 509/6:264). Hegel's argument will be that everything that is merely implicit in the notion of substance is made explicit in the Concept. More specifically, and looking ahead to the Subjective Logic, Hegel aims to transform Spinoza's metaphysics of substance, attributes, and modes into the three determinations of the Concept, as universal, particular, and individual.[12] To begin to understand how Hegel effects this transformation, we can now turn directly to the chapter called "The Absolute."

4.3.2 Substance as Absolute

Hegel's argument in the first chapter of the section on "Actuality" can be framed in terms of two interpretive questions. The first is relatively straightforward: Why have we already reached the absolute at this point in the *Science of Logic*? Initially, it appears to be a rather uncharacteristic place for the absolute to make an appearance, given that Hegel usually reserves the denomination for the final conclusion of his texts. The second question concerns the status of the absolute at this juncture and its connection to actuality: Why is the absolute the first moment or determination of the actual? How does the absolute function here as a step toward the development of the idea of activity of form?

To address the first question, we can begin by noting that Hegel's use of the term at this particular moment in the *Logic* is self-consciously ambivalent. There is something clearly premature about the announcement of the absolute in the Doctrine of Essence, and yet there are nonetheless good reasons for its appearance as the first moment of actuality. One clue that the presentation of the absolute here is premature can be found in Hegel's use of absolute

---

[12] See WL 504–505/6:239–240, 529–549/6:273–301; and VGP 3:260/20:170.

in the nominative, which, while not by any means unprecedented, is unusual and deviates from his more official uses of the term. Within Hegel's system, the term "absolute" usually appears in an adjectival form, describing a specific determination of something—*Wissen, Form, Idee, Geist*—rather than denoting something substantial in itself.[13] Our form of knowing is absolute, for example, when it is self-consciously determined and carried out in a certain way, mode, or manner, something that is only possible as the result of a particular development. Absolute spirit—art, religion, and philosophy—consists of specifically defined *modes* of self-knowledge that are essential for understanding human freedom. *The* absolute, then, as a substantive, is something rather empty and indeterminate, and "the absolute itself appears only as the negation of all predicates and as the void" (WL 466/6:187). To develop the concept of the absolute into something determinate and actual, Hegel will ultimately conclude the chapter by turning to the mode (*Modus*) of the absolute as the absolute's "*way and manner*," the way and manner in which the absolute comes to be expressed, revealed, and made manifest (WL 470, 471/6:193, 194). The utter abstractness and obscurity of *the* absolute in its initial pronouncement is thus no accident, for we do not yet know exactly what it is that is being described as absolute.

Nonetheless, Hegel has good reasons for introducing the absolute at this moment in the Doctrine of Essence, for it is an important marker of both an *end* and a *beginning* at once. As the marker of an ending, the absolute is the result of the cumulative determinations of the *Seins-* and *Wesenslogik* which make up the first volume of the *Science of Logic*. The absolute is thus a "negative outcome," and we can read the progression of the *Logic* thus far, the entire movement through the categories of being and essence, as "the *negative exposition* of the absolute" (WL 466, 467/6:187, 189). As negative, the absolute denotes the end of the Objective Logic and can be viewed as a refutation of the modes of thinking expounded by its categories—in particular, the metaphysical realism of being and the irreconcilable, unself-conscious dualisms of essence.[14] The absolute is "the ground in which [the previous determinations] have been engulfed," expressing at once the insufficiencies of an Objective Logic and providing the true basis presupposed by being

---

[13] On some of the different uses of the term "absolute" as an adjective, see Nuzzo (2003).

[14] Pippin (1989, 181) argues that the Doctrine of Being presents an argument against classical metaphysical realism, whereas the Doctrine of Essence argues against notions of "reflected being" while beginning to present Hegel's own idealism by attempting to reconcile traditional dualisms between essence and existence.

and essence, a presupposition that has now been posited and made explicit through the exposition of the prior categories (WL 467/6:188). However, as ground, the absolute is not only something negative but also "has itself a *positive* side" and represents a new beginning (WL 468/6:189). The beginning for which this section provides the transition is, as mentioned before, the Doctrine of the Concept or the Subjective Logic, the final book and undoubtedly the key to the *Logic* as a whole. In laying the ground for the determination of the Concept, the absolute in the beginning of its exposition is not only abstract but, further, can only be spoken of from a limited, external perspective. If the absolute is nothing ahead of displaying and exhibiting its content, nothing ahead of the very process of its own exposition (*Auslegung*), then at the outset, and in referring to it as a substantive rather than exhibiting it as a mode, the beginning can only be "the *absolute of an external reflection*" (WL 468–469/6:190).[15] Qua beginning, the absolute is not yet actual but a mere seeming (*ein Scheinen*), a merely relative absolute that is as yet premature.

Turning to the second interpretive question concerning the status of the absolute and its connection to actuality, we see that the main goal of Hegel's discussion in this admittedly obscure chapter is to present Spinoza's concept of substance in rough outline and, through that presentation, introduce the idea that the exposition or manifestation of absolute substance should be understood essentially as activity. Although the importance of the notion of activity is made much more explicit in the *Encyclopaedia Logic* account, there are nonetheless clear indications in the greater *Logic* that Hegel's overarching goals are consistent across the two texts.[16] What Hegel refers to as activity and "activity of form" (*Formtätigkeit*) in the lesser *Logic* are denoted in the greater *Logic* by references to the absolute's own "act" (*Tun*) and absolute form (EL §§147–151; WL 467–468, 471/6:189–190, 193–194). Hegel divides the chapter on "The Absolute" into three moments that reflect the three moments of substance according to Spinoza: the absolute itself, or the exposition of the absolute; the absolute attribute; and the mode of the absolute. In Spinoza's *Ethics*, substance (God or nature) is defined as infinite, indivisible, eternal, self-caused, necessary in its existence, and encompassing all actuality in its causal power. Although substance itself is one, its infinite

---

[15] Hegel discusses external reflection as one of the three forms of reflection in the first chapter of the Doctrine of Essence on *Schein* (seeming or "illusory being"), WL 348–351/6:28–32. External reflection relates to "something immediately given that is alien to it, and considers itself to be a merely formal operation that receives its material content from outside and of itself is only a movement conditioned by that content" (WL 350–351/6:31).

[16] Longuenesse (2007, 151) also makes the same suggestion.

nature means that it expresses itself through an infinite number of attributes or essences, of which the human mind can only perceive two: thought and extension. Affections of substance, or dependent, finite things, are called modes: "Particular things are nothing but affections of God's attributes, *or* modes by which the attributes of God are expressed in a certain and determinate way."[17] In Hegel's version of the presentation of substance, attributes, and modes, we can note two divergences that begin to signal his dissatisfaction with Spinoza's account. The first is his resistance to Spinoza's definitional approach to substance or the absolute, coupled with his general complaint that Spinoza's axiomatic, geometrical method is inappropriate for the topic of substance and can regard it only from the perspective of external reflection.[18] We saw in chapter 3 that Hegel defends a conception of method that is identical with its content, insofar as method expresses the content's essential structure or form. Here, Hegel and Spinoza appear to be in agreement, for Spinoza contends that the necessity expressed in the geometric method reflects the necessity of substance itself, that all the determinations of substance follow necessarily from it in the manner of a mathematical deduction. However, Hegel contends that the geometric method is external to and entirely inappropriate for the topic of self-causing substance, and distorts the essential form of its activity and development.[19] For Hegel, the exposition of the absolute requires its own distinctive method, one that cannot be borrowed from other topics and one which can only be revealed as the result of his investigation at the very end of the *Logic*. Vindicating Hegel on this score will thus have to wait until the discussion of absolute method in chapter 7; nonetheless, Hegel's chapter on "The Absolute" must be understood against the background of his dissatisfaction with Spinoza's "external" method.

The second divergence from Spinoza concerns Hegel's complaint that substance lacks personality (*Persönlichkeit*) and subjectivity, leading to a reversal of priority where the order of modes, as the most determinate and concrete

---

[17] Spinoza, *Ethics*, IP25C.

[18] On Hegel's understanding and critique of a definitional approach to theoretical cognition, see WL 708–713/6:512–519. As if to emphasize the absurdity of such stipulative definitions, Hegel refers to the first moment as "the absolute absolute" (a redundancy) and the second moment as "the relative absolute" (a contradiction in terms), in order to convey his dissatisfaction with Spinoza's threefold definition of substance, which in effect turns one absolute into three (WL 469/6:190–191).

[19] See WL 472–473/6:195–197; and VGP 3:282–287/20:158–187. See Goetschel (2004, 32), who stresses that Spinoza's *mos geometricus* is not a method in the sense of meta-theoretical reflection, but that *mos* "suggests custom, habit, manner, mores, law, prescription, order. . . . [T]he semantic field of *mos* points to ethical and moral connotations."

manifestation of substance, is presented as what is actual and as having priority over the abstract identity of substance and attributes. Hegel writes: "In actual fact, therefore, the absolute is first posited as absolute identity *only in the mode*" (WL 470/6:193; my emphasis). In suggesting that it is only in the order of modes that substance is determined as actual absolute identity, Hegel is presenting his critique of Spinoza's philosophy as an "acosmism," which contends that Spinoza's notion of substance amounts to the denial of the reality of finite individuals or modes and the belief that only God is real. Hegel's charge of acosmism is controversial, but rather than assess whether or not Hegel's charge applies fairly to Spinoza, I want to instead focus on what Hegel's objection tells us about his own philosophical commitments, especially as they pertain to the concept of actuality.[20] Here is a passage from Hegel's *Encyclopaedia* concerning Spinoza's treatment of modes that motivates his reversal of priority:

> [Spinoza's] philosophy does not give the principle of difference or finitude its due; and this means that this system should be called, not atheism, but "acosmism" instead. For there is not, properly speaking, any world at all in it (in the sense of something that positively is). . . . Substance, as it is apprehended immediately by Spinoza . . . is only the dark, shapeless abyss, so to speak, in which all determinate content is swallowed up as radically null and void. (EL §151Z)[21]

According to Hegel, Spinoza's treatment of substance amounts to a notion of the absolute in which the order of individual, finite things is treated as mere

[20] There are, as to be expected, many Spinozist rejoinders to Hegel's charge. Yitzhak Melamed (2010), for example, defends Spinoza by arguing that while individuals may be conceived as weak and functional in Spinoza, they are not illusory or unreal in any sense. Melamed also points out, correctly I think, that the real worry behind the acosmism charge is not the elimination of finite modes in general, but the elimination of the significance of *human* subjectivity and Spinoza's anti-humanism more broadly, which is surely reflected in Hegel's complaint about the lack of "personality." On Hegel's Spinoza critique, see also, Schmusli (1970), Parkinson (1977), Machery (2011), Ravven (2003), and Newlands (2011).

[21] See also VGP 3:281–283/20:163:

> Spinozism might really just as well or even better have been termed acosmism, since according to its teaching it is not to the world, finite existence, the universe, that reality and permanency are to be ascribed, but rather to God alone as the substantial. Spinoza maintains that there is no such thing as what is known as the world; it is merely a form of God, and in and for itself it is nothing. The world has no true reality, and all this that we know as the world has been cast into the abyss of the one identity. There is therefore no such thing as finite reality, it has no truth whatever; according to Spinoza what is, is God, and God alone. Therefore the allegations of those who accuse Spinoza of atheism are the direct opposite of the truth; with him there is too much God.

privation; hence, it has no positive reality of its own and, at an extreme, is considered mere illusion.[22] It is surprising to hear Hegel speak on behalf of the finite, given his propensity to criticize forms of *Verstand* that cling to finitude and "bad infinity." However, Hegel's point here is not to defend the finite per se but, rather, to defend the priority of the actual over the potential (where the modes are what is truly actual and substance represents an indeterminate power or potential), and to do so in a way such that the order of modes or individuality—which include thought-determinations and individual subjects or the I—can be regarded as self-determining on its own account, and not simply on account of the self-causing power of substance. Instead, Hegel regards the determination of modes themselves as "self-relating negativity, as *reflective seeming* [Scheinen] that is posited *as reflective seeming*" (WL 470/6:193). The idea of *Scheinen* posited *as Scheinen* means that *Schein* (seeming or illusory being) is no longer treated as mere illusory seeming or even mere appearance but, rather, through the activity of reflection, seeming and appearance are posited as actuality. In suggesting that it is in the order of modes that the absolute is posited, determined, and actualized, Hegel is claiming that substance is dependent on modes for content and determinacy, that absent the determinations of modes, substance is nothing but a "dark, shapeless abyss" of which nothing determinate can be said at all. At best, substance constitutes power and potentiality that is actualized in modes, and if the absolute is the exposition of the absolute, this activity is manifest primarily in the order of modes rather than absolute substance, which explains Hegel's transition to the discussion of modality in the following chapter. To be sure, although the chapter on "The Absolute" is more suggestive than substantive, it nonetheless sets the stage for Hegel's immanent deduction and, at the very least, presents the terms of Spinoza's substance as the basis for his own development of the Concept.

4.4 Modality: The Process of Actualization

Hegel's chapter on the modal categories consists of his most direct treatment of the relation between the actual, the possible, the necessary, and the contingent. The aim of the chapter is to develop a conception of absolute necessity,

---

[22] This criticism clearly recalls Hegel's objection to Schellingian conceptions of the absolute "as the night in which all cows are black" (PhG ¶16/3:22).

one that will both return us to the problem of substance and lay the ground for reconciling necessity and freedom. To begin, it will help to unpack in a little more detail two theses that have been briefly mentioned, and which underlie Hegel's treatment of actuality as the mode and manifestation of the absolute. The first is that actuality is not simply what exists, what is contingently there, what is tangible, or what is given in sensible intuition; not everything that *exists* is *actual*.[23] The distinction between existence and actuality demonstrates clearly that Hegel's prioritizing of modes over substance is not a prioritization of contingent, finite things but, rather, a prioritization of concrete and determinate forms of self-determining activity, over and above the sheer indeterminate, infinite power of substance. Actuality has a particular kind of self-determined, rational form, and things that are actual must live up to their own inner principle or standard of truth and activity. To use two of Hegel's favorite examples: a body separated from its soul or life exists as a contingent and finite thing but is not actual as a self-determined unity of form and matter; a state that does not live up to its own constitution also exists but is not actual insofar as it fails to realize its own self-determined laws and ends. The concept of purpose or function appears to be central for Hegel's understanding of actuality insofar as that which is actual constitutes a form-activity in which self-determined ends are realized. As noted, although the activities of life and reason are the central manifestations of self-actualizing form, certain artifacts of this activity—constitutions, ethical institutions, artworks, philosophical knowledge—can also be deemed actual not only because they manifest the form of freedom (for example, in the case of beauty) but, more importantly, because these artifacts in turn become the conditions for the further development and realization of the freedom of life and spirit. In the strictly logical context, actuality is defined as self-manifestation, a necessary relation between inner and outer, form and content, as self-expression. In order to be *self*-expression, actuality must be inherently divided against itself; it is not merely contingent existence but also a "self-differentiating and self-determining movement," a "form-unity" of existence and essence, and hence, "the determination of *immediacy* over against the determination of reflection-into-self" (WL 478/6:201, 202). More specifically, the negativity

---

[23] See, for example, EL §6, §142Z and WL 477–478/6:201. Hegel writes: "In common life people may happen to call every brainwave, error, evil and suchlike 'actual,' as well as very existence, however wilted and transient it may be. But even for our ordinary feeling, a contingent existence does not deserve to be called something-actual in the emphatic sense of the word; what contingently exists has no greater value than that which something-*possible* has; it is an existence which (although it is) can just as well *not be*" (EL §6Z).

of actuality is expressed as "an *actuality as against a possibility*"—that is, actuality is more than what it is, and it already contains within itself a relation between actuality and possibility. Understanding how actuality is more than itself, how it goes beyond itself, and how it contains the power and potentiality within itself to become something else, to produce a new actuality, is what it means for actuality to be "absolute."

The second Hegelian thesis central for this chapter is the priority of actuality over possibility.[24] In fact, and from looking at the title of Hegel's chapter alone, we can infer that there is properly speaking only *one* modality out of which all other modes are determined—namely, absolute actuality itself.[25] The claim here is, unsurprisingly, thoroughly Aristotelian: only actuality can beget another actuality, meaning that understanding potentiality—the "conditions of possibility," the power of some reality to bring about, express, and determine another reality—is to understand something about actuality itself as a dynamic process of the actualization of its own potentialities. As Aristotle writes in *Metaphysics*: "potentiality is discovered from actuality."[26] In effect, possibility, contingency, and necessity are all modes or determinations *of* actuality, ways in which actuality come to be determined. Very briefly, Aristotle defends three different ways of thinking about the priority of actuality, all of which are adopted by Hegel in his own understanding of modality, playing an important role in his approach to the genesis of the Concept which arises from the determination of actuality as activity of form. The first is priority in terms of formula or definition (*logos*): to define potentiality, one must in principle make reference to what is actual, to what the actualization of that potential would be. Potentialities are thus determined only in relation to actualities: being capable of seeing is defined in relation to actually seeing, and being visible is defined in relation to being actually seen.[27] The second is priority in terms of time, but specifically in the sense of species: although for an individual thing, potentiality precedes actuality in time (an individual seed is prior in time to its development into corn), every potential thing is preceded by an actual thing of the same species (mature corn precedes and produces seeds). Aristotle writes,

---

[24] In the contemporary scholarship on Hegel, Redding (2017, 2019a, 2019b, 2020) is the most forceful defender of the view that Hegel should be understood as a modal actualist.

[25] Regarding Kant's understanding of modality, Hegel pithily writes: "Possibility should come second; in abstract thought, however, the empty conception comes first" (VGP 3:439/20:345). See also Marcuse (1987, 89).

[26] Aristotle, *Metaphysics* 1051a30.

[27] See Aristotle, *Metaphysics* 1049b13–16.

[T]he actual member of a species is prior to the potential member of the same species, though the individual is potential before it is actual. . . . For from the potential the actual is always produced by an actual thing, e.g., man by man, musician by musician; there is always a first mover, and the mover already exists actually. We have said in our account of substance that everything that is produced is something produced from something and by something, and is the same in species as it.[28]

This second sense of priority will be particularly important for understanding Hegel's genesis argument: if the Concept "comes to be" from substance (understood as actuality and activity of form), then that from which the Concept arises must be of the same "species" as the Concept. To anticipate somewhat, Hegel's central claim will be that the Concept arises from the actuality of living, purposive form, and in particular, that the *self-conscious* Concept is an actualization of that form, belonging to the same species of activity. Finally, the third sense of the priority of actuality is priority in terms of substance, or more specifically, priority in terms of form or end. An adult is prior to the child and has a fully realized form that the child can potentially become, and the end of adulthood precedes the child in terms of determining its trajectory of development. In adopting these different ways of understanding the priority of actuality, Hegel aims to set the stage for interpreting actuality and Concept in terms of the purposiveness of form, and further, he aims to provide the conceptual framework for understanding the determination of life as the first actuality or immediacy of the Concept.[29]

Hegel moves swiftly in this chapter through three moments of actuality: formal modality (or contingency), real modality (or relative necessity), and absolute necessity.[30] Although Hegel is often thought of as a necessitarian that preaches the cold march toward history's end, here it becomes clear that he is in fact not only attuned to the role of contingency in the course of actual events but, further, that understanding the constitutive role of contingency is

---

[28] Aristotle, *Metaphysics* 1049b17–29.

[29] Here are some standard examples used by Aristotle to describe first and second actuality: knowledge and the exercise of knowledge; being asleep and being awake; eyes shut and eyes seeing; the power of an axe and an axe cutting; being capable of building and actually building. Hegel refers to *Geist* as "sleeping" in nature at PG §384Z, and to nature as "petrified intelligence" at PN §247Z.

[30] Longuenesse (2007, 121) notes that the three moments of actuality (formal, real, absolute) mirror the three moments of determinate ground. On the three moments of determinate ground, see WL 397–409/6:96–112.

central to his account of necessity.[31] Nonetheless, Hegel does begin his argument by presenting a critique of a *certain* understanding of contingency, one that finds its beginnings in a merely formal (or logical) notion of possibility. According to formal possibility, anything that is not self-contradictory is possible. This leaves the realm of formal possibility open to a "boundless multiplicity" (WL 479/6:203): the moon could be made of cheese, the sun may not rise tomorrow, aliens could abduct me in my sleep—the list of possibilities in the formal sense is potentially endless. To make matters worse, contradiction, a category presented earlier in the Doctrine of Essence, is in fact essential to the reflected determination of all finite things, meaning that everything is in fact self-contradictory, and hence, nothing is possible.[32] In the dialectic between formal possibility and impossibility, Hegel is suggesting that understanding the relation between the actual and the possible according to a formal conception of possibility amounts not to a determination of actuality at all but, rather, to a determination of *contingency* or mere existence. He writes: "The contingent is an actual which is at the same time determined as only possible, an actual whose other or opposite equally is" (WL 480/6:205). We could call this initial, merely formal sense of contingency a naïve or one-sided contingency, which amounts to the thought that everything that exists could equally well not exist, the thought that everything is determined *only* by chance. This formal sense of contingency is akin to the threat of contingency thematized in Kant's third *Critique*, where the boundless heterogeneity and contingency of nature threatened to make judgment's powers ineffective and non-actual. How does Hegel demonstrate the need to move beyond this

---

[31] On the necessity of contingency in Hegel, see, for example, Henrich (2010), Houlgate (1995), di Giovanni (1980), Lampert (2005), and Burbidge (2007). For a critique of Hegel on the necessity of contingency and a defense of Schelling, see Gabriel (2009, 2011). On Hegel's argument against necessitarianism in connection with Spinoza, see Knappik (2015).

[32] "*[E]verything is possible that does not contradict itself*; the realm of possibility is therefore boundless multiplicity. But each of these manifold entities is *determined in itself* and *as against an other*: it possesses negation within itself. Indifferent *diversity* passes over as such into *opposition*; but opposition is contradiction. Therefore, all things are just as much contradictory and hence *impossible*" (WL 479/6:302; see also WL 374–385/6:64–78). Hegel writes: "Finite things, in their indifferent multiplicity, are therefore simply this: to be contradictory, *internally fractured and bound to return into their ground*" (WL 385/6:79). Much has been written on Hegel's doctrine of contradiction, particularly concerning whether or not he means through his theory to deny the principle of non-contradiction. The most famous critic of Hegel's supposed denial is Popper (1940). For a defense of Hegel, particularly against Russell's accusation that Hegel confuses the "is" of predication and the "is" of identity, see Pippin (1978). Pippin also argues that contradiction is key particularly for grasping (i) the *essence* of things, and (ii) natural growth, change, and development. De Boer (2010) offers a defense of Hegel by suggesting that Hegel's theory does not in fact deny the principle of non-contradiction (see also Wolff 1999). For a reading of Hegel's system based on a "naturalized" reading of the theory of contradiction, see Hahn (2007). Finally, see Redding's (2007, chap. 7) critique of applying Priest's paraconsistent logic to a reading of Hegel.

determination of contingency that threatens to undermine the very category of actuality, making futile the attempt to determine what exists as having any essential form, internal potential, or self-determined end?

It is important to note that Hegel does not deny that this one-sided form of contingency has an important place in the world, and even a place in our own sense of self-understanding. Contingency "deserves its due in the world of objects," both when we are considering the realm of nature, where contingency has a certain degree of "free rein," and when we are considering the realm of spirit, where arbitrariness or freedom of choice (*Willkür*), despite its limitations as a determination of freedom, is an irreducible element of the human will (EL §145Z). To put it plainly, Hegel does not deny that many determinations are contingent in this sense, that many determinations constitute existence rather than actuality. The actual is rational, but it would be absurd to ascribe to Hegel the view that every possible determination should be deemed rational in the robust sense of having a self-determined end. Most things fall along the spectrum somewhere between existence and actuality, and the deduction of the Concept as self-actualization does not require that *everything* is determined as actual in the sense under consideration. Nonetheless, contingency as it arises out of the notion of formal possibility remains caught between two one-sided moments that make it incoherent as an exhaustive determination of "everything." When we refer to an object, event, act, or state of affairs as merely contingent, what we mean to say is that it has no ground, that it has no sufficient reason for being one way rather than another. However, as a possible object, event, act, or state of affairs, it must have *some* ground, it must have arisen from some other object, event, act, or state of affairs; otherwise it would not be possible at all.[33] Hegel writes: "The contingent, then, has no ground because it is contingent; and, equally, it has a ground because it is contingent" (WL 481/6:206). In fluctuating between these two determinations, we come to realize that this back and forth between groundlessness and groundedness is in fact necessary for grasping this mode of formal contingency. Contingency as this "*absolute unrest*" is *necessary* for the determination of actuality according to this formal account of

---

[33] See Hegel's discussion of the principle of sufficient reason at WL 388/6:82–83. Strictly speaking, a sufficient *Grund* has to be something actual in the sense of having an internal end or Concept. Determinacies that are merely "*externally* and *contingently conjoined*" as in "causes belonging to the sphere of mechanism" are, for Hegel, insufficient; rather, "[t]hat connection, the whole as essential unity, is to be found only in the *Concept*, in *purpose* or *end*" (WL 388/6:83).

modality in that according to formal contingency, actuality is said to be necessarily contingent in this particular sense.

For Hegel, the shortcoming of this initial understanding of the necessity of contingency is that those who wish to defend it lack sufficient awareness concerning the content of their own claim. In claiming that the fluctuation between groundlessness and groundedness is necessary, what one is really saying is that one lacks sufficient knowledge concerning the grounds in question, that one does not know the real conditions and circumstances that brought a particular actuality about. Thus, although Hegel acknowledges that sheer chance certainly plays a role in the determination of the actual, formal contingency operating as a complete and final determination of actuality is disingenuous insofar as it stops short of doing the work of understanding how particular things, events, acts, or states of affairs came to be actualized. This brings us to the second moment of real modality, which moves beyond the determination of formal possibility into considering *real* possibility, the concrete conditions and circumstances that bring some actuality into being. Hegel describes real possibility as follows:

> What is actual *can act* [*Was wirklich ist,* kann wirken]; something announces its actuality *through that which it produces.* . . . [W]hen we delve into the determinations, the circumstances, and the conditions of a fact [*Sache*] in order to ascertain its possibility, we do not stay with formal possibility but consider its real possibility. . . . The real possibility of a fact is therefore the existing multiplicity of circumstances that are connected with it. This existing multiplicity is, therefore, both possibility and actuality. . . . Real possibility constitutes the *totality of conditions*, a dispersed actuality. (WL 482–483/6:208–209)

Real possibility as the totality of conditions necessary for bringing something about determines actuality as something that can act, as something that has the power and potential to produce effects, only insofar as it is a process of actualization resulting from a determinate set of real conditions and circumstances. Thus, for the time being, it is not *really* possible—that is, the totality of real conditions are not present—for the moon to be made out of cheese or for the sun not to rise tomorrow. Moving beyond formal possibility as mere non-contradiction, but also beyond what Kant would call transcendental conditions of possibility, real modality determines the identity and difference of the actual and the possible by taking up actuality as a set of concrete, dispersed potentialities, as containing *within itself* the possibility of becoming a new configuration of conditions, and hence, a new actuality. What is actual can act, or has the power and potential to produce effects, insofar as a new configuration of circumstances and conditions can arise from the existing multiplicity of conditions. In the "movement of translating" real conditions and circumstances into new actualities and translating existing actualities into new, concrete conditions of possibility, Hegel is already beginning to present his notion of activity (*Tätigkeit*) (EL §148).[34] The movement of translation from the totality of conditions to actual fact is, Hegel says, "not a *transition* but *a joining with itself* [*nicht ein* Übergehen, *sondern ein Zusammengehen mit sich selbst*]" (WL 484/6:210): not a transition from formal possibility to actuality but a self-movement of conditions from actuality to actuality.[35] Conceiving of actuality as the process of actualizing real possibilities is to determine actuality as a dynamic movement that can produce effects, as a movement that "can act," as a kind of form-activity that produces and transforms itself on the basis of existing potentialities that are identical with itself. Once we move beyond formal possibility and contingency and do the work of determining and assessing the totality of conditions, actuality is seen not exclusively as the result of sheer chance but, rather, as a dynamic process of activity in which real conditions bring about real results.

In assessing the notion of activity Hegel is presenting here, we now can draw a distinction between activity as *absolute necessity* and activity as *purposive or free*. Although activity in the latter, fully developed sense will only be presented as the final moment in the transition to the Subjective Logic, it

---

[34] Hegel writes: "the immediate self-translation of the inner into the outer and of outer into the inner[, t]his self-movement of the form is *activity*" (EL §147).

[35] The same phrase appears at the end of the "Actuality" chapter: "Thus the externality is its inwardness; their relation is absolute identity; and the *transition* [Übergehen] of the actual into the possible, of being into nothing, is a *joining with itself* [*ein* Zusammengehen mit sich selbst]; contingency is absolute necessity; it is itself the presupposing of that first absolute actuality" (WL 488/6:217). Hegel's terminology is a little infelicitous here; he insists that the process of actualization in question is *not* a transition, but also repeatedly continues to employ the term transition to mark key moves in the *Logic* and also to mark key moves throughout his entire philosophical system. Despite the terminological inconsistencies, what I take Hegel to be insisting on is the claim that the process of actualization should be understood not as a transition between two categorically distinct modes but as a process that proceeds from actuality to actuality. The idea of "joining with itself" is meant to convey the notion of actualization that follows from the priority of actuality thesis. Insofar as Hegel adopts the priority of actuality thesis as a part of his deduction of the Concept, the key is that the "transition" to the Concept should not be understood as a transition to something categorically distinct from that which it is immanently deduced, but also as a transition in the sense of "joining with itself." I will say more about this notion of transition in what follows.

is helpful to have this goal in mind as we ascertain the significance and limitations of absolute necessity. To complete his account of real modality, Hegel writes: "When all the conditions of a fact are completely present, it enters into actuality" (WL 483/6:210). And he expresses this perhaps even more emphatically in the *Encyclopaedia*: "When *all conditions* are present, the fact [*Sache*] *must* become actual" (EL §147). In effect, real possibility is already real necessity because the totality of conditions is identical with a realized actuality, and thus, given a certain set of conditions, a certain actuality *necessarily* follows. Here again, however, Hegel shows himself to be attentive to the role of contingency in the determination of the actual, for in fact this kind of necessity remains *relative* because "it has its *starting point* in the *contingent*" (WL 484/6:211). Although given a certain set of conditions, a certain actuality necessarily follows, the multiplicity of existing circumstances are themselves contingent, leading to the necessity of contingency now in a deeper and more fully developed sense. Unlike the *formal* determination of contingency as a fluctuation between groundlessness and groundedness, the *real* determination of contingency requires us to grasp the constitutive role of contingency in the necessary progression of conditions into that which is actualized. What Hegel calls *absolute* necessity is simply the awareness that contingency is constitutive in the process of actualization, that the progression of contingent conditions is "*necessity's own* becoming" (WL 486/6:213). Contingency is necessity's own becoming because it is constitutive of—that is, *absolutely necessary* for—the determination of actuality and its ongoing process of actualizing potentialities. Although contingency is constitutive of the process of actualization, real modality nonetheless rules out what formal modality could not—namely, the complete determination of possibility and actuality in accordance with sheer chance.

In the conclusion of the "Actuality" chapter, Hegel goes on to suggest that absolute necessity is "*blind*" and "*light-shy*" (WL 487, 488/6:216). The progression of absolute necessity is blind, insofar as

> *purpose* [Zweck] is still not present *for-itself* as such in the process of necessity. The process of necessity begins with the existence of dispersed circumstances that seem to have no concern with one another and no inward coherence. These circumstances are an immediate actuality that collapses inwardly, and from this negation a new actuality emerges. . . . [H]ence the necessity that constitutes this process is called "blind." By

contrast if we consider purposive activity [*zweckmäßige Tätigkeit*] . . . this
activity is not blind but sighted [*sehend*]. (EL§147Z)

There are two claims that should be highlighted here concerning Hegel's understanding of absolute necessity. First, the notion of activity present in absolute necessity is limited and incomplete. Purpose, a sense of goal-directed
activity or activity that aims at an end, is not yet explicitly present, is not yet
present in a fully developed or self-determined sense. That purposiveness is
not yet present *for-itself* implies that at the stage of absolute necessity, purposiveness or activity is only present *in-itself*—that is, in an implicit or yet to
be developed sense. Absolute necessity is blind because the progression of
contingent conditions has no explicit self-determined purpose or goal, and
further, the conditions and circumstances themselves are only indifferently
related to one another in their ongoing progression. The sense of activity
in which a contingently combined set of conditions translates into a set of
effects conveys the necessity of contingency in processes of actualization but
clearly falls short of a notion of activity that could be called self-determined
or free. Second, purposive activity, where purpose is present *for-itself*, results
in a form of activity that is not blind but, rather, sighted. What exactly does
Hegel mean by "seeing" here? Purposive activity is a form of seeing activity
insofar as its ends and goals are self-determined. Conditions are actively
shaped such that they are not indifferently related and have an internal coherence; the progression of conditions are goal-directed and self-organized.
Nonetheless, although purposive activity determines its own ends, "seeing"
here does not entail that the totality of conditions and circumstances are fully
in view, or are at one's disposal, in advance of or in the midst of carrying
out an end. Even in the most conscientious activity, prospectively, we never
have complete knowledge of the circumstances and conditions surrounding
any particular act.[36] This lack of complete knowledge concerning the totality
of conditions is simply a part of our self-consciousness regarding the necessity of contingency in the progression of conditions into effects. Behind this
thought is a familiar Hegelian theme—namely, that the totality of conditions
can only be recollected retrospectively, that the actual is truly determined
and grasped as rational only after the fact. Here, on the cusp of the transition

---

[36] Hegel writes in the section on conscience in the *Phenomenology*: "This actuality is a plurality
of circumstances which breaks up and spreads out endlessly in all directions, backwards into their
conditions, sideways into their connections, forwards in their consequences. The conscientious
mind is aware of this nature of the fact and of its relation to it" (PhG ¶642/3:472).

to freedom or the Concept, Hegel reminds us that self-actualization must be grasped not only from a forward-looking perspective, with conditions marching ever onward into their results. Rather, self-actualization must also be grasped, and in fact, can only be *fully* grasped, from a retrospective, backward-looking perspective, one that carefully gathers up a dispersed actuality and determines it as the rational result of purposive, free activity.

With respect to the immanent deduction of the Concept, Hegel's understanding of the process of actualization is important because it establishes the framework within which the Concept can be said to be the ground of actuality as an activity of self-actualization. In the "Actuality" chapter, the conclusion is largely negative: *without* the unity and coherence provided by a self-determined purpose or the Concept, the process of actualization can only be grasped as absolute necessity or as the necessity of contingency, for the totality of conditions remains a bundle of externally related factors that aim at no particular result, even though certain results follow necessarily from certain conditions. That there is no *aim* internal to the totality of conditions is what makes the progression of conditions to results "blind," and what cannot yet be "seen" or discerned is the unity afforded by the purposiveness of form. When the totality of conditions is unified by the Concept such that activity has an overarching goal (survival and reproduction of the individual and the species, the pursuit of the true and the good), then the process of actualization is not blind or absolutely necessary but, rather, purposive and *self*-actualizing—it is an activity unified by a self, an activity unified by an end, an activity unified by the power of the Concept.

4.5 The Absolute Relation: Reciprocity and Power

The problem of the third and final chapter, titled "The Absolute Relation," is how to make the transition from a notion of activity where purpose is implicit (absolute necessity) to a notion of activity where purpose is explicitly self-determined and constitutes a relation-to-self. Establishing the latter completes the final stage of the genesis of the Concept; in fact, Hegel suggests that a self-determining, purposive self-relation simply *is* the Concept. Initially, Hegel's strategy in this chapter, like the overall strategy of his deduction, can appear somewhat artificial: he returns first to the problem of substance (the absolutely necessary), taking up the relation between substance and accidents; next, he takes up the relation of causality—in particular, the causal relations characteristic of mechanism; and finally, Hegel concludes the Objective Logic with the category of reciprocity or reciprocal action (*Wechselwirkung*), a reciprocal relation and interaction between causes and effects posited as a self-relation, determining purposive activity as the relation that is absolute.

Despite a certain artificiality in Hegel's progression, the final chapter of the Doctrine of Essence in fact takes up all three of Kant's categories of relation and can be read as an (unorthodox) attempt at rewriting the analogies of experience found in the first *Critique*.[37] There, Kant claimed that "[t]he general principle of the three analogies rests on the necessary *unity* of apperception," and Hegel, too, is suggesting that the determination of actuality outlined thus far rests upon the self-relation of the Concept (A177/B220). However, there is also a decidedly un-Kantian moment in Hegel's final step of the genesis or deduction of the Concept. Hegel claims that with reciprocity, the relation of finite or external causality called mechanism "is sublated" (WL 503/6:237).[38] This understanding of reciprocity as the "sublation" of mechanism is clearly not Kant's. For Kant, it is certainly not the case that the third analogy "sublates" the second analogy; rather, they are compatible and complementary, providing the rules under which the time-determinations of succession and simultaneity can appear.[39] Hegel's concept of reciprocity is instead much closer to Schelling's, who writes:

> Organization is thus the higher power of the category of reciprocity, which, viewed universally, leads to the concept of nature or of universal organization. . . . The basic character of organization is therefore that it be in reciprocity with itself, at once both producer and product, and this concept is the principle of the whole theory of organic nature. (SI 126/495)

---

[37] Unorthodox because Hegel is not concerned with experience or the time-determinations of appearances, but with the determination of actuality in his technical sense, which differs from Kant's understanding of actuality as tied to perception and sensation (see A80/B106 and A176–218/B218–265). For helpful reconstructions of this chapter that also discuss Hegel's rewriting of Kant's analogies, see Houlgate (2000) and Iber (2003). See also Redding (2007, 106–114) for a discussion of reciprocity in Kant. For a reconstruction that stresses the priority of teleology over mechanism whereby mechanistic explanations presuppose teleology, see Yeomans (2012, chap. 10). Kreines (2015) also argues for the priority of teleology over mechanism in terms of explanation, but he draws primarily from the "Mechanism" chapter that appears later in the Subjective Logic.

[38] "In der Wechselwirkung ist nun dieser Mechanismus aufgehoben" (WL 503/6:237).

[39] On the connection between the second and third analogy, see Watkins (2005, chaps. 3 and 4). As Watkins notes, "mutual interaction [occurs] in light of Newton's law of the equality of action and reaction, the action of the repulsive force of the one corresponds to the reaction of the repulsive force of the other" (137). (See also Watkins 2005, 249–250; and the section on mechanics in MN 4:536–4:553.)

Thus, in the final stage of the deduction of the Concept, Hegel once again (and not for the last time in the *Logic*) takes up the problem of constitutive inner purposiveness, trying to show that the determination of the Concept hinges on the presentation and vindication of a reciprocal self-relation in which something is the *cause and effect of itself*. The two most important points of reference for Hegel's idea of self-cause should by now be evident. The first is Spinoza's definition of substance; but as noted earlier, Hegel will suggest that the self-relation of being the cause and effect of oneself presupposes and requires the determination of subjectivity as coextensive with substance. The absolute must be determined not only as substance but equally as subject, because the notion of *causa sui* is unintelligible without some conception of the self. Commenting on Spinoza's philosophy, Hegel writes: "Absolute substance is the truth, but it is not the whole truth; it must also be thought of as in itself *active and living* [*in sich* tätig, lebendig], and by that very means it must determine itself as mind [*Geist*]" (VGP 3:257/20:166). The connection between *active* and *living* is key: only living activity suffices for determining the purposiveness characteristic of subjectivity or the Concept. The fully developed conception of activity as unified by a purpose is at once the concept of life, and in the reciprocity displayed by the concept of life, we have "at the same time attained the *Concept* itself" (WL 504/6:238). In Hegel's deduction, the terms activity, life, and Concept thus form a tightly knit circle, where each term ultimately refers to all the others. The second point of reference is an orienting focus of this study—namely, Kant's definition of a natural purpose (*Naturzweck*) or a living thing as "both cause and effect of itself." As we have already seen, Kant takes the attribution of intrinsic purposiveness to be fundamentally prohibited according to the laws of mechanistic causality, leading to an antinomy between mechanism and teleology (a version of the antinomy between necessity and freedom) and the relegation of purposiveness to a regulative status. In turning to the category of *Wechselwirkung*, understood as the reciprocal self-relation of cause and effect, Hegel means to challenge directly Kant's restriction and argue that *the* Concept is the activity and purposiveness of form that grounds what is actual, expressing the activity and form of subjectivity and freedom. The argument for purposiveness's constitutive status is thus a necessary feature of the deduction of the Concept, and Hegel's reference to the sublation of mechanism by reciprocity can be understood as part of his ongoing efforts to inscribe the activity of life into the activities of self-consciousness and freedom.

Hegel's argument for the determination of reciprocity is continuous with the development of the concept of actuality we have been tracking thus far, taking its departure from the question of how conditions are actualized into their effects. The determination of absolute necessity allows Hegel to return to the problem of substance, but this time, the power of substance to actualize effects is considered through the relation of substance and accidents whereby substance differentiates itself into a "*flux of accidents* [der Wechsel der Akzidenzen]," which are a "plurality" (WL 491/6:220). Hegel quickly dismisses this way of thinking about the power of substance, partly on account of the fact that the flux and plurality of accidents do not cohere into a genuine unity, and partly on account of the fact that the differentiation of accidents does not express "*real*" or inner difference, a lack of self-differentiation where the accidents "have *no power* over each other" (WL 492, 491/6:221). The lack of unity and inner difference in Hegel's characterization, whereby accidents remain externally related, leads him to dismiss this model for thinking about the power of substance as self-actualization, with the chapter moving on to the relation of causality or the relation of cause and effect. The three parts of Hegel's discussion (formal causality, the determinate relation of causality, and action and reaction) roughly follow, and can be read as his highly stylized gloss on, Newton's three laws of motion, also taken up by Kant in the third chapter of his *Metaphysical Foundations of Natural Science*.[40] It is more appropriate to read Hegel as responding to Kant here, rather than to Newton, and responding to Kant directly on the issue of the causality and form expressed in living activity. In their respective discussions of Newton's second law, both Kant and Hegel reflect on the problem of life in relation to a mechanistic understanding of causality as follows:

[Kant] This mechanical law must alone be called the law of *inertia*. . . . The inertia of matter is, and means, nothing else than its *lifelessness*. . . . *Life* is the faculty of a *substance* to determine itself to act from an *internal principle*, of a *finite substance* to change, and of a *material substance* [to determine itself] to motion or rest, as change of its state. Now we know no other internal principle in a substance for changing its state except *desiring*, and no other internal activity at all except *thinking*, together with that which depends on it, the *feeling* of pleasure or displeasure, and *desire* or willing. But these actions and grounds of determination in no way belong to representation

---

[40] See Yeomans's (2012, 219–222) discussion of Hegel on Newton's third law.

of the outer senses, and so neither [do they belong] to the determinations of matter as matter. Hence all matter, as such, is *lifeless*. (MN 4:544)

[Hegel] But it is the *inadmissible application* of the relation of causality to *the relations of physico-organic and spiritual life* that must be noted above all. Here that which is called the cause does indeed show itself to be of a different content than the effect, *but this is because* anything that has an effect on a living thing is independently determined, altered, and transmuted by the latter, *for the living thing will not let the cause come to its effect*, that is, it sublates it as cause. Thus it is inadmissible to say that nourishment is the *cause* of blood, or that such and such a dish, or chill and humidity, are the *causes* of fever or of what have you; it is equally inadmissible to give the Ionic climate as *the cause* of Homer's works, or Caesar's ambition as the *cause* of the fall of Rome's republican constitution. In *history* in general there are indeed spiritual masses and individuals at play and in reciprocal determination [*Wechselbestimmung*] with one another; but it is of the nature of spirit, in a much higher sense than it is of the character of living things, that it will not *receive into itself another originating thing* [*nicht ein* anderes Ursprüngliches in sich aufzunehmen], or not to let a cause continue itself into it but to break it off and to transmute it [*sondern sie abzubrechen und zu verwandeln*].—But these relations belong to the *Idea*, and will come up for discussion then. (WL 496/6:227–228)

Hegel's assertion here that an exclusively mechanical understanding of causality is inadmissible for grasping the activity of both organic and spiritual life is a direct response to Kant's assertion in the wake of Newton's second law that all matter is lifeless. Note that Kant's definition of life—the power of a substance to determine itself to act from an internal principle—is *exactly* what Hegel is trying to establish in order to complete his deduction of the Concept. Hegel's tying together of organic and spiritual life in this passage is also absolutely crucial: it signals that the justification for the sublation of mechanism, the justification for the *legitimate* application of the concept of purpose, must take place within the context of understanding the relation between the organic and the spiritual and the essential form of their mutual activity, rather than within the context of a general theory of matter. Thus, Kant is correct to associate life with desire, and even thought, but wrong to suggest that they are non-actual; for Hegel, the activities of desire and thought display the very form of the actual, and life is the activity through which there can be a genuine unity of matter and form.

Elaborating very broadly on the idea that "[e]very change in matter has an external cause," Hegel considers how this general principle might apply to our understanding of causes and effects in the process of actualization according the account of actuality provided thus far (MN 4:543). When we consider the actualization of causes (the totality of conditions) into their effects (the resulting actuality), Hegel suggests that living things and living minds *alter, transmute*, and even *break off* a cause, transforming external causes and conditions by means of their own activity. In other words, living things "sublate" external causes: they are metabolized, broken down, incorporated, absorbed, reshaped, and reconstituted, all in accordance with the internal demands of an individual organism acting within the context of a species. In the flow of causes and effects determined according to mechanism, however, this process can only be understood at the level of blind contingency: conditions are dispersed, external, and indifferent to one another, expressing no internal unity or coherence. We can consider an example offered by Hegel in this context: Suppose a man developed a talent, say, for music—how do we understand the causes of his talent? The talent was developed as a result of the man losing his father, so his father's death was the cause of his talent. But his father was shot while at war, so the shot and then the war were the causes. This kind of reasoning is potentially endless and can include all sorts of other contingencies such as the following: the gun was made with steel, so steel caused the man's talent; his father was shot on a foggy day, so fog was the cause of his talent; an overzealous monarch caused the war, and so he in fact caused the man's talent. Hegel contends that what we are speaking of here "is not a cause at all but only a single *moment* which belonged to the *circumstances of the possibility*" (WL 496/6:227). When actuality is understood exclusively according to the external causal connections of mechanism understood in this broad sense, the totality of conditions that constitute a given actuality are forever under- and overdetermined in such a way that actuality cannot be determined as something that "can act," as something that can display its power to produce effects. Mechanism underdetermines because there is an infinite regress of causes, so the set of conditions is never complete; mechanism overdetermines because there are too many causes and provides no criteria of its own with which to distinguish genuine, essential causes from accidental, non-essential ones. In the prior example, what mechanism cannot grasp is the development of musical talent as, irreducibly, a matter of purposive, self-determination, even while it takes place in the midst of a plurality of circumstances and events that provide a necessary context of action. The development of a passion and talent for music in the face of the grief of losing a parent is a process in which external causes and circumstances are transmuted, metabolized, incorporated, and reshaped in accordance with internal purposes and demands.

In claiming that the relation of causality defined broadly here as mechanism is "inadmissible" in the context of organic and spiritual life, and that mechanism is "sublated" by reciprocity, it is important to distinguish different ways of interpreting Hegel's point. On a weaker reading, we can understand Hegel to be claiming that there are simply distinct domains that require distinct forms of explanation. For example, while physics might be a powerful explanatory paradigm when we are trying to understand planetary orbits, it is less helpful when we are trying to understand the behavior and habits of orangutans, the role of gladiatorial spectacles in ancient Rome, or why a grieving son came to acquire a passion and talent for music. This means that there are different explanatory paradigms for different domains, and a paradigm that has great explanatory powers in one domain will radically under- and overdetermine in another domain. What Hegel is suggesting, then, is that mechanical causal relationships, while suitable in other domains, have very limited powers of explanation for organic and spiritual life, and we should employ other kinds of explanations in those domains. The weaker reading is easier to grant, and the claim about under- and overdetermination is an important aspect of Hegel's anti-reductionist argument. On a stronger reading, Hegel is not simply suggesting that different domains require different kinds of explanation; rather, Hegel is claiming a *priority* for teleological explanations such that mechanical explanations in some sense require or presuppose teleological ones.[41] In my view, the key for the plausibility of the stronger claim depends upon understanding the "self-reflective" teleological perspective from which the distinction between mechanical and teleological relationships is first drawn.[42] Thus, it is not simply that there happens to exist a domain—organic and spiritual life—within which mechanical relations do not adequately determine their objects. Rather, the actuality of

---

[41] In Hegel's own words: "the *purposive relation* [Zweckbeziehung] has proved to be the truth of *mechanism*" (WL 652/6:437–438). Kreines (2004, 2015), Yeomans (2012), and deVries (1991) all defend versions of the stronger reading.

[42] DeVries (1991, 54) argues that Kant's view on the non-objectivity of teleology "makes it impossible for knowledge to be self-reflective, for knowledge to know what knowledge is."

teleologically organized activity—the actuality of life and spirit—is what first establishes the distinction between a mechanical and teleological relationship, the distinction between non-life and life (the actuality of living activity is what first divides life from non-life). The priority of teleology, or the sublation of mechanism by reciprocity, must be understood from *within* the perspective of teleologically organized processes of actualization—processes which provide a perspective from which the distinction between mechanical and purposive actualization is first rendered intelligible. Organic and spiritual life sublates, metabolizes, and transmutes external causes in accordance with internal demands and aims, and it is only from the perspective of such self-determining activity that there is a meaningful, intelligible distinction between mechanism and teleology, and a priority of the latter over the former. Dividing itself from external causes is a self-determining act that is actualized only in living and spiritual activity.[43] To understand this claim, let us turn to the final stages of Hegel's deduction where the insufficiencies of mechanism bring us to reciprocity and the Concept.

Hegel refers to the external determinations of mechanism as a form of violence: "Violence is the *appearance of power*, or *power as external*" (WL 501/ 6:235).[44] Although this might sound like Hegelian dramatic flair, external power appears as violence because it does not allow actuality to be determined as something that *can act*, destroying the determination of actuality as something with the power to determine itself. In the mechanistic determination of causes and effects, actuality is determined as something acted upon by a variety of indifferent causes, a passive substance that "suffers *violence*" from causes acting as external powers. Insofar as it suffers violence, what is presupposed is a cause that can be an "*act* of violence . . . an *act* of power" (WL 501/6:235; my emphasis). It appears that even according to mechanism's own determinations, an external cause must be determined as a cause with the *power* to act upon some effect, the effect has to *suffer* some alteration; otherwise, neither cause nor effect would be what it is along the descending mechanistic chain of causes to their effects.[45] In cause, a power

---

[43] In the chapters that follow, I will discuss Hegel's account of life as "original division" at length.

[44] I discuss Hegel's use of the term "violence" in the "Objectivity" section of the Subjective Logic in section 6.2.

[45] In stating that in causality we presuppose a power (*Macht*) to act, there is an important argument that Hegel is assuming here from earlier sections of the Doctrine of Essence—namely, that the positing of laws and forces within the mechanistic paradigm does not help to explain or determine the fact or *Sache* with necessity, or as a matter of *essence* (see the chapter on "Appearance," WL 437–448/ 6:147–164; and the section on force and its expression and its resolution in the unity of inner and outer, WL 455–464/6:172–185). This argument is also famous from the "Force and Understanding"

to act is presupposed that is only realized or posited in the effect; in the alteration suffered in the effect, what is again presupposed is a power to act again as cause. Substance is thus determined as both active and passive, as actuality that can be both an act of power and vulnerable to acts of power. Notice here how Hegel is already demonstrating a reciprocity at work between cause and effect, agent and patient, within the paradigm of mechanism itself: a cause would not be able to act as cause without at the same time having the "capacity" to passively suffer some alteration by another cause; an effect cannot be an effect unless the alteration it suffers is again a power to act as some new cause. At first, the power of passive substance to act again as cause is determined as a *reaction*: as reaction, passive substance is divided as both the effect of a previous cause and as its own power of causality. It is both passive substance and reactive substance at once. Now, the difference between reaction and self-determined action, like the transition from real to absolute necessity, is not only subtle but, in fact, also "the hardest" (EL §159).[46] In reciprocity, causality is "*bent around* and becomes an action that returns into itself, an infinite *reciprocal action*" (WL 503/6:237). In bending around and turning back, passivity is taken up as a product of self-activity, and the entire series of conditions acting upon passive substance is broken off and transmuted into the active becoming of substance itself. Substance as reciprocity is

passive and active at once . . . is mediated *by itself*, is produced by its own activity, and is thus the *passivity posited by its own activity*. Causality is conditioned and conditioning . . . cause not only *has* an effect, but in the effect it stands, *as cause* in relation to itself. Causality has hereby returned to its *absolute Concept*, and at the same time has attained to the Concept itself. . . . In reciprocity, originative causality displays itself as an *arising* from its

chapter in the *Phenomenology*. Laws and forces belong to a previous shape of essence called "appearance"; they were posited as two different shapes of essence that belonged to a view in which existence was determined merely as appearance, with forces and laws standing behind appearances as their truth. They do not belong to the sphere of actuality because in actuality, we have already achieved the standpoint of the unity of inner and outer as expression and manifestation, meaning that laws and forces that stand behind appearances are no longer valid as explanatory for actuality. The unity of inner and outer is what allows Hegel to suppose that a power to act is presupposed in the expression of a cause. For an excellent account of Hegel's critique of forces and laws in relation to his critique of mechanism, see Kreines (2004; 2015, chap. 1).

[46] "The passage from necessity to freedom, or from the actual into the Concept, is the hardest one" (EL §159).

negation, from passivity, and as a *passing away* into the same, as a *becoming*. (WL 503–504/6:238–239)

Two things are happening at once in the logic of reciprocity, the logic of bending around and turning back: the first is the explicit determination of *purpose* in the reciprocity of active and passive substance; the second is the determination of the self-conscious Concept insofar as it turns back on the first relation and thereby determines its own reciprocity—its freedom—as both substance and subject. How is it that the determination of reciprocity realizes both relations at once?

4.6 The Life of the Concept

The transition from reciprocity to the freedom of the Concept can appear hasty, and Hegel is not wrong to suggest that it is "the hardest," insofar as he sets his sights on nothing less than overcoming the opposition between necessity and freedom. Beginning with Hegel's determination of actuality as the relation between inner and outer as manifestation, we can now reconstruct the stages of Hegel's genesis argument as follows:

A1. The unity and relation of the inner and outer is the culmination of the relation between essence and appearance: the relation between inner and outer is understood as manifestation, expression, and absolute form. (WL 461–465/6:181–186; EL §142)

A2. The modal determination of the unity and relation between inner and outer is the unity and relation between the actual and the possible. (WL 477–478/6:200–202)

A3. The process of actualization, the transformation of real possibility (the totality of conditions) into actuality and actuality into real possibility forms the basis for the determination of activity (*Tätigkeit*). (WL 482–485/6:207–13; EL §§147–149)

A4. We call this activity absolute necessity when the actualization of conditions into effects is not unified by an internal purpose or goal, where the set of conditions are contingently and externally combined as a mere aggregate, bundle, or plurality. (WL 485–488/6:213–217; EL §147)

A5. Absolute necessity as an aggregated plurality of conditions and effects is manifest in the notion of substance and accidents, and in the mechanistic conception of causality. (WL 490–500/6:219–233)

A6. According to the mechanistic conception of causality, the same substance can be both cause and effect in the process of actualization (action and reaction). (WL 500–503/6:233–237)

A7. Given the unity and relation of inner and outer, the external manifestation of substance as both cause and effect (action and reaction) can be inwardly reflected in a substance that is the cause and effect of itself (reciprocity). (WL 502–504/6:235–240)

A8. Substance that is cause and effect of itself is subjectivity, Concept, and freedom. (WL 504–505/6:238–240)

On this line of argument, reciprocity is the internalization of the external manifestation of the mechanistic progression of causes and effects: insofar as we can think the unity and relation of inner and outer (or essence and appearance), the external determination of action and reaction can be inwardly reflected as the internal reciprocity of a substance that is the cause and effect of itself.[47] This follows from Hegel's account in the passage discussed earlier, where he describes the living thing as not letting a cause come into its effect; rather, the living thing sublates, breaks, transmutes, and internalizes the cause, such that the effects produced are now a result of the activity of sublating, breaking, transmuting, and internalizing in accordance with its own aims, and not simply the result of the blind flow of absolute necessity. The simplest way of putting the point is that living and spiritual activity can interrupt the flow of causes and effects even while remaining dependent on the totality of conditions that provide a context of action. When Hegel claims that reciprocity sublates mechanism, we can understand this as the internalization or interiorization of mechanism—bending around and returning into itself—such that the activity of translating conditions into actuality is

---

[47] Yeomans (2012, 198) uses the helpful phrase "internalization of perspective" to describe the kind of substance-causation that Hegel is defending.

interiorized into a purposive locus of subjectivity. Mechanism, Hegel writes, is the "*externality* of causality," and it is "*inwardness*" that "sublates the movement of causality" (WL 503, 504/6:237, 239). The interiorization of the process of actualization brings about self-actualization, "the realm of *subjectivity* or of *freedom*" (WL 505/6:240). Once the process of actualization is interiorized into a locus of purposive activity, the immanent deduction of the Concept is complete, bringing forth the transition to the Subjective Logic.

The similarities between Hegel's argument here in the deduction of the Concept and his argument in the *Phenomenology* for the constitution of self-consciousness are striking. In both cases, it is the determination of interiority, of the self-relation of inner difference, that allows consciousness and thought to arrive at the notion of infinity and "infinite *reciprocal action*." In the phenomenological context, grasping the unity and distinction of inner and outer allowed for the double constitution of self-consciousness in its essential relation to life; in the logical context, Hegel argues that with reciprocity, we have attained to the Concept, determining the form of inner purposiveness and freedom. The parallel nature of these argumentative strategies becomes even more evident when, in the introductory section of the Subjective Logic, Hegel writes: "The Concept, when it has progressed to a concrete existence which is itself free, is none other than the 'I' or pure self-consciousness" (WL 514/6:253). To make clear that the determination of the Concept likewise has a double constitution, Hegel reiterates the relation between life and self-consciousness in the context of understanding the Concept's self-actualization:

[T]he Concept is to be regarded not as the act of the self-conscious understanding [*Verstandes*], not as the *subjective understanding*, but as the Concept in and for itself which constitutes a *stage* of *nature* as well as of *spirit*. Life, or organic nature, is the stage of nature at which the Concept comes on the scene, but as blind, as unaware of itself and unthinking; the Concept that is self-conscious and thinks pertains solely to spirit. (WL 517/6:257)[48]

---

[48] Hegel goes on to say that the logical form of the Concept is "independent" (*unabhängig*) of both spiritual and non-spiritual shapes, which is to say that the logical form of the Concept is independent of the philosophy of nature and the philosophy of spirit. Nonetheless, Hegel will argue in the Subjective Logic that there is a logical form of life and a logical form of self-conscious cognition or spirit, which suggests that the independence of the logical Concept from *Realphilosophie* in no way renders the relation between life and self-consciousness irrelevant.

The Concept determined *in and for itself*, the Concept understood as the *"absolute foundation"* that has *"made* itself the foundation," emerges unconsciously with the form-activity of life, and in its actualization, it becomes self-conscious form-activity or spirit (WL 508/6:245). In the transition to the Doctrine of the Concept, substance becomes subject in two senses at once: first, in the determination of substance as reciprocity—substance as living, active, and self-caused; and second, in bending around and turning back on the reciprocity of substance, self-conscious subjectivity is actualized. Reciprocity thus denotes both the form of freedom and life and their reciprocal, absolute relation. In the Subjective Logic, Hegel will develop distinctly *logical* ways of understanding the determinations of and the relation between life and spirit as the foundation of his entire philosophical system. But to conclude this present discussion, I want to return briefly to two ideas that have been important orienting foci in this chapter.

The first concerns the Aristotelian notion of actuality as activity of form and Hegel's adoption of the priority of actuality thesis. It should now be evident that Hegel means to understand *Formtätigkeit* in terms of purposiveness and *Lebensformtätigkeit*, the form of activity characteristic of life, or the activity of life-form. If the potential becomes actual through actuality, if actuality begets actuality, then the form of activity of life and the form of activity of the self-conscious Concept must, in a sense, belong to the same species, or admit of the same form. Hegel's discussion of the process of actualization is thus at once an attempt to think through the reciprocal relation between life and spirit such that the genesis of the Concept is "not a *transition* but *a joining with itself* [*nicht ein* Übergehen, *sondern* ein Zusammengehen mit sich selbst]" (WL 484/6:210).[49] The genesis and immanent deduction of the Concept is not a *transition* from substance to subject, or a *transition* from the internal purposiveness of life to self-conscious subjectivity, where the two sides of the transition would be categorically distinct; rather, it is a process of actualization or a "joining and going together with itself" such that the latter are immanent within the determinations of the former, and in their reciprocity, they constitute the absolute activity of form that is the ground of actuality. In the determination of mechanism, there is indeed a problem of transition, insofar as substance and subject stand in a relation of external causality or conditioning. We can recall here Hegel's earlier objection to Fichte's understanding of the relation between the I and not-I as

---

[49] See the discussion of this passage in section 4.3 and footnote 35, this chapter.

a fixed, external determination between free activity and dead, non-active nature. Given Hegel's objection, his own understanding of the relation between substance and subject must operate on a different "relational mode," or *Verhältnisweise*, a mode of relationship in which the form of activity of self-conscious subjectivity can be grasped as an *actualization* of the form of activity of living substance.[50] This understanding of actualization is key for Hegel's concluding argument of the *Logic* in which self-conscious cognition is determined as an actualization of the logical form of life, in a mode of relationship that Hegel calls the absolute Idea. The claim that the process of actualization is not a transition is also important for understanding the relation between the different parts of Hegel's system, in which the transitions from logic to nature, and from nature to spirit, are also importantly not transitions but, rather, a "joining with itself" understood as the absolute activity of form. The category of actuality in the *Logic* thus provides the basic framework for understanding the sense of movement, development, and purposive activity that ties together the different parts of Hegel's system, forming the basis for his understanding of the self-actualization of reason. The genesis and immanent deduction of the Concept is the actualization of purposiveness of form, from its manifestation as life to its manifestation as the self-conscious Concept.

A second orienting focus of this chapter has been Spinoza's conception of substance as *Deus sive Natura* and its significance for Hegel's deduction of the Concept. In addition to articulating the form of self-causation or self-determination common to both spirit and life, Hegel aims specifically to transform Spinoza's metaphysics of substance, attributes, and modes into the self-relating Concept determined as *universality, particularity,* and *individuality* (or singularity, *Einzelheit*). For Hegel, when something is comprehended in its Concept, when something is rationally comprehended (*begriffen*) and determined by thought as actual, what is grasped is the internal and reciprocal relation between that something as universal (its type, genus, or species), that something as particular (its being a token of a type, identical and interchangeable with other tokens of the same type), and that something as individual (its uniqueness or singularity as *this* individual in distinction from other members of its species, or tokens of its

---

[50] Hegel uses the term *Verhältnisweise* at WL 509/6:246: "Thus the Concept is the *truth* of substance, and since *necessity* is the determinate relational mode [*Verhältnisweise*] of substance, *freedom* reveals itself to be the *truth of necessity* and *the relational mode of the Concept*."

type). This strategy of articulating a *Sache* as the unity and relationship of these three determinations is present everywhere in Hegel's system, and an obvious question to ask is why we should accept Hegel's approach as adequately grasping its objects of investigation in their truth and objectivity.[51] If the Concept is immanent in actuality, then the three determinations of universality, particularity, and individuality likewise need to be immanent to actuality understood as activity of form. To understand Hegel's reasoning here, we can return to Kant's original definition of a natural purpose, where he distinguished three different ways that organisms can be understood as being the causes and effects of themselves: first, in relation to their species, by generating others of their own kind; second, in relation to themselves as individuals, by assimilating materials from their environment; and third, in the reciprocal relation of their parts to each other (leaves, branches, roots), and their parts to the whole. The three determinations of the activity of natural purposes are manifest in the three determinations of the Concept as universal, particular, and individual, respectively, such that unity of the Concept is constituted by the unity of internally purposive form. Life is thus constitutive of the Concept in a very direct sense, insofar as the unity of the Concept is constituted by the unity of organic activity and form. This way of understanding the three moments of Hegel's Concept also allows us to understand the connection between Hegel's idiosyncratic talk of *the* Concept and our ordinary way of speaking when we talk of concepts of *x* or *y*. Hegel is often thought to hold a theory of immanent concepts or universals, where the concept of something is the substance or kind of an object treated "as an irreducible whole, in so far as it exemplifies a universal from the category of substance (like 'man,' 'dog,' or 'rose') which constitutes the essential nature of the individual as a totality."[52] This surely captures a central part of what

---

[51] Perhaps the most famous execution of this approach is found in §§5–7 of the *Philosophy of Right* where Hegel deduces the concept of the will.

[52] See Stern (1990, 3–4). Stern argues for a strictly realist position in which the unity of the object is entirely independent of the "synthesizing activity" of Kant's transcendental subject and, further, the object as structured by a concept as substance-kind "exist[s] *independently* of the activity of the subject" and "is not tied in with the synthesizing activity of any *subject*" (5, 112). This does not appear to fit well with Hegel's alignment of substance and subject, nor does it fit well with Hegel's association of the Concept with subjectivity, especially given Hegel's claim that subjectivity and selfhood are present in organic activity. See also the defense of concrete universals in Stern (2009). More recently, Kreines (2015) has also attributed a theory of immanent concepts to Hegel. Kreines couples his view of immanent concepts with an argument for Hegel's epistemological monism and idealism in which the intelligibility of such concepts depends upon the absolute Idea, understood as "any reciprocal process of concept or kind and individual where thinking or reflection establishes freedom as immanent purpose" (2015, 230).

Hegel means when he claims that something is grasped in its Concept or essential form, and also partly explains how a concept can be the ground of the object's actuality. However, concepts of x or y, understood as immanent universals or substance-kinds, remain tied for Hegel to the activity of *the* Concept, whether this is the Concept as immediate qua life or the Concept as self-consciousness and thought. Hegel's understanding of the purposiveness of form as the ground of actuality is thus still idealist in that the unity of the object is constituted in its essential connection with the unity of the subject; or more specifically, Hegel's idealism remains tied to subject-object identity in the sense that has been defended in this book. In the context of understanding the Doctrine of the Concept as the *Subjective* Logic, as presenting the very form and shape of subjectivity, actuality and the unity of objects remain fundamentally tied to the purposive activity of subjects in the broad sense, encompassing both living and self-conscious subjectivity.[53] In the next chapter, we will see with more clarity how Hegel integrates an understanding of substance-kinds or immanent species-concepts with a theory of judgment—a theory of judgment that continues to be inspired by Kant's purposiveness theme.

---

[53] Hegel repeatedly associates life with subjectivity but for an especially perspicuous discussion, see the opening section of "Organics" in PN §337.

5

Life as Ground, and the Limits of the Subjective Concept

In the remainder of this study, my goal is to provide a reading of the Subjective Logic as Hegel's own version of a "critique of judgment," as his own accounting of the limitations and ultimate ground of judgment's powers, concluding that these powers are all grounded in a logical concept of life.[1] My argument will be that the Subjective Logic makes good on Hegel's suggestion that internal purposiveness serves a positive function with respect to reasoning activity as such, and that the trajectory of the sections on "Subjectivity, "Objectivity," and "The Idea" each contribute to the thought that life opens up the space of reasons, that self-conscious reasoning activities are actualizations of the immediate form of activity of life. Not surprisingly, the keystone of Hegel's argument will be found in the conclusion of the *Science of Logic* as a whole, where the determinations of the Idea—life, cognition, and the absolute Idea—provide the ground and method of his entire philosophical system. Central to understanding Hegel's Idea is providing a detailed account of why he claims that *life* is the *immediate Idea*, an *immediate* unity of Concept and objectivity (or Concept and reality), and most important, an activity of primitive, *original judgment*. Although a detailed interpretation of Hegel's Idea will need to wait until chapters 7 and 8, chapters 5 and 6 provide accounts of the sections on "Subjectivity" and "Objectivity" with the aim of demonstrating the need for turning to the logical concept of life, retracing in detail the steps of Hegel's argument that lead him to the conclusion of the *Logic*.

In this chapter, I discuss the three chapters in the "Subjectivity" section of the *Begriffslogik* that make up what Hegel calls the subjective Concept— namely, the forms of Concept, judgment, and syllogism. I defend two central interpretive claims that make headway toward the larger thesis that Hegel's Subjective Logic can be read as his "critique of judgment." The first claim

---

[1] Hanna (1986, 311) also refers to Hegel's "critique of judgment" in connection with Hegel's critique of "common" or formal logic, particularly as employed by Kant.

Hegel's Concept of Life. Karen Ng, Oxford University Press (2020) © Oxford University Press 2020.
DOI: 10.1093/oso/9780190947613.001.0001

is that although the third *Critique* is the most important background text for understanding the Subjective Logic as a whole, the core framework for Hegel's understanding of judgment is more directly taken from Hölderlin, who conceives of judging activity in terms of "original division." Combining insights from the third *Critique* concerning the constitutive import of purposiveness for judgment, alongside Hölderlin's understanding of judgment as grounded in "Being," Hegel recasts the activity of judgment as grounded in what he calls "the original judgment of life [*das ursprüngliche Urteil des Lebens*]," suggesting that judgment's powers are at once enabled and delimited according to the form of this activity. The Hölderlinian framework of Hegel's approach to judgment, moreover, sheds light on the continuing importance of Fichte and Schelling for Hegel's understanding of idealism and reveals how the speculative identity thesis is carried forward in Hegel's *Logic*. In section 5.1, I offer an outline of Hegel's overall argument with respect to the original judgment of life, which will continue to be defended in more detail in chapters 6, 7, and 8.

The second interpretive claim, defended at length in section 5.2, is that Hegel's discussion of the subjective Concept, and in particular the discussion of the "Judgment" chapter, reveals that judgment's forms are measured according to their ability or inability to express the unity displayed by life, or the unity of what Kant called a natural purpose. Moreover, in his presentation of the highest and final form of judgment, the judgment of the Concept, which represents what judgment is in its objectivity and truth, Hegel argues that the relation between subject and predicate, their possible correspondence or non-correspondence, is grounded in the subject's essential constitution or *Gattung*, the subject's genus, species, or kind. In light of this, I will argue that Hegel's understanding of judgment is best understood on the model of teleological judgments or *life-form judgments*, which take the *Gattung* of the subject as their ground.[2] A careful consideration of the subjective Concept

---

[2] In what follows, I interpret Hegel's use of the term *Gattung* broadly in terms of genus, species, and most generally, something's kind. Hegel himself uses the term in these various ways, and given that the term plays a central role in his account of the powers of judgment, a narrow understanding of the term exclusively in terms of biological classifications does not seem appropriate in this context. Although the term *Gattung* is employed in this broad sense, I will also argue that the general model for Hegel's understanding of *Gattung*-concepts is the idea of a life-form, which is conceived on the basis of Kant's notion of a natural purpose. Obviously, although not everything identified by judgment can be said to have a life-form in the strict sense, Hegel's overall claim will be that the individuality of things is determined essentially in relation to their *Gattung*-concept such that judgment itself is modeled on teleological judging, insofar as judgment seeks the unity exemplified in the unity between an individual instance and its *Gattung*. In the section on the "Idea," Hegel will explicitly discuss the fully developed sense of *Gattung* in terms of a life-form.

reveals two additional features of Hegel's approach to judgment that further show his indebtedness to Hölderlin and the third *Critique*. The first is that Hegel treats the subject of judgment in terms of "original division," an idea that allows him to draw an important idealist connection between judgment as the unity and relation between subjects and predicates in propositions, and judgment understood broadly in terms of the activity of the subject who judges, the activity of self-consciousness or the I. Although in the present chapter I will mostly be concerned with judgment in the first sense, much of Hegel's account, and especially his use of terminology (such as *Gattung* and original division), is meant to anticipate judgment in the broader idealist sense, which he discusses in detail in the section on the "Idea." The second feature of Hegel's approach to judgment that reveals his indebtedness to the third *Critique* in particular is that judgments of the Concept are essentially understood on the model of *reflective judgments*. As reflective judgments, what they seek to identify is a relation of exemplarity between subject and predicate such that the subject is an exemplar of its predicate, a relation of exemplarity that is modeled on the way individuals are exemplars of their kinds. Importantly, because they are reflective judgments, I will argue that the rational status of judgments of the Concept are not reducible to their being conclusions of sound syllogisms, an irreducibility that is signaled by a structural peculiarity in Hegel's presentation whereby there are four forms of judgment but only three forms of syllogism. In defending the importance of reflective judgments and their irreducibility, I will follow Paul Redding,[3] who has argued that Hegel should be interpreted as subscribing only to a *weak* inferentialism, and not to the strong inferentialism ascribed to him by Robert Brandom. On the whole, my discussions of Concept (section 5.2.1), judgment (section 5.2.2), and syllogism (section 5.2.3) will reveal that the *subjective* Concept is limited with respect to its ability to determine an individual *as an individual*, which signals the need for a transition to "Objectivity" and "The Idea."

---

[3] See especially Redding's (2015) article on Brandom's analytic pragmatism.

5.1 Hegel's Critique of Judgment: The Influence of Hölderlin and Life as a Logical Problem

In chapter 4, I argued that Hegel presents his genesis of the Concept argument by means of the problem of actualization: the genesis of the Concept is the genesis of an activity of form such that the translation of conditions into effects can be grasped as reciprocity or self-determination. The argumentative strategy in the transition from Objective to Subjective Logic was to make manifest the very process of actualization, displaying the formation and emergence of the Concept from its origins in the determination of actuality. The argumentative strategy of the first two sections of the Subjective Logic ("Subjectivity" and "Objectivity") is, in a sense, to try to go in the other direction: rather than displaying the process of actualization, the Subjective Logic presents a series of arguments that retreat into the ground of the determinations of subjectivity (Concept, judgment, and syllogism) and objectivity (mechanism, chemism, and teleology), where Hegel's aim is to demonstrate that these determinations are ultimately grounded in the unity and activity of form characteristic of life. The thought-forms of subjectivity, objectivity, and their reciprocal relation are revealed to presuppose life as their mutual ground, and the positive outline of life as ground and first actuality is presented in the opening chapter of the final section of the Subjective Logic on the "Idea" (see figure 5.1).

With the retreat into life as the ground of subjectivity and objectivity, we are finally in a position to fully grasp what Hegel, referring to Kant's great service to philosophy, called the "positive function" of inner purposiveness—namely, that it not only is constitutive of judgment's activities but also is posited by judgment as its own condition of actuality, as its own presupposition and self-determined ground. The argumentative strategy of the Subjective Logic clearly draws its inspiration from Kant's argument in the third *Critique* that the principle of purposiveness is the condition for the

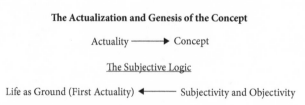

Figure 5.1. Hegel's argumentative strategies

effective actualization of judgment's power, where the unity of concept and object sought by judgment's activity is the unity of internally purposive form exhibited objectively in an organism or *Naturzweck*. Hegel's version of this claim can be found in an enigmatic passage in the introductory section of the chapter on "Life," where he writes:

> The original *judgment* of life [*Das ursprüngliche* Urteil *des Lebens*] consists therefore in this, that it separates itself off as individual subject from the objective, and in constituting itself as the negative unity of the Concept, makes the *presupposition* of an immediate objectivity. (WL 678/6:473)

The phrase "the original judgment of life" captures Hegel's goal of making good on the positive function of inner purposiveness, and further, it articulates the sense in which he will take up life as a distinctively logical problem in his own version of a critique of judgment that operates more in the manner of a genealogy by uncovering judgment's origin and source. We can interpret the idea of the original judgment of life by considering Hegel's use of the term "judgment," which appears to encompass both broader and narrower meanings. In its broadest sense, Hegel is clearly alluding to the Hölderlinian idea of judgment as *Ur-Teilung*, or *ursprüngliche Teilung*, an original, primordial, and primitive division of an original oneness and unity.[4] In the chapter on "Judgment," Hegel, fully endorsing Hölderlin's idea, writes: "Judgment is the self-diremption of the Concept . . . the *original division* of original unity; the word *Urteil* thus refers to what judgment is in and for itself" (WL 552/6:304). Far from being an isolated endorsement, this use of the term "judgment" as division and separation is present in all of Hegel's texts, a use that attests to the ongoing indebtedness of Hegel's thought to Hölderlin.[5] There are two ways of reading Hölderlin's all-important idea here, an idea that in many ways cuts to the very heart of German idealism and

---

[4] Hölderlin's notion of judgment is developed as a critique of Fichte, challenging the idea that I=I, or a principle of subjectivity, can be posited as the absolute, underived foundation of knowledge. Hölderlin writes: "*Judgment*—is in the highest and most strict sense the original separation of the most tight unity of object and subject in intellectual intuition, that separation which makes object and subject first possible, the judgment [*Ur-theilung*, original-separation]. The concept of judgment already contains the concept of the reciprocal relation of subject and object to each other, as well as the necessary precondition of a whole of which object and subject are the parts" (2003a, 191–192). See also Hölderlin's (2003b) letter to Hegel of January 26, 1795. On the origins of Hölderlin's fragment and its place in understanding the origins of German idealism, see Henrich (1997c).

[5] See Henrich (1997a, 1997b) for the definitive accounts of the influence of Hölderlin on Hegel. Henrich also suggests that it is through the lens of the influence of Hölderlin that the relationship between Hegel and Schelling should be understood.

romanticism. The first is more properly Hölderlinian: judgment as original division and separation presupposes the original unity of absolute Being as its ground, a unity that forever eludes judgment as an act of the mind and with which judgment cannot be reunifed without annihilating itself.[6] This results in the approach of *unendliche Annäherung,* or an infinite approximation toward the unity and infinity of Being that is in principle impossible to attain, for no act of judgment qua division can grasp the ground of absolute Being.[7] Given Hegel's consistent and unwavering critique of all notions of infinite striving toward a transcendent "beyond," his adoption of Hölderlian terminology here will clearly need an alternative reading, one that is more in line with Hegelian commitments. This brings us to the second, Hegelian reading of Hölderlin's idea: rather than judgment as original division presupposing an infinite, original unity as a ground that forever eludes judgment's grasp, original division and original unity are understood as equiprimordial in the activity and relationship that Hegel calls the original judgment of life.[8] Life manifests and enacts both original division and original unity, both inner difference and self-relatedness at once, expressing itself as an actuality of the equiprimordiality of Hölderlin's two poles. It is important to see that Hegel's transformation of Hölderlin's idea here is truly radical: whereas Hölderlin names "Being" as the mysterious and ultimately unreachable ground of

---

[6] "Being" is capitalized in this section when I am referring to Hölderlin's notion of Being as original unity and ground. Henrich writes, concerning Being as ground in Hölderlin: "Hölderlin calls this undifferentiated ground, 'Being,' because bare 'Being' seems to be inaccessible to any separation. And he *opposes* to 'Being' what he calls 'judgment'.... [T]he ground is thus 'Being' and the mind is 'judgment'.... There is no way back to undifferentiated 'Being' once the mind has originated" (2003, 293).

[7] Manfred Frank (1997, 2014) bases his interpretation of early German romanticism on the idea of *unendliche Annäherung,* a turn of phrase and idea that is found in Hölderlin, Novalis, and Friedrich Schlegel. Frank argues that early German romanticism should be distinguished carefully from the project of German idealism on account of the early romantics' ontological and epistemological realism, which leads to the idea that knowledge is a project of infinite approximation. Against Frank, Beiser (2002, 2003, 2014) argues for the continuity between romantic and idealist projects, a continuity that is most evident in their common approach to an organic view of nature. For the purposes of my argument, it is enough to note that the influence of Hölderlin on Hegel is indisputable and, equally, that the idea of infinite approximation is clearly one that is ruthlessly criticized by Hegel.

[8] See also GW 69–90/2:304–326. In *Faith and Knowledge,* Hegel also discusses the problem of synthetic a priori judgments in Kant with reference to the Hölderlinian idea of original identity/unity and original division/separation. He associates this idea with various Kantian operations, including reason, the original synthetic unity of apperception, figurative synthesis and the productive activity of the transcendental imagination, and the intuitive understanding, all of which Kant (according to Hegel) fails to follow through on or unduly restricts in some way. In the conclusion of his discussion, Hegel writes, "The deduction of the categories, setting out from the organic Idea of productive imagination, loses itself in the mechanical relation of a unity of self-consciousness which stands in antithesis to the empirical manifold, either determining it or reflecting on it" (GW 92/6:328). The discussion in *Faith and Knowledge* also includes his well-known critique of an "absolute beyond," which suggests that Hegel clearly adopts his own interpretation of judgment as *Ur-teil* that does not require any notion of *unendliche Annäherung* (GW 96/6:332).

judgment, Hegel names *life* as both original judgment and original unity, which means that life takes the place of Being as the ground of determinate acts of judgment in which subject and predicate, individual and universal, are distinguished and conjoined to form propositions (*Sätze*).[9] This radical Hegelian transformation of Hölderlin's idea has a number of consequences for our understanding of life as a logical problem (see figure 5.2).

First, as reflected in the passage quoted earlier from Hegel's "Life" chapter, the original division in question is the division or separation of subject and object, an act of self-separation that at once constitutes the "negative unity of the Concept." It is evident that for both Hölderlin and Hegel, the key point of reference for the act of self-division into subject and object is Fichte's self-positing activity of the I, whose very act of self-positing at once sets into place the division and reciprocity between I and not-I, or subject and object. In tracing Fichte's original act of division and self-positing to the original judgment of life, Hegel is suggesting that the basic categorical framework founded upon subject-object relation and opposition finds its first actuality in living activity and form, providing the ground for the actualization of judgment in the narrower, ordinary sense of joining subject and predicate, or in Kant's terms, judgment as the ability to think the particular as contained under a universal. The claim is that the original judgment of life is the ground and presupposition of judgment in the narrower sense, whose form of activity is taken up by Hegel under the heading of the subjective Concept. We can further note that, technically speaking, Hegel refers to life using all three forms of the subjective Concept, determining life as the immediate Concept, the original judgment, and also as syllogism.[10] Although one might suspect that Hegel is simply guilty of careless equivocation here (or the overuse of metaphors), I will demonstrate here, and in the chapters that follow, that this

---

[9] Hegel distinguishes between judgment proper (*Urteil*) and propositions or sentences (*Sätze*) (or "posits"; see Martin [2016]). See, for example, WL 552–553/6:305. Roughly, propositions express correctness but not truth, where correctness suggests an external relationship between subject and predicate rather than the genuine unity of Concept and object characteristic of truth. Henrich argues that Hegel replaces Hölderlin's Being not with life but with spirit (1997a, 139). I am arguing that this suggestion is not borne out in the text of the Subjective Logic, and cannot account for Hegel's term, the "original judgment of life," or more broadly, the indispensable role of the *logical* concept of life in Hegel's determination of the Idea. As I will argue in chapter 7, the ultimate foundation of Hegel's system is not simply life but also the reciprocal relation between life and cognition that Hegel calls absolute method. Nonetheless, to understand the trajectory of Hegel's argument in the Subjective Logic, I am suggesting that we must read Hegel as replacing Hölderlin's Being with life, a move that is much more in line with Hegel's own critique of Fichte that I discussed in chapter 3.

[10] For Hegel's references to life as Concept, judgment, and syllogism, see WL 517, 678, 679/6:257, 473, 474. See also EL §§ 160–161 and §§216–218.

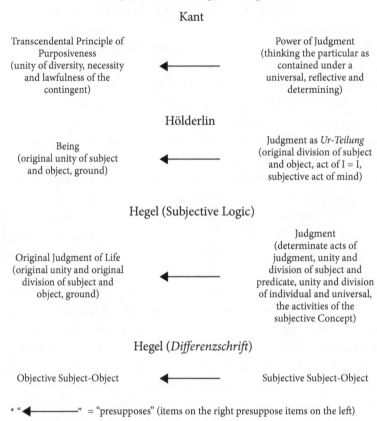

Critique and Genealogy of Judgment*

Kant

| Transcendental Principle of Purposiveness (unity of diversity, necessity and lawfulness of the contingent) | ← | Power of Judgment (thinking the particular as contained under a universal, reflective and determining) |

Hölderlin

| Being (original unity of subject and object, ground) | ← | Judgment as *Ur-Teilung* (original division of subject and object, act of I = I, subjective act of mind) |

Hegel (Subjective Logic)

| Original Judgment of Life (original unity and original division of subject and object, ground) | ← | Judgment (determinate acts of judgment, unity and division of subject and predicate, unity and division of individual and universal, the activities of the subjective Concept) |

Hegel (*Differenzschrift*)

| Objective Subject-Object | ← | Subjective Subject-Object |

* "←" = "presupposes" (items on the right presuppose items on the left)

Figure 5.2. Critique and genealogy of judgment in Kant, Hölderlin, and Hegel

is not the case. Instead, Hegel means to show that the unified activities of the subjective Concept have their ground in the immediate form of activity provided by a logical concept of life, a form of activity that both empowers and constrains their self-actualization. Ultimately, in combining Hölderlin's critique of Fichte with his own, Hegel means to demonstrate that the unity of the subject, the unity of the object, *and* the unity of subject and object are grounded in the logical form of life. This transforms two fundamental idealist theses that are at the heart of Kantian and post-Kantian philosophy: first, "that the structure and unity of the *concept* is the same as the structure and unity of the *self*," or the unity of the I;[11] and second, that the unity of the Concept or the I is the ground of the unity of the object, the source of the very form of objectivity.[12] In transforming these two well-known idealist arguments, Hegel's goal is to claim that the unity of the Concept qua subject, self-consciousness, or the I, and the unity of the Concept qua object, are both grounded in the unity and teleological form of life.

Second, interpreting Hegel's Subjective Logic as a critique and genealogy of judgment forces us to face up to what appears to be a blatant circularity on the part of both Kant and Hegel with respect to the relation between judgment and life. For Kant, the account of teleological judging amounts to saying something like the following: we must presuppose a concept of life in order to judge life (perhaps to judge anything at all), and further, the concept of life that we presuppose is objectively exhibited in the living thing that we mean to judge. Purposiveness in the third *Critique* is a way for judgment to pull itself up by its own bootstraps (so to speak), providing a self-given guarantee that judgment has the power to perform its stated function of unifying particulars under universals in a non-arbitrary fashion. This bootstrapping is indexed directly to the problem of life insofar as the unity sought by judgment is the unity displayed in organic form and, more broadly, in the purposiveness of nature as a teleological system. Hegel, never one to shy away from circles, makes this problem of circularity even more evident in referring to life as a primitive, "original judgment," resulting in the idea that what judgment presupposes in the concept of life is nothing but a concept of itself.[13] Hegel faces an even deeper difficulty, for if he is indeed trying to ground

---

[11] Brandom (2002, 210) calls this "the idealist thesis." For Hegel's version of this claim, see the famous discussion praising Kant's transcendental unity of apperception from WL 514–515/6:253–254. Brandom's "second idealist claim" is "that Spirit as a whole should be understood as a *self . . .* that Spirit has the structure and unity of the self" (227). The idealist thesis operates on three dimensions that for Brandom are all modeled on reciprocal recognition: a social dimension, an inferential dimension, and a historical dimension. In all three cases he attempts to demonstrate a structural analogy between a self constituted by mutual recognition and bound by the autonomy thesis (bound only to norms or authorities that I endorse/recognize/author as binding), and a form of the Concept (namely, Concept qua (roughly) ethical life, Concept qua an inferential system of the application of determinate concepts in judgments, and Concept qua a developmental process of history).

[12] See A89–90/B122 and A111. "The *a priori* conditions of a possible experience in general are at the same time conditions of the possibility of the objects of experience. Now I assert that the *categories* that have just been adduced are nothing other than the *conditions of thinking in a possible experience. . . .* They are therefore also fundamental concepts for thinking objects in general for the appearances, and they therefore have *a priori* objective validity, which was just what we really wanted to know" (A111). For Hegel's statement of this thesis, see WL 515–516/6:254–255.

[13] Another way of approaching this issue is to argue that judgments of life are irreducible and that they have a distinctive form. This view has been defended by Thompson (2008), who argues that judgments of life, or "natural historical judgments," constitute an a priori form of thought that is irreducible to other judgment types.

judgment in life as I am suggesting, then his view is potentially caught between two unappealing options: *either* Hegel is guilty of vicious circularity by arguing that judgment is grounded in life, only to define both in precisely the same terms; *or*, if he is not engaged in viciously circular reasoning, then he is blatantly committing the naturalistic fallacy by grounding an indisputably normative exercise in a natural, non-normative determination. That neither of these accusations obtain can be seen by considering exactly what Hegel is appealing to when life is determined as the ground of judgment and as the immediate Idea. Insofar as we are concerned with Hegel's treatment of life in the *Logic*, the determination of life at stake is categorical and a priori, and it concerns the form of activity of life insofar as this is presupposed by the form of activity of thought. What Hegel is appealing to in the logical concept of life is the fundamental form of all acts of unity and division that are potentially productive of determinacy and truth, the fundamental form of a type of self-determining activity that both manifests and produces the unity of concept and object that is the aim of judgment's activities. Rather than appealing to something non-normative or non-rational ("bare" nature), or to something categorically distinct from that which it grounds (as in the case of "Being"), the appeal to life is a relation between actuality and actuality, a relation between two determinations that share an identity of form. Most directly, and in referring to life as original judgment, Hegel is proposing that self-conscious acts of judgment presuppose an immediate and more primitive mode of judging activity manifest in the form of activity of life, one that expresses a primitive normativity and unity of form that underlies and enables more sophisticated modes of normativity and unity.[14] Life as ground is Hegel's version of the Kantian thought that purposiveness defines the space of judgment: life opens up the space of reasons because it is the necessary enabling condition of any possible system of rendering intelligible, the necessary horizon within which intelligibility as such becomes a problem and a possibility. In contrast to Hölderlin's grounding of

---

[14] Ginsborg defends an interpretation of Kant on reflective judgment that presents a version of the bootstrapping story. She writes: "My reading is based on the suggestion that we can account for a subject's grasp of a rule in terms of her adopting a normative attitude towards her mental activity. This suggestion presupposes that we can make sense of her as adopting this normative attitude without in turn assuming that she grasps a specific rule to which her mental activity is subject" (2006b, 53). This primitive normative attitude for Ginsborg stems from natural "associative dispositions" and "sorting inclinations" such that "her own activity exemplifies a rule that is universally valid" (55, 56). Ginsborg's understanding of normativity is largely informed by Kant's understanding of purposiveness in the third *Critique* (see Ginsborg 1997a, 2014); see also Ginsborg's (2011) article on primitive normativity. I return to the problem of reflective judgment in section 5.2.3.

judgment and intelligibility in Being, Hegel's ground of judgment is immanent, naturalized, non-mysterious, and fully accessible to determinate acts
of judging, eliminating the need for any notion of *unendliche Annäherung*.
To be clear, that life enables and circumscribes the possibility of any space
of reasons does not entail that non-living things are unintelligible, or that
they are somehow "outside" the space of reasons. Rather, the claim is that the
latter only become intelligible *as* the things that they are from *within* a space
of reasons opened up by living activity and form. Life as the ground of judgment means that intelligibility as such is possible and actual only *for* living
activity, and from the perspective of that activity.

Third, in substituting life in the place of Being, Hegel makes clear the importance of a claim I discussed in chapter 3 (especially in section 3.2, the
thesis of speculative identity beginning with S1)—namely, the Aristotelian
idea that there is an identity of being and life for things that live, that for
life and living activity, to be is to live. This, of course, does not mean that all
being is life, but it does suggest that the *relevant* sense of being that can be
determined as the actual ground of judgment is *being as life*, and not an overarching sense of sheer, undifferentiated Being—"*Being, pure being*, without
any further determination" (WL 59/5:82)—to which judgment stands opposed.[15] In beginning the *Logic* with pure, indeterminate, undifferentiated
being, Hegel is arguing that being is the relevant shape of immediacy only
when thinking is determined as formal reflection; however, when thinking
is determined as the power of the self-actualizing Concept, the relevant
immediacy in question is no longer being but life.[16] Although it is often
remarked that Hegel is the "great foe of 'immediacy,'"[17] what the logical concept of life makes evident is that not all immediacies are equal, that different
senses of immediacy contain different potential for development, and most
important, that the relevant and appropriate immediacy for understanding
the Idea—the unity of Concept and objectivity that manifests the very actuality of reason—is not sheer being but living activity and form.[18] We can
think about the problem of finding the right immediacy in connection with
Hegel's well-known complaint that Kantian *Verstand* and its concepts remain

[15] On the way in which the beginning of Hegel's *Science of Logic* engages with and challenges
Hölderlin's argument in "Judgment and Being," see Henrich (1997a, 137–138).

[16] See section 8.2 for a discussion of Hegel's critique of being as an "impoverished" beginning in
contrast to the beginning of absolute method.

[17] Sellars 1997, 14.

[18] Hegel discusses the different immediacies relative to different contexts in the *Logic* at WL 628/
6:406.

merely empty and formal, being dependent on intuitions for their content and actuality. Hegel's rejection of Kant's intuition theory is often cited as evidence for his rampant and unchecked rationalism, but in fact his position is much more subtle. Blind, sheer intuitions are the appropriate determination of immediacy when concepts are defined as that which is empty and formal, but Hegel's contention is that intuitions are the wrong immediacy to turn to when tracing the genealogy of the logical Concept. Importantly, in denying that intuitions are the relevant immediacy for logical form, Hegel is *not* denying the relevance of intuitions for knowledge in general: in the section on "Psychology" in the *Philosophy of Mind*, intuitions in space and time, differentiated into the three moments of feeling (*Gefühl*), attention (*Aufmerksamkeit*), and intuition proper (*Anschauung*), are determined as the immediacy of theoretical mind, the immediate shape of theoretical mind or intelligence (PG §§446–450). Thus, intuitions indeed have a role to play in the activities of the theoretical mind in the *Realphilosophie*, but they have *no role* in determining the *logical form* of the Concept as the unity and relationship of universality, particularity, and individuality. As noted in chapter 4, the relevant immediacy for understanding the unity and relationship of those three determinations are the three forms of reciprocity expressed by a *Naturzweck*, the three ways in which life manifests its being a cause and effect of itself: reproducing itself as an individual, reproducing itself as a member of a species, and reproducing the species itself. Hegel is thus less of a "foe" of immediacy than is usually assumed, and he is much more concerned with finding the *right kind of immediacy* relative to the end or purpose to be actualized. From the general claim that immediacies are ultimately sublated, posited, and subject to all manner of mediation, it does not follow that all immediacies contain the same potential for development, or that immediacy simply and entirely disappears into its mediated developments, playing no role in shaping the direction, content, or actuality of its developed forms. In chapter 7, I will argue that *life* and *cognition* in the conclusion of the *Logic* should be understood as replacing the functions of Kant's *intuitions* and *concepts*, suggesting that the logical concept of life places specific *form-constraints* on the actualization of self-conscious cognition and judgment. For now, we can simply reiterate that in replacing Hölderlin's Being with life, Hegel is arguing that the *relevant* immediacy for understanding the necessary relation between Concept and object sought after by judgment is the immediacy of the activity of life.

Fourth, in putting life in place of Being as ground, Hegel changes the very meaning of ground and argues that the form of a *sufficient ground* is the teleological form of the Concept, a form that is *immediately* manifest in the logical concept of life. He writes that "to be a *ground in a teleological sense* [*der teleologische Grund*] is a property of the Concept and of mediation by the Concept, which is reason [*Vernunft*]" (WL 388/6:83). A ground that has a teleological form is technically speaking no longer a ground (*Grund*) but reason (*Vernunft*), and that which it grounds is not simply grounded (*begründet*) but also rational (*vernünftig*). In order to understand Hegel's claim here, we can once again constrast Hölderlin and Hegel's respective approaches in determining the ground of judgment. For Hölderlin, the relation between judgment and its ground is a relation between two entirely heterogeneous elements separated by an unbridgeable gulf. Through various modes of remembrance or recollection, primarily enabled by poetry rather than conceptual thought, we can approximate the absolute ground of Being without ever being fully at one with it, for Being is ultimately a ground that forever eludes judgment's grasp.[19] For Hegel, if the relation between judgment and its ground is a relation between heterogeneous, unbridgeable elements, then judgment is, in a sense, not sufficiently grounded at all. For the form of judgment to contain the potential (or real possibility) for expressing truth— where truth is the unity of Concept and objectivity, or the Idea—it must be grounded in something that contains the totality of conditions for the actuality of that unity of form. Put somewhat differently, Hegel is suggesting that the potential for truth-aptness contained in the form of judgment must be grounded in an actuality that can display its power to produce the very truth at which judgment aims. This is why the priority of actuality thesis is so important: every potential thing is preceded by an actual thing of the same species, or again, every potential thing is grounded in and produced by an actual thing that has the same form. The only determination sufficient for grounding the potential for truth-aptness contained in the form of judgment, the only determination that displays that power as a sufficient ground, is the unity of form displayed by the activity of life.

This provides us with a rough overview of the sense in which Hegel's argumentative strategy in the Subjective Logic can be viewed as his approach

---

[19] Hegel's own approach to recollection in the *Phenomenology*, the "forgotten path" of despair that is likewise the science of the experience of consciousness, is surely also indebted to Hölderlin's thought.

to the critique of judgment, as his argument for the claim that judgment is grounded in a logical determination of life. Stated in its simplest form, Hegel is suggesting that if the first *Critique* yielded essentially negative results by setting the *limits* of pure reason, the concept of life and inner purposiveness serves the positive function of providing a *ground* for pure reason and, more specifically, its power to think the particular as contained under a universal in the form of judgments.

5.2 The Subjective Concept

In order to understand the three chapters on "Concept," "Judgment," and "Syllogism" that make up the "Subjectivity" section of the Subjective Logic, there are two interpretive problems that need to be noted at the outset. First, if Hegel means to provide a catalogue or "table" of the basic forms of judgment and inference, a quick look at his headings tells us that he provides nothing new in this regard, for he appears to be presenting forms and problems that are familiar from the history of logic and especially from the logic textbooks of his own time. At least in outline, the most important chapter of the section on judgment is nearly identical to Kant's table of judgments from the metaphysical deduction of the first *Critique*, discussing the same judgment forms, with the only noticeable difference being that Hegel reverses the order of quantity and quality by placing qualitative judgments first.[20] This is puzzling, given Hegel's accusation that Kant's categories are merely "borrowed" and, worse, entirely subjective and empirical in their derivation from the table of judgments, an accusation against Kant that is echoed in Fichte and Schelling, and one that largely shapes their own attempts at providing something akin to a deduction of the fundamental categories of thought. Concerning Kant's "*empirical logic*," Hegel writes that there is no justification for such a logic except that

we find the named species and that they show up in *experience*. What we have in this manner is an *empirical* logic—an odd science indeed, an *irrational* cognition of the *rational*. . . . the Kantian philosophy incurs a further

---

[20] See A70/B95. Hegel makes the same move in the Doctrine of Being, discussing the categories of quality before quantity. This is another way in which Hegel affirms, systematically, the priority of actuality in the *Logic*.

inconsequence by *borrowing* the categories for the *transcendental logic*, as so-called root concepts, from the subjective logic where they were assumed empirically. (WL 541/6:289)

Hegel's complaint here appears to concern the derivation of Kant's transcendental logic from merely empirical and subjective sources, which suggests that, in essence, transcendental logic has no proper ground. Putting aside for the purposes of our discussion possible Kantian responses to this complaint,[21] Hegel's accusation raises the question of how his own, nearly identical "table" of judgments is to be understood, given that he traces these very same forms in Kant to illegitimate sources or grounds.[22]

The second interpretive problem for understanding Hegel's presentation of the subjective Concept concerns the fact that, ultimately, Concept, judgment, and syllogism all fall short of fulfilling their purported function of articulating genuine unity and synthesis between a universal and an individual, and thereby, ultimately fall short as self-sufficient forms that allow us to determine an individual *as* an individual. If Concept, judgment, and syllogism provide us with a map of what Hegel understands to be the basic components and operations of thought, then Hegel's somewhat surprising conclusion is that the subjective Concept, on the whole, is limited as a self-sufficient operation that can be identified with the form of objectivity, that it is limited as an operation of thought that seeks to bring non-contingent unity to an object, allowing us to identify it successfully as some individual thing. To be clear, this limitation on the subjective Concept is surprising *for Hegel* because it is often surmised that his *Logic* preaches hyper-rationalism (or hyper-conceptualism) to the degree that the self-sufficient Concept encompasses all thought and reality, leaving nothing outside its grasp. For

---

[21] For defenses of Kant, arguing that the "subjectivity" charge applies only to forms of intuitions (and so schematized categories), but not to the categories themselves, see Ameriks (1985) and Guyer (1993). For a defense of Hegel's critique on charges of subjectivism, see Bristow (2002) and Sedgwick (2012).

[22] As we will see, Hegel's treatment of the forms of judgment resemble Kant's only in a superficial sense, and actually differ quite significantly in their substantive content. On the similarities and differences between Kant and Hegel on judgment, see EL §171Z; and Longuenesse (2007, chap. 6). Longuenesse also suggests that Hegel's complaint concerns Kant's "lame justification" and is not an outright dismissal of the logical forms of the table itself (209). Longuenesse also parses the difference between Kant and Hegel's treatment of the table as follows: "for Kant, *any* discursive judgment (combinations of concepts, as general and reflected representations) is analyzable as to its quantity, as to its quality, as to the relation between an assertion and its condition, and as to its modality. In contrast, in Hegel's presentation, the four titles of judgment characterize four *distinct* types of judgments" (209–210).

Kant, this limitation of the subjective Concept is simply a description of the proper limitations of thought, which remains dependent on intuitions to fulfill the function of referring to individuals.[23] Since this path is not available to Hegel, given his unrelenting critique of Kant's intuition theory, the specific shortcomings of the subjective Concept raise the question of what *would* suffice to ground the unity of an object such that it can be determined as an individual, *without* the reliance on intuitions. We can further note that the limitations of the subjective Concept should not in any way be understood as Hegel's rejection of its traditional forms. It is clear that the contents of the subjective Concept *do* indeed constitute the basic operations of thought, *and* that they remain non-self-sufficient insofar as they are unable, on their own, to successfully fulfill the task of individuation. The key however, is that contrary to nearly all interpretations of Hegel, interpretations from both friends and foes, the internal relations of the various determinations of the subjective Concept alone do not suffice for the determination of an individual, which suggests that Hegel *must* supply a replacement framework to fulfill the *function* of Kant's intuition theory, despite his outright rejection of it.

I will argue that both of these interpretive problems—Hegel's appeal to Kant's table of judgments and the problem of determining something as distinctly individual—lead us directly to the logical determination of life as their proper solution. Hegel can appeal to the same judgment-forms he criticized as having an empirical and subjective derivation in Kant because Hegel will instead trace their source to the a priori unity and activity of life-form; likewise, the shortcomings of the subjective Concept in determining an individual *as* an individual will find their solution in the determination of individuality within the context of a logical concept of life as the immediate Idea. Life is the appropriate ground for judgment because it is the immediate, a priori form of subject-object identity and distinction; it is the immediacy and actuality of the "unity of Concept and objectivity" or the "unity of Concept and reality" (WL 671, 672/6:464, 465). Put more directly, the specific limitations of the subjective Concept all point to life or the immediate Idea as the solution for overcoming those same limitations. Again, although the full defense of these claims will take us to the end of this study, here I take up the specific shortcomings or limitations of the subjective Concept in

---

[23] For a discussion of the problem of individuation in Kant and Hegel, see Redding (2007, chap. 3). Redding puts the point succinctly: "Kant insisted that conceptual specification *alone* could never be sufficient to render a thought capable of referring to an individual thing" (88).

order to demonstrate the necessity of turning to life as the immediate shape of the Idea.

5.2.1 Concept

The following subsections will treat Concept, judgment, and syllogism in turn, but it is important to emphasize that these three determinations are more properly considered by Hegel to constitute a single, unified operation of thought insofar as they mutually entail one another. Stated all at once (with more detailed elaboration to follow): Concept is determined as universality that particularizes itself as individuality; insofar as Concept determines itself by joining and dividing universal and individual in the judgments, "the individual is universal" or "the universal is individual," the self-determined determinacy of the Concept *is* or already takes the form of judgment; the form of judgment, in turn, is the sort of form that enables it to be a premise or conclusion of an inference, and thereby presupposes inferential reasoning as its proper context. That Concept, judgment, and syllogism all operate together to make up the complete activity of the subjective Concept is demonstrated most clearly in the highest and final form of judgment—what Hegel calls the apodictic judgment of Concept, which takes the form: *this* x *constituted so and so is true/good/beautiful.*[24] The apodictic judgment can be broken down into the following syllogism:

All *x* constituted so and so are good.
This *x* is constituted so and so.
Therefore, this *x* is good.

Thus, in the progression of the three chapters of the subjective Concept, Hegel demonstrates that Concept presupposes and posits itself as judgment, and judgment presupposes and posits itself as syllogism, making syllogism

---

[24] See WL 582, 585–587/6:344, 349–351; and EL §§178–180. Di Giovanni mistakenly omits "beautiful" in his translation. For simplicity's sake, I am employing the predicates, true, good, and beautiful as the paradigmatic predicates for the apodictic judgment of the Concept. Technically, Hegel includes their negations, and the complete list reads as follows: *gut, schlecht, wahr, schön, richtig, recht,* and *passend.* Hegel refers most often to *gut* and *schlecht,* which reflects the importance of the transition from the Idea of the true to the Idea of the good or the practical Idea in the chapter on "The Idea of Cognition." I discuss the judgment of the Concept in section 5.2.2.

the very "*form* of reason," or more emphatically, that "*everything rational is a syllogism*" (WL 588/6:352).

In addition to Concept, judgment, and syllogism operating together to constitute the activity of the subjective Concept, Hegel's presentation of each form has both a negative and a positive aim. Negatively, Hegel's analysis exposes the limitations of the various forms of judgment and syllogism to establish a necessary connection between universality and individuality—limitations that, in each case, drive the *Logic* toward a subsequent thought determination that is meant to overcome the limitation of the previous determination. One of the central questions at play in the progression of the subjective Concept, then, is the following: Why is it necessary to transition from subjectivity to objectivity at all? What are the specific limitations of the subjective Concept and, particularly, the limitations of its final determination of syllogism that make it necessary to turn to the determinations of objectivity? Another way of thinking about the limitations of the subjective Concept is to consider the difference between Concept and Idea, two terms that are notoriously slippery but, in the *Logic*, are used by Hegel quite precisely. In the chapter on "The Concept," he writes: "But the *adequate* Concept is something higher; it properly denotes the agreement of the Concept with reality, and this is not the Concept as such but the *Idea*" (WL 542/6:290). This passage tells us three crucial things: first, the Concept is somehow *inadequate*—there is something that the Concept *is not equal to*; second, what the Concept is *unequal to* is reality (*Realität*)—Concept and reality do not *immediately* agree or correspond; third, the adequate Concept, or the Concept that is equal to reality, that agrees with reality, is *not* Concept at all, but Idea. By this alone it should be evident that the subjective Concept is not self-sufficient and subject to certain limitations, the most important of which is its inability, on its own, to determine something as individual.

There are two important and related movements in the chapter on "The Concept" in which this limitation is signaled. The first is what Hegel calls the outward directedness of the Concept: in developing the relations between universality, particularity, and individuality, Hegel describes the determinateness of the Concept in terms of a double movement of "seeming" (*der Doppelschein*), where it appears (in the sense of mere seeming) as both inwardly and outwardly directed, "*der Schein* nach innen" and "*der Schein* nach außen" (WL 533/6:278).[25] Although the Concept will be described throughout the chapter in terms of both movements, as both reference and

---

[25] Hegel references the idea of *Doppelschein* again in his discussion of individuality at WL 546/6:296. The choice of *Schein* as the mode of determinateness and appearing of the Concept itself

reflection inward and outward, it is the *reference outward* that drives the movement of the Concept toward increasing determinateness from universality to particularity, and finally, to individuality.[26] The idea that the Concept gains increasing determinateness and approaches particularization and individuation through a movement, reference, and directedness toward being outside itself suggests that the power of the Concept to become actual (and not mere *Schein*), the power of the Concept to determine an individual reality, depends upon its continually maintaining this reference outward. Hegel writes: "In so far as the seeming is *inwardly directed* [*insofern es Scheinen* nach innen *ist*], the particular remains a universal; through outwardly directed seeming [*durch das Scheinen nach außen*], it is a *determinate particular*" (WL 546/6:296). Second, and related to the determinateness and particularization of the Concept as an outward reference, Hegel describes the moment of individuality in terms of a loss of the Concept, a *Verlust*.[27] Speaking in somewhat animistic terms, Hegel writes that in becoming individuality, the Concept "becomes *external to itself* and steps into actuality" (WL 548/6:299). Thus, in determining itself as something distinctly individual, the Concept has "lost itself [*hat sich verloren*]"—the Concept is outside itself and alienated from itself (WL 549/6:301). In the *Encyclopaedia Logic*, Hegel further reminds us that "[t]he individual is the same as the actual," which suggests that the Concept must "lose itself" in order to determine some actual, individual reality, and that in doing so, it is no longer *just* Concept (EL §163). In the immediate context of Hegel's discussion, the Concept "loses itself" by becoming judgment; however, as we will see, judgment and syllogism will likewise reveal themselves to be limited in different ways—limitations that will all ultimately concern the problem of individuation.

Positively, each of the determinations of the subjective Concept anticipate and point toward the Idea of life as ground. The forms of the subjective Concept come closest to establishing a necessary connection between universal and individual when they are able to mimic or express the unity displayed in a universal substance-kind or genus (*Gattung*), when they are

---

suggests that determinateness of the Concept at this stage is relatively weak, not yet fully actual, falling below even appearance (*Erscheinung*) proper.

[26] Hegel writes of the movement of particularization that it is "the side of the determinate Concept which is outwardly directed [*die nach außen geht*]" (WL 533/6:279). He also writes that the Concept qua particular is "*outside itself* (außer sich)" (WL 537/6:283).

[27] "But individuality is not only the return of the Concept into itself, but immediately its loss [*Verlust*]" (WL 548/6:299).

able to mimic or express the necessary connection displayed in the relation between a biological *Gattung* and its members.[28] This is a recurring theme throughout the three chapters on the subjective Concept, and Hegel explicitly ties this theme to the development of objectivity; that is, whenever the forms of the subjective Concept come close to expressing the unity of internally purposive form, Hegel will associate that form of subjectivity with objectivity.[29] The form of activity of *Naturzwecke* thus sets the standard against which objectivity is measured: insofar as a judgment or syllogism qua activity of the subjective Concept is more or less able to express the relation between universal and individual displayed in organic form, and thereby actually determine something *as* individual, that judgment or syllogism is more or less objective, more or less able to convey the truth of its subject matter.[30] In the context of the chapter on "The Concept," the internal relationship of the three determinations of universality, particularity, and individuality are meant to express the unified activity of a natural purpose as a cause and effect of itself. Hegel stresses that the universality of the Concept is a concrete universality, having "the character that belongs to the *genus* as the determinateness that is not separated from the universal" (WL 533/6:278). Hegel also writes that the universal is the "*essence*" and "*substance* of its determinations," that which is "formative and creative," expressing "*free power* . . . without *doing violence*" and is "*free love*" (WL 531–532/6:276–277). All these formulations are meant to express the relation between a biological species or kind and its individual members that is manifest in the Concept, but the more metaphorical elaborations of free power and free love are also instructive. In stating that the Concept does not do violence, Hegel is alluding to a relationship that he described earlier as violence—namely, mechanism: "violence is the *appearance of power* or *power as external*" (WL 501/6:235).[31] The external relation of

---

[28] The classic interpretation of Hegel's approach to substance-kind universals can be found in Stern (1990).

[29] For example, in his discussions of the judgment and syllogism of necessity, which I take up later.

[30] In his presentation of the Concept as particular, Hegel discusses the "impotence of nature," suggesting that nature's forms remain "Conceptless," which would appear to pose a problem for my suggestion that the subjective Concept comes closest to objectivity when it expresses the unity of organic form (WL 536/6:282). As I noted in chapter 3, the key is to maintain a distinction here between nature and the a priori concept of life that is at stake for Hegel in the *Logic*. Nature's self-organization and existence is full disorder and contingency, but this contingent existence is not to be identified with the a priori form of activity characteristic of life. That spirit realizes this activity of form with a higher degree of necessity and systematicity than nature is surely the case, but this does not alter Hegel's thesis that internally purposive form is the standard for objectivity.

[31] See also WL 639, 646, 663, 667/6:420–421, 431, 452–453, 458. Although mechanism is characteristic of this type of external relationship, Hegel uses the term "violence" to describe external power in other contexts as well, including the chemical process and external teleological relations. I discuss Hegel's use of the term "violence" in more detail in section 6.2.

mechanistic causality is thus the point of contrast for the non-violent power of the Concept, a power that takes an internally purposive, teleological form. Hegel also speaks of the Concept in terms of non-domination in the preface to the second edition, stressing the need for the Concept to accord with reality, rather than forcefully imposing its form on things:

> [W]hen we speak of *things*, we call their *nature* or *essence* their Concept, and this Concept is only for thought; but still less shall we say of the concepts of things that we dominate them, or that the thought determinations of which they are the complex are at our service. On the contrary, our thought must accord with them, and our choice or freedom ought not to want to fit them to its purpose. (WL 16/5:25)

And of the determination of the individual in relation to a universal *Gattung* (genus, species, or kind):

> [T]he *nature*, the specific *essence*, that which is truly *permanent* and *substantial* in the manifold and contingency of appearance and fleeting externalization, is the *Concept* of the thing, *the immanent universal*, and that each human individual though infinitely unique is so primarily because he is a *human*, and each individual animal is such an individual primarily because it is an *animal*: if this is true then there is no saying what such an individual should still be if this foundation were removed, no matter how many other predicates with which the individual would still be otherwise adorned—if, that is, such a foundation can equally be called a predicate like the rest. (WL 16–17/5:26)[32]

The individual can only be determined *as* an individual insofar as it is an individual *of* a certain species or kind. Without this immanent universal or Concept, and no matter how many other predicates are attached to it, Hegel states there is no saying what such an individual *should be*, which suggests that the determination of individuality is necessarily connected with our ability to determine something's species or kind.[33] Hegel then raises the question

---

[32] See also WL 533/6:279, where Hegel discusses life, I, spirit, and absolute Concept as concrete universals.

[33] In the passage, Hegel is alluding to the idea that something's Concept, something's species or kind, speaks to what an individual of that kind *ought to be*, claiming that *without* the Concept, we cannot say "*was so ein Individuum noch sein sollte.*" This fits in with Kant's understanding of teleological judgments, which also tell us something about how an object ought to be, and Hegel will raise this issue again in his discussion of the judgment of the Concept.

of whether or not universals like "human" or "animal" can be treated like other predicates, with the implication that the answer is definitively no, given that he just claimed that no number of predicates *absent* the Concept are sufficient to determine individuality. This has important implications for how we understand Hegel's claim associating individuality with the loss of the Concept, which appears to contradict the claim in the prior passage asserting that the Concept is the sine qua non of determining individuals. That Hegel is not contradicting himself can be shown by returning to the specific context of discussion where this loss is described. The loss of the Concept takes place within the context of its stepping into actuality qua individual and thereby becoming the form of judgment; what started as the universal is now individual: "the individual is the universal." This suggests that it is *judgment*, and not individuality as such, that is the loss of the Concept, that it is the determination of individuality in the form of judgment (at least initially, and to an extent that Hegel will now explore) which brings about this loss and entails it. In other words, the form of judgment in its initial determination is the loss of the Concept because it will not be able to capture the mode of unity displayed by organic form. The limitations of the forms of judgment discussed by Hegel thus all speak to this "loss," a loss that is manifest in the subsequent difficulties faced by the judgment's forms to unite universal and individual in the manner of the Concept.[34]

5.2.2   Judgment

Although it is not the final chapter of the section on "Subjectivity," the chapter on "Judgment" is arguably the keystone of the section and captures what is most important concerning Hegel's at once negative and positive assessment of the forms of the subjective Concept. In this chapter, it becomes evident that Hegel's analyses of the various judgment forms are all measured against the standard of their ability or inability to express the objective universality of the relation between genus and species, or a species and its individual members. Hegel's treatment of judgment is thus quite directly a critique of judgment, insofar as he identifies the various limitations and powers

---

[34] Hegel ends the chapter on "The Concept" by discussing the way in which an individual can be referred to by being "*pointed at* by someone external to it," recalling his famous discussion of the "this" of sense-certainty from the *Phenomenology* (WL 549/6:300). Hegel concludes that this way of determining individuals is a "*posited abstraction*" that cannot truly resolve the problem of individuation.

of judgment as all indexed to the unity of internal purposiveness, making the problem of teleological judging central to his overall understanding of the activity of judgment as a whole. In addition to the fact that reference to the genus or species (*Gattung*) as objective universality is the constant refrain of this chapter, Hegel's treatment of the final and most developed form of judgment, the judgment of the Concept, also takes up the specific normative dimension of teleological judgments in which something's genus or species is the source of our understanding of what an individual *ought to be*.[35] Here, I will argue that Hegel's understanding of the judgment of the Concept is best understood on the model of teleological judgments, or *life-form judgments*, which take the genus of the subject as their ground.[36] Hegel's analysis of judgment thus revolves entirely around the problem of life, with each form failing or succeeding relative to its ability to capture this objectivity of form.

A further consideration that makes Hegel's treatment of judgment so important is a structural issue within the context of the divisions and headings of the subjective Concept: although the forms of judgment both anticipate and eventually develop into the forms of syllogism, there is, surprisingly, no fourth form of the syllogism that corresponds to the judgment of the Concept.[37] That is, although there are four forms of judgment (of existence,

---

[35] The importance of judgments of the Concept for Hegel's *Logic* is underappreciated, and Hegel reaffirms their importance both in the introduction to the section on "Objectivity" and in the introductory discussion of "The Idea of the True." See WL 629, 697/6:407, 499.

[36] Hegel's understanding of judgment thus shares important affinities with Michael Thompson's (2008) understanding of natural-historical judgments. Redding (2007, chap. 6) argues that the judgment of the Concept, as an evaluative judgment, can be compared with Kant's treatment of aesthetic judgments. I discuss the importance of reflective judgments in section 5.2.3.

[37] On this asymmetry, see Moyar (2018). Moyar's insightful and detailed analysis of the Subjective Logic argues that the missing fourth form of syllogism finds resolution in the "Teleology" chapter in the section on "Objectivity." He suggests that teleology resolves the two main conceptual puzzles that are explored in the chapters on "Judgment" and "Syllogism"—namely, the genus/species relation and the ground/consequent relation. For Moyar, both of these models for thinking about individuals (the substantial model and the conditional model) are united in Hegel's account of teleology, which all finally point to what he calls the "ultimacy of the practical." I am mostly in agreement with Moyar's account, and given the emphasis given to the concept of life in this book, I am very sympathetic to the idea that the limitations of syllogism find their resolution in a notion of teleology. One difference between Moyar's analysis and my own is his emphasis on inference over judgment in understanding the argument of the Subjective Logic. Judgment is foregrounded in my account insofar as I frame Hegel's approach to these issues in relation to Kant's third *Critique* and Hölderlin's understanding of original division, with the aim of providing an account of the overarching importance of what Hegel calls the "original judgment of life." However, insofar as Concept, judgment, and syllogism all constitute one unified activity (and as I have noted, Hegel refers to the immediate shapes of all three as life), I don't think that this difference between us is necessarily a substantial one. One way in which the difference between our interpretations is more substantial concerns what I will say concerning the irreducibility of the rational status of judgments of the Concept to their being conclusions of sound syllogisms. Essentially, I argue that Hegel understands judgments of the Concept in terms of exemplarity, which suggests that such judgments are not finally reducible to their being conclusions of sound syllogistic reasoning. Herrmann-Sinai (2016) argues that Hegel's forms of syllogism are completed first, with an

of reflection, of necessity, and of the Concept), there are only three forms of syllogism, which correspond to the first three forms of judgment (of existence, of reflection, and of necessity). This is puzzling not only due to Hegel's obsessive attention to systematicity but, moreover, given the importance that is usually (and not incorrectly) ascribed to syllogism for understanding Hegel's notion of reason. The types of relations discussed by Hegel in the final form of syllogism under the heading of the syllogisms of necessity are identical to the types of relations discussed under the heading of the judgments of necessity, none of which are sufficient for grasping the necessary relation between universality and individuality characteristic of the Concept (for example, ground/consequent relations and relations of exclusion). That there is no fourth form of the syllogism to correspond with the final form of judgment suggests that the rational status of the kinds of evaluative judgments Hegel discusses under the heading of the judgment of the Concept are *not reducible to their being conclusions of sound syllogisms*. Explaining and defending this claim will take us to the end of the chapter, but to anticipate, I will argue that judgments of the Concept, or judgments that employ evaluative predicates such as true, good, and beautiful, in addition to being modeled on teleological judgments, are at bottom also reflective judgments. In a way this should be unsurprising, since for Kant, teleological judgments are a species of reflective judgment. In addition to the structural peculiarity of there being no fourth "syllogism of the Concept," we can point to an additional clue that hints at the enduring importance of reflective judgments— namely, that Hegel crucially includes the predicate "beautiful" in his list of predicates for the judgment of the Concept in both the greater *Logic* and the *Encyclopaedia Logic*.[38] The inclusion of the predicate beautiful is relevant insofar as few philosophers (perhaps none, and certainly not Hegel)

---

account of the practical syllogism in the "Teleology" chapter, and second, with the syllogism of the good in the "Cognition" chapter. I am not sure that there is a difference between what Herrmann-Sinai calls the syllogism of the good and the syllogism of internal purposiveness discussed at the end of the "Teleology" chapter. In section 6.3, I discuss the practical syllogism, and there I will argue that the action that is the conclusion of the practical syllogism should not be understood as operating on the model of applying rules to cases but, instead, that even here reflective judgment will continue to play an important role.

[38] See WL 582/6:344 and EL §178A. As I have noted, "beautiful" is mistakenly omitted in the di Giovanni translation. It is also important to note that in treating the predicates "true," "good," and "beautiful" together in the judgment of the Concept, Hegel is arguing that there is no categorical difference in how judgment operates in these three cases, arguing that all these judgments indeed share the same form. In the literature on Kant, scholars are increasingly defending the importance of Kant's views on aesthetics for his theory of cognition more broadly; here, I would suggest that that lesson is likewise significant for understanding Hegel on similar issues.

would defend the view that judgments of beauty are the result of applying rules to cases, or even that they are the result of inferential reasoning broadly construed. Although it is clear that Hegel pursues a non-atomistic approach to judgment that will indeed emphasize its embeddedness in a holistic, inferential context, it is equally clear that he reserves pride of place for reflective, teleological judgments in his account. Following Redding, this suggests that Hegel's inferentialism is *weak* rather than *strong*, where weak inferentialism is the thesis that "inferential articulation is *necessary* for specifically *conceptual* contentfulness" and strong inferentialism contends that inferential articulation is "*sufficient.*"[39] Judgments of the Concept thus represent the key for understanding the entire section on the subjective Concept, and my argument will be that it is this form of judgment, and not any of the forms of syllogism, that comes closest to capturing the form of objectivity.[40]

We can begin by considering the transition from Concept to judgment, picking up from the idea that judgment constitutes the loss of the Concept. Hegel opens the chapter on judgment by identifying two of its central features in relation to the Concept: first, that judgment is the self-posited determinateness of the Concept, or, the self-dividing of the Concept into the relation between subject and predicate; second, as this determinateness, judgment is the "proximate [*nächste*] *realization* of the Concept, inasmuch as reality denotes in general the entry into *existence* as a *determinate* being" (WL 550/6:302). That judgment is the *proximate* realization of the Concept suggests that judgment will come very close to expressing the unity of universality, particularity, and individuality expressed by the Concept, but it will fall short of actually *realizing* that unity. This is signaled by Hegel even in his

---

[39] See Brandom (1994, 131). Although I follow Redding in interpreting Hegel as a weak inferentialist, my reading of the progression of the "Judgment" chapter differs significantly from his. In claiming that Hegel "demand[s] a place for both *judgements* that are thought of as expressive of *de re* attitudes *and* ones of expressive of *de dicto* attitudes," Redding argues that what Hegel calls judgments of existence track the former and what he calls judgments of reflection track the latter (2015, 675). Brandom's (2007, 657–658) defense of strong inferentialism hinges a lot on the qualification of "broadly" in his understanding of inferential articulation. Redding (2015) provides a helpful catalogue of criticisms faced by Brandom's strong inferentialism from a Hegelian perspective. In my own discussion in what follows, I will not at all be concerned with refuting the Brandomian thesis directly; all I need for the claim that judgments of the Concept are modeled on teleological, reflective judgments to go through is that *Hegel* should be read as a weak rather than strong inferentialist.

[40] Against an Aristotelian background, Redding raises the question of the place of judgments about individuals within inferential reasoning (2007, 89, 119). His approach to the judgment of the Concept emphasizes two dimensions of this judgment form that suggests the import of its place in an inferential context: first, the contestability of this type of evaluative judgment, which leads to the recognitive relation between subjects as the "ultimate ground of the objectivity of the judgment" (189); and second, that the proper inferential context for evaluative judgments is "*inference through analogy*," which Hegel takes up under the heading of the syllogism of reflection (189–199).

discussion of the final and highest form of judgment, where he continues to insist that reality may or may not conform with the unity expressed in judgment (WL 582/6:344).[41] Throughout the chapter, Hegel develops various ways of thinking about the relation between subject and predicate, but he also insists that what subject and predicate are cannot be determined ahead of or apart from their determination and development in specific judgment forms.[42] Each form of judgment thus expresses a specific type of relationship between subject and predicate, with each progressive form getting closer to approximating the unity displayed in the Concept.[43] What drives the argument of the "Judgment" chapter is the progressive determination of different kinds of predicates (namely, abstract universals, empirical universals, objective universals or *Gattungen*, and normative, evaluative predicates or the Concept), predicates that in turn suggest different relationships between predicate and subject.[44] Let us now turn directly to each of the judgment forms taken up by Hegel.

The first two forms of judgment discussed by Hegel are judgments of existence (*die Urteile des Daseins*) (the positive, negative, and infinite judgment) and judgments of reflection (the singular, particular, and universal judgment). Judgments of existence are essentially judgments of *inherence*, expressing a relation in which a predicate inheres or is contained in the subject; judgments of reflection are judgments of *subsumption*, expressing a relation in which the subject is *subsumed* under the predicate.[45] The problems with the inherence model of judgment roughly track the problems explored in the "Perception" chapter from the *Phenomenology*, where Hegel considers how the model of a thing and its properties insufficiently conceives of the unity of an object. First, in saying that "the rose is red" where redness inheres in the rose as one of its properties, the judgment of existence expresses a relation between a substance and its accidents, without any indication of whether such a property is essential or non-essential with respect to the subject.

---

[41] Hegel also writes that the Concept is present in judgment as "*appearance* [Erscheinung]," which is an advance from the *Doppelschein* of the previous chapter (WL 552/3:304).

[42] Hegel's discussion of judgment recalls his discussion of the speculative proposition in the preface of the *Phenomenology* in a variety of ways, the most important of which is his understanding of the relation between subject and predicate in terms of speculative identity and reciprocity. See the preface to PhG.

[43] On the relation between the correspondence of concept and object and the agreement of subject and predicate, see Longuenesse (2007, 206–208).

[44] See the chart on the four forms of judgment that follows.

[45] For an excellent and comprehensive account of Hegel's treatment of judgments of inherence and subsumption in relation to the history of logic, see Redding (2014).

Redness as a predicate can inhere in any number of subjects (balloons, stop signs, cardinals, fire hydrants), and so in a judgment of inherence, "the predicate is of wider scope and therefore does not correspond to [the subject]" (WL 561/3:316). Second, the predicate "red" is only one of many properties of the subject, meaning that the rose is not *just* red but also fragrant, prickly, blooming, and romantic. This makes the subject a "bad infinite plurality" of properties, and *not* the one single property identified by the predicate (WL 561/6:317). The relation of inherence turns out to be far too indeterminate for the determination of the subject (the individual entity or object "rose"), and Hegel moves on to consider judgments of reflection in which the subject is subsumed under the predicate. In judgments of reflection, the predicate (or universal) aims to be an essential determination of the subject (the individual) such that the predicate can tell us something about the relationship between the individual entities that are subsumed under it. The progression of the quantifier from "one" to "some" to "all" corresponds with the increasing determinacy of the predicate to establish an essential relation with the subject, "anticipating" as Hegel says, a "*universal* nature or *species*" (WL 571/3:330). When we say, "all humans are mortal," and subsume the subject under the predicate, there are different ways of understanding the subject "all humans." One way of understanding the subject is in terms of a plurality, where all the individual instances are added up and aggregated; a related way of construing the subject is in terms of an "*empirical* universality," where this universality remains a "*task*" and an "*ought*," allowing plurality to count as "*allness*" insofar as a no exception has yet been found (WL 573/6:331–332).[46] But yet another way of understanding the subject "all humans" is in terms of a genus or species, which is implied by the fact that we can drop the quantifier "all" in certain cases and simply say, "human being is mortal." With the determination of this type of universality, Hegel claims that we have moved beyond *both* relations of inherence and relations and subsumption:

> The universality that has thereby arisen is *the genus*, or the universality which is *concrete* in its universality. The genus does not *inhere* in the subject; it is not *one* property of it or a property at all; it contains all the single determinacies dissolved in its substantial solidity. —Because it is thus posited as this negative self-identity, it is for that reason essentially subject,

---

[46] Hegel ties this idea of empirical universality to the problem of induction, which he discusses in the next chapter in the corresponding section on the syllogism of reflection.

but one that is no longer *subsumed* under its predicate. Consequently the nature of the judgment of reflection is now altogether altered. (WL 574/ 6:333–334)

Neither inherence nor subsumption can capture the relationship or "negative self-identity" of the genus, for "*what belongs to all the individuals of a genus belongs to the genus by its nature*" (WL 575/6:334). This leads Hegel to the third form of judgment: the judgment of necessity.

The judgment of necessity introduces a new type of relationship between subject and predicate such that the predicate is the "*universality which is in and for itself* or *objective universality*" (WL 575/6:335). This new type of predicate is the genus or species, and the judgment of necessity aims to express a relationship between subject and predicate as the relationship expressed by natural kinds—that is, as the relation between an individual and its species or the species and its genus. Hegel discusses three types of judgments under the heading of the judgment of necessity: the categorical judgment, the hypothetical judgment, and the disjunctive judgment. With respect to the first type, Hegel emphasizes that what he calls the categorical judgment must be definitively distinguished from the positive and negative judgments discussed under the heading of the judgment of existence ("the rose is red," "the rose is not red") (WL 576/6:336). To articulate the difference, Hegel contrasts "the rose is red" with "the rose is a plant," and claims that in the former case, the predicate is merely an external, contingent property, whereas in the latter case, the expressed relationship between subject and predicate is one of *necessity*. To understand Hegel's point here, we can recall the passage quoted earlier where Hegel raised the question of whether or not something's Concept (taken in his specific sense) can be understood as a predicate that is on a par with all other predicates. It is clear that Hegel answers no to this question, and in the presentation of the categorical judgment, he is suggesting that a predicate that expresses a universal genus or species introduces an entirely new type of relationship to its subject that relationships of inherence and subsumption completely obscure, a relationship that expresses both necessity and objectivity.

Looking more carefully at the judgment, "the rose is a plant," Hegel contends that the subject represents the "immediacy of external existence" and the objective universality of the predicate is an "*immediate* particularization" (WL 575/6:335). The reference to immediacy suggests that the relationship expressed by the judgment, "the rose is a plant," contains the potential for further development, that implicit in this relationship is a relationship that we need to make explicit. We can think about what is implied by "the rose is a plant" by comparing it to "the rose is red." Hegel suggests that the relationship implied in the categorical judgment is the relationship between ground and consequent, or condition and conditioned (WL 577/6:338). That is, when we say, "the rose is a plant," the implied relationship between subject and predicate is the following: "if the rose is, then it is a plant"—the hypothetical judgment. Of course, we can also say, "if the rose is, then it is red," but the relation expressed in this case between ground and consequent does not admit of the kind of necessity expressed in the former statement. In understanding the type of relationship that Hegel is identifying in judgments of necessity, it is important not to fall back on the previous model of subsumption where we understand "all roses" (as an aggregated plurality, with as yet no exception) to be subsumed under the predicate "plant." In moving beyond this subsumptive relationship, Hegel is arguing that the necessary relation between subject and predicate expressed by judgments of necessity is of an entirely different kind—one that cannot be determined by adding up "all roses" and discovering that they are, in fact, all plants. This can be seen when we take up another example, one used by Michael Thompson: the statement, "The yellow finch breeds in the spring."[47] If we understand this statement on the subsumptive model, then we would take this to mean that all yellow finches breed in the spring, and should we find a single yellow finch that did *not* breed in the spring, then our judgment would turn out to be false. But, as Hegel contends, this would be a "vulgar apprehension" indeed (WL 576/

---

[47] See Thompson (2008, 65). Thompson's argument operates by considering and rejecting certain candidates for reduction to more familiar judgment forms, where universal propositions ("All S's are F"), universal propositions with ceteris paribus clauses ("All S's are F under normal circumstances"), statistical generalizations ("Most S's are F"), generics ("S's are F"), universal propositions with normatively restricted subjects ("All properly constituted S's are F"), all fail to capture the distinctive logical form of the kinds of statements he has in mind. Of course, Thompson also emphasizes "that the same concrete thought might at once exhibit many such forms of predication," so the irreducibility of the form of thought he identifies with natural historical judgments does not exclude them from being expressed some other way (17; see also Thompson 2004). Hegel's strategy here is less fine-grained, but appears to operate in a similar way where judgments of inherence and judgments of reflection fail to capture the necessary relation between subject and predicate that obtains when the relation identified is one between a species and its genus, or an individual and its species. See also Harrelson (2013), who argues that Hegel's "Judgment" chapter presents a domain-specific logical theory, where "the form of judgment or inference is specific to the subject of judgment" (1259). Harrelson suggests that Hegelian logic is expansive and ontologically sensitive, arguing against the global application of formal logics on the basis of domain neutrality. Hanna (1986) also argues that Hegel's critique of "common logic" should be understood as stemming from ontological commitments. See also Rand (2015) for an argument that despite the similarities between Hegel and Thompson on evaluative judgments, Hegel, unlike Thompson, maintains a clear distinction between natural and spiritual defect.

6:336); in finding this judgment false on the basis of the subsumptive model, we are entirely misunderstanding the relation expressed here between subject and predicate. The mistake here is treating an objective universality as if it were an empirical one, treating the subject "the yellow finch" as amounting to the aggregated plurality of all yellow finches. The necessary relation between subject and predicate implied by judgments of necessity is thus entirely missed or obscured on the models of inherence and subsumption, and this is made explicit for Hegel when the categorical judgment is developed into the ground/consequent relation expressed in the hypothetical form.

The hypothetical judgment is presented by Hegel as follows: "*If A is, then B is;* or, *the being of A is not its own being, but the being of another, of B.*—What is posited in this judgment is the *necessary connection* of immediate determinacies" (WL 576/6:337). The necessary connection described by Hegel here is the same necessary connection between concept and object described by Kant in the third *Critique* as characteristic of teleological form. The object A (in the subject position) is not its own being, but the being of another, of concept B (in the predicate position). This necessary connection obtains when B is an objective universal or genus, being the ground for the actuality of A.[48] If this relation of necessary connection where B is the ground of A obtains, then B as the genus also contains "the *principle* of its particularization into species," which brings Hegel to the disjunctive judgment (WL 581/6:343): A (objective universal genus) is B (species), as well as C (species) (for example, contained in the genus *Homo* are *Homo erectus* and *Homo sapiens*); and A (individual of a genus) is either B (species) or C (species) (for example, an individual of the genus *Homo* is either a *Homo habilis*, a *Homo erectus*, a *Homo neanderthalensis*, or a *Homo sapiens*, etc.). Hegel stresses that taken in the empirical sense, the disjunctive judgment "lacks necessity," due to the fact that the specification of empirical species is subject to all kinds of contingencies (for example, it is not clear whether or not Neanderthals are a distinct species or are a subspecies of *Homo sapiens*, an uncertainty that weakens the necessary connection of the relation between the genus *Homo* and its various species) (WL 579/6:340). The genus in the disjunctive judgment is therefore determined as the "*proximate genus,*"

---

[48] This is exactly how Kant defines the purposiveness of form in the third *Critique*: "[I]nsofar as the concept of an object also contains the ground for the object's actuality, the concept is called the thing's *purpose* and a thing's conformity with that character of things which is possible only through purposes is called the *purposiveness* of its form" (KU 5:180). And again: "[A] purpose is the object of a concept insofar as we regard this concept as the object's cause (the real ground of its possibility); and the causality that a *concept* has with regard to its *object* is purposiveness (*forma finalis*)" (KU 5:220).

which suggests that judgments of necessity—categorical, hypothetical, and disjunctive judgments—are still ultimately unable to express the strict necessity of the relation between individual, particular, and universal displayed by the unity of the Concept (WL 579/6:341).

Hegel begins his discussion of the judgment of the Concept by comparing the forms discussed thus far:

> To know how to form *judgments of existence*, such as "the rose is red," "the snow is white," etc., hardly counts as a sign of the great power of judgment [*Urteilskraft*]. The *judgments of reflection* are more in the nature of *propositions* [Sätze]; in the judgment of necessity the object [*Gegenstand*] is present, it is true, in its objective universality, but it is only in the judgment now to be considered that *its relation to the Concept is found*. In this judgment, the Concept is laid down as the basis, and since it is in relation to the object, it is an *ought-to-be* to which reality may or may not conform. (WL 581–582/6:344)

In the transition to the judgment of Concept, Hegel thus stresses two important things: first, that what distinguishes the judgment of the Concept from the other forms of judgment is that here the Concept (predicate) determines what the object (subject) *ought to be*, suggesting that the Concept has normative, law-like powers with respect to its object; second, reality (still) may or may not conform to what is expressed in this judgment, reminding us again of the limitations of the subjective Concept, that the Concept as the *ought to be* is not yet Idea. There is something strange about needing to emphasize that judgment may or may not conform with reality, but given how often Hegel is accused of not understanding this simple point, it is important to note instances where Hegel states this explicitly and beyond all doubt (again, thought and being are not *immediately* adequate to one another; otherwise we cannot make sense of the difference between Concept and Idea). What was implicit in judgments of necessity is explicit in judgments of the Concept: the objective universality of the genus has normative powers with respect to that which belongs to it, determining, in some sense, what the members of the genus ought to be. This normative power was implicit in the objective universality of the genus, but in the disjunctive judgment, the genus was revealed to have a *proximate* character that could not entirely express the intended relation of necessity between subject and predicate. Hegel frames this limitation of the previous form of judgment by saying that it "has not yet determined itself to the third moment, that of *individuality*" (WL 582–583/6:345). Judgments of necessity, like the previous forms of judgment, only get as far as particularization and cannot individuate something qua individual. The judgment of the Concept brings us from the proximate genus to the genus that has a normative, law-like relationship to that which individuates its objective universality, representing the highest and final form of judgment— one that has no correspondent in the chapter on "Syllogism."

In arriving at the ought-character of the judgment of the Concept, Hegel has in mind a dimension of teleological judgments described by Kant as follows:

> A teleological judgment compares the concept of a product of nature as it is with one of what it *ought to be* [*was es* sein soll]. Here the judging of its possibility is grounded in a concept (of the end) that precedes it *a priori.* (EE 20:240)

It is important to note that Hegel arrives at the normative power of the Concept *by way of* the objective universality of the genus from the previous form of judgment; that is, the normative power of the predicates Hegel associates with judgments of the Concept—good, bad, true, beautiful, correct, right, suitable—is essentially indexed to the genus—what Hegel calls the "*constitution* [Beschaffenheit]" of the subject, a constitution that "contains the *ground* why a predicate of the judgment of the Concept applies or does not apply to the *whole subject*, that is, whether the subject corresponds to its Concept or not" (WL 585/6:349). In other words, Hegel is suggesting that the ground of the relation between subject and predicate in the judgment of the Concept is the genus or the constitution of the subject—that *the Gattung-concept of the subject constitutes the ground of the potential correspondence or non-correspondence between subject and predicate.* To unpack this claim, let us turn to the progression of the three types of judgment Hegel considers under the heading of the judgment of the Concept: assertoric, problematic, and apodictic.[49]

The assertoric judgment is described as follows: "The subject is a concrete individual in general, and the predicate expresses this same individual as the *relation* of its *actuality*, determinateness, or *constitution* to its Concept. (This

---

[49] Hegel again places the actual first by discussing the assertoric judgment before the problematic one, reversing Kant's order.

house is *bad*, this action is *good*.)" (WL 583/6:346). What makes this an advance from the previous form of judgment is the following: first, the predicate tells us what the subject ought to be, making explicit what was implicit in the relation between genus and species; second, the subject is now an individual with a particular actuality, determinateness, or constitution—that is, the subject is not a sheer immediacy, but an individual of a particular kind, an individual with a substantial nature and essential makeup, making explicit what was implicit in the categorical judgment, "the rose is a plant."[50] However, *that* the individual has a particular constitution is not yet explicit in the assertoric judgment, which *simply* states that this house or this action is bad or good, without explicit reference to the genus or type of thing that a house or an action is. This makes the judgment *merely* assertoric in that the only "*verification is a subjective assurance*" (WL 583/6:346)—this house is bad because I say so! However, Hegel continues that, of course, what I mean when I say that this house is bad is not that it is only bad according to my "*subjective consciousness*" but also that the house is bad in itself, independent of whether or not *I* think so—that badness is a predicate of the house itself. Implicitly, then, the relation between subject and predicate is presupposing some "external third factor" that has yet to be made explicit—namely, the constitution of this house in relation to the genus "house." Without explicit reference to this third factor, the assertoric judgment is entirely ungrounded: *I* say that the house is bad, but *you* say that the house is good, and both statements are equally justified (in their lack of justification). This brings us to the problematic judgment, which combines the positive and negative sides of the assertoric judgment: "the house is good as well as bad"; or, "the house is either good or bad."

What is problematic in the problematic judgment is the subject rather than the predicate: it is the *house* that is indeterminate between good and bad. In this contingency and indeterminacy, it becomes evident that the house is good or bad "*according to how it is constituted*" (WL 584/6:348). In order to grasp the constitution of the problematic subject, Hegel suggests that the subject is divided into two moments, that there is an ambiguity in the subject that can now be clarified and made explicit:[51] first, the subject (the house) is

---

[50] And its subsequent developments: "if the rose is, then it is a plant"; "contained in the genus plant are roses, as well as shrubs, as well as trees, etc."; "an individual plant is either a rose, a shrub, or a tree, etc." All these judgments suggest that individuals are not just bare individuals but, instead, necessarily belong to a kind or species.

[51] See also the discussion of ambiguity (*Zweideutigkeit*) and negativity in the *Phenomenology* in chapter 3, this volume.

a contingent existence that has a particular constitution (it has three floors, vaulted ceilings, and was built in 1923); second, the subject is an "objective nature" or Concept, an objective universality expressive of what it ought to be (houses are constituted to provide shelter from the elements, to provide space for gathering, rest, storage, solitude, etc.) (WL 584–585/6:348). Thus, when we say, "the house is good," the subject "house" is taken in both of these senses at once such that the predicate "good" can properly attach to it *only* if the subject is taken in both of these senses at once: we would not be able to say that the house is good if we had no idea what houses are for; likewise, even if we know what houses are for, we could not say whether a specific house is good without any knowledge regarding its particular constitution. Hegel refers to this ambiguity or two-sidedness as the "original division [*ursprüngliche Teilung*]" of the subject, a "division [*Teilung*] which is the judgment itself" (WL 585/6:348). And again: "As this duplicity [*Gedoppelte*], the *subject* of the judgment is here posited." It is *as* this duality and original division that Hegel writes of the subject that "it contains the *ground* of its *being* or *not being* what it *ought to be*." That is to say, the original division of the subject as a concrete individual constituted in a particular way according to its genus is the ground of whether or not the subject corresponds to its predicate (good, bad, true, beautiful, correct, right, suitable), the ground of whether or not the subject is or is not as it ought to be.

In making explicit that the relation between subject and predicate is grounded in the original division and two-sidedness of the subject in the mentioned sense, Hegel arrives at the final and fully developed form of judgment, the apodictic judgment: "the house *constituted* so and so is *good*, the action *constituted* so and so is *right*" (WL 585/6:349). The apodictic judgment is "*truly* objective" or "the *truth* of *judgment* in general." The objectivity of the apodictic judgment is grounded in the constitution of the subject, which is now the concrete universality of the "two moments, the objective universal of the *genus*, and the *individualized* universal." The truth of judgment, therefore, is that its objectivity is grounded in the original division of the subject as an individual of a genus, bringing us back to Hegel's Hölderlinian thesis concerning the original judgment of life. The chapter on "Judgment" brings us quite far with respect to this thesis, but I want to argue that Hegel ends his chapter by reminding us of the limitations of the *subjective* Concept and withholds the completion of his thesis until the chapter on "Life" in the final section of the *Logic* on the "Idea."

The subject of judgment, in being the unity and division of the two moments, refers to an actual fact (*Sache*): an actual house, an actual act. The subject need not only correspond to the predicate; for if the judgment is to be true, the subject, Hegel says, must also correspond to the fact of the matter, an actual given fact in reality that has a particular determinateness. We can recall that earlier, Hegel claimed that the particularization, individuation, and determinateness of the Concept is a movement and reference outward, which suggests that the judgment of the Concept must have the same outward reference. The notion of outward reference suggests that the subjective Concept strives to correspond with reality and approximates it, but ultimately remains inadequate and unequal to reality until we reach what Hegel calls the Idea. What does it mean, then, that *life* is the *immediate Idea*, the immediate unity and division of Concept and reality? Roughly, I think it means the following: life qua Idea not only is the ground of the correspondence between subject and predicate in judgment but must also be the ground of a schema of reality, allowing reality to take shape for and appear to the judging subject in a way that corresponds with its powers of judgment. That is, in order for reality to potentially correspond or not correspond to judgments of the Concept, reality must appear immediately to the judging subject in a particular way. This reality is not the immediacy of sheer being, nor is it the immediacy of intuition in the form of space and time; rather, it is the immediate schema of the form of life, a form that Hegel outlines in the chapter on "Life" according to three poles: corporeality, externality, and process of the species. Reality for Hegel is thus not the immediacy of sheer being or bare givenness but, rather, always appears as shaped by the specific constitution of one's life-form, and all life-forms immediately experience reality according to the specific constitution of these three poles. This argument, however—that the logical concept of life will help replace the function served by Kant's intuition theory, providing an immediate schema of reality—takes us well beyond the present discussion, and its elaboration and defense will be taken up in chapter 7. In this section, I have defended the thesis that judgments of the Concept, which represent Hegel's account of evaluative judgments, should be understood on the model of teleological judgments or life-form judgments, taking the *Gattung*-concept of the subject as their ground; in the next section, turning to the chapter on "Syllogism," I will argue that judgments of the Concept are also reflective judgments, and as such, that their rational status is not reducible to their being conclusions of sound syllogisms (see figure 5.3).

The Four Forms of Judgment

Form of Judgment	Types	Relation between S & P	Type of Predicate	Examples
Judgment of Existence (Quality)	Positive, Negative, Infinite	Inherence (thing and properties)	Abstract Universal	"the rose is red"
Judgment of Reflection (Quantity)	Singular, Particular, Universal	Subsumption	Empirical Universal	"all humans are mortal"
Judgment of Necessity (Relation)	Categorical	Genus/Species		"the rose is a plant"
	Hypothetical	Ground/Consequent		"if the rose is, then it is a plant" ("*if A is, then B is; or, the being of A is not its own being, but the being of another, of B*")
	Disjunctive	as well as	Objective Universal, the *Gattung*	"contained in the genus *Homo* are *Homo erectus* as well as *Homo sapiens*, etc." (A is B as well as C)
		either/or		"an individual of the genus *Homo* is either a *Homo habilis*, a *Homo erectus*, a *Homo neanderthalensis*, or a *Homo sapiens*, etc." (A is either B or C)
Judgment of the Concept (Modality)	Assertoric			"this house is *bad*, this action is *good*"
	Problematic	ought-to-be	Concept	"the house is good as well as bad" "the house is either good or bad"
	Apodictic			"the house *constituted* so and so is *good*, the action *constituted* so and so is *right*"

Figure 5.3. The four forms of judgment

5.2.3 Syllogism

In the foregoing discussion of judgment, I noted a structural peculiarity concerning the chapter on "Syllogism"—namely, that whereas Hegel presents four forms of judgment, there are only three forms of syllogism, and most important, there is no corresponding form of syllogism for the highest form of judgment, the judgment of the Concept. The most direct reason for this omission is Hegel's concern, in the chapters on the subjective Concept, with the determination of individuality or singularity, and the problem of how thought can determine something qua individual. Aristotelian categorical logic can only include individuals as subjects or predicates of judgments in syllogisms insofar as those individuals are treated as universals or members of a class, which renders them as *particular* rather than as distinctly *individual* in Hegel's (and Aristotle's) sense.[52] As Hegel noted, the subject of the judgment of the Concept is "an *immediate individual*" or "a concrete individual in general," which suggests that what is determined in the judgment of the Concept—the specific determinateness that is captured by this judgment form—cannot be completely captured or determined by syllogistic form (WL 583/6:345–356). In the progressive development of the various forms of syllogism, Hegel appears to be suggesting that syllogism *underdetermines* individuality or singularity relative to the judgment of the Concept, that inferential reasoning underdetermines the subject of judgment as an individual with a specific constitution relative to its kind or species. How are we to square this with Hegel's more positive and all-encompassing claims concerning syllogism—"*everything rational is a syllogism*"[53]—as identical with reason as such? How are we to understand Hegel's positive assessment of syllogism alongside the relatively negative outcomes of the "Syllogism" chapter, in which none of the forms of syllogism are able to express the specific determinacy captured by the judgment of the Concept?

To begin to address this puzzle, we can turn to Hegel's transition from judgment to syllogism, and consider in more detail the exact nature of Hegel's positive assessment of syllogism. As I mentioned earlier, concept, judgment, and syllogism are taken by Hegel to constitute one, unified operation of thought. In his analysis of the various forms of judgment, Hegel presents them in such a way as to already anticipate the forms of syllogism explored in the next chapter: for example, the progression of the determination of the subject from one to some to all in the judgment of reflection anticipates Hegel's discussion of induction and analogy in the syllogism of reflection; or again, the ground/consequent relation and the relations of

---

[52] On "the exclusion of singularity from syllogistic reasoning," and the Aristotelian background of Kant's intuition theory, see Redding (2007, 89–90, 119).

[53] See also EL §181. Again, understanding Hegel as a weak inferentialist is central to my argument. See the discussion in Redding and Bubbio (2014, 479–480), who write: "But in contrast to Brandom, we understand Hegel as a 'weak' rather than a 'strong' inferentialist, in that while necessary, the fact of a judgment's standing in such inferential relations is not sufficient for it to have content" (279). See also Redding (2007, 81, 117), who argues that Hegel incorporates elements of both representationalism and inferentialism, and elsewhere (Redding 2015) presents a defense of Hegel's weak inferentialism and a detailed critique of Brandom's strong inferentialism from a Hegelian perspective.

exclusion that Hegel discusses under the headings of hypothetical and dis-junctive judgments anticipate his discussion of the hypothetical and disjunc-tive syllogisms, respectively. It is therefore evident that inferential reasoning is already implied by Hegel's analysis of the various judgment forms, and this also has to be the case with respect to the judgment of the Concept, which, of all the judgment forms, is most explicitly already a syllogism.[54] The transition from judgment to syllogism is thus entirely seamless: the unity and relation-ship expressed by the copula in the judgment of the Concept is already the unity and relationship of syllogism, or again, what the copula expresses in the judgment of the Concept simply *is* the unity and relationship of premises and conclusion in a syllogism. The apodictic judgment, "the house constituted so and so is good," is thus already a syllogism such as the following:

> All houses that provide shelter from the elements are good.
> This house provides shelter from the elements.
> Therefore, this house is good.

In the judgment of the Concept, the ground of the correspondence be-tween subject and predicate is the constitution of the subject in rela-tion to its genus (the house that does or does not provide shelter from the elements); in this syllogism, what was the ground of the judgment of the Concept is now the middle term of the syllogism that unites the minor and major terms in the conclusion ("house" and "good"), thereby becoming the ground of the syllogism. Hegel writes: "The essential feature of the syllo-gism is the *unity* of the extremes, the *middle term* that unites them and the *ground* that supports them" (WL 589/6:353). The three terms highlighted by Hegel—*unity, middle term* (Mitte), *ground*—are importantly and essen-tially related: the middle term is the ground of the syllogism insofar as it provides the required unity that is the basis for drawing the conclusion. If the progression of the "Judgment" chapter tracked the development of dif-ferent types of predicates—from abstract universals to empirical universals to objective universals or the *Gattung* to the Concept—then the progres-sion of the "Syllogism" chapter will track the development of different types

---

[54] See section 5.2.1. Kevin Harrelson puts the point well: "A complex and well-constructed prop-osition about a rich topic (like 'humanity,' 'justice,' or 'jazz') approaches the form of argument and theory.... [A] sentence like 'a well-constructed house is one that can weather heavy storms' already makes an argument . . . e.g., withstanding a heavy storm is one of the premises from which one identifies a house as a well-constructed one" (2013, 1272).

of middle terms and assess their respective abilities to bring genuine, non-contingent unity to the extremes, and thereby assess their sufficiency as grounds for drawing conclusions. Thus, just as different types of predicates expressed different types of relationships between subject and predicate in judgment—from inherence to subsumption to necessity to normativity and law-likeness—different types of middle terms will ground varying degrees of unity and necessity of the extremes in the conclusion—a conclusion that in turn is a judgment that expresses a specific relationship between a subject and predicate. In Hegel's presentation of the three forms of syllogism (of existence, of reflection, and of necessity), each will employ a different type of middle term that will produce a conclusion that expresses the relation between subject and predicate in its corresponding form of judgment—that is, the conclusion of a syllogism of existence, whose middle term is "*abstract*," is a judgment of existence; the conclusion of a syllogism of reflection, whose middle term is a "*totality*" that aggregates individuals into "allness," is a judgment of reflection; and finally, the conclusion of a syllogism of necessity, whose middle term is the "*genus*" or "*objective* universality," is a judgment of necessity (WL 595, 609–610, 617/6:361–362, 380–381, 391).[55]

Strictly speaking, then, although it is the case that inferential reasoning is implied in and presupposed by the judgment of the Concept, Hegel does not present a form of syllogism in the "Syllogism" chapter that can produce a judgment of the Concept as its proper conclusion. There are several reasons for this, reasons which I will explore within the context of the "Syllogism" chapter itself, and also in chapter 6 within the context of Hegel's understanding of objectivity. For now, let me provide a rough overview of the problem at hand. First, and most generally speaking, insofar as the subject of the judgment of the Concept is an *individual* and not only a particular, this distinctive individuality of the subject is not something that can be deductively inferred. More specifically, the determinate constitution of the individual of a genus to which distinctively normative predicates are attached (not merely externally but also as a matter of the essential constitution of the subject) is not primarily a matter of deductive reasoning. Second, that Hegel ends his discussion of syllogism with the syllogism of necessity in which the middle term is a *Gattung* suggests both that the *Gattung* is the "whole" or inferential context in which individual judgments become meaningful *and*

---

[55] See also WL 624/6:400–401 for Hegel's summing up of the progression of the different middle terms explored in the chapter.

that there is what John McDowell calls a "logical weakness" or "deductive impotence" of the *Gattung* with respect to its individual instantiations such that individuals cannot be exhaustively determined by their species-concept.[56] Individuals are not only *not* exhaustively determined by nor deducible from their species-concept; moreover, individuals have positive powers of determination with respect to their species-concept and can express their *Gattung* in unique ways that can transform its substance and boundaries.

Third, the proper determinacy of the individual subject in the judgment of the Concept is therefore *exemplarity*: the individual is an exemplar of its species or kind such that its actuality is irreducibly both individual and universal at once. Qua exemplar, the subject is the ground of its relation to its predicate not according to a pre-given rule but, rather, according to its specific constitution in which it positively or negatively exemplifies its species.[57] When this same subject qua exemplar becomes the middle term of a syllogism, its exemplarity its lost insofar as it becomes a rule from which a particular case is deduced (as in the earlier example: All houses that provide shelter from the elements are good; this house provides shelter from the elements; therefore, this house is good).[58] As an exemplar, the individual subject of the judgment of the Concept is *a law unto itself* rather than a rule applying to particular cases. If we return to the predicates Hegel employs in the context of the judgment of the Concept (good, bad, true, beautiful, correct, right, suitable), the inclusion of the predicate "beautiful" is particularly instructive for understanding why there is no syllogism of the Concept: when we say of some individual x that it is beautiful, even adding that this x *constituted so and so* is beautiful, beauty cannot thereby be deduced by turning the subject into a generalized rule such as "all x constituted so and so are beautiful."[59] The relation between subject and predicate in the judgment of the Concept is normative, or an "ought-to-be" as Hegel says, but in the case of an *actual* correspondence between subject and predicate, this correspondence is not

[56] McDowell 1998b, 171–174.

[57] This can also be a model for thinking about what Hegel means by "ethical dispositions," which are realized in individuals within an institutional action-context by means of habituation and upbringing. If we consider the relation between the individual and its relevant institutional action-context (where the action-context plays the role of the *Gattung*), the statements, "Antigone, who does thus and so, is a good sister," or "Antigone, who does thus and so, is a bad citizen," express the thoughts that Antigone is a positive or negative exemplar of what it is to be a sister or citizen, given the contexts of the institutions of the family and the state in which sisterhood and citizenship are determinate, meaningful social roles.

[58] See also Redding's (2007, 194–195) discussion of rule and cases.

[59] See Hegel's discussion of the syllogism of allness where he stresses the futility of deducing beauty from rules such as "*regularity*" (WL 610/6:382).

a relation of inherence, subsumption, or even the necessity of a genus but, rather, a relation of exemplarity in which the individual subject exemplifies and is a realization of the predicate, where exemplarity is delimited by a horizon of determinacy provided by the genus as the objective universal of the individual. Put somewhat differently, the predicates of judgments of the Concept are neither properties of the subject, nor rules under which the subject can be subsumed, nor deducible from the genus of the individual, even while the genus provides the very condition and context of all predication; rather, predicates of judgments of the Concept are *exemplified* in the subject, which means that the correspondence between subject and predicate in such cases cannot be deduced from a general rule. Thus, when we say, "the house constituted so and so is good," what we are saying is that *this* house is an exemplar of the kind "house," and its exemplarity is not readily deducible from general rules we may construct concerning all houses, even while *this* house can only be an exemplar insofar as it is indeed an instance of the kind "house."

Fourth and finally, insofar as Hegel conceives of the subject of the judgment of the Concept as an individual exemplar that is a law unto itself within the context of its *Gattung* (the original division of the individual subject into "two moments, the objective universal of the *genus*, and the *individualized universal*"), the moment of individuality is ultimately a manifestation of self-individuation:[60] in the case of judgment in the narrow sense taken as the relation between subject and predicate, individuality is indexed to the manifestation of the *object* identified by the subject-concept (an actual exemplary house); in the case of judgment in the broader and encompassing idealist sense that takes the subject of judgment to be the living I or self-consciousness (i.e., the subject who judges), individuality is an activity of self-determination and self-constitution, an "original judgment" of the living I in which individuality with a particular constitution is self-posited as an exemplification of its *Gattung*.

Let me briefly say something about the first two forms of syllogism before turning to a more detailed discussion of the syllogism of necessity, the account of which provides the transition from Hegel's discussion of the subjective Concept or "Subjectivity" to the section on "Objectivity." In the syllogism of existence, the middle term is characterized by Hegel as an abstract determinacy that is only contingently and arbitrarily related to its extremes such

---

[60] On Hegel's understanding of individuality as self-individuation, see the discussion in section 6.1.

that the unity of the minor and major terms in the conclusion is external, tenuous, and in some cases even nonsensical and absurd. In addition to claiming that all the terms of the syllogism of existence are "*abstract*," Hegel also suggests that the relationships implied between the terms of the syllogism of existence are ones of inherence and subsumption.[61] Take the classic example:

> All humans are mortal.
> Gaius is a human.
> Therefore, Gaius is mortal.[62]

The key to Hegel's analysis is the type of relationship implied by the middle term. In the syllogism of existence, two types of relationship are being implied. First, being human inheres as a property of Gaius, and mortality in turn inheres as a property of being human, allowing us to infer that mortality inheres as a property of Gaius. Second, Gaius is subsumed under the category "human," and human is subsumed under the category "mortal," allowing us to infer that Gaius can also be subsumed under the category "mortal." Hegel's analysis here mirrors his analysis in the "Judgment" chapter in which relations of inherence and subsumption, while surely applicable in many contexts, nonetheless fail to establish sufficient unity between subject and predicate in the conclusion such that the subject can be identified as distinctly individual. Hegel writes that in the syllogism of existence, it is "*completely contingent* and *arbitrary* which of the many properties of a thing is adopted for the purpose of connecting it with a predicate" (WL 594/6:359).

---

[61] See WL 591–592/6:356–357 on inherence and subsumption in the syllogism. On the abstractness of the terms, Hegel writes:

> The extreme of individuality, as *abstract individuality*, is the *immediate* concrete, consequently the infinite or indeterminable manifold; the middle term is equally *abstract particularity*, consequently a *single* one of these manifold qualities, and similarly the other extreme is the *abstract universal*. Therefore it is essentially on account of its form that the formal syllogism is wholly contingent as regards its content; and contingent, not in the sense that it is contingent for the syllogism whether *this* or *another* object be submitted to it—logic abstracts from this content—but insofar as a subject forms the basis it is contingent what kind of content determinations the syllogism shall infer from it. (WL 595/6:361–362).

On Hegel's critique of formal syllogisms, or syllogisms of the understanding, see Schick (2003).

[62] Note that Hegel will use this example again in his discussion of the syllogism of allness, and of course, this categorical syllogism can also be an example of what *Hegel* calls the categorical syllogism, which is the first form of the syllogism of necessity. What changes in the progressive development of syllogisms is the relation implied by our understanding of the middle term, which is what allows Hegel to use the same example under different headings.

Whereas the middle term is treated as a contingent property in the syllogism of existence, in the syllogism of reflection, Hegel transitions to considering the middle term as an essential property that has the character of "allness." The middle term of the syllogism of reflection is "the *totality* of the terms," "the form of *allness* . . . [that] gathers the individual externally into universality," an allness that anticipates "*the genus*" (WL 609–610/6:380–381). This echoes Hegel's discussion of the judgment of reflection in which the predicate was an empirical universal or plurality. In this example, the middle term is now no longer taken as a contingent property but, instead, as an aggregate of all individual humans, which leads Hegel to the syllogisms of induction and analogy. In anticipating the genus, the unity suggested by "allness" is one that we assume by generalizing from particular cases, where the aggregated plurality of cases counts for universality or "allness" insofar as no exception has yet been found. On the basis of "allness," we can also establish analogical relations between the individual instances of the universal "all," and in so doing, the middle term approaches "essential universality" and is "taken as something concrete which, in truth, is just as much a universal nature or genus as it is an individual" (WL 615/6:389).[63] Again, echoing his earlier argument from the "Judgment" chapter, "allness" as the middle term already implies the objective universality of the genus, and in the syllogism of necessity, Hegel takes up the genus as the middle term or ground of syllogism under three headings: categorical, hypothetical, and disjunctive.

To understand Hegel's treatment of the syllogism of necessity and the transition to "Objectivity," we can return to considering the positive and negative dimensions of his analysis. Positively, the syllogism of necessity has for its middle term "the *universal nature* of the fact [*Sache*], the *genus*" (WL 617/6:391). With the genus as the middle term, the unity and relationship expressed by the syllogism is one of necessity, because the genus is the "inner identity" of the extremes rather than a contingent property that is only externally related to the major and minor terms. Just as the categorical judgment ("the rose is a plant") looked superficially similar to the judgment of existence ("the rose is red"), Hegel says that "superficially" the categorical syllogism (in his sense) can look similar to the syllogism of inherence (WL 618/6:392). However, Hegel makes clear that the premises of the categorical

---

[63] Or again, "[T]he mediating element is *allness*. But *individuality* appears as the essential ground of allness and universality only as an external determination in it, as *completeness*. But universality is *essential* to the individual if it is to be a middle term that unites; the individual is therefore to be taken as an existing universal *in itself*" (WL 617/6:390–391).

syllogism are themselves categorical judgments; using the same example, the middle term of the syllogism is now "human being" taken as a substance-kind or *Gattung*: "the middle term is the essential *nature* of the individual and not *just any* of its determinacies or properties" (WL 618/6:393). With the genus as the mediating middle that pervades all the terms of the syllogism, Hegel claims that the categorical syllogism is no longer subjective but, instead, expresses an identity in which "objectivity begins" (WL 619/6:394). Objectivity begins with the categorical syllogism because the genus is the ground that unites the terms in a necessary manner and produces a conclusion in which the relation between subject and predicate is likewise one of necessity. Almost immediately after announcing the beginning of objectivity, however, Hegel claims that the categorical syllogism still contains a subjective element, where subjectivity in this context signals a lack of genuine unity between the middle term and the extremes. This brings us to the negative dimension of Hegel's analysis of the syllogism of necessity, which as I have noted, can be understood in terms of the "logical weakness" or "deductive impotence" of the genus.

After elaborating on the objectivity and power of the genus as the middle term, Hegel goes on to explain its logical weakness in relation to an immediately posited individual:

> What is really immediate in the syllogism is the *individual*. The individual is subsumed under its genus as middle term; but under the same genus come also an *indeterminate number of many* other individuals; it is therefore *contingent* that only *this* individual is posited as subsumed under it. —But further, this contingency does not merely belong to the *external reflection* that finds the individual posited in the syllogism to be contingent by *comparison* with others; on the contrary, it is because the individual itself is related to the middle term as to its objective universality that it is posited as *contingent*, as a subjective actuality. From the other side, because the subject is an *immediate* individual, it contains determinations that are not contained in the middle term as the universal nature; it also has, therefore, a determinate existence which is indifferent to the middle term, determined for itself and with a content of its own. (WL 619/6:394)

We can reconstruct Hegel's point as follows. First, the immediate individual that was the subject of the judgment of the Concept is now the immediate individual of the syllogism ("Gaius"), which is subsumed under the genus ("human being") as the middle term. However, second, an indefinite number of many other individuals also fall within the genus "human being," so it is entirely contingent that Gaius is the individual identified by the middle term, "human," rather than Cleopatra or Socrates. Third, the contingency in question here is *not* the same contingency that was present in the syllogism of reflection, in which the middle term was taken to be "allness," a contingency connected with an individual's place in comparison with other individuals within an aggregated plurality; rather, this is a specific contingency of the individual *in relation to its Gattung* as an objective universality, a specific contingency that Hegel calls an individual's "subjective actuality." Fourth, the specific contingency of the individual in relation to its *Gattung* is the following: the immediate individual has determinations *for itself* that are not contained in and indifferent to its *Gattung*, the specific existence of an individual can have determinations that are indifferent to its *Gattung* altogether, even while the individual remains, necessarily, an individual instance of its kind. For example, Cleopatra supposedly committed suicide with a self-inflicted bite from a poisonous snake, a specific determinateness with respect to her individual mortality that is entirely indifferent to and not contained in what it means to be human or mortal. The individual thus remains contingent in relation to the genus as middle term, and the middle term underdetermines the individual *qua individual*, which leads Hegel to turn from the categorical syllogism to the hypothetical syllogism.[64]

It is important to note that Hegel defends two claims regarding the power of the genus in his discussion of the syllogism of necessity. On the

---

[64] McDowell's discussion of deductive impotence occurs in the context of his analysis of the transformation that takes place when rational reflection enters the picture of our consideration of Aristotelian categoricals. He considers two levels of this deductive impotence associated with two conceptions of nature. The first is that from the statement, "human beings have thirty-two teeth," it does not follow that *this* individual human, John McDowell, has thirty-two teeth. This kind of deductive impotence, however, raises "no practical problem" for non-rational beings (1998b, 172). The second level of deductive impotence concerns the relation of rational beings to their species. For rational beings, there is a practical problem concerning the fact that "the predicate of an 'Aristotelian categorical' about the species cannot be deductively transferred to its individual members." The practical problem is summed up as follows: "With the onset of reason, then, the nature of the species abdicates from a previously unquestionable authority over the behavior of the individual animal" (1998b, 172). Hegel's discussion in the "Syllogism" chapter is, of course, not concerned with the practical dimensions of this deductive impotence; rather, Hegel is using the idea of deductive impotence in order to shed light on the nature of individuality as such, where individuality that is necessarily an instantiation of a species is nonetheless irreducible to and non-deducible from its species. This conceptual point concerning individuality holds across Hegel's work, but later in the *Logic*, he will suggest that the genus has a much tighter grip on the individuals of non-rational species in contrast to the power of the genus over the individuals of a rational species. Nonetheless, the general point about deductive impotence is central for understanding Hegel's approach to the problem of individuality, especially as this appears in the chapter on "Syllogism."

one hand, the genus expresses a concrete universality in which "objectivity begins," meaning that the genus provides the objective context for the determination of individuals. On the other hand, individuals, although they are necessarily individuals of a certain kind, also necessarily manifest specific determinations and characteristics that are indifferent to their genus, meaning that individuals are never exhaustively determined by their genus concept. In defending both these claims, Hegel means to argue that the syllogism of necessity, whose forms develop around the genus as the mediating factor, underdetermines individuality, even while the genus provides the necessary context for its specification. This underdetermination is evidenced in the earlier passage, and by the fact that none of the syllogisms of necessity can produce a judgment of the Concept as a conclusion, where the predicates of judgments of the Concept can only belong to individuals with a specific constitution, a specific constitution that can never simply be deduced from the genus. Hegel's analysis of the categorical syllogism and the deductive impotence of the genus is thus central for understanding the limitations of syllogism and why there is no syllogism of the Concept. Given that the progression of middle terms mirrors the progression of the predicates of judgment, one can safely infer that a syllogism of the Concept would have *the Concept* as a middle term, and this is what Hegel suggests in his discussion of the disjunctive syllogism. However, when the "totality of the Concept" is the posited mediating factor, Hegel writes that this is in fact "*no longer a syllogism* at all" (WL 623/6:399). To understand why this is the case, we can turn to the hypothetical and disjunctive syllogisms.

Like the hypothetical judgment, the hypothetical syllogism expresses the relation of ground and consequent, or condition and conditioned:

If A is, then B is,
But A is,
Therefore, B is.

Just as the hypothetical judgment expressed the truth of the categorical judgment, the hypothetical syllogism is the truth of the categorical syllogism insofar as it expresses the necessity that is implied by the genus, namely: "*If A is, then B is; or, the being of A is not its own being, but the being of another, of B.*" In the hypothetical judgment, the necessary connection expressed was that B (genus) is the ground for the actuality of A (species); in the hypothetical syllogism, Hegel suggests that B is the "*totality of conditions*" and A is "*actuality*" (WL 620/6:396).[65] This way of speaking clearly recalls Hegel's treatment of the category of actuality in the Doctrine of Essence and, more specifically, his discussion of real modality in which the translation of a totality of conditions (real possibility) into actuality and actuality itself being a totality of conditions formed the basis for the concepts of *activity* and *activity of form*. Indeed, Hegel goes on to elaborate on A as the mediating factor of the hypothetical syllogism and claims that it "determines itself as *activity*, since this middle term is the contradiction of the *objective univer-sality* . . . and the *indifferent immediacy*"; and again: it is "the *form-activity* of translating the conditioning actuality into the conditioned" (WL 621–622/ 6:397). The mediating element that is the ground of the unity of the hypo-thetical syllogism is now determined in two ways that are essentially related. First, the mediating element is the genus or an objective universal *and* an indifferent, immediate individual *at once*; it is what Hegel called a "subjec-tive actuality." Just as the subject of the judgment of the Concept was posited as the original division of these two moments (genus and individual), here Hegel claims that the mediating element is the contradiction of these two moments: Cleopatra is the "contradiction" between the genus that inevitably shapes and defines her, and her indifferent, immediate individuality with a specific constitution that resists the deductive powers of the genus, being a unique manifestation of individuality that may even transform and redefine the genus "human" by means of her activity. This brings us to the second fea-ture of the mediating middle: as a manifestation of the contradiction between the objective universality of the genus and an individual subjective actuality, the mediating element is now an activity or activity of form, a "*self-related negativity*" and "absolute form" (WL 622/6:398). The contradiction between the genus and the individual is not external, inert, or fixed in its opposition but, rather, constitutes an activity of form in which there is an ongoing re-ciprocal action between genus and individual, one that constitutes a locus of subjective actuality. In associating the mediating element with activity, Hegel is anticipating the next step in the disjunctive syllogism in which this ele-ment ought to contain all three moments of the Concept as "universality as well as particularity and individuality," repeating the moves of his genesis of the Concept, in which the deduction of internally purposive activity was at

---

[65] However, insofar as actuality is understood to be identical with the totality of conditions, Hegel suggests that it is "indifferent which side is taken as universality and which as individuality" (WL 620/6:396).

the same time the deduction of the Concept. To elaborate on the mediating element as activity of form, Hegel transitions to the disjunctive syllogism, which, like the disjunctive judgment, expresses the principle of specification or the "particularization" of the "genus differentiated into its species":

A is either B or C or D,		A is either B or C or D,
But A is B,	or	But A is neither C nor D,
Therefore, A is neither C nor D.		Therefore, A is B.

In the first premise, the subject, A, is universal; in the second premise, the subject is determined as a particular; in the conclusion, the subject is posited as an "*individual* determinateness . . . as exclusive individuality" (WL 623/6:399). Hegel then claims that A, posited in the disjunctive syllogism as "the *universal* sphere of its particularizations . . . determined as an *individual*," is "the truth of the hypothetical syllogism . . . which for this reason is equally *no longer a syllogism* at all." That is, when the mediating element is posited as universal, particular, and individual at once—that is, as Concept—the form of activity is no longer syllogism at all; instead, this totality is now posited as the object. We can reconstruct Hegel's reasoning here in three stages.

First, A as described in the disjunctive syllogism has the same constitution as the subject and ground of the judgment of the Concept: an immediate, concrete individual constituted in a particular way according to its objective, universal genus. Second, as I briefly noted earlier, each form of syllogism has a conclusion that is a judgment of the corresponding judgment form: the conclusion of a syllogism of existence is a judgment of existence ("Gaius is mortal," where mortality is understood as a contingent property of Gaius); the conclusion of a syllogism of reflection is a judgment of reflection (Gaius is subsumed under the aggregated plurality of "all humans," and insofar as we have not yet encountered a human who is not mortal, Gaius can likewise be subsumed under the category "mortal" until we find an exception); the conclusion of a syllogism of necessity is a judgment of necessity (Gaius's mortality belongs to the universal nature of being human such that Gaius would not be human if he were not mortal). This brings us to the third stage: Why does Hegel suggest that we cannot construct a syllogism that produces a judgment of the Concept as its conclusion, or that in such cases, the form of activity in question is no longer a syllogism? Contrary to Hegel's suggestion, such a syllogism can indeed be easily constructed. For example:

> If we are working within the context of modernist architecture, then the house constituted so and so is good.
> We are working within the context of modernist architecture.
> Therefore, the house constituted so and so is good.

There are two things we can note about this syllogism. First, although it indeed produces a judgment of the Concept as its conclusion, there is also already a judgment of the Concept contained as the consequent of the conditional in the first premise. This suggests that in order to produce a normative judgment as a conclusion, there must already be a normative judgment contained in the premise; that is, one cannot deduce a normative conclusion from a non-normative premise. This specific point about normative judgments is mirrored more broadly in Hegel's discussion of the other forms of syllogism, in which the premises and conclusions are likewise composed of judgments of the same form (i.e., from premises about contingent properties, we can only arrive at conclusions about the contingent properties of a subject; from premises about an aggregated plurality of subjects, we can only arrive at conclusions about the subject that are statistical probabilities; from premises about the genus or species, we can only arrive at conclusions about the subject concerning the nature of its kind). Nonetheless, the specific point about normative judgments is particularly important, since it establishes the autonomy of the normative domain such that normative conclusions cannot be derived from non-normative premises. But this still does not explain why there is no syllogism of the Concept. Moreover, this omission should *not* be understood as suggesting that we thereby cannot reason inferentially concerning normative claims, drawing normative conclusions from normative premises, which of course we can and do.

This brings us to the second point: if we isolate the judgments of the Concept in this syllogism, we can ask, "What *makes* the house constituted so and so good?" According to the syllogism, the goodness of the house is inferred from working within the context of modernist architecture, and it appears that we have two options for understanding the relationship between antecedent and consequent: either the context of modernist architecture constitutes a determinate set of rules from which the goodness of the house can be deduced, or the house is a positive exemplification of modernist architecture in its specific, individual constitution, a rule unto itself. However, the first option is ruled out according to the deductive impotence of the genus outlined by Hegel in his analysis of the categorical syllogism: neither specific individuals nor the particular constitution of specific individuals can be deduced from the genus. The goodness or badness of the house therefore rests on its being a positive or negative exemplification of modernist architecture, in which case the normative judgment that the house is good does not depend on the premises of a syllogism but, rather, depends upon the *actual exemplary object* referred to by the subject-concept "house." Judgments of the Concept, then, in addition to expressing the normative dimension of the genus characteristic of teleological judgments, are also, at bottom, *reflective judgments*. As reflective judgments, they are characterized by two essential features. First, judgments of the Concept presuppose a "principle of purposiveness" as their ground, which for Hegel means the following: the *Gattung* or life-form of the subject defines the space of judgment, or again, the subject belongs essentially to a *Gattung* or life-form which provides the necessary horizon of determinacy and context of predication.[66] Second, the relation between subject and predicate is one of exemplification in which the subject exemplifies the predicate insofar as it is also an exemplar of its kind.[67] As a relation of exemplarity, the judgment of the Concept qua reflective judgment cannot be deduced from a general rule, and its truth can only be confirmed or disconfirmed by reference to the manifestation and constitution of the actual object identified by the subject-concept in relation to a judging subject. The manifestation and constitution of the actual object is not a bare "this," nor the immediacy of sheer being, but is always already an individual thing of a particular kind, an individual exemplar of a *Gattung* where the relation between individual and *Gattung* is determined as reciprocal action. As an objective universality manifest in the object, the *Gattung* is the objective context of all actual judging, rather than a merely subjective, transcendental principle of judgment.[68]

Insofar as judgments of the Concept are, for Hegel, the objective truth of judgment as such, their status as reflective judgments have far-reaching implications for understanding the *Logic*, as well as for understanding his

[66] This marks a deep disagreement between Hegel and Schelling on the ground of predication, despite the fact that Hegel develops his speculative identity thesis on the basis of earlier Schellingian insights. On Schelling's understanding of the ground of predication in terms of "unprethinkable being," see Gabriel (2015). On Schelling's theory of judgment, see García (2015).

[67] See Gadamer (1976, 59), who also describes the relation between individual and species in terms of exemplarity. See also Kant's discussion in §§17 and 18 of KU, where he discusses exemplarity and the idea of reason.

[68] Although Hegel rejects the language of reflective judgment and raises characteristic concerns about Kant's specific understanding of this activity, he also writes that when the Concept is determined as purpose, this is an "*objective judgment*" that "judges *objectively*," where an objective judgment appears to replace what Kant called reflective judgment (WL 656/6:443–444). Given Hegel's

entire philosophical system. Recall that reflective judgment for Kant was characterized as the power of judgment to ascend from a particular to a universal in cases where no pre-given universal rule or concept sufficed to determine the particular in question. On the basis of the power of reflection that Kant associates with the "faculty of judging" as such—the power "to consider . . . to compare and to hold together given representations either with others or with one's faculty of cognition, in relation to a concept thereby made possible . . . which goes on even in animals, although only instinctively"—judgment apprehends the particular as a rule unto itself in accordance with the principle of purposiveness, judging it to be beautiful or alive, or simply as the kind of the thing that it is such that empirical nature can be grasped as a scientific system (EE 20:211). Far from being a special case of judgment restricted to a narrow domain, the power of reflection is arguably operative in nearly all cases of judgment, and it underwrites the power of determining judgment to apply rules to cases insofar as it allows judgment to ascertain particulars such that they can be identified as *appropriate* for subsumption under available rules.[69] In this chapter, I have argued that judgments of the Concept should be understood as follows: first, that these judgments are grounded in appropriate *Gattung*-concepts and the idea of the *Gattung* as such as objective universality, which govern the ascription of evaluative predicates (true, good, beautiful, etc.); second, that they should be understood on the model of reflective judgment, insofar as no form of syllogism is presented in which a judgment of the Concept is produced as a possible conclusion. This second feature of the *Logic's* analysis of the subjective Concept suggests that judgments of the Concept are not primarily understood by Hegel to be the result of the application of rules to cases but, instead, are the result of a judging activity that *cannot* be understood exclusively on the model of subsuming particulars under pre-given rules or universals (i.e., as determining judgment).[70] Reflective judgment and the power of reflection

---

high praise of inner purposiveness in the same discussion, his complaint about reflective judgment clearly concerns Kant's insistence on its merely subjective validity and does not amount to a wholesale dismissal of the very idea as such. I discuss Hegel's idea of objective judgment in the next chapter, section 6.3.

[69] See Ginsborg's (2006b) discussion of how judgment takes certain associations as "appropriate." The power of reflecting is closely related to the power of schematism, and I discuss Hegel's logical concept of life as a priori schema in chapter 7, this volume.

[70] Hegel claims that determining judgment is a mere abstraction. Regarding the distinction between reflective and determining judgment and its connection with purposiveness, Hegel writes:

point toward primitive and immediate capacities, processes, and forms of activity that, as Kant says, "goes on even in animals, although only instinctively," taking us beyond what is presented in the chapters on the subjective Concept and toward the processes Hegel discusses under the heading of a logical notion of life. In leaving open an important role for reflective judgment in his analysis of the subjective Concept, my argument is that Hegel should only be read as a weak inferentialist. The limitations of the subjective Concept are fully compatible with Hegel's stronger claims regarding the importance of syllogism—"*everything rational is a syllogism*"—insofar as a judgment's standing in inferential relations is necessary but not sufficient for it to have content.

The conclusion of the "Syllogism" chapter is also the transition to objectivity, an objectivity that begins with the determination of the genus as middle term, and one that is completed with the determination of a mediating element that constitutes the activity of form of the Concept. Within the confines of the forms of syllogism, Hegel repeats that the Concept as middle term is an "*ought-to-be* [Sollen]," that for syllogism there is merely "a *demand* [*Forderung*] [my emphasis] that the mediating factor shall be the Concept's totality" (WL 624/6:400). Once the mediating element is *realized* as the activity of the Concept, subjectivity transitions into objectivity, and Hegel's discussion moves to a consideration of the *reality* of the Concept under the headings of mechanism, chemism, and teleology. To understand Hegel's transition and, further, to understand the trajectory of the Subjective Logic as moving toward a discussion of the Idea, it is important to return to the narrower and broader meanings of judgment that Hegel employs as part of his transformation of the Hölderlinian paradigm of judgment as original division. On the narrower understanding of judgment whose primary topic of analysis is the relation between a subject-concept and a predicate-concept in a proposition, Hegel's conclusion is that the truth of judgment refers to the actual object identified by the subject-concept, "a *fact* [Sache] that is *in*

However unsatisfactory is for this reason Kant's discussion of the teleological principle with respect to its essential viewpoint, still worthy of note is the place that Kant assigns to it. Since he ascribes it to a *reflective power of judgment*, he makes it into a *mediating link* between the *universal of reason* and the *individual of intuition*; further, he distinguishes this *reflective* power of judgment from the *determining* power of judgment, the latter one that merely *subsumes* the particular under the universal. Such a universal that only *subsumes* is an *abstraction* that becomes *concrete* only in an *other*, in the particular. (WL 656/6:443)

and for itself—objectivity" (WL 624/6:401).[71] The chapters of the section on
"Objectivity" thus take up the reality to which the activities of the subjective
Concept refer, the reality to which—insofar as Concept is not yet Idea—the
subjective Concept may or may not correspond. In the progression from the
determination of mechanism to chemism to teleology, reality (the actual
things or *Sachen* to which thought refers) comes closest to corresponding
to the developed forms of the subjective Concept when reality itself has the
shape of an internal purpose or end. When Concept and objectivity or reality correspond, when subjectivity and objectivity both have the shape of the
subject-object, Hegel arrives at the determination of the Idea, the actual correspondence of Concept and reality that is characteristic of all truth.

The narrower understanding of judgment already points toward judgment in the broader, more encompassing idealist sense insofar as the unity
of the former is ultimately grounded in the unity and activity of living self-
consciousness or the I, the unity and activity of the subject who judges. The
unity and activity of form of the subject who judges, taken as the mediating
element, cannot be deduced from general rules but, as a law unto itself, is an
original act of self-positing in which the I posits itself as an exemplar of its
species, an original act of self-consciousness that is the ground for the unity
of judgment in the narrow sense through which experience takes form. This
understanding of the Concept as the unity of self-consciousness is established
by Hegel in the introduction of the Subjective Logic, and Hegel returns to the
topic of self-consciousness in the chapter on "The Idea of Cognition." In my
interpretation of the judgment of the Concept, I argued that an individual
subject with a particular constitution in relation to its *Gattung* operates as the
ground of judgment in the narrow sense, the ground of whether or not a subject corresponds or does not correspond to its predicate. In chapter 7, I will
argue that this same principle applies to the broader sense of judgment where
the subject of judgment is self-consciousness or the I: the individual I with a
particular constitution in relation to its life-form is the ground of the unity of
Concept and objectivity, or Concept and reality. Hegel begins his argument
for this claim by reference to "the original judgment of life," in which a living
subject constitutes itself qua subject by setting itself in opposition and in relation to objectivity. The form of activity of the living subject becomes the

---

[71] The term "*Sache*" plays an important role in the *Logic*, particularly in the chapter on "Ground" in
the transition to the section on "Appearance" (see WL 414–417/6:119–123). Bowman, who translates
Sache as reality, argues that Hegel "intends to treat 'Concept' and *Sache* as synonymous" (2013, 17).
See also Bowman's (2013, chap. 6) discussion of determinate intentional content.

ground of its unity and relationship with reality, a unity and relationship that produces determinate truths and goods. Although there are, of course, significant differences between a merely living individual and a self-conscious I, the chapter on "Life" remains absolutely central insofar as it defines the parameters for how reality or objectivity take shape for *all* living individuals, presenting the form of activity of life as an a priori determination. Thus, insofar as life serves a positive function as the ground of judgment, it is not only the horizon of determinacy and the context of all predication; life as the ground of judgment is also the source of all actual unity and correspondence between subjective Concept and reality, a unity and correspondence that Hegel calls the Idea.

6

The Objectivity of the Concept

In the previous chapter on the subjective Concept, I argued that the objective universality of a *Gattung*, broadly understood as a genus, species, or kind, and whose fully developed shape can be understood as a life-form, constitutes the ground of judgment. In referring to the genus in terms of an *objective* universality, Hegel means to suggest that *Gattung*-concepts are objective with respect to the determination of individuals, that individuals are always essentially individuals of a certain kind, and moreover, that the kind of thing an individual is provides the standard and context for the ascription of normative predicates.[1] My conclusion was that what Hegel calls the judgment of the Concept, which has no corresponding syllogism form, is best understood in terms of *reflective judgment*, in which the relation between subject and predicate is determined as a relation of exemplarity, where the subject exemplifies the predicate insofar as it is also a positive or negative exemplar of its kind. Judgments of the Concept thus presuppose the objective context of the genus as their necessary ground, a context without which subject and predicate could not be brought into unity and relation.

Hegel's goal in the "Objectivity" section is to show that the objective universality of the genus is not simply the necessary context of predication but also the necessary context of something's existence and reality, an objective context that determines the degree to which self-determining activity can be realized. In the present chapter, I will argue that mechanical, chemical, and teleological processes all manifest varying degrees of activity, but it is only when Hegel arrives at the determination of internal purposiveness in the chapter on "Teleology" that self-determining activity is fully realized. Whereas the treatment of the subjective Concept was primarily focused on the forms and operations of thought, the treatment of objectivity concerns the objective reality and existence of the Concept, and the degree to which that objective reality can be understood as part of processes of self-determination. Key to Hegel's account of the objectivity of the Concept is the

[1] See deVries (1991, 65).

Hegel's Concept of Life. Karen Ng, Oxford University Press (2020) © Oxford University Press 2020.
DOI: 10.1093/oso/9780190947613.001.0001

question of how we can understand judgment as something objective, an objectivity that hinges, unsurprisingly, on the determination of internally purposive form. Rather than offering a comprehensive account of "Mechanism," "Chemism," and "Teleology," my goal in this chapter is to continue the argument from the previous chapter that Hegel's Subjective Logic can be understood as his "critique of judgment" by tracing the role of the genus in the determination of the objective reality of the Concept. In that vein, I will continue to emphasize the importance of judgment in my account, with the aim of showing how the section on "Objectivity" leads us finally to the original judgment of life.

This chapter will proceed as follows. First, I provide a short defense of Hegel's treatment of the ontological proof for the existence of God in the transition from subjectivity to objectivity, and I argue that in the context of Hegel's argument, being should be understood essentially as activity (section 6.1). Second, I argue that mechanism, chemism, and external purposiveness all fall short of self-determining activity insofar as Hegel refers to their processes in terms of "striving" (*Streben*) and "violence" (*Gewalt*) (section 6.2). The shortcomings of mechanical, chemical, and externally purposive processes continue to reveal the important role that Hegel ascribes to the objective context of the genus, whose power in relation to the individual determines the degree to which self-determining activity is manifest. Third, I take up the problem of what Hegel calls "objective judgment" and provide a brief analysis of the "Teleology" chapter through a discussion of the practical syllogism (section 6.3). Although the practical syllogism manifests the form of activity of the Concept, I argue that Hegel continues to reserve an irreducible role for the self-determining activity of judgment, which brings us finally to the determination of the Idea.

6.1 The Transition to Objectivity: Being as Activity

The transition to the section on "Objectivity" in the *Logic* is notoriously difficult to understand and defend, in large part because of Hegel's discussion in the introduction to that section comparing the transition from the subjective Concept to objectivity with the ontological proof for the existence of God. Hegel suggests that the transition from the subjective Concept to its self-determined reality is essentially "the same" as the inference from the concept of God to God's existence, which has been the source of reactions ranging from ire, to confusion, to mockery, depending on one's philosophical disposition and context (WL 625/6:402).[2] Nonetheless, I think that Hegel's position not only is defensible but, moreover, that the identification of the *realization* of the Concept with the ontological proof tells us something essential about his understanding of both judgment and objectivity.[3]

To begin, we can return to the relation between subject and predicate in judgment. In attempting to make his case for identifying the transition to objectivity with the ontological proof, Hegel reminds us of his discussion of judgment in which he suggested the following:

> the subject first obtains determinateness and content in its predicate; until then . . . for conceptual cognition it is only a *name*; but in the predicate with its determinateness there begins, at the same time, *realization* in general [Realisation *überhaupt*] . . . in judgment, the *realization* of the Concept is not yet complete. (WL 626/6:403)

Having completed his account of the subjective Concept, Hegel now specifies that the fully developed unity of subject and predicate (the copula "fulfilled") is to be understood in terms of *realization*: in an objectively true judgment, the subject is realized in the predicate and the predicate is an

---

[2] Schelling clearly thinks that this identification of Concept with God is "monstrous," but the exact nature of this identification is not always clear (1994, 136). At one point, Hegel gives priority to the logical determination of the "proof" and suggests that the ontological proof is simply an application of a broader logical point (WL 626/6:403). Later on, Hegel entirely identifies the "absolute, divine Concept" with "God's self-determination" such that the relation of application no longer obtains (WL 627/6:405). Depending on the perspective and emphasis of such an identification (which has an important family resemblance with both Spinoza's identification of God with nature and Aristotle's identification of God with thought thinking itself), Hegel's claim is either sacriligious or deeply pious (or perhaps atheistic or pantheistic). Although I do not think there can be a final decision on this score, the undeniable and essential connection that Hegel draws between the Concept and the *Gattung*, along with his ruthless critique of all transcendence and an absolute "beyond," speak in favor of a naturalist or non-theistic reading, which is the preferred reading in my interpretation.

[3] Harrelson argues that Hegel's innovation with respect to the ontological proof should be understood in terms of unifying human and divine reason, such that knowledge of God is also our reunification with God, making our knowledge of God essential to God's nature (2009, 204–205). He writes that

> to the extent that human consciousness possesses knowledge of God, it is the divine in the human that possesses this knowledge. To that same extent, then, the divinity constitutes the intellect, and our knowledge of God is God's self-knowledge, a point that Spinoza also raises in the context of his discussion of the 'intellectual love of God.' God's self-knowledge is, of course, not substantially distinct from its object. . . . It would indeed follow from our idea of God that he exists *if our idea of God were God's idea of himself.* (2009, 205)

On the ontological proof in Hegel, see also Lauer (1982), Nuzzo (1995), Hodgson (2007), Redding and Bubbio (2014), and Williams (2017).

expression of the realization of the subject.[4] In the judgment, "this action is good," the predicate "good" is the mode of the realization of the subject such that goodness is manifest in the action, or the action is a manifestation and realization of goodness. Whereas relations of inherence and subsumption in judgments of existence and reflection obscure the relation of realization, the relation of realization is first made possible in judgments of necessity where the predicate is determined as a genus, species, or kind (what it is to be a plant is realized in the rose, and the rose is a realization or manifestation of what it is to be a plant). This is why Hegel suggests, in his presentation of both judgments and syllogisms of necessity, that it is only within the context of a determinate *Gattung* that "objectivity begins." Objectivity begins with the *Gattung* because it is only within its context that *realization* in accordance with the Concept can take place; without the determinate context of a *Gattung*, the realization of the subject through the predicate remains vague, indeterminate, contingent, and incomplete.[5] We can also now determine a deeper sense in which the relation between subject and predicate in judgments of necessity is *necessary*—namely, the *Gattung*-predicate is a *necessary condition* for the realization of the subject. Without the *Gattung*-predicate, the subject cannot be realized qua something objective according to its Concept, neither from the perspective of thought nor from the perspective of the existence of the object itself. Something's genus, species, or kind is now determined as a necessary condition for its objective realization. At the end of the foregoing passage, Hegel reminds us that in judgment, "the *realization* of the Concept is not yet complete." In judgments of the Concept, the normative power of the genus as the necessary, objective context of realization is made explicit with the determination of distinctively normative predicates (true, good, beautiful), but the relation between subject and predicate in this form of judgment remains an "ought-to-be." With the transition to objectivity, *ought*

---

[4] Hegel discusses "objective judgment" and judging objectively in the chapter on "Teleology" while considering Kant's notion of reflective judgment (WL 656/6:443–444). I discuss objective judgment in section 6.3.

[5] One might say that in an objective judgment of existence, we see that redness is realized in the rose and that the rose is a realization of redness—why do we still need the objective universality of the genus in order to understand this relation of realization? For one thing, to say that it is the *rose* that is a realization of redness, and not simply that "redness is realized," we need to know what kind of thing the rose is. Moreover, while realization might be the correct way to understand the redness of the rose, the predicate "red" is not a necessary condition for the realization of the subject "rose." Many roses are realized without being red, but it is a necessary condition of being a rose that it is realized as a plant.

becomes *is* (being, existence) insofar as the predicate of the judgment of the Concept is realized in an individual object that is an exemplar of its kind. The key to Hegel's transition thus lies in the relation of realization by which judgment becomes something objective; the necessary condition for the realization of the individual subject-cum-object is the objective context of the *Gattung*.

However, even if it is conceded to Hegel that the genus provides the necessary condition for realization, it is evident from Hegel's own discussion of the categorical syllogism that the genus is not a sufficient condition for the determination of individuality and, here by extension, for the realization of an individual. All existing things exist as a thing of a certain kind, but obviously one cannot infer the existence of an individual thing simply from the concept of its kind. According to Hegel, the only case in which we can infer the existence of something from its concept is that of *the* Concept: only in the case of *the* Concept are concept and being identical. He writes: "[the] *realization* [Realisierung] of the Concept is the *object*," and, "objectivity has the meaning, first of all, of the *being in and for itself of the Concept*" (EL §193; WL 630/6:408). The comparison with the ontological proof thus has a very specific application, and everything hinges on Hegel's specification that the inference to being or existence only obtains for *the* Concept—the self-relating activity in which individuality, particularity, and universality are actualized as a unified whole. The inference from the Concept to its being or existence thus obtains only if that being or existence is itself determined as a kind of *activity*—that is, it is only when being or existence itself constitutes self-determining activity that we can talk about the *realization* of the Concept. Hegel makes this quite explicit at the end of the chapter on "Syllogism," on the cusp of the transition to objectivity, where he describes the hypothetical syllogism as "the *form-activity* [Formtätigkeit] of translating the conditioning actuality into the conditioned" (WL 622/6:397). When the mediating element of the syllogism is itself determined as a self-mediating activity—a self-mediation of the three moments of universality, particularity, and individuality at once—this mediation itself becomes objective, a mediation that is manifest in objective existence. In suggesting that it is only in the manifestation of self-determining, self-actualizing activity that Concept and its objective existence are one, Hegel is again appropriating Fichte's understanding of the self-positing I, in which the activity of absolute self-positing performatively enacts the existence of the I for-itself. As Fichte writes: "The act in question is simply the concept of the I, and the concept of the I is the concept of this act; both are exactly the same" (ZEWL 35/I: 460).[6] We can also recall that in identifying the concept of the I with activity, Fichte had specified that the intuited activity in question should not be associated with being, which is static, but with life. In Hegel's case, we can say more precisely not that being or existence is "inferred" from the Concept but, rather, that the being or existence of the Concept is nothing but the Concept's own activity of self-realization, and moreover, that the activity of self-realization of the Concept is itself an objective existence in which internally purposive form is manifest. Hegel elaborates on the importance of understanding being as activity in the context of his interpretation of the ontological proof as follows:

> God, as the living God, and still more as absolute spirit, is known only in his [*sic*] *activity* [Tun]. Humankind were directed early to recognize God in his *works* [Werken]; only from these can the *determinations* proceed that can be called his *properties*, and in which his being is also contained. Thus, the conceptual comprehension of God's *activity* [Wirken], that is of God himself, grasps the *Concept* of God in his *being* and his being in his Concept. *Being* [Sein] by itself, or even *existence* [Dasein], are such a poor and restricted determination, that the difficulty of finding them in the Concept may well be due to not having considered what *being* or *existence* themselves are. . . . The Concept, even as formal, already immediately contains *being* in a *truer* and *richer* form, in that, as self-related negativity, it is *individuality* [Einzelheit]. But of course the difficulty of finding *being* in the Concept in general, and equally so in the Concept of God, becomes insuperable if we expect being to be something that we find *in the context of outer experience* or *in the form of sensory perception*, like *the one hundred dollars in my finances*, as something graspable only by the hand, not by spirit, essentially visible to the outer and not the inner eye; in other words, when the name of being, reality, truth, is given to that which things possess as sensuous, temporal, and perishable. (WL 626–627/6:404)

In this passage, Hegel specifies the exact character of the being or existence in question when one is considering the objective realization of the Concept in relation to the ontological proof. First, being is understood in terms of activity and the products of activity—that is, being is understood

---

[6] Redding and Bubbio (2014) also suggest that it is Hegel's appropriation of Fichte's I=I that provides the right concept of the "Concept" for Hegel's understanding of the ontological proof.

primarily as *actuality*. God is known through God's deeds, works, acts, and effects; moreover, it is only through such deeds, works, acts, and effects that what are traditionally construed as the *properties* of God can be determined and discerned. The determination of properties is thus not only subordinate to the determination of the genus, which provides an objective context for distinguishing between essential and non-essential properties, but further, in instances where there is the presence of self-determining activity, properties are determined by and proceed from that activity. This understanding of being as activity, and more specifically as objectivity, is "much richer and higher than the *being or existence* of the ontological proof, as the pure Concept is richer and higher than that metaphysical void of the *sum total* of all *reality*" (WL 628/6:405). Grasping being as activity is therefore the crux of grasping the unity of being and Concept; or in other words, grasping something's activity is to grasp being and Concept at once.

Second, the truer, richer, and higher form of being is likewise being as self-related negativity or *individuality* (*Einzelheit*).[7] The moment of individuality, so elusive in Hegel's presentation of the forms of judgment and syllogism, is now explicitly determined as a self-relating activity such that individuality is primarily a self-posited, self-realized determination. The objective determination of individuality requires what Hegel calls activity of form, an activity of self-mediation by which subjectivity posits itself as an objective existence. At bottom, then, individuality is a self-determined, self-posited determination (as Fichte claimed: the concept of the I is the concept this act, both are exactly the same). In his discussion of the individual (or the singular, *das Einzelne*) in the "Concept" chapter, Hegel's key examples are "[l]ife, spirit, [and] God," and individuality in that context is likewise described as "self-related negativity," "the immediate identity of the negative with itself [that] *exists for itself*" (WL 547–548/6:297–300). But this account of individuality creates a puzzle: Why are rocks, clouds, planets, lumps of coal, drops of water—objects that we do not ordinarily associate with activity, life, negativity, or spirit—not quite individuals? Why are life and living activity prerequisites for individuality? Hegel's answer is that when we speak of non-living, non-self-determining things as individuals (*this* piece of rock, *this* cloud, *this* drop of water), their individuation into a "this" depends on their being "*pointed out*"—that is, individuation in such cases depends upon existing in relation to something

---

[7] See EL §163: "[T]he individual is the same as the actual"; and WL 548/6:299: "Through individuality, where the Concept is *internal to itself*, it becomes *external to itself* and steps into actuality."

that can actively point it out *as* a "this." This dialectic of immediacy is well known from the opening chapter of the *Phenomenology*, and in the *Logic*, Hegel writes: "A *this* . . . [is] a *posited* immediacy *pointed out* by someone external to it. The *this is*; it is *immediate*, it is a *this*, however, only in so far as it is *pointed out*" (WL 549/6:300). Hegel argues, however, that this mode of individuation is derivative and abstract: derivative because *thisness* depends entirely upon an activity and individuality external to what is pointed out, and abstract because the individuality of *thisness* is entirely severed from the object's own essential nature and constitution. Non-derivative and concrete individuals are always self-individuating individuals, and this activity of self-individuation (or self-relating negativity) is manifest immediately in the activity of form of living beings. Indeed, this is why Hegel begins the chapter on "Life" with a discussion of "the living individual."[8] Individuality is immediately manifest in the living being, or the living being immediately posits itself as an individual, dividing itself from what it is not, because it *matters* to the living being that it is itself and not something else: first, that it is itself and not a piece of inert, dead matter; second, that it is itself and not substitutable for another member of the same species (that I am an alpha and not a beta in my wolfpack, that I am Karen and not Isabel); third, that it is itself and not a member of another species (that I am a human being and not a wolf).[9] Only beings that can be *for themselves* can point things out *for them* as an individual *this*, and so for Hegel, anything that is individual *only* on account of being pointed out by something outside itself is not an individual in the strict sense. Rocks, clouds, lumps of coal, and drops of water are thus mere particulars rather than individuals. In the context of the ontological proof, then, the being that is identical with the Concept is its own activity, and this activity posits itself as self-determining individuality.[10]

---

[8] See the opening paragraphs of the section on "The Living Individual": "The infinite relation of the Concept to itself is as negativity a self-determining, the diremption of itself within itself *as subjective individuality* [subjektive Einzelheit] *and itself as indifferent universality*. . . . This *subject* is the Idea in the form of *individuality* [*der Form der* Einzelheit], as simple but negative self-identity—the *living individual* [*das* lebendige Individuum]" (WL 679–680/6:474–475).

[9] Individuality, then, can come in degrees. Whereas the first way that it matters to a living being that it is itself matters for *all* living things, the second and third ways in which it matters to a living being that it is itself tracks the degree to which the living being in question is a self-determining individual. For example, the second and third ways (non-substitutability and species-specificity) matter less for bacteria than for wolves and humans (the classification of bacteria is notoriously difficult, and the prevalence of horizontal gene transfer in the bacterial world makes both individuality and species-specificity weak determinations).

[10] In thinking about the individuality of the I, Fichte famously argues that one becomes an individual only insofar as one is recognized as an individual, a claim that Hegel also endorses. The recognition requirement can be read as an individual's necessary connection to its universal genus, which here is a relation that Hegel is trying to present *logically*. The recognition requirement is a

Third and finally, Hegel specifies how being is *not* to be taken when considering the objective realization of the Concept: being or existence is not to be taken as external, sensory perception or as experience, like the one hundred dollars in my finances which is there or not there to be perceived. In reference to Kant's refutation of the ontological proof in which he employs the infamous hundred thalers as an example, Hegel claims that Kant employs both an "untrue" concept of the concept and an "untrue" understanding of reality; that is, when concepts are taken as empty and abstract, and when reality or being is taken as sensory experience, then indeed, one can surely not infer the existence of a hundred thalers from its mere concept (WL 627/ 6:405).[11] However, given Hegel's defense and presentation of his own concept of the Concept, along with the objective context of realization provided by the genus, the comparison with the ontological proof is warranted in this specific sense: in the manifestation of self-determining, self-actualizing activity, an activity that takes an objective, determinate form within the context of a *Gattung*, to grasp that activity is to grasp the objective existence of the Concept.

It is against this background of the Concept's realization that the progression from mechanism to chemism to teleology can be understood. Each of these three determinations are manifestations of the objective reality of the Concept in two senses: first, they are manifestations of the Concept's *own reality*, the objective existence of the activity of the Concept itself; second, they are manifestations of the reality that corresponds with the Concept, manifestations of the reality to which the Concept refers. As the objective reality of the Concept taken in both of these senses, mechanism, chemism, and teleology manifest varying degrees of self-determining activity ranging across the following: self-subsistence; self-externality and indifference; reaction and interaction; power and violence; law; relation to otherness; affinity and tension; external purposiveness and instrumental action; and finally,

---

phenomenological, material, social, and historical expression of this logical point: only living creatures can be individuals in the strict sense, and living individuals are individuals only by virtue of their activity and membership within some life-form. Recognition (and its proto-forms—namely, the special relationship that obtains between members of the same species) is simply part and parcel of such membership. We can note some important differences between mere "pointing out" and recognition: pointing is unidirectional, whereas recognition must be reciprocal; pointing does not transform the constitution of the object, whereas recognition does; pointing is necessarily subjective, whereas recognition is objective; pointing can never determine the Concept of an object, whereas recognition does. On becoming an individual in Fichte, see GNR 18–84/III: 17–91.

[11] See A599/B627.

self-determined, internally purposive activity. These various determinations of mechanical, chemical, and teleological objects and their processes represent varying degrees of self-determination, but they also represent overlapping and simultaneous layers of activity contained within a single object. This becomes most evident in the chapter on "Life," where the living individual as both subject and object relates to itself, to its environment, and to other members of its species in the manner of all three types of processes at once;[12] but within the context of the three chapters on "Objectivity," Hegel illustrates this point by drawing comparisons to manifestations of mechanical, chemical, and teleological activity all at work in the domain of spirit. Examples of mechanical processes and activity are manifest in a "*mechanical mode of representation,* a *mechanical memory, habit,* a *mechanical mode of acting,* [which] signify that the pervasive presence that is proper to spirit is lacking in what spirit grasps or does" (WL 631/6:410). Hegel also refers to fate, law, rule, and government as manifestations of mechanical relationships in the spiritual domain (WL 639–640, 642–644/6:420–422, 424–428). Examples of chemical processes and activity, which operate in the mode of "*relation to other*," are manifest in living and spiritual relations as follows: "in living things, the sex relation falls under this schema, and the schema also constitutes the *formal* basis for the spiritual relations of love, friendship, and the like" (WL 645–646/6:429). To articulate the idea of a neutral medium that allows for the external community of chemical objects, Hegel also employs the example of language as an analogue, arguing that it fulfills the same function as its chemical counterpart in the spiritual domain (WL 647/6:431). Although teleological, purposive activity and processes are so characteristic of spirit that one hardly needs specific examples to see how teleology is manifest in the spiritual domain, Hegel nonetheless draws on the example of tool use in order to articulate the external relationship between means and ends in the case of instrumental action (WL 663, 666/6:453, 456–457). In drawing on these examples from the domain of spirit, Hegel aims to make clear that just as Concept, judgment, and syllogism constitute one unified operation of thought, mechanical, chemical, and teleological processes are all simultaneously manifest in the objective reality of the Concept in the two senses just noted: first, the Concept itself exists simultaneously as a mechanical, chemical, and teleological object and its activities range across mechanical, chemical, and teleological relationships; second, the reality that corresponds

---

[12] See, for example, WL 680–681, 684–685, 687/6:475–477, 480–483, 484–486.

to the Concept is likewise made up of mechanical, chemical, and teleological objects along with their interrelated processes, a differentiated totality that constitutes objective reality as such.

6.2 Mechanism, Chemism, and External Purposiveness: Striving and Violence

The trajectory of mechanism, chemism, and teleology is ultimately aimed at the determination of internally purposive activity and form, a determination that brings us from objectivity to life and the Idea. Just as subjectivity develops into objectivity, objectivity develops into a locus of self-determining subjectivity, a "*subject-object*" that is manifest immediately as the Idea of life and self-consciously manifest as the Idea of cognition (WL 673/6:466). In the progressive development of objectivity, Hegel presents the objective reality of the Concept manifest in mechanism, chemism, and external purposiveness as all falling short of the form of self-determination insofar as their respective objects remain fixed in their externality both with respect to themselves and with respect to their processes and relationships with other objects. Throughout his analysis, Hegel refers to the non-self-determining manifestations of objectivity in terms of *striving* (*Streben*) and *violence* (*Gewalt*).

Essentially, *striving* can be understood as a striving toward self-realization, and Hegel presents this process in terms of both a striving for self-unity and a striving for unity with otherness. The process of mechanism, in which mutually indifferent objects enter into external relationships governed by law, is described as a "*striving* towards the center" (WL 641/6:423)—that is, toward a center of gravity;[13] the process of chemism with "objects in tension . . . a relationship that is called their *affinity*" is a striving to sublate "the one-sidedness of its own existence" and a "striving to sublate the one-sidedness of the other object," a reciprocal relation of striving that reaches "*neutrality*" (WL 646–647/6:430–431);[14] in the activities of external purposiveness, Hegel writes that "[p]urpose, therefore, is the subjective Concept as an essential striving and drive to posit itself externally" (WL 657/6:445).[15] In describing these

---

[13] See also WL 642, 644/6:424–425, 428. See the discussion in Kreines (2015, chap. 1, esp. 49–54).
[14] On chemism, see Kreines (2015, chap. 7) and Burbidge (1996).
[15] See also WL 661, 668/6:450–451, 460.

processes in terms of striving, Hegel means to convey their relative *lack* of self-determination in contrast with the activity of internal purposiveness in which the objective reality of the Concept is fully realized. Although it might be tempting to accuse Hegel of unjustified anthropomorphism in his employment of the language of striving, I think there are better interpretive options here. First, given his argument for the priority of teleology over mechanism on the basis that the very distinction between teleological and mechanical processes is first opened up by the actuality of teleological activity,[16] it is clear that Hegel employs the striving language *from the perspective of the activity of the Concept* (this discussion is taking place *within* the Doctrine of the Concept). Second, in speaking metaphorically about lower levels of objectivity—mechanical, chemical, and externally purposive processes—in terms of striving, Hegel is implicitly defending a materialist point, namely that these processes have to be understood such that they *could* develop into internally purposive processes. Rather than unjustified anthropomorphism, striving as a metaphor is a marker for the materialist ambition that we can one day come to fully understand the emergence of living processes from non-living ones, while also continuing to grasp the importance of the life/non-life distinction as opening up any possible system of intelligibility. Although there is some unresolvable messiness here, Hegel is thus trying to hold together two claims that are equally important: first, that from the perspective of the self-determining activity of the Concept, determining the relative lack of self-determining power of lower level processes matters for its own relationship to itself (these lower-level processes are intelligible *as* the processes that they are only when intelligibility as such is opened up by living activity that divides itself from the non-living world); and second, to avoid problematic metaphysical dualisms or supernaturalisms, lower-level processes have to be understood and described such that they could become what ultimately develops from them—namely, life and living activity, as well as the cognitive activity that grows out of life (life and cognition are, after all, material processes). The language of striving is Hegel's (perhaps imperfect, but nonetheless instructive) way of trying to hold these two thoughts together.

These considerations should also be kept in mind with respect to the language of *violence*, and if striving moves toward self-realization and self-individuation, violence is the power that works against them. Hegel's

---

[16] See the discussion in section 4.5, this volume.

characterization of what he means by violence is made most evident in his discussion of the mechanical process: violence is power that is exercised as external, but more specifically, it is the power of an objective universality whose act of power disables, restricts, and even destroys the capacity of an object to "constitute itself as a *subject* in this universal, or make this latter its *predicate*" (WL 639/6:420). Power as violence, developed as an objective relationship, thus has three characteristics. First, it is the power of an objective universality "*against* the object"—that is, it is a power of the genus manifest as non-identical with the object's own individual self-relation (WL 639/6:421). Defined in this way, the determination of this external power appears to function in two ways: (a) in line with Hegel's earlier argument that objective universality simply *is* the genus, the genus or kind to which the object belongs provides the context and necessary condition for the object's processes and relationships by which it is realized; (b) this power of the objective context of the genus can be something external to the object such that the object's individual determinateness does not itself reflect the power of the genus. This non-identity between the external power of the genus and an individual object's determinateness is described in terms of extinction, perishableness, and finitude in general; as Hegel writes, "the fate of the living being is in general the *genus*."[17] Hegel then goes on to specify that more properly speaking, the term "fate" should be reserved only for self-consciousness because it is free, since without the freedom of self-determined action, the power of the genus cannot be determined or experienced as fate. When there is no manifestation of self-determining action, the power of the genus is simply the violence of blind contingency—a contingent, objective context for self-subsistence and external relationships; a contingent, objective context with which the object can neither identify nor be estranged from. Only in the presence of free action can the power of the genus be determined as fateful, as a source of alienation and self-estrangement.

For the second characteristic, Hegel presents the relation of violence in terms of the relation between subject and predicate: violence is the exercise of the external power of the genus that incapacitates the object in its ability to constitute itself as a subject by means of realization through a predicate. The ability of an object to constitute itself as a subject is thus defined, in the first instance, by the objective context provided by the genus; that is, the capacity or incapacity of an object to constitute itself as an individual subject depends

---

[17] For references to the genus in mechanism and chemism, see also WL 641, 646/6:423, 430.

first and foremost on the kind of thing the object is. For mechanical, chemical, and externally purposive objects, the power of the genus is determined essentially as violence insofar as these objects *cannot* constitute themselves as subjects through a predicate due to their very nature as defined by their genus. For example, a rock, qua rock, can be determined through a predicate externally—by means of external impact from other objects and forces (it can be crushed or cracked into pieces) or by means of human definition and conceptualization (*this* rock is igneous and *that one* is sedimentary)—but it cannot determine *itself* through a predicate and constitute itself as a subject by means of its own activity. The power of the object to constitute itself as a subject is necessarily defined in relation to its essential *Gattung*-predicate, a predicate that manifests the power of violence insofar as the object is unable to constitute itself as a subject by means of this very same predicate.

The third characteristic, finally, is that power as violence directs itself against individuality. In specifying that it is only in the presence of the freedom of self-consciousness that the power of the genus can be determined as fate, Hegel writes the following: "Only self-consciousness has fate in the strict sense, because it is *free*, and therefore in the *individuality* of its 'I' it absolutely exists *in and for itself* and can oppose itself to its objective universality and *alienate* itself from it" (WL 639/6:421). Individuality is thus defined as an existence in and for itself that can stand opposed to and be in contradiction with its objective universality or genus, while continuing to manifest the genus's power as identical with its own self-relation.[18] Without the ability to oppose its genus, the ability to be self-alienated with respect to its genus, the object is not, strictly speaking, an individual (it remains a mere particular, a token of its type entirely interchangeable with other tokens of the same type). Individuality is therefore not only the power of the object to constitute itself as a subject through its predicate, but moreover, this power of self-constitution is essentially also the power to oppose, contradict, and transform the genus by means of the genus's own power as manifest in the determinateness of an individual.

The determinations of striving and violence thus convey the power of the genus in relation to the relative power of self-determination manifest in the object, the relative power of the object to constitute itself as an individual, self-determining subject by means of the power of the genus reflected into itself. The activity of the object remains a striving, and the power of the genus

---

[18] See also the discussion in section 5.2.3, this volume.

manifests violence, insofar as the object does not realize the self-determining and self-constituting power of individual subjectivity. It is only at the very end of the "Teleology" chapter, when internally purposive self-determination has been achieved, that Hegel writes of subjective purpose that it "needs no violence," that it is no longer merely "an *ought-to be* and a *striving*" (WL 667, 669/6:458, 461).[19]

6.3 Objective Judgment: Internal Purposiveness and Transition to the Idea

If the relation of violence denotes the externality and non-identity of the power of the genus vis-à-vis the individual's power to constitute itself as a subject, internally purposive self-determination is characterized by the individual's power to constitute itself as a subject *by means* of the power of the genus, a power of the genus that is manifest and actualized in the individual's relation-to-self. At stake in the chapter on "Teleology," then, is how to finally understand the essential activity and reality of the Concept as self-determination. In order to present the objective form of self-determination, Hegel considers two types of activity: externally purposive, instrumental activity (which takes up the overwhelming majority of the chapter); and internally purposive, self-determining activity. It is, of course, in the introductory section of the "Teleology" chapter that Hegel praises Kant's concept of inner purposiveness for opening up the concept of life and the Idea, suggesting that it serves a positive function. Throughout the book, I have argued that this positive function can be understood as a claim for the constitutive (and not merely regulative) role of life for self-consciousness and thought, and more

---

[19] Like the language of striving, one might suspect that Hegel's use of the term "violence" in the context of his discussion of objectivity is overly metaphorical and unjustifiably anthropomorphic. In what sense, after all, can a genus or kind be said to exercise violence, particularly in the case of mechanical, chemical, or externally purposive objects? In using the term "violence," Hegel is surely working backwards from the genus defined with respect to living things; indeed, his example concerning the genus being the fate of the living being suggests that this is the model he has in mind. Although he employs the term "violence" throughout all three chapters, it might be helpful to make the following distinctions on Hegel's behalf: in the case of mechanical, chemical, and externally purposive objects, the "violence" of the genus with respect to the individual objects that belong to it is metaphorical and characterized by an external, indifferent contingency; in the case of self-consciousness and spirit, the power and violence of the genus can be characterized as fate, the cunning of reason, or even the slaughter bench of history; living beings fall somewhere in between, and Hegel writes of living things that they have no fate, *and* that their fate is the genus, depending on the perspective one takes on the living thing qua object.

directly, that Hegel ultimately grounds his entire system of reason on the basis of internally purposive form. Life opens up the space of reasons and defines the space of judgment, making intelligibility as such a problem and possibility. In preparing his transition to the Idea, Hegel frames his discussion of teleology by putting forward two claims that should, by now, be familiar. The first is that internally purposive activity has a certain priority over mechanical, chemical, and externally purposive activity and processes; the second is that internal purposiveness provides a "standard" or "criterion" of truth and is the basis for "*objective judgment*" (WL 651, 656/6:437, 443). As we will see, these two claims are essentially related, but let us briefly take up each in turn.

With respect to the priority claim, it is perhaps helpful to start with what Hegel does *not* mean: internal teleology is not prior in time with respect to the other determinations of objectivity, nor is it prior in the sense of being the cause of the other determinations.[20] The priority in question concerns which determination—specifically, mechanical causality or the causality of internal purposiveness—"possesses truth *in and for itself*" (WL 651/6:437). Thus, if there is a priority of internal teleology, then this priority should be understood in terms of truth, such that the objective form of this activity itself manifests, displays, and actualizes the form of truth. When Hegel defines the Idea ("truth as such") as the unity of subjective Concept and objectivity, or Concept and reality, this arises as a result of the objective determination of internally purposive activity, which suggests that this activity itself provides a standard for truth. Since "purpose is the Concept itself in its existence," this objective standard of truth is, of course, nothing but the Concept itself (WL 652/6:438). The idea that the internal purposiveness of the Concept provides a standard for truth is Hegel's transformation of Kant's all-important claim in the third *Critique* that purposiveness defines the space of judgment, and more specifically, that it is a condition of applying logic to nature. As a standard of truth, we have already seen that the inner purposiveness of the Concept operates in a variety of ways: it provides the standard for

---

[20] DeVries (1991), Yeomans (2012), and Kreines (2015) have all forcefully defended the explanatory priority of teleology in Hegel, arguing that mechanistic explanations presuppose teleological ones. I am largely in agreement with their accounts, and they provide much more detail concerning this question than I will do here, where my aim is simply to explain the connection between Hegel's priority claim and his understanding of objective judgment. In framing the priority of teleology in terms of explanation, it is important to recall Hegel's suggestion in the *Phenomenology* that the satisfaction afforded by explanation is essentially connected to self-consciousness's explanation of the form of its own activity (PhG ¶163/3:133–134).

the articulated unity between universality, particularity, and individuality; it provides a standard for understanding the unity and activity of judgment; it provides a standard for understanding the unity and mediation of syllogism; it provides a standard for understanding the necessary relation between Concept and objective reality; and most important in the context of the "Teleology" chapter, it provides a standard for understanding the activity of self-determination in which a subjective aim, purpose, or goal is realized as an objective existence in the world.

Understanding the sense of priority in question thus immediately brings us to Hegel's second claim that internal purposiveness is the standard or criterion of truth and the basis for judging objectively. As the basis for objective judgment, internal purposiveness is the activity that enables the relation of *realization* between subject and predicate in which an objective existence constitutes *itself* as a subject by means of its essential *Gattung*-predicate. In constituting itself as a subject through a predicate that is an objective universal, the predicate becomes something *for* the subject such that the subject's activity is both in and for itself. This process of objective judging—an act of self-determining, self-constituting, self-realizing subjectivity—is the process by which the object posits itself as a subject, bringing forth the subject of judgment in the broader, more encompassing sense of the subject who judges, the subject of judging activity as such. In the section on the "Idea," Hegel will discuss the two essential manifestations of this activity of objective judging: first, the activity of the living individual—the original judgment of life—in which a living individual constitutes itself as an objectively existing subject in a body, in relation to an environment, and as a manifestation of the power of the species; second, the activity of self-conscious cognition—the logical shape of spirit—in its pursuit of truth (understanding itself and the world through definitions, divisions, and theorems) and goodness (the realization of subjective and objective freedom by means of freely willed action). The notion of objective judgment whose standard is the activity of internal purposiveness completes Hegel's argument from the chapters on "Judgment" and "Syllogism," and in particular, completes the transition from considering the relation between subject and predicate to considering the relation between self-determining subjectivity and objectivity. Hegel writes:

> The Concept, as purpose, is of course an *objective judgment*, in which one determination, the subject, namely, the concrete Concept, is self-determined, while the other is not merely a predicate but external

objectivity. . . . [I]t is the truth that exists in and for itself and judges *ob-jectively*, determining external objectivity absolutely. Thus, the relation of purpose [*Zweckbeziehung*] is more than *judgment*; it is the *syllogism* of the self-sufficient [*selbständigen*] free Concept that unites itself with itself through objectivity. (WL 656/6:443–444)

In an objective judgment, the relation between subject and predicate is determined as the relation between a self-determining subject in relation to its external objectivity such that the subject is self-determined precisely by means of its relationship to an external objectivity that it determines for itself. At the beginning of this process, purpose is determined as "the subjective Concept as an essential striving and drive to posit itself externally" (WL 657/6:445). Earlier in the Subjective Logic (in the "Concept" chapter), Hegel had anticipated this striving to self-posit externally in terms of the outward reference and outward directedness of the Concept.[21] The striving of the subjective Concept to posit itself externally, which Hegel now calls the subjective *purpose*, signals the shift from considering the forms of judgment (explored in the "Judgment" chapter) to considering the objectivity of judgment, an objectivity that can be posited and determined *only* in relation to a judging subject. Judgment is objective, then, on account of two factors: first, judgment is objective in relation to the self-constituting activity of a judging subject who realizes itself by means of an objective universal or essential *Gattung*-predicate, where the power of that predicate is reflected in the subject's relation-to-self; second, judgment is objective on account of the relationship between a judging subject and an external objectivity that it determines "absolutely"—that is, an external objectivity that it determines according to its own internally purposive activity and form. These two features of objective judgment, and the relationship between subjectivity and objectivity that they represent, are the main topics of discussion in the final section of the *Logic* on the "Idea." The identification of internal purposiveness with the standard of truth and the form of objective judgment is thus the culmination of Hegel's argument that purposiveness serves a positive function for philosophy in contrast to the negative function of Kant's *Critique of Pure Reason*. Before turning to a discussion of the "Idea" in the next chapter, I want to return briefly to the question of syllogism and its role in Hegel's understanding of the objectivity of the Concept.

---

[21] See the discussion in section 5.2.1, this volume.

In writing in the earlier passage that objective judgment is the "syllogism of the self-sufficient free Concept," Hegel appears, finally, to be completing his discussion of the subjective Concept in which he presented four forms of judgment but only three forms of syllogism.[22] The missing "syllogism of the Concept," discussed at length in chapter 5, now finally makes an appearance, and Hegel seems to be suggesting that the relation of purposiveness is itself to be understood as the syllogism of the Concept. I now want to consider how this suggestion is compatible with and complementary to the argument I made in chapter 5 regarding the significance of the absence of the syllogism of the Concept from Hegel's earlier account of syllogism. My argument here will be that: (i) the syllogism of the Concept concerns the practical rather than the theoretical shape of reason; and (ii) the self-determining, which is to say the rational status of the actions Hegel has in mind with regard to the contrast between external and internal purposiveness, is likewise not reducible to such actions being the sound conclusions of practical syllogisms.

We can understand Hegel's claim here concerning syllogism in several ways. First, although in the previous passage Hegel states that the relation of purpose is "more than" judgment, it is in fact more accurate to say that the relation of purpose is *both* objective judgment and syllogism at once. This is due not only to the general inseparability of judgment and syllogism, defended in earlier chapters by Hegel, but also more directly, due to the specific way in which the judgment of the Concept—*this* x *constituted so and so is true/good/beautiful*—was articulated such that it already contained within itself a form of syllogistic reasoning. Given that the subjective form of the judgment of the Concept was already articulated as a syllogism, it should be no surprise that the objective and realized judgment of the Concept—one where a subject realizes and determines itself as true, good, or beautiful by reflecting the power of its genus—is likewise an articulated and objective syllogism. However, and as evidenced throughout Hegel's discussion of the Idea in which he continues to refer to the activity of self-determination in terms of judgment (the activity of the judging subject that divides itself from and realizes itself through its objective *Gattung*-predicate and the predicate of external objectivity),[23] it would be a mistake to read Hegel here as suggesting

---

[22] See the discussion in sections 5.2.2 and 5.2.3, this volume.
[23] Most notably but not exclusively in the reference to the original judgment of life, and also in the transition to cognition. See WL 678, 689/6:473, 487; and EL §213.

that syllogism somehow has priority over judgment, or that the latter is reducible to its role in the former.

Second, the purposive relation as a syllogism derives from Hegel's definition of the syllogism of necessity, "in which the mediating element is the
objective nature of the fact [*Sache*]" (WL 590/6:354). We can recall that at
stake in the progression of the syllogism of necessity was the determination
of a mediating element in which the power of the genus was reflected in an
individual so as to constitute an activity of form. Once the mediating element of the syllogism has been determined as self-actualizing activity, Hegel
transitions from subjectivity to objectivity, highlighting that the activity in
question is "*no longer a syllogism* at all" (WL 623/6:399). This suggests that
we can distinguish two senses of the term "syllogism," which are not clearly
demarcated by Hegel himself: the first refers to the subjective, theoretical activity of syllogizing whereby one infers, for example, Gauis's mortality from
the general rule that all humans are mortal; the second refers to the objective,
practical activity of self-realization whereby the internally purposive activity
of a subject is itself the mediating element that brings about a realized, objective end. This second sense of syllogism explains why Hegel refers to the
object as a syllogism throughout the chapters on objectivity: the object is a
syllogism to the degree that it manifests the mediation of self-determining
activity, the mediation of translating conditions into actuality. At the end of
the *Logic*, Hegel will take up the question of how theoretical and practical
syllogizing activities are united, but for now the identification of the purposive relation with syllogism concerns the second sense of syllogism as the
realization of an end mediated by self-determining activity.

This brings us to the third point: the purposive relation is a syllogism in
the sense of being a practical syllogism, whose form is reflected by the three
sections of the chapter on "Teleology": the major premise is an initial subjective purpose or aim ("I want to farm the land"), the minor premise is the
means required to carry out that purpose ("Turning the soil with a plough
is a necessary means to farming the land"), and the conclusion is the action
that employs the means to carry out the initial purpose ("I turn the soil with a
plough in order to farm the land").[24] This example of the practical syllogism

---

[24] Herrmann-Sinai (2016) argues that whereas in the "Teleology" chapter Hegel takes up the practical syllogism, the syllogism of the Concept properly understood only appears in the chapter on
"Cognition" in Hegel's discussion of the Idea of the good. As I noted previously, I do not think there is
a difference between the syllogism of internal purposiveness and the syllogism of the good. See also
the discussion of the practical syllogism in Moyar (2018). Moyar argues that the practical syllogism

is clearly an instance of external purposiveness. We can understand this externality in two ways. First, in external purposiveness, the means, however "honorable" the tool in question, suffers the destiny of being "used up" and "worn away," for it is in the very nature of being a mere means to be used in the service of an external end (WL 663, 666/6:453, 457).[25] This recalls the relation of violence discussed earlier: the means, governed by the relation of external purposiveness, is unable to function as self-determining and is always subsumed by the external end that it serves. It is by definition a *mere* means, and not an end in itself.[26] Second, in a relation of external purposiveness, the means is used to realize an end that is itself simply another means; the ends of external purposiveness "are only relative ends, or essentially nothing but means" (WL 666/6:457). In ploughing the soil to farm the land, farming the land is itself a means in service to the end of feeding the population. These two senses of externality give us a clue as to how Hegel conceives of internally purposive action: in internally purposive action, the means is an end in itself such that it reflects the totality and unity of the syllogism within itself as an objective judgment. Consider the following example:

> I am your friend.
> Friends visit their friends in the hospital.
> I visit you in the hospital.

In this case, the act of visiting a friend in the hospital is not a mere means to being a good friend; rather, the act of visiting a friend in the hospital expresses and is itself a realization of the end of friendship, such that means and ends are identical. To treat visiting your friend as a mere means (to friendship, to winning favors that your friend is in a position to give, to appear virtuous to others, to be able to hold it over your friend later on) would not only reveal a complete misunderstanding of what friendship is but it would also render the action externally purposive (not to mention subject to disapprobation).

---

is the syllogism of the Concept, and here I argue that while there is a sense in which this is correct, Hegel continues to argue that the content of judgment is not exhausted by its role in syllogisms.

[25] See Hegel's discussion of how the plough is more "honorable" than the purposes it serves, at WL 663/6:453.

[26] Hegel compares external purposiveness to mechanical and chemical relations, writing: "Their process in this relation is none other than the mechanical or chemical one; in this objective externality the previous relationships emerge but under the dominance [*Herrschaft*] of the end ... [this] may be regarded as *violence*" (WL 662–663/6:452).

If we formulate this syllogism as a *subjective* judgment of the Concept, we could say the following: "The act of visiting a friend in the hospital is an act of good friendship." As an *objective* judgment of the Concept, we would say this: "Visiting a friend in the hospital is a *realization* of good friendship." In the second, the subject is realized through the predicate, or the subject posits and individuates itself in external objectivity as an end in itself. In chapter 5, I argued that the subjective judgment of the Concept is best understood as a reflective judgment: the goodness of the act of visiting my friend is not deduced from a general set of rules concerning friendship; rather, the goodness of the act is an exemplification of friendship where the act can only show up as exemplary given the context of the genus "friendship." Note, of course, that this does not mean that the concept of friendship is rationally opaque; we can articulate the concept of friendship quite vividly, and do so, for example, in both philosophy (think: Aristotle) and art (think: Elena Ferrante's *Neapolitan Quartet*) (just as critics and art historians write tomes expressing in detail the essence of modernist architecture, which allow us to understand what makes particular houses exemplary, helping us to improve our judgment). Nonetheless, the relation between subject and predicate in the subjective judgment of the Concept is not simply deduced from the genus, even while the genus provides the necessary context of predication and, in particular, is the absolute context for the ascription of normative predicates.

In an objective judgment of the Concept, the genus is the necessary context of *action*: the subject constitutes itself and is realized by reflecting the power of the genus in external objectivity. Our example thus looks like this: visiting a friend in the hospital is an act that expresses the power of friendship in external objectivity, constituting the subject as an exemplary friend through the self-determining activity of the subject. The act of visiting your friend realizes good friendship, *not* because it is deduced from the practical syllogism, but because it is an act of self-determination, an act of self-determination that can only take place by reflecting the power of an objective universality or genus—in this case, the rational, ethical institution of friendship, which itself exists within the more encompassing objective universality of ethical life (*Sittlichkeit*). It is particularly important that the genus of friendship in the syllogism does not operate primarily or exclusively as a set of rules from which my good action is necessarily deduced: in the case of subjective judgments of the Concept, this followed from the deductive impotence of the genus; in the case of objective judgments of the Concept, the operation of the genus exclusively and primarily as a fixed set of rules or laws that apply with necessity incapacitates the self-determining activity of an individual subject, who can be self-determining only insofar as she can alienate herself from the genus by means of the power of the genus itself. When we are not yet fully self-determining with respect to the institution of friendship as children (or as adults for that matter), we may be taught a set of rules by which it operates (friends are loyal, sympathetic, share confidences, have shared interests, etc.). If a friendship is new or goes stale, the rules can still be mechanically applied by rote, and sometimes with reluctance such that the rules appear as an imposition on my freedom ("I *have* to attend my friend's baby shower"). When friendship enables my self-determination and is a realization of internal purposiveness, being an exemplary friend is an act of self-determination such that I can rationally reflect upon the institution of friendship while inhabiting it wholeheartedly in a way that reflects my individuality at the same time.[27] In such instances of self-determination, this activity, while reflecting the practical syllogism, also renders the practical syllogism superfluous. More precisely, self-determining, internally purposive activity cannot be reduced to being the conclusion of a sound practical syllogism but is irreducibly an objective judgment of the Concept.[28]

---

[27] This is what Neuhouser (2000) and Honneth (2014) call "social freedom."

[28] In the *Philosophy of Right*, this thought is reflected in Hegel's discussion of the inelimable role of the judge, whose role consists in exercising the capacity of reflective judgment. Hegel writes: "Collisions arise in the application of the law, where the understanding of the judge has its place; this is entirely necessary, for the implementation of the law would otherwise be a completely mechanical process" (PR §211Z). My argument here owes much to McDowell (1998a, 1998c). Echoing Aristotle, McDowell writes: "Action that displays the ethical character of its agent does so by virtue of the purposiveness that is operative in it" (1998a, 23); and, "As Aristotle consistently says, the best generalizations about how one should live hold only for the most part" (1998c, 58). Key to McDowell's critique of the rule and cases model of ethical deliberation and action is the argument that what plays the role of the major premise in the practical syllogism is "the virtuous person's conception of the sort of life a human being should lead," and that this conception of how to live is not "codifiable in universal principles" (1998c, 66–67). In the foregoing example, the claim would be that the conception of ethical life that I inhabit in which friendship plays an essential role, is not the kind of thing that can be finally codifiable in universal principles (a set of rules concerning friendship nested within a wider set of rules governing all the other institutions of ethical life), and hence, that one cannot simply deduce the right thing to do in a particular case from a set of articulated rules. If friendship operated on a rule and case model, acts of friendship would be, as Hegel writes, "a completely mechanical process." Moyar (2011, 37–38) argues against reading the practical syllogism as a "mechanical affair," and he also argues that the disjunctive syllogism plays an important role in ethical deliberation (138–142). For a reading that argues against associating Hegel with McDowell's uncodifiability thesis, see Novakovic (2017, 56–64). While I am very sympathetic with her account of principled habits and her reading of Hegel, my difference from Novakovic concerns the reading of McDowell on the meaning of "uncodifiability." The uncodifiability of ethical life does not mean that codified laws and principles, along with many other explicitly articulated rules, do not play an absolutely essential role in the cultivation, sustaining, critique, and refinement of ethical habits. Hegel undoubtedly affirms the importance of such laws and principles, but simply insists on their non-sufficiency (they are necessary but not sufficient), thereby reserving an irreducible role for reflective judgment and the non-codifiable ethical habituation connected with its operation and ongoing refinement.

To the question of whether or not the practical syllogism is the syllogism of the Concept, then, the answer is both yes and no. The practical syllogism is the syllogism of the Concept insofar as it expresses the form of purposiveness as rational, self-determined action. The Concept is objective because it is an activity of self-realization, an activity of self-realization that is enabled by the power of an objective universality in relation to an external world. The form of this activity reflects the unity of the practical syllogism, and all self-determined action can in principle be explicitly articulated as a practical syllogism. However, the objectivity of the Concept cannot be reduced to the soundness and unity of the practical syllogism, but is irreducibly a self-determining act of objective judgment by which a subject posits itself externally in objective reality. The immediate, original manifestation of this self-determining activity is what Hegel calls the original judgment of life, an original judgment that is at once the immediate manifestation of the Idea.

7

Life as the Immediate Idea

7.1 The Idea

A collection of Hegel's classic definitions of the Idea runs as follows: the unity of subjective Concept and objectivity; the unity of Concept and reality; the objective realization of the Concept; the adequate Concept and truth as such; the unconditioned; and finally, reason as such and the rational.[1] In the introduction to the section on the "Idea," Hegel emphasizes that the Idea is something *actual*, that the unity of the Idea is not a goal or "beyond" toward which we strive, but a manifest, objective reality with a determinate existence; and more strikingly, that things are actual only by possessing and expressing the Idea. To clarify the transition from "Teleology" to the "Idea," Hegel offers the following as a more precise characterization of his final topic of discussion in the *Logic*, a characterization that makes clear how internal purposiveness opens up the concept of life and the Idea:

> This identity [of the Idea] has therefore rightly been defined as the *subject-object*, for it is as well the formal or subjective Concept as it is the object as such. But this must be understood more precisely. The Concept, inasmuch as it has truly attained its reality, is the absolute judgment whose *subject* distinguishes itself as self-relating negative unity from its objectivity and is the latter's being-in-and-for-itself; but it refers to it essentially through itself and is, therefore, *an end-in-itself* [Selbstzweck] and *drive* [Trieb]. For this very reason, however, the subject does not possess objectivity immediately in it (it would then be only the totality of the object as such, a totality lost in the objectivity) but objectivity is the realization of purpose [*die Realisation des Zwecks*]—an objectivity *posited* [gesetzt] by virtue of the activity of the

---

[1] In the preface of the *Phenomenology*, Hegel had already defined the Idea in terms of concrete universality and species or kind. He writes: "Anaxagoras first took cognizance of *Nous* as the essence. Those who succeeded him grasped the nature of existence more determinately as *Eidos* or *Idea*, which is to say as *determinate universality*, as a *kind* (Art). The term, '*kind*,' perhaps seems too ordinary and too petty for the ideas which are all the rage nowadays, such as beauty, holiness, and the eternal. However, Idea means neither more nor less than kind or species" (PhG ¶55/3:54).

Hegel's Concept of Life. Karen Ng, Oxford University Press (2020) © Oxford University Press 2020.
DOI: 10.1093/oso/9780190947613.001.0001

purpose [*die Tätigkeit des Zwecks*], one which, as *positedness* [Gesetztsein], has its substance and its form only as permeated by its subject. (WL 673–674/6:466–467)

In this passage, Hegel combines a variety of terms and frameworks that I have discussed at length in this book in order to arrive at the culminating characterization of the Idea. First, Hegel returns here to his earlier terminology of "the *subject-object*," claiming that the unity and identity at stake in the Idea finds its correct definition with this term.[2] In the *Differenzschrift*, discussed in chapter 3, Hegel had distinguished between the *subjective* subject-object and the *objective* subject-object in order to articulate the *speculative identity* of self-consciousness and living nature as absolute. That both sides are designated as subject-object means the following: on the side of the subject, the self-positing, self-relating activity of the I is essentially life-activity that is *for-itself* and self-aware, such that self-consciousness's objective modes of knowing and acting are thoroughly permeated and mediated by life; on the side of the object, living nature displays the form and activity of self-production and inner purposiveness *in-itself*, without the reflexive mediation of thought. Although much of the *Differenzschrift* takes up Schelling's ideas from the same period, we can now see that Hegel unequivocally and consistently endorses the fundamental insight of that text with respect to the absolute, essential relation between self-consciousness and life. In the context of the *Science of Logic*, the speculative identity of subjective and objective subject-objects is reproduced at a variety of levels and finds its ultimate result and foundation in the Idea. First, the *Logic* as a whole is divided into the Objective Logic and Subjective Logic; second, the Subjective Logic itself contains sections on subjectivity and objectivity, the activities of which are determined largely in relation to the unity and power of the genus; third, the unity and relation of subjectivity and objectivity in the Subjective Logic is grounded in the Idea, which is itself divided into the Idea as life (the objective subject-object) and the Idea as self-conscious cognition (the subjective subject-object). In developing this notion of the subject-object at multiple, overlapping levels, and concluding the *Logic* with a presentation of the dialectic between life and cognition, the Idea completes an argument that Hegel began in outline in the *Differenzschrift*, thereby providing his system with an absolute, scientific method.

---

[2] See also EL §214.

Second, Hegel presents the necessary relation between subject and object expressed in the Idea in terms of *purposive activity*. Although this fundamental insight has Fichtean roots, Fichte's conception of sheer activity remains relatively opaque, which creates an opening that is seized upon by Hegel. Activity in general is defined by Hegel as the translation of a totality of conditions into actuality. In the "Actuality" section of the Objective Logic, discussed in chapter 4, this process of translation was presented as potentially expressive of a variety of modalities, from contingency, to real possibility, to necessity. Self-determined activity expresses a *reciprocity* between conditions and actualized effects such that actuality is the realized result of a totality of conditions unified and organized according to a purpose. With the internalization of reciprocal causality into a locus of self-determining power that can be characterized as subjectivity, Hegel arrives at the determination of the Concept, whose self-relation displays the reciprocity of being a cause and effect of itself by producing itself as universal, particular, and individual all at once. Already in the introduction to the Subjective Logic, Hegel had suggested that this internalized locus of self-determining power has a double manifestation: as immediate and unconscious in living subjectivity; and as self-aware and thinking in self-conscious subjectivity. In the foregoing passage, this self-determining power is characterized as an end-in-itself and an essential drive to posit subjective purposes and aims as objective reality. This process of actualization whereby objectivity is realized takes place by means of the activity of the subject, such that objectivity is posited as shaped and permeated by the purposes of the subject. Purposive activity is the realization of the reciprocity between subject and object, a reciprocity that is, in turn, as Hegel will outline in the Idea of cognition, the condition for the realization of truth and goodness.

Third and finally, Hegel calls the self-realizing, self-determining activity of the Concept—the *adequate* Idea—"the absolute judgment."[3] Throughout chapters 5 and 6, I argued that Hegel's argumentative strategy in the Subjective Logic is best understood in terms of a critique of judgment, a framework inherited from Kant's third *Critique* and Hölderlin, with the aim of demonstrating the positive function of inner purposiveness as the ground for the activities of reason. In the first section of the Subjective Logic, Hegel presented the forms of the subjective Concept with respect to their abilities to express the unity of universality, particularity, and

---

[3] On the Idea as judgment, see also EL §§213–214.

individuality in terms of the unity of subject and predicate in judgments, and the unity of premises and conclusion in syllogisms. Judgment, I argued, is understood by Hegel as an act of original division, or *ursprüngliche Teilung*: in subjective judgment, this division is more narrowly understood as the distinction and relation between subject and predicate; in objective, and now, "absolute," judgment, this division is more broadly understood as a self-constituting act of the judging subject whereby it is realized as an individual of a genus in distinction from and in relation to external objectivity. A further consideration also unites these two senses of judgment: in subjective judgment, the genus of the subject-term provides the necessary context of predication and governs the ascription of normative, evaluative predicates (true, good, beautiful) in which the relation between subject and predicate is understood in terms of exemplarity; in objective, absolute judgment, the genus of the judging subject provides the necessary context of self-realizing, self-individuating activity such that the realization of subjective purposes can be determined as objectively true or good—the objective realization of exemplarity. In presenting the unity and activity of the Idea in terms of "absolute judgment," Hegel will now turn to the absolute ground of all judging activities by taking up the "original judgment of life," an original judgment that, importantly, has a double manifestation. First, the original judgment of life is life-activity *in-itself* (*Lebensformtätigkeit* in-itself), the form of activity of the realization of subjective ends as objective *in general*. Second, the original judgment of life is an act of self-division by which life-activity becomes *for-itself* or "*cognition* in general," a judgment of life in which "the Idea is doubled" (WL 689/6:487). I will discuss this doubling of the Idea in more detail, but for now it is important to note that Hegel refers to *both* life and cognition as a *judgment of life*. That is, the doubling at stake in the Idea is life that is *in-itself* and life that is *for-itself*, unconscious life and self-conscious life, rather than a distinction between two categorically distinct determinations. This way of understanding the doubling of the Idea not only is consistent with Hegel's other treatments of the general relation between life and self-consciousness, but, and more specifically within the context of the arguments from the *Logic*, it also follows from his understanding of the process of actualization in which the relation between a totality of conditions and its realized actuality is "not a *transition* but *a joining with itself* [*nicht ein* Übergehen, *sondern* ein Zusammengehen mit sich selbst]" (SL 484/6:210).[4] The doubling of the original judgment of life in Hegel's discussion of the Idea reflects this process of self-actualization.

7.2 Two Interpretive Claims: Ground and Doubling

In this chapter and chapter 8, I will discuss the concluding chapters of the *Science of Logic* against the background of two interpretive claims. The first is that the contents of the section on the "Idea" have a different status from the other thought-determinations taken up in the *Logic* thus far: life, cognition, and the absolute Idea are not to be treated as simply further thought-determinations generated by thought thinking itself, on a par with the other categories of the *Logic*. Rather, and continuing the argument I made in chapter 5 in which I claimed that what Hegel calls the original judgment of life functions as a ground, the determination of the Idea should be understood as the ground of the thought-determinations of the *Logic* as a whole and, moreover, as the ground and method of Hegel's entire philosophical system. There is ample textual evidence suggesting that Hegel intends for the Idea to serve the function of grounding the *Logic* as a whole: insofar as the subject matter of logic (and philosophy) is "*truth* itself [Wahrheit *selbst*]," and the Idea is the "objectively *true*, or the *true as such*," it is clear that Hegel means to present the Idea as the answer to the question of the nature of truth (WL 507, 670/6:244, 462). More emphatically, Hegel writes: "If anything has truth, it possesses it through its Idea, or, *something possesses truth only insofar as it is Idea*" (WL 670/6:462). In another well-known passage, Hegel claims that the Concept is the absolute foundation (*Grundlage*) that has *made itself* the foundation, which suggests that as the *realized Concept*, the foundation in question is again the Idea (WL 508/6:245). The status of the Idea as a ground is also evident in the introductions to the *Philosophy of Nature* and the *Philosophy of Mind*, which take up the manifestations or actualizations of the Idea in the domains of nature and spirit, respectively. There is thus ample textual evidence that the Idea, and specifically the chapters in the *Logic* that take up this determination, has a different status from the other contents of that book, and more directly, that Hegel means for the Idea to fulfill the

---

[4] See the discussion of this passage in chapter 4, this volume.

function of grounding his philosophical system, providing it with a scientific, absolute method.

Apart from the textual evidence, there are broader philosophical considerations that provide good reasons for interpreting Hegel's Idea along the lines of ground. In addition to the fact that the problem of grounding is a general preoccupation of post-Kantian philosophy, the progression of the *Science of Logic* itself raises a puzzle that has yet to be addressed, and whose solution can likewise be found in the Idea. Thus far, every thought-determination of the *Logic* has revealed itself to be insufficient in some way; at the most general level, this insufficiency can be understood in terms of the failure of particular categories to adequately capture what is absolute.[5] Very often in Hegel, these failures are couched in terms of one-sidedness, fixed dualisms, abstractions, or internal inconsistencies, and as the *Logic* progresses, subsequent thought-determinations are enlisted to resolve the insufficiencies of earlier ones (for example, becoming resolves the one-sided determinations of being and nothing; actuality resolves the various one-sided determinations of essence and appearance). Usually, the way of addressing the insufficiency of particular categories is to refer to Hegel's *holistic* understanding of the *Logic* in which all the categories are taken to constitute a systematic whole such that each single category, while insufficient on its own, finds its truth only relation to the whole. However, although holism can guarantee the internal coherence of the system of categories, holism cannot guarantee that the *whole itself* is non-arbitrary and objective. Even if the *Logic* is non-arbitrary in its progression and displays complete internal coherence, there could be other, equally internally coherent sets of categories, and holism alone would not allow us to decide between these various internally coherent sets. In serving the function of grounding, the Idea allows Hegel to demonstrate that the system of thought-determinations presented in the *Logic* is the necessary and objective set of categories for self-conscious life. That is, it is only insofar as the thought-determinations are grounded in the Idea that they gain their legitimacy, authority, and objectivity.

The second interpretive claim I will defend with respect to the concluding section of the *Logic* concerns what Hegel calls the "doubling" or "duplication" of the Idea, a doubling in which the Idea is manifest as *immediate* in life

---

[5] On the progression of the *Logic* in terms of definitions of the absolute (along with some reservations concerning the abstractions of various attempts at definition), see WL 51–52/5:74; EL §85; and EL §86Z. Hegel also writes at EL §213: "The definition *of the absolute* as the Idea is now itself absolute. All definitions given previously return into this one."

and as *thought, self-consciousness,* and *spirit* in cognition. Contrary to most interpretations in which the former is taken to be superseded and overcome without remainder by the latter, I will argue that this doubling of the Idea is Hegel's attempt to replace Kant's doctrine of the two stems of knowledge, where *life* and *cognition* take the place of *intuitions* and *concepts*. As two entirely heterogeneous stems,[6] finding a solution to the problem of combining intuitions and concepts takes up a large part of the first *Critique*, and ultimately, as I argued in chapter 2, the broader problem of judgment leads Kant to seek a solution in the principle of purposiveness in the third *Critique*. To understand how life and cognition qua Idea come to replace pure intuitions and concepts, we can turn briefly to Kant's canonical statements concerning these two stems:

> [T]here are two stems of human cognition, which may perhaps arise from a common but to us unknown root, namely sensibility and understanding, through the first of which objects are given to us, but through the second of which they are thought. (A15/B29)

> Objects are therefore given to us by means of sensibility, and it alone affords us intuitions; but they are *thought* through the understanding, and from it arise concepts. (A19/B33)

> Thoughts without content are empty, intuitions without concepts are blind.... Only from their unification can cognition arise. (A51–52/B75–76)

Famously, Hegel not only generally rejects Kant's dualistic approach to intuitions and concepts as entirely heterogeneous but, more specifically, consistently rejects Kant's theory in which sensible intuitions appearing under the a priori forms of space and time provide the content for thought. Instead, Hegel (and the idealists) turn to exploring what Kant, in the first passage, calls a "common root," which is the absolute, original ground of the unity of heterogeneous elements. In chapter 3, I considered some of the ways in which Fichte and Schelling conceived of this absolute unity and identity, and

---

[6] Kant writes in the Schematism chapter: "Now pure concepts of the understanding, however, in comparison with empirical (indeed in general sensible) intuitions, are entirely heterogeneous, and can never be encountered in any intuition.... Now it is clear that there must be a third thing, which must stand in homogeneity with the category on the one hand and the appearance on the other, and makes possible the application of the former to the latter" (A137–A138/B176–B177).

Hegel likewise has proposed various candidates for this common root using Kant's own terminology in his earlier work, including transcendental imagination, intuitive understanding, the original synthetic unity of apperception, and reason.[7] The Idea represents Hegel's mature and fully developed position with respect to this "common root," becoming the primary term of art and framework for the final presentation of his philosophical system. An important passage from *Faith and Knowledge* sums up Hegel's approach with respect to Kant's distinction between intuitions and concepts, and also provides the context for understanding Hegel's mature position:

> Reason is nothing else but the identity of heterogeneous elements of this kind . . . in the deduction of the categories. . . . [T]he original synthetic unity of apperception is recognized also as the principle of figurative synthesis, i.e., of the forms of intuition; space and time are themselves conceived as synthetic unities, and spontaneity, the absolute synthetic activity of the productive imagination, is conceived as the principle of the very sensibility which was previously characterized only as receptivity. This original synthetic unity must be conceived, not as produced out of opposites, but as a truly necessary, absolute, original identity of opposites. As such, it is the principle both of productive imagination, which is the unity that is blind, i.e., immersed in the difference and not detaching itself from it; and of the understanding, which is the unity that posits the difference as identical but distinguishes itself from the different. This shows that the Kantian forms of intuition and the forms of thought cannot be kept apart at all as the particular, isolated faculties which they are usually represented as. One and the same synthetic unity—we have just now determined what this means here—is the principle of intuition and of the understanding. The understanding is only the higher potency; in it the identity which in intuition is totally immersed in the manifold, simultaneously posits itself against the manifold, and constitutes itself within itself as universality, which is what makes it the higher potency. (GW 69–70/2:304–305)

In this admittedly dense passage, Hegel claims, on the basis of the Kantian letter itself, that the unity of the manifold of intuition and the unity of the understanding as the faculty of judgment originate from "one and the same synthetic unity"—namely, the original synthetic unity of apperception. The

---

[7] See also the section on transcendental intuition in DS 109–111/2:41–43.

key for Hegel appears to lie in Kant's suggestion in the B-Deduction that the forms of intuition are themselves already synthetic unities that are the result of spontaneity, and not simply attributable to a heterogeneous faculty of receptivity as Kant had suggested in the Transcendental Aesthetic.[8] The suggestion is that intuitions themselves, rather than constituting a separate contribution, are at bottom always already conceptually mediated by means of one and the same act of original synthetic unification.[9] This means that there is indeed a common root that is the ground of unity for both intuition and the understanding, which entails that the two stems are *not* in fact heterogeneous, as Kant (generally, with some noted exceptions) takes them to be. From this passage, it is usually inferred that Hegel therefore does away with an intuition theory altogether and concentrates instead on a theory of thought's autonomous self-determination, of which the *Science of Logic* is the flagship. However, contrary to this assumption, I will argue that this passage contains the clues to a different solution to the problem of the heterogeneity of Kant's two stems, a solution that hinges on Hegel's insistence on the "doubling" of the Idea.

The first thing to notice is that Hegel, in sourcing the unity of intuition and the unity of the understanding to the same root, nonetheless continues to discuss them as *two kinds of unities* that, despite their common principle, nonetheless have different descriptions. Two differences in their respective descriptions are of particular note. First, Hegel describes the unity of intuition, a result of the productive imagination, as "blind," "immersed in difference and not detaching itself from it." The unity of the understanding is "the unity that posits the difference as identical but distinguishes itself from the different." This clearly echoes Hegel's characterization of the unity and division of life as blind and unreflective, in contrast with the unity and division of cognition as self-consciously posited. The key here is that there remain two kinds of unity at stake that, in their identity and difference, cannot be reduced to one. Hegel is thus describing the two unities in terms of his own speculative identity thesis, which should not be surprising given that the

---

[8] In connection with Kant's discussion of figurative synthesis in the B-Deduction, Pippin (1989, 30–31) makes the footnote at B160 the key for his reading of Hegel's idealism.

[9] Another important passage in this regard appears in §10: "The same function that gives unity to the different representations *in a judgment* also gives unity to the mere synthesis of different representations *in an intuition*, which, expressed generally, is called the pure concept of the understanding" (A79/B105). See McDowell's (2009) discussion of this passage in connection with a reading of Sellars.

Differenzschrift and *Faith and Knowledge* were published only a year apart, and both in the journal co-edited by Hegel and Schelling.

Second, Hegel describes the understanding as the "higher potency" in contrast with lower potency of intuition. The understanding constitutes itself as the higher potency by positing itself against the blind unity of the manifold, and in so doing, attains to a universality within itself. The language of potencies is adopted from Schelling, but Hegel's own, developed approach to the process of actualization proceeding from real possibilities is more instructive here. In describing the two unities in terms of higher and lower potencies, we can interpret Hegel as suggesting that the higher potency (the unity of the understanding) is an *actualization* of the lower potency (the unity of intuition). The same identity, which in intuition is engulfed in the manifold, is, in the understanding, self-actualized in opposition to the manifold and constitutes itself as universal. Put somewhat differently, the constitution of the higher potency is the process by which unity and identity *in-itself* becomes unity and identity *for-itself*. What all this suggests is that although Hegel indeed affirms that intuitions always already constitute a synthetic unity produced by spontaneity, he nonetheless continues to differentiate between two irreducible modes of unity: one that is blind, immediate, and engulfed; and one that is self-posited in opposition to the former, constituting a unity for-itself. Most importantly, the higher potency of the understanding can only constitute and actualize itself *as* the higher potency in opposition and relation to the lower potency of intuition.[10]

Hegel's dismissive remarks concerning Kant's intuition theory thus need careful reconsideration. Although it is the case that Hegel rejects the Kantian language of sensible intuition and understanding, consistently speaking pejoratively of these terms and the view they represent, what Hegel does *not* reject is the necessary and reciprocal relationship between two stems of knowing in which some element that is manifest as *immediate* is posited in opposition and relation to self-conscious thought. Moreover, self-conscious thought constitutes itself as such through this act of opposing and relating, and is a higher potency or actualization of an immediacy that contains the potential within itself to realize that higher potency. What Hegel objects to with respect to Kant's intuition theory is thus the following: (1) that intuitions and

---

[10] See GW 73–74/2:309, where Hegel writes, "Thus the in-itself was established in the potency of imagination." In the same discussion, he also speaks of the "duplicity [*Duplizität*] of this potency," which in Kant remains "relative" and "fixed" in opposition.

concepts are heterogeneous; (2) that what is immediately given to thought can be isolated through a faculty of *pure* receptivity, such as sensibility in which no activity or spontaneity is present; (3) that what is immediately given to thought can be given without any immediate unity or organization, that what is immediately given lacks *any* intrinsic unity or organization at all; and (4) that the appropriate register for a theory of *sensible* intuition is the psychology of the human mind, and not a transcendental doctrine of elements providing the a priori conditions for knowledge.[11] The doubling of the Idea as life and cognition avoids the heterogeneity of Kant's two stems, while allowing them to fulfill similar functions. Life and cognition are not heterogeneous insofar as they are both realizations of the unity of Concept and objectivity; life is that unity as "blind . . . immersed in difference and not detaching itself from it," whereas cognition "is the unity the posits the difference as identical but distinguishes itself from the different." However, they remain two distinct modes of unity and division that cannot be reduced to one in the production of knowledge and truth, for cognition is actualized only insofar as it stands in opposition and relation to the immediacy of life. As the immediate Idea, or the "blind" unity and division of Concept and objectivity, life in the *Logic* therefore serves a similar function as the synthetic unity of the forms of intuition, "which [allow] the manifold of appearance to be ordered in certain relations" (A20/B34). The logical form of life is the logical form of an intuition, the a priori synthetic unity—the original synthetic a priori judgment—that is the condition of anything's being an object of thought at all.[12] Although it would be misleading to try to map all of Hegel's terminology and framework directly onto its potential Kantian counterparts, it would perhaps be more accurate to say that the logical form of activity of life (*Lebensformtätigkeit*) is the *schema* of reality in which Concept and objectivity are an immediate unity. In tying together both intuition and schema, the logical form of life is at once what enables objects to be immediately given and present to subjects, *and* what immediately provides objectivity with a determinate shape and form in accordance with the life-form or *Gattung*-concept of the subject. The three moments of the chapter on "Life" spell out this trajectory: the corporeality of the living individual is the power of inner sense; the externality of the life-process is the power of outer sense; and the *Gattung* or life-form of the judging subject is the objective determinateness

---

[11] See PG §§446–450.
[12] I borrow the phrase, "the logical form of an intuition," from McDowell (2009, esp. 30–35).

of the first two moments, providing the context for the realization of those powers in accordance with the unity of the Concept. Hegel's reference to the productive imagination in the earlier passage is also particularly important in this regard:[13] insofar as the productive imagination is the source of the figurative synthesis of the manifold of intuition (B151–152) *and* the source of the schemata of the pure concepts of the understanding by which concepts attain their *"significance"* (A146/B185), Hegel appears to be claiming that the blind synthetic unity of intuition is always already unified under schematized concepts—that is, that it is always already unified by the form of activity of life. Life in the *Logic* functions as the logical form of the blind unity that in *Faith and Knowledge* Hegel had attributed to the productive imagination, functioning as the relevant immediacy or "lower potency" out of which self-conscious cognition is realized.[14] In providing the schema of reality in which Concept and objectivity are immediately manifest in their unity and division, the Idea of life replaces Kant's theory of intuitions and offers an alternative account of the "two stems" of knowledge that avoids the problem of heterogeneity, while nonetheless providing content and constraint for thought.[15]

---

[13] "The main point is that productive imagination is a truly speculative Idea" (GW 71/2:306).

[14] See PN §357A, where Hegel refers to the Idea of life as an "inner unconscious creative principle." In the third *Critique*, Kant describes the power of productive imagination as "the *free lawfulness* of the imagination . . . this power . . . [is] productive and spontaneous . . . in harmony with the *understanding's lawfulness* in general" (KU 5:240–241). Hegel's mature position which ascribes to life the power of the productive imagination thus also finds some precedent in Kant, since the free play of the imagination and the understanding in judgments of taste are guided by the principle of purposiveness. See also Wretzel's (2018) discussion of organic imagination.

[15] I follow Michael Pendlebury here in thinking of the power of schematism as primitive synthesizing "capacities, dispositions, and processes," or as primitive synthesizing processes which involve "grouping-dispositions" that allow us to immediately place what is immediately present to us into a certain "similarity-class" or kind (1995, 786, 785). Kant writes: "We will call this formal and pure condition of the sensibility, to which the use of the concept of the understanding is restricted, the schema of this concept of the understanding, and we will call the procedure of the understanding with these schemata the *schematism* of the pure understanding. The schema is in itself always only a product of the imagination" (A140/B179). Schelling writes in his *New Deduction of Natural Right* that life is the "schema" of freedom: "Thus it must unite in itself both autonomy and heteronomy. The name of this causality is *life*. Life is the autonomy in the phenomenon; it is the schema of freedom, insofar as it reveals itself in nature. This is why, of necessity, I become a *living* being" (1980, §§8–9). W. H. Walsh has also argued that organic form can provide an alternative to Kant's understanding of schematism in terms of time, a reading that appears to be in line with Schelling's analysis of the role of the organism in allowing consciousness to determine itself as active in the temporal succession of presentations. Walsh writes:

> Even if [one is] sympathetic to the idea of schematism as such . . . [one] may well wonder whether alternative methods of schematizing could not be come by . . . to give real body to it we need to know what an alternative set of schemata would be like . . . [for example] if we considered the possibility of making sense of the categories in organic as opposed to mechanical terms. Elements in an organic complex would here take the place of elements in a temporal situation. Substance might be interpreted in terms of growth and form as opposed to what underlies mechanical change, and causality be thought of in terms of

In the next two sections (7.3 and 7.4), I defend this thesis of doubling by providing a detailed account of Hegel's concept of life in the *Logic*. The key to understanding this "scandalous" chapter lies not only in the details of its contents, which find similar expression in other parts of Hegel's system,[16] but more importantly in understanding the specific *status* and *function* that Hegel is attributing to life in the logical context. With respect to the status of life in the *Logic*, I argue that life as the immediate Idea is the a priori form of activity (*Formtätigkeit*) in which the unity and division of Concept and objectivity are immediately manifest. In referring to life as "original judgment," I argue that the function of the logical concept of life is to replace the synthetic unity of intuition as the "lower potency" out of which the "higher potency" of self-conscious cognition is realized. The form of activity of life thus provides an immediate schema of reality that at once realizes and constrains the activities of cognition, providing the condition for their self-actualization. Once Hegel's logical concept of life is in view, chapter 8 will complete my argument for the two interpretive claims outlined in this section by turning, first, to a discussion of theoretical and practical cognition and, finally, to absolute method as the dialectic between life and cognition.

7.3 The Immediate Idea: The Original Judgment of Life

Hegel opens the chapter on "Life" somewhat defensively, suggesting that it will appear to most as if he has entered discussion of "a subject matter so concrete, and if you will so real, that in dealing with it one may seem to have overstepped the domain of logic as it is commonly conceived" (WL 676/ 6:469). Hegel's first line of defense is to distinguish his discussion of *logical* life as "pure Idea" from discussions of *natural* life in the philosophy of nature, and from discussions of life in connection with *spirit*, both of which are more familiar domains in which the determinacy of life has an obvious place (WL 677/6:470–471). In distinguishing logical life from natural and

---

purpose and function. If such a set of ideas could be worked out in detail, we should find ourselves with an alternative account of the presuppositions of experience, an alternative empirical use for the categories and thus in effect an alternative metaphysics. (1957, 105–106)

[16] Most notably, in the account of the organism in the *Philosophy of Nature*, and also in Chapter IV of the *Phenomenology*.

spiritual life, Hegel stresses that logical life is free from all presuppositions of "external actuality" (WL 677/6:471): the Idea of life in no way presupposes the formations of nature, nor does it presuppose the ends and activities of spirit. Whereas natural and spiritual life possess a determinateness owing to their "*externality*," logical life remains "enclosed within the form of the Concept," presupposing only the subjective and objective forms of the Concept presented in the preceding sections of the Subjective Logic (WL 678, 677/6:472, 471).

In addition to distinguishing logical life from its natural and spiritual shapes, Hegel also proposes two positive considerations that make the treatment of life as the immediate Idea necessary: first, the treatment of life is necessary insofar as it is a "presupposition" of cognition; second, the treatment of life is necessary if logic is *not* to be an "empty affair devoid of determination [*Leeres und Bestimmungsloses*]" (WL 676–677/6:470).[17] The positive contribution of a logical concept of life can thus be summed up as follows: life is logical cognition in the shape of immediacy, an immediate unity of Concept and objectivity that is the *necessary presupposition* of cognition in its self-conscious form. As the necessary presupposition of cognition, what life contributes is a determinacy or determinateness (*Bestimmtheit*) without which logic would be entirely empty (*leer*). The first claim concerning life as a presupposition of cognition should not be surprising, insofar as Hegel presents other versions of this claim throughout his philosophical system, most notably in the *Phenomenology of Spirit* and the *Philosophy of Mind*. In the logical context, however, life refers to the form of activity in which the unity and division of Concept and objectivity are immediately realized, and moreover, is a form of activity that contains the potential for the self-actualization of cognition. The second claim concerning life as the antidote to the emptiness of logic is somewhat more surprising, given that from the very beginning of Hegel's investigation he has insisted that logic is concerned with both form and content, and that the assumption that logical forms are empty is a mistaken and impoverished understanding of the activity of thought.[18] Nonetheless, in claiming that life supplies an immediate determinateness that prevents logical form from being empty, it is evident that there is room in Hegel's account for something that replaces the

---

[17] Concerning emptiness, Hegel also writes: "[I]f logic were to contain nothing but empty, dead forms of thought, then there could be no talk in it at all of such a content as the Idea, or life" (WL 676/6:469).

[18] See, for example, WL 29/5:43–44.

function of the forms of intuition, even if such a replacement can no longer be adequately described along the lines of the "forms of intuition" in Kant's sense. In the conclusion of the *Logic*, Hegel is stating unequivocally that the consideration of logical cognition alone is not sufficient for avoiding emptiness and the lack of determination. Insofar as life has the character of immediacy *and* prevents logic from being empty, life must play a role in enabling objects to be immediately given and present to a knowing subject, providing an a priori form in which objects can appear as such. For Kant, famously, concepts without intuitions are empty, and intuitions are representations that are both immediate and singular.[19] Rejecting Kant's view in which judgment involves the problem of enjoining two heterogeneous elements (concepts and intuitions, universals and particulars, mediated generality and immediate singularity), Hegel proposes instead that we understand the problem of judgment in terms of the relationship between two *modes* of judgment: one that is immediate and primitive, a form of activity manifest in all living things that enables anything to be presented as an intelligible object of cognition at all; and one that is mediated and self-conscious, a form of activity manifest primarily (though perhaps not exclusively) in human beings. Judgment in its more familiar self-conscious form presupposes judgment in its more primitive form, and the more primitive form of judging activity is what prevents self-conscious judgment from being empty, from being *mere* thought without content. Although the system of thought-determinations of the *Logic* prior to the Idea are immanently developed by the self-determining activity of thought thinking itself, Hegel is now claiming that the *reality* of those thought-forms, what enables their *realization*, is the unity of the Idea and, more specifically, the immediacy of the Idea manifest in living activity. Here it is important to note again that the determinations of the Idea are not simply further determinations of thought on a par with the other thought-forms of the *Logic*, but have a different status and function. The Idea is the ground of the thought-determinations insofar as it secures their mode of realization, ensuring that they correspond with reality.

Hegel's claim that logical life is a necessary presupposition of cognition that prevents its forms from being empty suggests that we can read the three

---

[19] See Allais (2009, 389): "[T]he crucial features of intuitions are that they are representations that are immediate and singular. I suggest that the most straightforward reading of immediacy and singularity is that intuitions are representations that involve *the presence to consciousness of the particular they represent* [my emphasis]. In other words, intuitions represent objects *immediately* because they *present* the particular object itself. . . . The singularity of intuitions can be understood as the idea that an intuition presents a specific particular thing."

sections of the chapter on "Life"—the living individual, the life-process, and the genus—as "*three processes*" that at once enable and constrain the realization of self-conscious cognition (EL §217).[20] Through these three processes, which can be separated for the purposes of analysis but are essentially unified and integrated in their actualization, the unity and division of Concept and objectivity are immediately realized, constituting the form of activity that Hegel calls the "original *judgment* of life" (WL 678/6:473).[21] In referring to logical life in terms of a primitive or "original judgment," Hegel is in fact combining two features of Kant's theory of judgment that were never explicitly integrated by Kant himself. The first is the general claim, explored throughout this book, that the power of judgment presupposes purposiveness and, more specifically, *internal purposiveness* as a condition of its operation: purposiveness defines the space of judgment and is "the condition under which it is possible to apply logic to nature" (KU 20:212). The second is a suggestion I made earlier—namely, that life provides the schema that brings immediate unity to concepts and intuitions (for Hegel, Concept and objectivity) as part of a transcendental doctrine of judgment. In the first *Critique*, the schematism functioned as the mediating "third thing" (A138/B177) between heterogeneous concepts and intuitions by being homogenous with both, thereby ensuring the possibility of judgment in which intuitions are subsumed under concepts. As a product of the transcendental synthesis of the imagination, the "schemata of sensibility first *realize* the categories, yet they likewise also *restrict* them, i.e., limit them to conditions that lie outside the understanding (namely, in sensibility)" (A146/B186; my emphasis).[22] Life in the *Logic* combines these two features of Kant's theory of judgment by presenting the form of activity of life (or the form of purposiveness) as the a priori schema by which logical cognition is both enabled and constrained. The logical processes of life first *realize* cognition's forms, yet they likewise also *restrict* them—that is, limit them to conditions that lie outside cognition (namely, in life). Life is an a priori schema because it enables objects to be immediately given and present to subjects, not only as a purely uncategorized *this*, but always already as a concrete individual shaped minimally and immediately by

---

[20] See also EL §215, where Hegel refers to the Idea as "essentially *process.*"

[21] See section 5.1, this volume, for a discussion of the "original judgment of life" in connection with Hölderlin's conception of judgment.

[22] Kant's descriptions of schemata in the third *Critique* are also instructive: "Establishing that our concepts have reality always requires intuitions. If the concepts are empirical, the intuitions are called examples. If they are pure concepts of the understanding, the intuitions are called schemata.... Schemata contain direct ... exhibitions of the concept" (KU 5:351–352).

the *Gattung*-concept of the judging subject (a *this-such*).[23] That living things have objects immediately present to them as *this-such*es does not, of course, mean that life qua mere life operates with the sophisticated, fine-grained, and abstract concepts that we do; rather, it simply means that even at the level of the activity of mere life, objects are not given to subjects as entirely uncategorized *this*es. A *this* is always already a *this* to be avoided or pursued, a *this* to be eaten, a *this* to be mated with, a *this* to hide and rest under, a *this* to protect and defend, a *this* to infect and invade, a *this* that is the same as *these* and different from *those*, where the *Gattung* or life-form of the subject provides the objective context for and fundamentally shapes all these imme-diately given determinations.[24] For Hegel, even the most immediate and sin-gular representation of an object is always already given as minimally shaped by *the* Concept, where the Concept is understood immediately as the unity of a living *Gattung*, and in its more mediated, self-actualized determination, the unity of spirit and the self-conscious I.

In referring to life as "original judgment," then, Hegel is arguing that the relevant immediacy for cognition—that what is immediately "given" in cognition—is always already a synthetic unity that is the product of a primi-tive activity of judging manifest in all living things. Describing logical life as the "soul which is simple self-relation [that] remains one in the manifoldness [*Mannigfaltigkeit*] belonging to objective being," Hegel compares the external manifold appearing in the a priori forms of "space and time" with the man-ifold as permeated by the a priori form of activity of life (WL 678/6:472).[25] The comparison is cautious, since space and time are determinations that belong more properly to the philosophy of nature (Hegel qualifies his ref-erence to space and time by adding the clause, "if these could already be mentioned here"), but it is also telling, since Hegel is clearly comparing the unity that logical life brings to the manifold with the unity of the manifold resulting from a priori forms of intuition, which implies that they serve sim-ilar functions. Whereas the manifold appearing under the forms of space and time is "an indifferent subsistence . . . a mutual externality of wholly diverse

---

[23] On schemata as primitive grouping dispositions accordance with classes and kinds, see Pendlebury (1995); on schemata as holistic representations, see Matherne (2014, 188). Pippin (1976, 167) refers to schematic representations as "a whole, a kind, a this-such."

[24] Regarding the role of negation and universality in identifying a *this*, Hegel, in the "Sense-Certainty" chapter of the PhG writes: "Nor are the animas excluded from this wisdom" (PhG ¶109/ 3:91).

[25] Hegel also discusses space and time in the presentation of life in the *Phenomenology*. See PhG ¶169/3:140.

and independent [*selbständiges*] elements," the external manifold permeated by the a priori form of life is the "*simple determinateness* of its Concept . . . the soul is an omnipresent outpouring of itself into this manifold but remains at the same time the simple oneness of the concrete Concept with itself." That is to say: whereas space and time as the a priori forms of intuition leave the manifold relatively underdetermined and lacking in genuine unity, the a priori form of life permeates and realizes the unity of the manifold according to the form of the Concept. In a highly condensed summary of the trajectory from the first to the third *Critique*, Hegel goes on to suggest that the manifold appearing in space and time according to the Kantian view is an "absolute multiplicity of atomistic matter," or to use Kant's own words, "a crude chaotic aggregate without any trace of a system" (EE 20:209).[26] The Kantian view thus finds itself in a contradiction, insofar as it must "admit the actuality of this Idea [of life]" in order to block empirical atomicity and chaos, while at the same time, life for Kant remains "an *incomprehensible mystery*" (WL 678/6:473). Charting the path of "Kant's great service to philosophy" in which internal purposiveness comes to serve a positive function, Hegel begins the conclusion of the *Logic* by presenting the a priori activity of life as the unconscious, immediate, original synthetic unity of the manifold, the original judgment that at once enables cognition and constrains it, providing a schema of determinateness that is a necessary presupposition of self-conscious cognition.

7.4 The Processes of Life as Form-Constraints: Corporeality, Externality, and the Genus

To get a better understanding of how life functions as an a priori schema, I want to turn now directly to the three processes outlined in the "Life" chapter and argue that they provide three *form-constraints* presupposed by the self-actualization of cognition. Each process represents a determinate aspect of the original judgment of life, which Hegel describes as follows:

---

[26] Immediately following this passage, Kant speaks of the "*unity of nature in space and time,*" suggesting that this unity is not sufficient to block the "disturbing boundless heterogeneity" of nature, and thus, that judgment requires a transcendental presupposition of the purposiveness of nature (see EE 20:209–211).

The original *judgment* of life [*Das ursprüngliche* Urteil *des Lebens*] consists therefore in this, that it separates itself off as individual subject from the objective, and in constituting itself as the negative unity of the Concept, makes the *presupposition* of an immediate objectivity. (WL 678/6:473)

The original judgment of life is the purposive activity by means of which an individual subject constitutes itself in opposition and relation to objectivity. Picking up from the conclusion of the "Teleology" chapter that immediately precedes the chapter on "Life," the original judgment of life is the general form of internally purposive activity in which subjective purposes, aims, and ends are realized as objective. The immediate form of this activity is manifest in three determinate processes: first, a living individual subject constitutes itself in objectivity by possessing a specific *corporeality* (*Leiblichkeit*), the locus of inner sense; second, a living being realizes subjective ends as objective through life-processes in relation to an external environment, directing itself toward an *externality* or *outwardness* (*Äußerlichkeit*) that it posits as conformable with the form of its activity, the locus of outer sense; third, a living being realizes subjective ends as objective in relation to the processes of its genus or species (*die Gattung*), where the genus or species provides the necessary context in which corporeality and externality have a determinate shape. These three processes—which reflect the three moments of the Concept as individual, particular, and universal—make up the form of activity that Hegel calls the original judgment of life. The unified activity constituted by these three processes are the source of an immediate, unconscious, synthetic unity of the manifold, an immediate unity of Concept and objectivity that at once enables and constrains the activity of self-conscious cognition.

7.4.1 The Living Individual: Corporeality (*Leiblichkeit*)

In setting the stage for his discussion of the living individual (*das lebendige Individuum*), the formulation of the "original judgment of life" is meant to be a general gloss on Hegel's understanding of idealism in which the self-determining activity of the Concept posits itself in relation and opposition to objectivity (WL 679/6:474). This self-positing activity of distinguishing and relating, an activity that at once constitutes the judging subject and sets in place the opposition between subject and object as the schema of knowing, represents Hegel's mature position on the ground of his idealism, and clearly manifests both Fichtean and Schellingian roots.[27] On the Fichtean side, Hegel continues to adopt the general schema of the self-positing activity of the I that sets itself in opposition to a not-I, an activity and relationship that for Fichte is the ground of all theoretical and practical knowing. In tracing the immediate form of this activity and schema to the original judgment of life, Hegel continues to develop and transform Schelling's insight that life provides the most "obvious proof" of transcendental idealism, insofar as the form of its activity is an immediate manifestation of the idealist conception of knowing. The opening paragraphs of "The Living Individual" describe, in very general terms, the fundamental character of Hegel's idealism, but the following passage from the opening of the "Organics" section of the *Philosophy of Nature* is perhaps even more instructive in this regard:

> Life, therefore, can be grasped only speculatively; for it is precisely in life that the speculative has an existence. *The perpetual action of life is thus absolute idealism* [my emphasis]; it becomes an other which, however, is always sublated. If life were a realist, it would have respect for the outer world; but it always inhibits the reality of the other and transforms it into its own self. Thus it is in life that what is the *true* first exists. (PN §337Z)

The perpetual action of life simply *is* absolute idealism: the form of its activity is the immediate shape of knowing in which truth first has an existence. The activity of life pervades reality with the form of its own self, transforming the outer world into a posited determinateness. Turning directly to the determination of the living individual and its place in this activity, Hegel finally and definitively describes the living individual in terms of the subject of judgment:

> Having proceeded from the Idea, self-subsisting objectivity is therefore immediate being only as the *predicate* of the judgment of the Concept's self-determination—a being that is indeed distinct from the subject but is at the same time essentially posited as a *moment* of the Concept. With respect to content, this objectivity is the totality of the Concept—a totality, however, that has the subjectivity of the Concept, or its negative unity standing over

---

[27] See also Hegel's gloss on Reinhold's principle of consciousness in the *Phenomenology*: "Consciousness *distinguishes* something from itself and at the same time it *relates* itself to it. Or, as this should be expressed: There is something *for consciousness*, and the determinate aspect of this *relating*, or the *being* of something *for a consciousness*, is knowledge" (PhG ¶82/3:76).

against it, and this subjectivity or negativity is what constitutes the true centrality, namely, the Concept's free unity with itself. This *subject* is the Idea
in the form of *individuality*, as simple but negative self-identity—the *living
individual*. (WL 680/6:475)

This passage establishes three essential features of Hegel's idealism,
characterized here according to the activity of the judgment of life. First,
referring again to the all-important judgment of the Concept, Hegel is now
discussing what he takes to be the *objective realization* of the judgment of the
Concept, as opposed to its merely subjective form.[28] Objectivity is the "*predicate* of the judgment of the Concept's self-determination": objectivity is not
treated simply as "immediate being" but is also posited through an act of self-
determination in which a subject is realized through its predicate.

Second, through this act of self-positing, objectivity is permeated by the
form of the Concept; however, the true "centrality" of the Concept, the locus
of its self-determining activity and internalized perspective, is the subject. In
identifying the "centrality" of the Concept with subjectivity, Hegel is simply
reiterating that subjectivity is synonymous with the internalized locus of self-
determining power which constitutes the perspective from which objectivity
can be determined as intelligible at all. In other words, things can only be
determined as objective *from* the perspective of a self-determining subject;
without that perspective, objectivity has no significance. Although objectivity is often understood to mean the *absence* of subjective perspectives or
contributions, Hegel is arguing that the very notion of objectivity as the absence of subjectivity only has meaning as posited by a subject.[29]

Third, the subject of judgment manifests the form of individuality, and
more specifically, the subject who judges is the *living individual*. In determining the subject of judgment as the living individual, Hegel is not simply
referring to an empirical instance of a living thing, just as when the idealists
refer to self-consciousness or the I as the ground of knowledge, they are not
referring to an empirical instance of a particular self-conscious, phenomenological perspective. Rather, and similar to Fichte's determination of the *absolute I*, the living individual as the subject of the original judgment of life is
an absolute perspective, at once universal and individual, an a priori, formal

---

[28] Regarding the judgment of life as an objective judgment of the Concept, Hegel writes: "Through
this self-determining, the *universal* life becomes a *particular;* it has thus split [*entzweit*] itself into the
two extremes of judgment, which immediately becomes syllogism" (WL 679/6:474).

[29] This is arguably the position of theoretical cognition, which I discuss in section 8.1.

determination that gives shape to empirical instances. As an "initiating, self-moving *principle*," the living individual is "life as *soul*," a soul that "*in its immediacy* is immediately external and possesses an objective being within itself" (WL 680/6:475). As a principle of self-movement, or more precisely a principle of internal purposiveness, the living individual as soul immediately possesses *corporeality* (*Leiblichkeit*), a corporeality that is the means through which the living individual is immediately united with objective reality. Hegel writes:

> This living individual is in the first place life as *soul*, as the Concept of itself, fully determined within itself, the initiating, self-moving *principle*. . . . [T]his soul is *in its immediacy* immediately external, and has an objective being within itself—a reality that is subjugated to the purpose, the immediate *means*, in the first instance, objectivity as *predicate* of the subject, but also, objectivity is the *middle term* of the syllogism; the corporeality of the soul is that whereby the soul unites itself with external objectivity [*die Leiblichkeit der Seele ist das, wodurch sie sich mit der äußerlichen Objectivität zusammenschließst*]. — The living being possesses corporeality in the first instance as a reality that is immediately identical with the Concept; to this extent, corporeality has this reality in general by *nature*. (WL 680/6:475)[30]

Qua self-moving principle, the living individual at stake here is not an individual, empirical living thing but, rather, an a priori form of activity that Hegel refers to as *soul*. The form of activity of the soul has an immediate, corporeal reality by nature that is the *means*—the predicate, the middle term[31]—by which it is immediately united with external objectivity. In other words, the corporeality of the living individual is the means by which Concept and objectivity are immediately united. Corporeality is a formal constraint that enables the realization of the living individual qua subjective purpose as external objectivity; it is a schema, or "third thing," that enables and constrains the immediate unity of Concept and objectivity. Although corporeality, or the specific embodiment of a living individual, may appear to be an empirical

---

[30] See also EL §216 and §216Z: "The Concept is realized as soul, in a *body*. . . . The Concept of life is the soul, and this Concept has the body for its reality."

[31] Hegel is not conflating these terms here; in associating them, I take it that he means to draw our attention to the way in which he has already established that the predicate and the middle term (qua genus and qua Concept) bring unity to judgment and syllogism.

determination, the function that Hegel is identifying with respect to corporeality here is decidedly formal: Hegel is not specifying any determinate details
concerning what specific instances of living corporeality may entail, but is
simply identifying the formal role that is played by corporeality—whatever
determinate, empirical shape it takes—with respect to the principle of self-
movement. Corporeality is presented here as an a priori condition for the
activity of judging in which Concept and objectivity are united in the processual actuality of reason that Hegel calls the Idea. The corporeal form of the
living individual provides a schema of immediate synthetic unity that at once
enables and constrains its internally purposive activity, allowing it to transform its subjective purposes and aims into objective reality.[32]

In presenting the determination of the living individual as the absolute,
original subject of judgment, Hegel naturalizes the terms of his idealism and
fundamentally transforms our understanding of the ground of cognition and
knowing. With respect to the shape or structure of the living individual and
its corporeality, Hegel elaborates by turning once again to the form of inner
purposiveness, but this time with explicit reference to the self-organizing
shape of an organism or natural purpose. Two features are of particular importance. First, the corporeality of the individual itself constitutes an internally purposive unity, such that "the organism is a manifold, not of *parts* but
of *members*" (WL 681/6:476). The subjective unity of the living individual
manifests the organization of internal purposiveness, and even though the
organism is indeed "*capable*" of mechanical and chemical relationships,
Hegel suggests that in such relations the living being is "treated as something
dead." Insofar as it is treated as a living being, the parts of the organism cannot
be separated from the whole and still remain what they are: "when separated,
they revert to the mechanical and chemical relationships of common objectivity." Rather, the unity of the organism is a drive (*Trieb*) in which it is at once
an activity and process of production *and* the resulting product at once; that
is, the unity of the organism is a drive in which it is the cause and effect of itself (WL 681–682/6:477).

Second, Hegel describes the "*Concept* of the *living subject* and *its process*"
in terms of the three moments of the Concept: the universality of the organism is manifest as *sensibility*; the particularity of the organism is manifest

---

[32] See Nuzzo (2008) for an argument that Kant's theory of sensibility needs to be understood in
connection with a notion of "transcendental embodiment."

as *irritability*; and the individuality of the organism is manifest as *reproduction*.[33] These three powers of the living individual, which are actualized by means of its corporeal reality, reflect both the potentiality of the individual organism as it realizes subjective purposes as objective and the general processes of life-activity as a whole corresponding to the three sections in the chapter on "Life." Thus, whereas irritability corresponds broadly to the life-process in which the individual directs itself toward externality, and reproduction corresponds broadly to the process of the genus, sensibility ought to be highlighted here in particular in the context of the determination of the corporeality of the living individual. Sensibility denotes several features of the living individual that are important with respect to the form-constraint of corporeality: sensibility constitutes the inwardness of the organism insofar as it has a capacity for receptivity and self-feeling. The inclusion of sensibility as a moment of the process of the living subject is particularly noteworthy given Hegel's rejection of sensibility as an independent faculty of pure receptivity as one of the two heterogeneous stems of knowledge. Sensibility, in Hegel's characterization, is indeed an "infinitely *determinable* receptivity," but the determinateness of "the so-called *impression*" is inwardly and spontaneously reflected to generate *self-feeling*—an immediate sense of self that constitutes the interiority or inwardness of the living subject (WL 682/6:478). Enabled by the corporeality of the living subject, sensibility is the "determinate being of the inwardly existent soul [*das Dasein der in sich seienden Seele*]," or what can be called *inner sense*. The embodiment of the living subject is thus the enabling condition of self-feeling or inner sense, the means by which an immediate interiority of activity and perspective is actualized.

In presenting self-feeling and inner sense as enabled by corporeality, Hegel presents an alternative to the account given by Kant in the Transcendental Aesthetic in which time is determined as the a priori form of inner sense. Where Kant writes, "[T]ime is nothing other than the form of inner sense, i.e., of the intuition of our self and our inner state" (A33/B49), Hegel would say that the power of sensibility, enabled by the corporeality of the living

---

[33] See also Hegel's discussion of sensibility, irritability, and reproduction in PN §§353–356; and his discussion of the organism in the section, "Observation of Nature," in the *Phenomenology*. Although the account provided in the *Logic* mirrors Hegel's discussion in the *Philosophy of Nature*, it is again important to stress that what Hegel discusses in the *Logic* has a different status and function. Insofar as these determinations belong to logic, they are part of the formal constraints for the self-realization of cognition, rather than general descriptions of the organic formations of nature. For an anticipation of this idea that life can be a logical concept and not just an empirical one, see also PhG ¶285/ 3:215–216.

subject, is the form of inner sense.[34] Far from being pure receptivity, sensibility is a capacity for receptivity that is at once inwardly and spontaneously reflected to generate self-feeling, an immediate sense of our self and our inner state. Although I have highlighted the way in which corporeality enables the determination of inner sense in the present section, it is important to note that, strictly speaking, all three powers—sensibility, irritability, and reproduction—flow from the corporeality of the living individual as the subject of judgment, constituting a unified totality in their processes of actualization. In order to understand the shape of the second power, that of irritability, I turn now to Hegel's discussion of the form-constraint of externality or outer sense, which he discusses under the heading of "The Life-Process."

7.4.2 The Life-Process: Externality and Outwardness (*Äußerlichkeit*)

The second moment of the Idea of life in which the living individual is outwardly directed toward a presupposed objective world is already implied by and intrinsically connected to the first moment of inner sense. Like the self-positing act of the I, inwardness and outwardness, subjectivity and objectivity, are established in one and the same act, and the living individual is continually sustained through its positing of this distinction and relation. Hegel writes: "In shaping itself inwardly, the living individual tenses itself against its original act of presupposition, and as a subject existing in and for itself, sets itself in opposition to the presupposed objective world" (WL 684/6:480).[35] The process of self-production embodied in the living

---

[34] For Hegel, time, as well as space, which are the first determinations of the *Philosophy of Nature*, are determinations of "self-externality [*Außereinander*] in complete abstraction" (PN §253). Hegel also discusses the significance of space and time in connection with theoretical mind or intelligence, describing them as "the *forms* in which intelligence is intuitive" (PG §448). However, insofar as space and time are determinations of nature, Hegel continues to insist, against Kant, that space and time are not merely subjective forms. He writes: "But when we said that what is sensed receives from the *intuiting mind* the form of the spatial and temporal, this statement must not be understood to mean that space and time are *only subjective* forms. This is what *Kant* wanted to make space and time. However, things are in truth *themselves* spatial and temporal; this double form of asunderness is not one-sidedly imposed on them by our intuition" (PG §448A). He also continues to refer to space and time as "abstract" and "meagre," suggesting that "things get very little from these forms" by way of unity, especially in contrast with the unity grasped by the cognition of things according to their Concept.

[35] See also PN §357: "The self-feeling of individuality is also directly exclusive and in a state of tension with a non-organic nature which stands over against it as its *external* condition and material."

individual is, thus, at once inwardly and outwardly directed:[36] as a process of internal self-production, the sensibility of the living individual produces self-feeling and inner sense, enabled and constrained by corporeality; as a process of self-production directed outside itself, the realization of subjective ends as objective is enabled and constrained by an external, objective world shaped by outer sense, or what Hegel calls irritability.[37] What drives the life-process as the relation between the living individual and externality is *need* (*Bedürfnis*): the living individual is driven outside itself by need, and is itself "the drive to posit this *other* world *for itself*, similar to itself, to sublate it and to objectify *itself*" (WL 684/6:481). If need is the impetus of the life-process, its aim and goal is the objective truth of self-certainty in which the living subject successfully sublates the otherness of the world and posits externality as conformable with the self. The conformability of externality with the living subject is the second form-constraint for the self-realization of cognition: an externality conformable with the self is a necessary means through which subjective ends are realized as objective, a necessary condition for the unity and correspondence of Concept and objectivity.

In elaborating on the schema of a conformable externality, Hegel primarily focuses on what drives the living subject outside itself, along with its activities of assimilation, as it attempts to satisfy its needs. This suggests that the immediate conformability of the external world, at least insofar as one is concerned with the presuppositions of cognition, is primarily shaped by the needs of the living subject. Externality is rendered conformable (Hegel uses the terms *angemessen* and *entsprechend*)[38] by means of the living subject's activity: driven by the feeling of need, which Hegel characterizes in terms of contradiction, diremption (*Entzweiung*), and pain, the living being seeks to sublate the feeling of need by seizing, appropriating, and assimilating objects outside itself such that "externality [*Äußerlichkeit*] [is] transformed into interiority [*Innerlichkeit*]" (WL 685/6:482). Although it may again appear that Hegel has crossed the line into empirical considerations concerning the organism, it important to stress that the conformability of externality is treated

---

[36] Hegel calls irritability, "a direction outwards [*einer Richtung nach außen*]" (WL 683/6:479), and a "*relation outwards* [Beziehung nach außen]" (WL 682/480). In the *Philosophy of Nature*, assimilation is "the process outwards [*Der Prozeß nach außen*]" (PN §357A). See also section 5.2.1 for a discussion of the inward and outward directedness of the Concept.

[37] Recall Kant's discussion of outer sense in the Transcendental Aesthetic: "By means of outer sense (a property of our mind) we represent to ourselves objects as outside us, and all as in space" (A22/B37).

[38] See WL 684–685/6:481–482.

here with respect to its function as an a priori condition of judgment. Insofar as externality at once enables and constrains the activity of judgment, Hegel presents this condition in the following terms:

> Because the living being is drive (*Trieb*), externality approaches and enters it only insofar as it is already in and for itself *within the living being*; therefore, the effect [*Einwirkung*] on the subject consists solely in the latter finding the externality [*Äußerlichkeit*] presented to it as *conformable*. This externality may not be conformable with the subject's totality, but at least it must correspond to a particular side of it. (WL 685/6:482)

The relation between the living subject and externality, and the effect or impact of externality on the subject, can take a variety of shapes, shapes that reflect the determinations presented in the "Objectivity" section of the Subjective Logic. Externality can affect the subject according to mechanical and chemical relations, but within such relationships, the living being is not affected qua living being, and externality acts merely as a "cause" upon the living being qua mechanical or chemical object. When the living being is affected by externality qua living being, externality "*excites* it," which means that in such cases, externality responds or corresponds to a felt need of the living subject. Insofar as externality corresponds to a felt need, the subject, in addition to its existing mechanical and chemical relations, enters into a relation of external purposiveness with the outer world, using and shaping the outer world as a means to achieve subjective aims. Externality is transformed into interiority and an "inner process"—external purposiveness becomes internal purposiveness and "reciprocal action [*Wechselwirkung*]"[39]—when the subject seizes, appropriates, and assimilates the object, pervading the object with the form of its own subjectivity as part of its process of self-reproduction. The result of the process in which the living subject relates to a conformable externality is a confirmation of its self-feeling, or the truth of its inner self-certainty: "the living being posits itself as self-identical *for-itself*. . . . [T]hrough the objective process, the living being gives itself its *feeling of self*" (WL 686/6:483). Insofar as the process both begins and ends with self-feeling, what the relation to externality enables is the transformation of self-feeling as the inwardness of receptive sensibility to self-feeling as

---

[39] See WL 683/6:479.

outwardly posited self-certainty. In short, the relation to externality allows the living individual to sublate its particularity and raise itself to universality (WL 686/6:484).

Two features of Hegel's analysis of the life-process are particularly striking. First and foremost, Hegel describes the schema of conformable externality primarily in terms of the needs of the living subject: the subject is driven outward by need, and externality is conformable to the subject insofar as it corresponds to felt needs. This can make Hegel's idealism appear overly subjective in a pejorative and problematic sense, insofar as the external world is given shape (at least immediately) entirely through the lens of the needs of the subject. Another way of expressing Hegel's point would be to say that the external world is conformable to the subject only insofar as it is interest-laden—the world is both shaped by our interests and responds (positively or negatively) to them. Externality could not in fact be conformable to the subject if it did not in any way respond to the subject's needs and interests; correspondingly, a subject without needs or interests (if this is even conceivable) would entirely lack outer sense. To prevent the outward directedness of the living being from being *merely* subjective, however, a second feature of Hegel's analysis needs to combined with the first—namely, that the aim of the life-process is to transform *certainty* into *truth*, rendering the *particularity* of the subject *universal*. The key to this transformation is the process of assimilation by which the subject successfully reproduces itself, pervading the substance and constitution of the object with its own form—that is, with the form of the Concept.[40] Take the following example: Driven by the need to satisfy its hunger, a living being seizes upon the fruit of a tree, appropriates the fruit for itself, and assimilates the object. Through this process, the subjective and particular aim of the living being (to alleviate hunger by eating fruit) is transformed in a variety of ways: first, insofar as assimilation successfully alleviates hunger, the subjective purpose of the living being has been objectively realized in a course of action, and the living being receives confirmation that the world is conformable to its aims, at least in part; second, in alleviating its hunger, the subject receives confirmation of the certainty of its own self-feeling insofar as it has found satisfaction for its

---

[40] In the *Philosophy of Nature*, Hegel specifies that the process of assimilation has both a theoretical and practical dimension, anticipating the theoretical and practical dimensions of self-conscious cognition. See PN §§357–365. Concerning assimilation, Hegel writes, "The organism must therefore posit what is external as subjective, appropriate it, and identify it with itself; and this is *assimilation*" (PN §357Z).

needs, a certainty of self that is sustained through ongoing, successful reproduction; third, the activity by which the individual successfully reproduces
itself points beyond the individual toward the reproduction of its life-form
or species, insofar as the activity in question, under normal circumstances,
allows other individuals of the same species to find the same forms of confirmation described here. Certainty is transformed into truth insofar as subjectivity and objectivity (or Concept and objectivity) find correspondence
and reciprocity, a correspondence that is brought about by the life-process
of the subject. Particularity posits itself as "real universal life" insofar as the
life-process by which the individual reproduces itself is at the same time a
process by which a universal species is reproduced (WL 686/6:484). Far from
being merely particular, the life-process of the living individual is an *exemplification* of the universal life of the species, and part of a larger process of the
reproduction of the species as a whole.

In his analysis of the life-process, Hegel presents conformable externality
as a necessary condition for judgment, describing the immediate schema in
which subjectivity and objectivity correspond to produce the truth of self-
certainty. In the final section of the "Life" chapter, Hegel proceeds to argue
that the life-process can only be grasped as part of a larger process of the
genus or species, a process of the wider context of a life-form that constitutes
the third form-constraint for the actualization of self-conscious cognition.

7.4.3 The Genus (*Die Gattung*)

In chapters 5 and 6, I argued that the determination of the genus plays a
foundational role in Hegel's understanding of the subjective and objective
Concept, driving the progression of the Subjective Logic toward its conclusion in the Idea. Within the present context of Hegel's discussion of logical
life, the determination of the genus as an a priori schema serves three important functions which allow him to complete his argument that logical life is
a necessary presupposition of cognition that prevents its forms from being
empty. Hegel's first and most general claim with respect to the process of the
genus follows directly from his discussion of the life-process: the life-process
by which an individual reproduces itself always already presupposes the process of the genus; and conversely, the process of the genus presupposes the
life-process of the individual. The genus is reflected in the individual in two
ways: first, the individual is a manifestation of and *exemplifies* its genus such

that its own processes are at once individual and universal; second, the individual is a *member* of a genus such that it is a part of a larger whole, as an organ is to the whole organism. Here, it is important to recall the function of the genus in Hegel's discussions of the subjective and objective Concept, where the genus is the ground of predication and the realization of the subject, respectively. The power of the living individual to judge reflects the power of the genus as its own power of self-determination, and the process by which the individual attains the truth of self-certainty presupposes the process of the genus as its necessary, universal context. In opening up the universal context of the living individual, Hegel writes that in the genus process, there is a "duplication of the individual—a presupposing of an objectivity that is identical with it, and a relating of the living being to itself as to another living being" (WL 687/6:484). The genus process emerges as part of the same process in which the living being presupposes an external objectivity, with the specification that the presupposed objectivity in this case is not simply conformable with the subject but also *identical* with it. In this type of relationship, the self-relation of the individual is identical with its relation to another living individual; or as Hegel has described this relationship in another context, being-for-itself and being-for-another are one and the same. Adding to the relation of excitation in which a conformable externality responds to the needs of the subject, the relation between living individuals of the same species, where each individual is a drive, is "contradiction," in "tension," a "longing [*Verlangen*]," and "immediately reciprocal" (WL 687/6:485). Insofar as the presupposed objectivity of the living subject is now identical with the subject itself rather than simply conformable with it, the wider context of the genus process allows the subject to attain a higher, more universal truth of self-certainty than was available in its relation to a merely conformable externality. Through the wider context of a life-form, the individual finds confirmation of its own self-feeling in relation to an objective reality that is identical with itself.

Hegel's second claim is that the genus process is an enabling condition of the judging activities of the living individual, and at the same time, that it constrains those activities in a variety of ways. Although corporeality, externality, and the genus are decidedly not three discrete processes, it is the determination of the genus that best allows us to view these processes as a unified and determinate activity of form. With respect to corporeality and externality, the genus process determines to a large degree the specific shape and features of the inner and outer sense of the living individual. When

Hegel suggests that the genus process consists in the relation between living individuals that are identical, their identity and reciprocity rests entirely on their being members of the same genus, which specifically renders their corporeality and life-process identical. The genus determines the specific shape of corporeality and provides the criterion for what constitutes successful reproduction for the individual as it confronts a conformable externality. Moreover, the genus process provides the criterion for the successful "duplication" of individuals, or the reproduction of the species as a whole. In short, the genus sets the parameters for the judging activities of the living individual as it seeks to realize subjective ends as objective. The dual function of enabling and constraining the activities of judgment can be most vividly illustrated in the reciprocal relation between living individuals, a relation that constitutes the immediacy of the relation of recognition between self-consciousnesses that is the hallmark of Hegel's conception of spirit. Hegel characterizes the relation between living individuals in terms of a longing (*Verlangen*), a term that at once connotes desire, urge, and appetite, as well as request and demand.[41] The relation between living individuals enables and facilitates the life-process in which an individual reproduces its own self-feeling, but this same relation to another can likewise thwart, restrict, oppose, and even destroy the process of individual reproduction. Most important, the reciprocal relationship between living individuals is the means through which the genus itself is reproduced, resulting in the product of "the *realized genus*" (WL 688/6:486). The reciprocal activity of living individuals is the process of reproducing the life-form itself, a process of unity, identity, and reciprocity alongside contradiction, diremption, conflict, and constraint.

Hegel's third claim with respect to the genus concerns the relationship between an individual and its life-form, especially as it pertains to the power of the life-form over and against the individual. As he suggested earlier in the section on "Objectivity," the genus is the ultimate fate of the living individual;[42] here, Hegel writes: "In the genus process, the separated individualities of individual life perish" (WL 688/6:486). The relative power of the individual vis-à-vis its life-form is thus an important determining factor in establishing the degree of self-determination available to the individual: the degree to which the individual can oppose itself to its life-form,

---

[41] Hegel also describes the genus-process in terms of sexual differentiation, opposition, and relation. See WL 688/6:486; EL §220; and PN §§368–369.

[42] See the discussion in section 6.2, this volume.

be self-alienated from its life-form, and therefore, exist not as immediately engulfed by its life-form but have life-form as such exist *for it*—all of this represents the power and potentiality of the judgment of life to divide itself from itself in the positing of self-conscious cognition. The key is not simply that the individual has the power to oppose the process of the genus, but more important, and insofar as the individual has self-conscious awareness of the form of activity of life itself, the individual has the power to determine and transform the genus process, reshaping the very terms of individual and collective reproduction. In Hegel's presentation, this power of self-conscious self-determination is decidedly *not* available in the immediacy of mere life, a lack of power that is signaled by the power of the genus *over* the individual. The transition from the Idea of life to the Idea of cognition is itself characterized as an act of judgment in which life divides itself from itself, gains an awareness of its own activity of form, and in so doing, constitutes itself as self-conscious cognition. Hegel writes in the last lines of the chapter on "Life":

> The Idea, which is *in-itself* [an sich] as genus, is now *for-itself* [für sich], in that it has sublated its particularity that constituted the living species, and has thereby given itself a *reality* which is *itself simple universality*; thus it is the Idea that *relates itself to itself as Idea*, the universal that has universality for its determinateness and existence. This is the *Idea of cognition*. (WL 688/ 6:486–487)

And in the first lines of the chapter on "Cognition":

> Life is the immediate Idea, or the Idea as its *Concept* not realized in its own self. In its *judgment*, the Idea is cognition in general. (WL 689/6:487)

The difference between the Idea as life and the Idea as cognition is the distinction between the genus *in-itself* and the genus *for-itself*, or again, it is the difference between the Idea as engulfed in immediacy and the Idea that relates to itself with an awareness of the determination of the Idea. The self-constitution of self-conscious cognition is itself a judgment of life, in that it is *life* that divides itself from itself, an act of division in which self-consciousness is first constituted. The result of this judgment (or self-division) is not an overcoming, an erasure, or even a complete transformation of the form of life; rather, the result of this judgment is a *doubling* of the Idea: "Through this judgment the Idea is doubled, into the subjective Concept whose reality is the Concept itself, and into the objective Concept which is as life" (WL 689/6:487).[43] In referring to the doubling of the Idea, Hegel is insisting, as I have argued (in sections 7.2 and 7.3), that cognition consists of a relation of reciprocity and actualization between two synthetic acts of unification—one immediate and engulfed, the other self-consciously posited—that cannot be reduced into one without extinguishing cognition altogether. Although in Hegel's characterization, the Idea of life and the Idea of cognition are indeed *not* heterogeneous (both manifest the form and activity of the Concept), it remains the case that life without cognition is unconscious and blind, and cognition without life is entirely empty. Life is the animating principle of cognition that cognition posits as its own presupposition; the doubling of the Idea is the ongoing process of cognition's self-realization.

The determination of the genus as an enabling and constraining pre-supposition of cognition is of particular importance within the larger context of Hegel's philosophical system, insofar as it is consistently the means through which Hegel arrives at the determination of self-consciousness and spirit. Both are consistently defined in terms of the genus that is *for-itself*, as self-conscious life, as the life-form that is aware of itself as a life-form. There are two ways of understanding Hegel's claim with respect to the role of the genus here, and I will recommend that the second way is the preferred in-terpretation, at least with regard to understanding the logical Idea. In de-termining self-consciousness and spirit as the genus that is *for-itself*, one way of interpreting Hegel's point is to read him as suggesting that there is a continuity between mere life and self-conscious life that is often overlooked in assessing the capacities and activities of reason. What Hegel is interested in highlighting, then, is the deep continuity between rational animals and non-rational animals—that, indeed, human animals share much in common with non-human animals which warrants consideration when coming to grips with how cognition operates. This strand of thinking is perhaps most perspicuously evident in the transition from the *Philosophy of Nature* to the *Philosophy of Mind*, where the discussion of the animal organism continues almost seamlessly into the anthropology's discussion of the natural soul, which describes the immediate and natural features of embodied human existence.[44]

---

[43] On the doubling of the Idea, see also EL §§223–225.

[44] Malabou (2005, 26) calls this move from nature to spirit, a "*reduplication*."

Without denying the deep continuities between rational and non-rational animals (and without needing to commit Hegel to its denial either), I want to argue that there is a second way of interpreting Hegel's presentation of spirit and self-consciousness as the genus that is *for-itself*. Rather than simply being a claim about the continuity between animal and rational life, the specific identity and difference between the Idea of life and the Idea of cognition should be understood in terms of a *logical* identity and difference. On the side of identity, Hegel's claim is that judgments of life and judgments of cognition have the same logical form: both are grounded in the determination of the genus, which provides a universal context and standard of evaluation with respect to their theoretical and practical activities of realizing subjective purposes as objective. When a living individual or self-conscious I judges, that activity reflects the power of its life-form, which sets the parameters for the correspondence of Concept and objectivity.

On the side of difference, we can turn to what Aristotle calls a "difference in the genus":[45] according to Aristotle, although both horses and humans are animals, their respective animality is not identical; rather, their common animality is expressed in entirely different ways according to the specificities of their respective life-forms.[46] The animality of horses and the animality of humans are distinct because they are governed by distinct life-form contexts; what we identify as common between them at a logical level is not anything substantial about their animality but simply the logical form of life-activity as such, which on its own provides no substantive content with respect to how their respective animalities are realized. If this is the case, then the first interpretation that emphasizes the continuities between animal and human life on a linear scale can be somewhat misleading, insofar as the "animality" of

---

[45] See Boyle's (2016, 2018) discussions of Aristotle on this idea.

[46] The key difference at stake here is how the introduction of rationality modifies and transforms what it is to be an animal. Aristotle writes:

> For by genus I mean that one identical thing which is predicated of both and is differentiated in no merely accidental way. . . . For not only must the common nature attach to the different things, e.g. not only must both be animals, but this very animality must also be different for each (e.g. in the one case equinity, in the other humanity), and so this common nature is specifically different for each from what it is for the other. One, then, will be in virtue of its own nature one sort of animal, and the other another, e.g. one a horse and the other a human. This difference, then, must be an otherness of the genus. For I give the name of 'difference in the genus' to an otherness which makes the genus itself other. (Aristotle, *Metaphysics* 1057b38–1058a8)

each is in fact quite distinct.[47] What the continuity view overlooks is the absolute importance of species-specificity with regard to ascertaining cognitive capacities. On Hegel's view of life as an a priori schema, cognitive capacities are indexed entirely by the immediate form of activity of life, which means that all cognitive capacities are fundamentally shaped by the corporeal reality and the relation to the environment actualized in particular species. Species-*specificity* is not species-solipsism, and the importance of species-specificity in no way rules out complex interspecies relations, including forms of imaginative and affective identification with the points of view of other life-forms. It simply means that all these possibilities are internal to and opened up by one's own life-form activity *from the inside*. With respect to the difference between life and self-conscious forms of cognition, the key logical difference lies in cognition's self-conscious reflexivity concerning its own life-form. This self-conscious reflexivity transforms the determination of life, but it does not eliminate its distinctive contribution as the immediate schema of any possible unity of Concept and objectivity. Moreover, although the form of activity of life will have different manifestations in different life-forms, the life-form that is *for-itself* is essentially constituted through the activity that Hegel calls the doubling of the Idea: the form of activity of self-conscious cognition is the processual activity of its self-division from and unity with the immediacy of its own life-form. To be sure, the immediacy of self-conscious life is very different from, say, the immediacy of life for a horse or a bat (each has a different corporeal shape and structure, with different capacities of sensibility that enable different relations to the external world), but this does not entail that there is *no* relevant immediacy of life that is required for the actualization of self-conscious cognition. The immediacy of self-conscious life is cognition's own presupposition; it is *our* "unconscious creative principle," distinct from the unconscious creative principles of horses and bats, but without it, the activities of cognition would be entirely empty (PN §357Z). More than empty, it would be even more accurate to say that without the immediate schema of life-activity, cognition would have no actuality. For self-conscious cognition, then, its essential activity is the reflexive doubling of the Idea, the activity in which life divides itself from itself. In the absence of this doubling, there could be no self-conscious

---

[47] McDowell emphasizes this point in *Mind and World*: "We do not need to say that we have what mere animals have.... Instead we can say that we have what mere animals have, perceptual sensitivity to features of our environment, but we have it in a special form" (1996, 64).

cognition at all. It is only in the relation and opposition between life and cognition, posited by the judgment of life itself, that there is "*thinking, spirit, self-consciousness*"—in other words, cognition's activity is the ongoing dialectic between its own immediate schema of life and the theoretical and practical activities of self-conscious spirit (WL 689/6:487).[48]

---

[48] My account here shares much with Khurana's understanding of the relation between life and spirit, and I am indebted to many conversations with him on this topic. In Khurana's discussion of Hegel's place in transformative theories of rationality, he highlights two aspects of Hegel's understanding that are overlooked by transformative theories: the first is that, according to Hegel, what animals and humans share is a "general form of organization," rather than particular capacities such as perception or action; the second is that Hegel understands transformation as an ongoing constitutive activity, rather than as a unified state of being that is the case simply due to species membership in a rational form of life. This leaves room for a "certain animality" within spirit insofar as transformative activity is understood in terms of a continual, internal, dialectical opposition in which spirit is constituted in its opposition and relation to life, an opposition and relation that has an essentially self-conscious form (Khurana 2017, 384–387). I am largely in agreement with Khurana's account, and here I attempt to highlight Hegel's version of this thought in the context of the logical Idea.

8

The Idea of Cognition and Absolute Method

In this chapter, I conclude my discussion of the Idea by offering an analysis of theoretical and practical cognition, which grow out of Hegel's account of logical life as an a priori schema. Cognition is the result of life's self-division from itself (the Idea "doubled"), which in more straightforward terms means that Hegel understands cognition in terms of self-conscious life. Whereas life as the immediate Idea provides an account of the a priori processes that enable the relation and opposition between subject and object, allowing objects to be immediately given and present to subjects, life becoming aware of itself produces various self-conceptions, which have various limitations and positive powers. In section 8.1, I discuss some of the limitations and powers of theoretical and practical cognition, and I argue that those same limitations are overcome by grasping their unity, a unity that results in absolute method. In section 8.2, I argue that absolute method is best understood as the ongoing dialectic between life and cognition, taking up Hegel's analysis of *beginning* and *dialectic* in the final chapter of the *Logic*.

8.1 Theoretical and Practical Cognition

One of the effects of reflexivity on the determination of logical life is a resulting dissatisfaction with respect to its mode of reproduction: from the perspective of self-conscious cognition, the form of activity of life is only "repetition" and an "infinite progress" (WL 688/6:486). From the perspective of self-consciousness, the immediate self-certainty that is produced through life-activity is extremely limited for the individual, reaching its height in the genus process with the propagation of the species, a process that results, necessarily, in the perishing of the individual. Of course, it is only once life is divided from itself that there can emerge a dissatisfaction with *mere* life. Without this division and doubling, individuals entirely immersed in the

Hegel's Concept of Life. Karen Ng, Oxford University Press (2020) © Oxford University Press 2020.
DOI: 10.1093/oso/9780190947613.001.0001

immediacy of life, who live out their life-processes unconsciously and largely by instinct, do not, as part of their self-feeling, experience mere life as a limitation or bad infinity. The key transformation that takes place with the emergence of self-conscious cognition is the ability to reshape the processes of life according to the purposes and aims of freedom rather than the immediate aims of ongoing reproduction. Put somewhat differently, the immediacy of life-form activity (corporeality, the relation to a conformable externality, and the relation to other members of the same species) becomes permeated by reason and thought. Although the three processes of life are fundamentally transformed by reason and thought, the logical form of life retains its power as an enabling and constraining presupposition of cognition insofar as its theoretical and practical activities are realized by means of the form-constraints of life: cognition realizes its aims in a specific body with determinate powers of thought and action, in relation to a conformable external world that it conceptualizes and actively shapes to respond to the aims of freedom, and in relations of recognition with other self-conscious individuals through which the life-form as a whole is reproduced as spirit.[1] The ongoing power and significance of the schema of logical life is seen most clearly in the section on Subjective Spirit in the *Philosophy of Mind*, where Hegel outlines, in a number of stages, the concrete, self-actualization of human mindedness insofar as reason comes to permeate all three dimensions of human life-activity. Hegel anticipates these developments in the opening of the chapter on "Cognition" by making reference to the determinations of spirit in anthropology, phenomenology, and psychology (WL 694–695/6:494–496). However, in the logical context, the Idea of spirit does not denote the embodied natural soul, phenomenological consciousness, or psychological mind but, rather, the I as both subject and object: as subject, the I is the subjective Concept, with the powers of judgment and inference outlined in the first section of the Subjective Logic; as object, the I is the objective Concept, with the powers of activity outlined in the second section of the Subjective Logic, most notably, the powers of externally and internally purposive action. Empowered by the schema of logical life, the living, self-conscious I, beginning as drive and inner purpose, once again seeks to realize itself as objective, but this time the

---

[1] Hegel now characterizes the doubling of the Idea as follows: "[I]t is from the *Idea of life* that the Idea of spirit has emerged, or what is the same thing, that the Idea of spirit has demonstrated itself to be the truth of the Idea of life" (WL 694/6:493).

result is the reproduction of self-certainty by means of the rational activity of pursuing the true and the good.[2]

The logical form of life thus opens up the theoretical and practical activities of cognition, or more directly, the logical form of life opens up the space of reasons. Both theoretical and practical cognition take the general form of the judgment of life, beginning as a subjective drive that distinguishes itself from and relates itself to a presupposed objectivity, and in that process, realizes subjective purposes by permeating objectivity with its own rational form. In the case of theoretical cognition, the subjective drive for truth is confronted by the givenness of its presupposed world, and by means of its powers of judgment and inference, it renders the world conformable by conceptual comprehension, aided by definitions, divisions, and theorems. In the case of practical cognition, the subjective drive to realize the good is achieved by transforming the external world according to its freely willed action, shaping the world in a way that furthers the aims of a self-determined, rational life. Although Hegel's discussion of both theoretical and practical cognition operates at a relatively high level of generality in order to stay within the bounds of a logical context, it is worth noting some important features of both in order to understand how he arrives at the final stage of the absolute Idea as the method for his philosophical system.

With respect to the general shape of theoretical cognition, it is instructive to consider both its ultimate limitations and its positive contribution to the production of truth. On the side of limitations, Hegel has in mind a type of finite cognition, or *Verstand*, in which cognition is fixed in its opposition to a given. Theoretical cognition receives its "determinate content and filling" from the givenness of the objective world, but at the same time, theoretical cognition cannot overcome the givenness of the object, which renders truth "an absolute *beyond*" according to its own self-description (WL 729, 698/6:542, 500). This general shape of finite cognition is discussed in Hegel's work in a variety of contexts, often in connection with a critique of Kant, and more broadly in connection with a critique of an "instrument" view of cognition where cognition is a filter or medium (passive or active) that fails to sufficiently bridge the absolute gulf between the I and its given object in the pursuit of truth.[3] Whereas the Idea of life is an immediate unity of Concept

---

[2] On the ongoing production of "real" or "absolute" truth of self-certainty, see WL 696, 697, 729/ 6:497, 498, 542.

[3] See PhG ¶¶73–76/3:68–72; and EL §10Z.

and objectivity, the Idea of cognition, in both its theoretical and its practical forms, initially finds itself on one side of an absolute gulf between subjectivity and objectivity that it has difficulty traversing in its attempt to realize the truth of its self-certainty. In the theoretical context, truth resides in the given object, which is an "unknown *thinghood-in-itself behind* cognition" that cognition can never reach; in the practical context, the good is an "*ought-to-be*" that can never be objectively realized (WL 698, 731/6:500, 544). In large part due to reflexivity and self-consciousness concerning its own form of activity, cognition in effect gets in its own way by positing an absolute distinction between itself and its object, making unity with objective reality in the shape of the true and the good unattainable *in principle*. There is a certain irony here, insofar as distinguishing itself from objectivity is essential to cognition's absolute act of self-constitution, but by this same act of self-division, cognition also creates the conditions for its own dissatisfaction. Although the living being may face all sorts of empirical obstacles in its life-processes that prevent it from successfully reproducing its feeling of self-certainty in relation to the external world, the self-conscious I can fail to reproduce its truth of self-certainty due to faulty and one-sided self-conceptions. The specific limitation of theoretical cognition lies in such a faulty self-conception: in conceiving of itself as absolutely separated from the truth that it seeks, theoretical cognition on its own cannot overcome the givenness of the object, remaining an external form that necessarily falls short of capturing the truth of the thing itself.

Despite its limitations, theoretical cognition nonetheless makes a positive contribution to the production of truth, constituting an essential part of cognition's activity. Hegel divides theoretical cognition into analytic and synthetic activities, with synthetic cognition making up the bulk of his discussion.[4] The three moments of synthetic cognition reflect the three moments of the Concept: definition attempts to cognize the universality of the object; division cognizes the particularization of the universal; and theorems cognize the individuality of the object "in its reality" (WL 718/6:527). When theoretical cognition operates to define and divide the objects of the external world, Hegel claims that it is already minimally operating at the level of judgments of necessity, in which objects are determined and divided according to genera and species (WL 708/6:512). Thus, for theoretical cognition to judge at all, it is always already judging according to *Gattung*-concepts. Although

---

[4] On the unity of analytic and synthetic cognition, see WL 741/6:557.

these definitions and divisions do not get beyond the "*proximate* genus," in-sofar as empirical determinations of genera and species remain inevitably plagued by a certain contingency and arbitrariness that is an eliminable fea-ture of nature, the "instinct of reason" nonetheless provides a ground for such divisions such that the sensible properties of nature can be "more adequate to the Concept" (WL 708, 717/6:512, 526).

Hegel is making two claims here. First, the division of nature into genera and species remains proximate and contingent, but this is because nature it-self *is* full of contingency in its divisions and distinctions. Although theo-retical cognition can, of course, make empirical errors, it is also not missing anything in determining nature according to relatively contingent, proxi-mate classifications, since nature itself *is* contingent. Second, the ground of these divisions and the very divisions themselves are a product of the instinct of reason. The sensible properties of nature, apprehended according to the powers of life and thought embodied in the self-conscious I, are indeed ade-quate to and conformable with the Concept; in fact, theoretical cognition is able to capture the "vital point [*Lebenspunkt*]" of animal life and the "highest point" of plant life, according to its systems of classification (WL 717–718/6:526). Specifically, by means of its definitions and divisions, cognition is able to determine the "individuality" of both plant and animal life, or the essential shape and structure of their internally purposive activity embodied in the unity of sensibility, irritability, and reproduction.[5] The instinct of reason is thus able to find *some* truth of self-certainty in its theoretical pursuits after all, despite the absolute distinction it has drawn between itself and the con-tingency of its given object.

Hegel's reference to the instinct of reason here should be noted in partic-ular. The most extended discussion of the instinct of reason can be found in the section, "Observation of Nature," in the *Phenomenology of Spirit*, where there is a similar analysis of the contingency of nature's divisions faced by observing reason in its attempts to classify nature according to definitions and laws. In that context, and comparing the instinct of the animal with the instinct of reason, Hegel defined the instinct of reason as follows:

[5] As an example, Hegel points specifically to the organs by which individuality is reproduced in an-imal and plant life—namely, the organs of eating for animals and the fertilizing organs for plants (WL 717–718/6:526).

Just as an animal's instinct is to seek and consume food, without its thereby bringing forth anything but itself, so too does the instinct of reason only find itself in its seeking. An animal stops with self-feeling. In contrast, the instinct of reason is at the same time self-consciousness. (PhG ¶258/ 3:199–200)[6]

In the life-process of assimilation, the animal finds the external world conformable and reproduces its own self-feeling; in the theoretical activity of defining and dividing up the external world, the instinct of reason finds nothing but reason itself. Specifically, the instinct of reason produces the truth of self-certainty in finding the external world adequate to its systems of classification, an adequacy that reaches its highest point for theoretical cognition when it grasps the form of inner purposiveness, the shape of living individuality itself, in the existences of organic nature.[7]

With respect to theorems, Hegel recommends that this type of cognition must be kept within its proper bounds, emphasizing that its method of construction and proof is inappropriate for philosophical investigations.[8] Essentially, what cognition finds in this method of proof is a mode of necessity that is contrary to its essentially self-determining form. To illustrate the inappropriateness of theorems with respect to philosophy, Hegel returns to his oft-repeated criticism of Spinoza, who employs a synthetic method appropriate for geometry to the philosophical investigation of substance: the axiomatic necessity of the geometric method is ill-suited for a subject matter whose essential activity is freedom (WL 727/6:539). Ultimately, theoretical cognition's abilities to produce self-certainty are limited insofar as none of its self-conceptions as analytic or synthetic cognition fully reflect the self-determining form of the Concept, and Hegel suggests that the transition to practical cognition is the same as the transition from necessity to freedom outlined earlier in the "*genesis of the Concept*" (WL 729/6:541). Without repeating that argument here, what generally motivates the transition to practical cognition is twofold: first, although its method of proof does not reflect the freedom of the Concept, the necessity produced in theorems overcomes the contingency of the object, transforming the very stance of theoretical

---

[6] Immediately before this, Hegel is discussing the relation between the concept of purpose and the instinct of reason, suggesting a formal parallel between the activity of internal purposiveness and the self-constitution of self-consciousness. See PhG ¶¶ 257–258/3:198–200.

[7] See also PhG ¶295/3:224: "[T]o observation, reason exists as *life as such*."

[8] See also EL §231.

cognition which began by simply *finding* its object as given; second, the absolute gulf posited by theoretical cognition between itself and the contingency of its given objects can be bridged by a transformation of its self-conception, a transformation that is already nascent in theoretical cognition's form of activity. As the drive for truth, cognition employed theoretical means toward the end of positing subjectivity as identical with its presupposed object, an activity that already manifests the form of the practical syllogism. We can formulate the activity of theoretical cognition as follows:

> Theoretical cognition is the drive for truth.
> The drive for truth involves the tools of analysis and synthesis (theoretical tools).
> Theoretical cognition employs theoretical tools in the pursuit of truth.

In the transformation of its self-conception, cognition, with a meta-awareness of the shape of its theoretical activity *as practical*, posits itself essentially as *willing*, or the drive to intentionally shape the world by means of action in accordance with self-determined ends. As the drive to realize the good, practical cognition emerges initially as "the syllogism of *external purposiveness*," employing finite means in the pursuit of finite and particular ends (WL 730/6:543).[9] Like theoretical cognition, however, practical cognition faces a number of difficulties in its attempt to realize the good through action. These difficulties amount to problems of contingency at a distinctly practical register: there are many different kinds of good to be realized, and the will may have difficulties resolving itself in choosing a particular good; my actions can be thwarted by external contingency and evil, and the good itself can become distorted due to irrational or unjust action contexts, alongside faulty and one-sided self-conceptions; finally, there can be a conflict of duties within the good such that its realization is contradictory or undermined. Hegel soberly admits that it may indeed be impossible to overcome the obstacles faced by the will in its pursuit of the good, which leads the will to determine the good as a mere *ought* that can never be realized.

Hegel's sober admission concerning the genuine obstacles the will faces in its drive for the good should be noted here, since it tempers the view of an unbridled Hegelian optimism with respect to the power of reason. Nevertheless, Hegel will not rest content with the determination of the good as a mere

---

[9] On the syllogism of external purposiveness, see section 6.3, this volume.

ought, and the difficulties faced by practical cognition are resolved by means of a reunification with theoretical cognition. To be clear, the reunification with theoretical cognition does not imply that the problems of practical contingency mentioned here cease to exist for the will; rather, what the reunification with theoretical cognition prevents is the will's faulty self-conception in which it pursues an *ought* that cannot be made actual *in principle*. That the problem for practical cognition concerns its own self-conception, rather than the genuine obstacles of practical contingency (which deserve a detailed and systematic investigation but cannot be the topic of a logical investigation), is stated quite clearly by Hegel when he writes: "It is the will itself, therefore, that alone stands in the way of attaining its goal, because it separates itself from cognition and because for it external actuality does not receive the form of a true existence. The Idea of the good can therefore find its completion only in the Idea of the true" (WL 732/6:545).[10] What exactly does theoretical cognition contribute, then, to the will's activity of realizing the good?

Insofar as what is in question is the will's self-conception, I want to suggest that what the reunification with theoretical cognition enables is a shift in stance and perspective, a shift that prevents the will from undermining its own actions on the basis of a faulty self-conception. From an admittedly high level of generality, the difference between theoretical and practical cognition can be described as follows: whereas theoretical cognition finds truth in its given external actuality and conceives of itself initially as empty of truth, practical cognition takes external actuality to be a "nullity [*Nichtige*]" without any intrinsic worth or truth until it is first determined by the will according to the ends of the good (WL 732/6:545). In short, for theoretical cognition, all truth is to be found in the external world, and for practical cognition, no truth is to be found in the external world. This stance of the will, in which the ends of the good reside within the will alone, and external actuality is, in-itself, empty of all worth, is what leads the will to conceive of the good as an unrealizable *ought*. The nullity of the world cannot be rendered conformable to the absolute worth of the good will, leaving "two worlds in opposition" (WL 731/6:544). What the unity of theoretical and practical standpoints allows is a reciprocity and mutual tempering of each such that cognition can be brought in relation to the external world while avoiding

---

[10] See also WL 733/6:547: "[W]hat still *limits* the objective Concept is its own *view* of itself. . . . Through this view the Concept stands in its own way, and thus what it has to do is to turn, not against an external actuality, but against itself."

the extreme vices of both stances: theoretical cognition's meta-awareness of its own activity as practical prevents the self-conception in which all content of truth is found in the givenness of the object; practical cognition's re-unification with theoretical cognition prevents the self-conception in which the will alone is the source of all goodness and worth. Theoretical cognition reminds the will that the contingency of the world can be made to conform with cognition's form of activity, that although it is *true* that there are ineliminable contingencies, this truth is something that cognition can grasp, and most importantly, it is not a fact that disables the activity of cognition *in principle*. Since theoretical cognition can find truth of self-certainty in the given contingency of the world—most notably, the instinct of reason finds itself in the form of inner purposiveness as such—nothing in principle prevents the will from finding the truth of self-certainty amid practical contingency, except for its faulty conception of itself. Far from a worthless nullity, the actuality confronting the will is already permeated by rational ends, "an objective world whose inner ground and actual subsistence is the Concept" (WL 734/6:548). That is, the external actuality confronting the will is always already a world shaped by the rationally realized ends of the will itself—ultimately, the world of objective spirit, and more directly, the world of ethical life. The insistence of the will that the good is a mere *ought* that cannot be realized is thus a misconception of both itself and its world—a misconception that theoretical cognition can help to correct. The unity of theoretical and practical cognition brings forth *the absolute Idea*, which, once more, returns us to the problem of life.

8.2 The Dialectic of Life and Cognition as Absolute Method

Why does the determination of the absolute Idea bring us back to the Idea of life? To leave no doubt that life plays an essential role in the final moment of the *Logic*, here is Hegel in the opening of the chapter on "The Absolute Idea":

> The absolute Idea has shown itself to be the identity of the theoretical and the practical Idea, each of which, of itself still one-sided, possesses the Idea only as a sought-for beyond and an unattained goal. . . . The absolute Idea, as the rational Concept, which in its reality joins only with itself [*nur mit sich selbst zusammengeht*], is by virtue of this immediacy of its objective

identity, on the one hand the return to *life*; but it has no less sublated this form of its immediacy, and contains within itself the highest opposition. (WL 735/6:548–549)

And in the *Encyclopaedia Logic*:

The absolute Idea is first of all the unity of the theoretical and the practical Idea, and hence equally the unity of the Idea of life with the Idea of cognition. . . . The deficiency of life consists in the fact that it is still only the Idea *in-itself*; cognition, on the contrary, is the Idea only as it is *for-itself*, in the same one-sided way. The unity and the truth of these two is the Idea that is *in* and *for itself*, and hence *absolute*. (EL §236Z)[11]

In the activity of the absolute Idea, there is at once a return to life and a sublating of its immediacy, an activity that contains the highest, internal opposition. The language of "joining with itself" recalls the language employed to describe the process of actualization, a process of actualization that, here, takes place by means of a return to life. That the immediacy of life is sublated in the return to life means that rational life is permeated by rational ends, but the absolute Idea remains doubled in its inner opposition, an opposition that constitutes the very process of its self-actualization. In the passage from the *Encyclopaedia*, the importance of the doubling of the Idea is even more apparent, with Hegel claiming not only that the absolute Idea is the unity of life and cognition but, further, that life and cognition on their own remain deficient and one-sided. What is especially noteworthy is the claim that *cognition* is equally one-sided when taken in isolation from its essential relation and opposition to life. Hegel thus continues to affirm his earlier claim that cognition *without* life would be an empty affair devoid of determination. I now want to consider what it means for the absolute Idea, as the ongoing dialectic between life and cognition, to be the method of Hegel's philosophical system.[12]

Like the account of cognition, the determination of the Idea as absolute method operates at a very high level of generality, and it is difficult to distill specific details concerning exactly how such a method is supposed to operate.

---

[11] See also EL §235, where Hegel refers to the speculative or absolute Idea as life.
[12] On Hegel's absolute method, see Nuzzo (1999, 2005, 2011), Forster (1993), Zambrana (2015, chap. 7), and Kreines (2015, chap. 10).

Despite the high level of generality, Hegel does not hesitate in making far-reaching claims concerning the scope of absolute method, calling it "absolute form," "the absolute foundation and ultimate truth," the *universal absolute activity*" in which "the *Concept is everything*," and a "self-determining and self-realizing movement" (WL 737/6:551). The absolute Idea is the method for *everything*, and there is no object or subject matter that is, in principle, outside method's grasp. Method is "reason's highest and sole *drive,* to find and cognize *itself by means of itself in everything*." Admittedly, the sheer outrageousness of these claims tries the patience of even the most generous reader. However, I take it that Hegel is putting forward absolute method as the method of his philosophical idealism: having excised Kant's thing-in-itself, there is no domain of objects that is, *in principle*, outside reason's grasp, and absolute method is both the subjective act of knowing and the means by which reason knows everything it comes to know. Having eliminated the thought that truth and goodness are beyond the grasp of reason in principle, the unity of theoretical and practical cognition is what allows Hegel to determine the scope of method as truly absolute, as having no meaningful "outside." Moreover, in claiming that method is at once identical with cognition's activity, and that it is cognition's "*instrument* and means," Hegel has finally produced the positive result of his long-stated position that method is not external to its content, but instead represents the essential form of its content, that method is "the structure of the whole in its pure essentiality."[13] Method is the way, manner, and mode by which reason operates, the essential form of reason's self-actualization. That reason operates by way of the unity and opposition between life and self-conscious cognition means the following: first, life opens up the possibility of rendering intelligible, allowing objects to be immediately given and presented to be known and appropriated, providing an a priori schema of reality shaped by the objective *Gattung* or life-form of the knowing subject; second, self-consciousness of one's own life-form activity (which can be vague, inchoate, mythical, religious, artistic, historical, ethical, scientific, literary, or philosophical, or any combination thereof) produces theoretical and practical self-conceptions that mediate and reshape the activity of life, enabling new and ever-changing powers of freedom, self-determination, and knowledge alongside new and ever-changing contingencies and problems. This method of reason is *absolute* because, as

---

[13] See PhG ¶48/3:47 and the discussion of Hegel's method in the *Phenomenology* in section 3.4.1, this volume.

noted, it has no meaningful "outside": there is nothing that is intelligible that is not rendered intelligible via this method, and even the intelligibility of what falls below the processes of life and cognition—mechanism, chemism, and external purposiveness—are only intelligible *as* the things that they are from *within* the bounds of method itself. The conceptual, then, taken in Hegel's broad and encompassing sense as opened up by the activity of life, is "unbounded; there is nothing outside it."[14]

Still operating at a very high level of generality, Hegel identifies two central features of absolute method as reason's processual activity: beginning and dialectic.[15] Although the beginning is, unsurprisingly, characterized by immediacy, there are three important qualifications on the immediacy of beginning as presented in the final chapter of the *Logic* that are worth noting. First, the immediacy of beginning in question here is an immediacy of *thinking*, and not the immediacy of sense experience or representation (WL 738/6:553). Hegel calls this immediacy of thinking, "*inner intuiting* [innerliches Anschauen]." Second, the immediacy in question is not inert but, rather, must already contain within itself the potential for its further development (WL 740/6:556). In containing this potential for development, the immediacy of beginning is somehow "deficient," "afflicted with a *negation*," and yet, "endowed with the *drive* to carry itself further" (WL 739/6:555).[16] Third, the immediacy in question is already a universal determination, and specifically is an "objective universal" *in-itself* not yet posited *for-itself*. Recall that the objective universal for Hegel is always the determination of a *Gattung*-concept—something's genus, species, or kind. All three of these qualifications make the immediacy of reason's beginning already quite complex: beginning is a determination that already contains both unity and generality by means of a *Gattung*-concept, alongside differentiation, negativity, and a potential for further development. The obvious choice for the beginning in question is, of course, the determination of "being" with which the *Logic* began, but Hegel claims that this determination is far too "impoverished," that the universality and relation-to-self expressed by "being" is far too abstract, to serve as the relevant immediacy that constitutes the true beginning of absolute method (WL 739/6:554). Instead, reason's beginning must already have the shape of the Concept *in-itself*: the immediacy of thinking is always already

---

[14] McDowell 1996, 44.

[15] In the *Encyclopaedia*, Hegel identifies three moments of absolute method: (1) beginning; (2) progression and judgment; and (3) the end. See EL §§238, 239, 242.

[16] See also PhG ¶22/3:26, where Hegel refers to purpose as the beginning.

determined as manifesting the form of the Concept. The beginning of absolute method is finally characterized as follows:

> [A] beginning which is *in itself* a concrete totality may as such also be *free* and its immediacy have the determination of an *external existence*; the *germ of the living being* and the *subjective purpose* in general have shown themselves to be such beginnings and therefore both are themselves *drives*. (WL 740/6:556)

Absolute method thus begins, in its immediacy, with living, subjective purposiveness—the drive for the truth of self-certainty, the drive to posit subjective purposes and aims as objective. Reason begins immediately as the subjective purposiveness manifest in living activity, a beginning that already contains within itself both universality and negation. It is an immediate universality that has the potential and drive within itself for development, advancement, and progress. The "advance [*Fortgang*]" is the process by which the immediate universality of the beginning determines and posits itself as universal *for itself* such that it is "equally an individual and a subject" (WL 740/6:555–556). For this advance to be possible, the objective universality of the beginning—the immediately relevant *Gattung* context—must be one that has the power and potential for rational self-actualization. That is, it must be a schema of living activity that has the power to posit itself as spiritual activity.

However, Hegel's account of the beginning of absolute method also presents a puzzle: it turns out that the beginning of absolute method is not the same as the beginning of the *Logic*, that in fact, the beginning cited here at the end of the *Logic* is entirely different from the beginning with which the *Logic* began. In short, absolute method begins with purposiveness and life, but the *Logic* itself begins with being (being, pure being, without any further determination). How are we to make sense of this? An initial answer to this question is that Hegel simply affirms this difference of beginnings. He writes:

> But the simple determination of *being* is in itself so impoverished that, if for that reason alone, not much fuss ought to be made about it. . . . [T]he demand [*Forderung*] that being should be exhibited [*das Sein aufzuzeigen*] has a further, inner meaning in which more is at issue than just this abstract determination; implied in it is the demand for the *realization of the Concept*, a realization that that does not lie in the *beginning* itself, but is

rather the goal and task of the entire subsequent development of cognition. (WL 739/6:554)

According to this passage, there are in fact two senses of beginning that need to be distinguished. The first is the beginning in "being," a determination that is so abstract and impoverished, that, now at the conclusion of the *Logic*, Hegel is at a loss to say anything substantial about it at all. Rather than make a fuss about this first sense of beginning, Hegel instead directs our attention to "the *demand* that being should be exhibited," and associates this demand with "the demand for the *realization of the Concept.*" That the latter demand is implied by the former means the following: being can only be exhibited, pointed out, shown, and ultimately rendered intelligible from the perspective of the realized Concept or the Idea. In the attempt to satisfy the demand that being be exhibited, the *Logic* comes to satisfy the demand for the realization of the Concept—the demand for an account of how being can be rendered intelligible at all. Hegel makes clear that the demand for the realization of the Concept is in fact *not* at the beginning understood in the first, impoverished sense, but that it is attained as the goal and task of the entire project, a project in which it is now clear that the Doctrine of the Concept plays a crucial, outsized role.[17] The second, truer sense of beginning is the beginning of absolute method thus outlined, which is only now made fully explicit at the end of the progression of the *Science of Logic*. Now at the end, we can see that the beginning in being was a demand that being be exhibited and rendered intelligible, a demand that is fulfilled via the realization of the Concept in absolute method. These two beginnings form a mutually illuminating circle, since absolute method allows us to grasp how being is exhibited and rendered intelligible, and being as an impoverished, abstract determination contains a demand to be exhibited and *rendered* intelligible, which ultimately develops into the demand for an absolute method.

The second moment of absolute method is dialectic, and it is also characterized as the moment of *judgment*—the moment in which reason is divided from itself as analytic and synthetic cognition. Dialectic has almost become synonymous with Hegelian thought itself, and its central characteristics are on full display in absolute method: in the advance and development

---

[17] The demand for the realization of the Concept, developing throughout the Objective Logic, is perhaps first made explicit in the genesis of the Concept argument in the "Actuality" section, which brings about the transition to the Subjective Logic.

of the immediate beginning, reason sets itself in opposition to a negative, and at the same time, it overcomes this contradiction in a positive, mediated determination that preserves and retains negativity in the process of its self-actualization. In a description that mirrors Hegel's discussion of method in the introduction of the *Phenomenology*, dialectic is described as a process of determinate negation whereby a *"first negative"* is rationally mediated into the determination of a *"second* negative" or "negative of the negative" (WL 744, 745/6:561, 563).[18] More concretely, dialectic transforms the immediate beginning of absolute method into a rationally mediated determination posited by cognition for itself. Through this dialectical process, the results posited by reason are immediately again a beginning, and beginning is again a drive that advances in its development as "cognition rolls onwards from content to content" (WL 750/6:569). The infinite advance of absolute method, continually enriching itself and increasing in concreteness through self-determined activity, expands into a philosophical system, consisting of logic, nature, and spirit. Famously, Hegel calls this a *"circle of circles,"* with absolute method constituting the essential form and activity of reason as such (WL 751/6:571). Importantly, the two moments of *beginning* and *dialectic* are inseparable in the determination and continual progression of absolute method. Without the immediate drive and subjective purpose of the beginning, shaped by an objective *Gattung*-context, there is no negativity and no advance, no possibility of self-division and opposition that brings about a posited, sublated determination. Absolute method, as the ongoing dialectic between life and cognition, returns again and again to its beginning in life, a return that is likewise the opening of intelligibility as such.

[18] The negative of the negative "is the innermost source of all activity, of all living and spiritual self-movement, the dialectical soul that everything true possesses and through which alone it is true; for on this subjectivity alone rests the sublation of the opposition between Concept and reality, and the unity that is truth. . . . [It is] the *innermost, most objective moment* of life and spirit, through which a *subject* is a *person*, is *free*" (WL 745–746/6:563).

References

Allais, Lucy. 2009. "Kant, Non-Conceptual Content, and the Representation of Space." *Journal of the History of Philosophy* 47 (2): 383–413.

Allais, Lucy. 2015. *Manifest Reality: Kant's Idealism and his Realism*. Oxford: Oxford University Press.

Allison, Henry. 1991. "Kant's Antinomy of Teleological Judgment." *The Southern Journal of Philosophy* 30 (Suppl.): 25–42.

Allison, Henry. 2000. "Is the Critique of Judgment 'Post-Critical'?" In *The Reception of Kant's Critical Philosophy: Fichte, Schelling, and Hegel*, edited by Sally Sedgwick, 78–92. Cambridge: Cambridge University Press.

Allison, Henry. 2001. *Kant's Theory of Taste: A Reading of the Critique of Aesthetic Judgment*. Cambridge: Cambridge University Press.

Ameriks, Karl. 1985. "Hegel's Critique of Kant's Theoretical Philosophy." *Philosophy and Phenomenological Research* 46 (1): 1–35.

Aristotle. 1984. *The Complete Works of Aristotle: The Revised Oxford Translation*. Edited by Jonathan Barnes. Princeton, NJ: Princeton University Press.

Baum, Manfred. 1990. "Kants Prinzip der Zweckmäßigkeit und Hegels Realisierung des Begriffs." In *Hegel und die "Kritik der Urteilskraft,"* edited by Hans-Friedrich Fulda and Rolf-Peter Horstmann, 158–173. Stuttgart: Klett-Cotta.

Beiser, Frederick C. 1987. *The Fate of Reason: German Philosophy from Kant to Fichte*. Cambridge, MA: Harvard University Press.

Beiser, Frederick C. 2002. *German Idealism: The Struggle against Subjectivism, 1781–1801*. Cambridge, MA: Harvard University Press.

Beiser, Frederick C. 2003. *The Romantic Imperative: The Concept of Early German Romanticism*. Cambridge, MA: Harvard University Press.

Beiser, Frederick C. 2005. *Hegel*. New York: Routledge.

Beiser, Frederick. 2014. "Romanticism and Idealism." In *The Relevance of Romanticism: Essays on German Romantic Philosophy*, edited by Dalia Nassar, 30–43. Oxford: Oxford University Press.

Bernstein, J. M. 2001. *Adorno: Disenchantment and Ethics*. Cambridge: Cambridge University Press.

Bowman, Brady. 2013. *Hegel and the Metaphysics of Absolute Negativity*. Cambridge: Cambridge University Press.

Boyle, Matthew. 2016. "Additive Theories of Rationality: A Critique." *European Journal of Philosophy* 24 (3): 527–555.

Boyle, Matthew. 2018. "A Different Kind of Mind?" In *The Routledge Handbook of Philosophy of Animal Minds*, edited by Kristin Andrews and Jacob Beck, 109–118. New York: Routledge.

Brandom, Robert. 1979. "Freedom and Constraint by Norms." *American Philosophical Quarterly* 16 (3): 187–196.

Brandom, Robert. 1994. *Making It Explicit: Reasoning, Representing, and Discursive Commitment*. Cambridge, MA: Harvard University Press.

Brandom, Robert. 2002. "Some Pragmatist Themes in Hegel's Idealism." In *Tales of the Mighty Dead: Historical Essays in the Metaphysics of Intentionality*, 210–234. Cambridge, MA: Harvard University Press.

Brandom, Robert. 2007. "The Structure of Desire and Recognition: Self-Consciousness and Self-Constitution." *Philosophy and Social Criticism* 33 (1): 127–150.

Breazeale, Daniel. 2013. *Thinking Through the Wissenschaftslehre: Themes from Fichte's Early Philosophy.* Oxford: Oxford University Press.

Bristow, William F. 2002. "Are Kant's Categories Subjective?" *Review of Metaphysics* 55 (3): 551–580.

Burbidge, John. 1996. *Real Process: How Logic and Chemistry Combine in Hegel's Philosophy of Nature.* Toronto: University of Toronto Press.

Burbidge, John. 2007. *Hegel's Systematic Contingency.* New York: Palgrave Macmillan.

Burmeister, John K. 2013. "Hegel's Living Logic." *Research in Phenomenology* 43 (2): 243–264.

Campbell, Joseph Keim, Michael O'Rourke, and Matthew H. Slater, eds. 2011. *Carving Nature at Its Joints: Natural Kinds in Metaphysics and Science.* Cambridge, MA: MIT Press.

Cerf, Walter. 1977. "Speculative Philosophy and Intellectual Intuition: An Introduction to Hegel's Essays." In G. W. F. Hegel, *The Difference Between Fichte's and Schelling's System of Philosophy*, edited by H. S. Harris and Walter Cerf, xi–xxxvi. Albany: SUNY Press.

Chaouli, Michel. 2017. *Thinking with Kant's "Critique of Judgment."* Cambridge, MA: Harvard University Press.

Cohen, Robert S., and Marx W. Wartofsky, eds. 1984. *Hegel and the Sciences.* Dordrecht: D'Reidel.

Dahlstrom, Daniel O. 1998. "Hegel's Appropriation of Kant's Account of Teleology in Nature." In *Hegel and the Philosophy of Nature*, edited by Stephen Houlgate, 167–188. Albany: SUNY Press.

De Boer, Karin. 2010. "Hegel's Account of Contradiction in the *Science of Logic* Reconsidered." *Journal of the History of Philosophy* 48 (3): 345–373.

deVries, Willem A. 1991. "The Dialectic of Teleology." *Philosophical Topics* 19 (2): 51–70.

di Giovanni, George. 1980. "The Category of Contingency in the Hegelian Logic." In *Art and Logic in Hegel's Philosophy*, edited by Warren E. Steinkraus and Kenneth L. Schmitz, 179–200. Atlantic Highlands, NJ: Humanities Press.

Dupré, John. 1995. *The Disorder of Things: Metaphysical Foundations of the Disunity of Science.* Cambridge, MA: Harvard University Press.

Düsing, Klaus. 1986a. "Ästhetische Einbildungskraft und intuitiver Verstand. Kants Lehre und Hegels spekulativ-idealistische Umdeutung." *Hegel-Studien* 21: 87–128.

Düsing, Klaus. 1986b. "Die Idee des Lebens in Hegels Logik." In *Hegels Philosophie der Natur*, edited by Rolf-Peter Horstmann and Michael John Petry, 276–289. Stuttgart: Klett-Cotta.

Ferrarin, Alfredo. 2001. *Hegel and Aristotle.* Cambridge: Cambridge University Press.

Ferrarin, Alfredo. 2006. "Hegel on Aristotle's *Energeia.*" *Hegel Bulletin* 27 (1/2): 69–80.

Ferrini, Cinzia. 2009. "From Geological to Animal Nature in Hegel's Idea of Life." *Hegel-Studien* 44: 45–93.

Ferrini, Cinzia. 2011. "The Transition to Organics: Hegel's Idea of Life." In *A Companion to Hegel*, edited by Stephen Houlgate and Michael Baur, 203–224. Oxford: Blackwell.

Fichte, J. G. 1971. "Eigene Meditationen zur Elementarphilosophie (Zweiter Teil: Practische Philosophie)." In *Gesamtausgabe: Nachgelassene Schriften Bd. 3: 1793–1795*. Suttgart-Bad Canstatt: Frommann.

Findlay, John. 1958. *Hegel: A Re-Examination*. London: George Allen & Unwin.

Förster, Eckart. 2009/2010. "The Significance of §§76 and 77 of the *Critique of Judgment* for the Development of Post-Kantian Philosophy (Parts 1 and 2)." *Graduate Faculty Philosophy Journal* 30 (2): 197–217 and 31 (2): 323–347.

Förster, Eckart. 2012. *The Twenty-Five Years of Philosophy: A Systematic Reconstruction*. Cambridge, MA: Harvard University Press.

Förster, Eckart, and Yitzhak Y. Melamed, eds. 2015. *Spinoza and German Idealism*. Cambridge: Cambridge University Press.

Forster, Michael. 1993. "Hegel's Dialectical Method." In *The Cambridge Companion to Hegel*, edited by Frederick C. Beiser, 130–170. Cambridge: Cambridge University Press.

Frank, Manfred. 1997. *"Unendliche Annäherung": Die Anfänge der philosophischen Frühromantik*. Frankfurt am Main: Suhrkamp.

Frank, Manfred. 2014. "What Is Early German Romantic Philosophy?" In *The Relevance of Romanticism: Essays on German Romantic Philosophy*, edited by Dalia Nassar, 15–29. Oxford: Oxford University Press.

Franks, Paul. 1997. "*Tatsache* and *Tathandlung* in the Development of Fichte's Jena *Wissenschaftslehre*." *Archiv für Geschichte der Philosophie* 79 (3): 310–323.

Franks, Paul. 2005. *All or Nothing: Systematicity, Transcendental Arguments, and Skepticism in German Idealism*. Cambridge, MA: Harvard University Press.

Friedman, Michael. 1991. "Regulative and Constitutive." *The Southern Journal of Philosophy* 30 (Suppl.): 73–102.

Gabriel, Markus. 2009. "The Mythological Being of Reflection: An Essay on Hegel, Schelling, and the Contingency of Necessity." In Markus Gabriel and Slavoj Žižek, *Mythology, Madness, and Laughter: Subjectivity in German Idealism*, 15–94. New York: Continuum.

Gabriel, Markus. 2011. "Contingency or Necessity? Schelling versus Hegel." In *Transcendental Ontology: Essays in German Idealism*, 102–136. New York: Continuum.

Gabriel, Markus. 2015. "Schelling (1775–1854)." In *The Oxford Handbook of German Philosophy in the Nineteenth-Century*, edited by Michael Forster and Kristin Gjesdal, 88–107. Oxford: Oxford University Press.

Gadamer, Hans-Georg. 1976. *Hegel's Dialectic: Five Hermeneutical Studies*. Translated by P. Christopher Smith. New Haven, CT: Yale University Press.

García, Marcela. 2015. "Schelling's Theory of Judgment and the Interpretation of the Copula." *Schelling-Studien* 3: 25–49.

García, Marcela. 2016. "Energeia vs. Entelecheia: Schelling vs. Hegel on *Metaphysics Lambda*." *Revista de Filosofía* 51: 113–137.

Gardner, Sebastian. 2007. "The Limits of Naturalism and the Metaphysics of German Idealism." In *German Idealism: Contemporary Perspectives*, edited by Espen Hammer, 19–49. New York: Routledge.

Gardner, Sebastian. 2011. "Idealism and Naturalism in the Nineteenth Century." In *The Edinburgh Critical History of Nineteenth-Century Philosophy*, edited by Alison Stone, 89–110. Edinburgh: Edinburgh University Press.

Gaukroger, Stephen. 2010. *The Collapse of Mechanism and the Rise of Sensibility: Science and the Shaping of Modernity 1680–1760*. Oxford: Oxford University Press.

Ginsborg, Hannah. 1997a. "Kant on Aesthetic and Biological Purposiveness." In *Reclaiming the History of Ethics: Essays for John Rawls*, edited by Andrews Reath, Barbara Herman, and Christine Korsgaard, 329–360. Cambridge: Cambridge University Press.

Ginsborg, Hannah. 1997b. "Lawfulness Without a Law: Kant on the Free Play of Imagination and Understanding." *Philosophical Topics* 25 (1): 37–81.

Ginsborg, Hannah. 2001. "Kant on Understanding Organisms as Natural Purposes." In *Kant and the Sciences*, edited by Eric Watkins, 231–258. Oxford: Oxford University Press.

Ginsborg, Hannah. 2004. "Two Kinds of Mechanical Inexplicability in Kant and Aristotle." *Journal of the History of Philosophy* 42 (1): 33–65.

Ginsborg, Hannah. 2006a. "Kant's Biological Teleology and Its Philosophical Significance." In *A Companion to Kant*, edited by Graham Bird, 455–469. London: Blackwell.

Ginsborg, Hannah. 2006b. "Thinking the Particular as Contained Under the Universal." In *Aesthetics and Cognition in Kant's Critical Philosophy*, edited by Rebecca Kukla, 35–60. Cambridge: Cambridge University Press.

Ginsborg, Hannah. 2011. "Primitive Normativity and Skepticism about Rules." *Journal of Philosophy* 108 (5): 227–254.

Ginsborg, Hannah. 2014. "Oughts Without Intentions: A Kantian Approach to Biological Functions." In *Kant's Theory of Biology*, edited by Ina Goy and Eric Watkins, 259–274. Berlin: De Gruyter.

Goetschel, Willi. 2004. *Spinoza's Modernity: Mendelssohn, Lessing, and Heine.* Madison: University of Wisconsin Press.

Goy, Ina, and Eric Watkins, eds. 2014. *Kant's Theory of Biology*. Berlin: De Gruyter.

Greene, Murray. 1980. "Hegel's Concept of Logical Life." In *Art and Logic in Hegel's Philosophy*, edited by Warren E. Steinkraus and Kennith I. Schmitz, 121–149. Atlantic Highlands, NJ: Humanities Press.

Guyer, Paul. 1993. "Thought and Being: Hegel's Critique of Kant's Theoretical Philosophy," in *The Cambridge Companion to Hegel*, edited by Frederick Beiser, 171–210. Cambridge: Cambridge University Press.

Guyer, Paul. 2001. "Organisms and the Unity of Science." In *Kant and the Sciences*, edited by Eric Watkins, 259–281. Oxford: Oxford University Press.

Hahn, Songsuk Susan. 2007. *Contradiction in Motion: Hegel's Organic Concept of Life and Value*. Ithaca, NY: Cornell University Press.

Hance, Allen. 1998. "The Art of Nature: Hegel and the Critique of Judgment." *International Journal of Philosophical Studies* 6 (1): 37–65.

Hanna, Robert. 1986. "From an Ontological Point of View: Hegel's Critique of Common Logic. *Review of Metaphysics* 40 (2): 305–338.

Hanna, Robert. 2008. "Kantian Non-Conceptualism." *Philosophical Studies* 137 (1): 41–64.

Harrelson, Kevin J. 2009. *The Ontological Argument from Descartes to Hegel.* Amherst, NY: Humanity Books.

Harrelson, Kevin J. 2013. "Logic and Ontology in Hegel's Theory of Predication." *European Journal of Philosophy* 23 (5): 1259–1280.

Harris, Errol. 1998. "How Final Is Hegel's Rejection of Evolution?" In *Hegel and the Philosophy of Nature*, edited by Stephen Houlgate, 189–208. Albany: SUNY Press.

Harris, H. S. 1977. "Introduction to the Difference Essay." In G. W. F. Hegel, *The Difference Between Fichte's and Schelling's System of Philosophy*, translated and edited by H. S. Harris and Walter Cerf. Albany: SUNY Press.

Hegel, G. W. F. 1969. *Science of Logic*. Translated by A. V. Miller. Amherst, NY: Humanity Books.

Hegel, G. W. F. 1977. *The Phenomenology of Spirit*. Translated by A. V. Miller. Oxford: Oxford University Press.

Henrich, Dieter. 1983. "Fichte's Original Insight." In *Contemporary German Philosophy*, vol. 1, edited by Darrel E. Christensen, 15–52. University Park: Penn State University Press.

Henrich, Dieter. 1997a. "Hegel and Hölderlin." In *The Course of Remembrance and Other Essays on Hölderlin*, edited by Eckart Förster, 119–140. Stanford, CA: Stanford University Press.

Henrich, Dieter. 1997b. "Hölderlin in Jena." In *The Course of Remembrance and Other Essays on Hölderlin*, edited by Eckart Förster, 90–118. Stanford, CA: Stanford University Press.

Henrich, Dieter. 1997c. "Hölderlin on Judgment and Being: A Study in the History of the Origins of Idealism." In *The Course of Remembrance and Other Essays on Hölderlin*, edited by Eckart Förster, 71–89. Stanford, CA: Stanford University Press.

Henrich, Dieter. 2003. *Between Kant and Hegel: Lectures on German Idealism*. Cambridge, MA: Harvard University Press.

Henrich, Dieter. 2010. "Hegels Theorie über den Zufall." In *Hegel im Kontext*, 158–187. Frankfurt am Main: Suhrkamp.

Herrmann-Sinai, Susanne. 2016. "Hegel's Metaphysics of Action." In *Hegel and Metaphysics: On Logic and Ontology in the System*, edited by Allegra de Laurentiis, 163–180. Berlin: De Gruyter.

Hodgson, Peter C. 2007. "Editorial Introduction: The Lectures on the Proofs of the Existence of God (1829)." In G. W. F. Hegel, *Lectures on the Proofs of the Existence of God*, edited by Peter C. Hodgson, 1–34. Oxford: Oxford University Press.

Hölderlin, Friedrich. 2003a. "Being Judgment Possibility (1795)." In *Classic and Romantic German Aesthetics*, edited by J. M. Bernstein, 191–192. Cambridge: Cambridge University Press.

Hölderlin, Friedrich. 2003b. "Letter to Hegel, 26 January 1795." In *Classic and Romantic German Aesthetics*, edited by J. M. Bernstein, 188–190. Cambridge: Cambridge University Press.

Honneth, Axel. 2014. *Freedom's Right*. Translated by Joseph Ganahl. New York: Columbia University Press.

Horstmann, Rolf-Peter. 1989. "Why Must There Be a Transcendental Deduction in Kant's Critique of Judgment?" In *Kant's Transcendental Deductions: The Three "Critiques" and the "Opus postumum,"* edited by Eckart Förster, 157–176. Stanford, CA: Stanford University Press.

Horstmann, Rolf-Peter. 2013. "The Problem of Purposiveness and the Objective Validity of Judgments in Kant's Theoretical Philosophy." *Washington University Jurisprudence Review* 6 (1): 81–97.

Horstmann, Rolf-Peter, and Michael John Petry, eds. 1986. *Hegels Philosophie der Natur*. Stuttgart: Klett-Cotta.

Houlgate, Stephen. 1995. "Necessity and Contingency in Hegel's *Science of Logic*." *Owl of Minerva* 27 (1): 37–49.

Houlgate, Stephen, ed. 1998. *Hegel and the Philosophy of Nature*. Albany: SUNY Press.

Houlgate, Stephen. 2000. "Substance, Causality, and the Question of Method in Hegel's Science of Logic." In *The Reception of Kant's Critical Philosophy: Fichte, Schelling, and Hegel*, edited by Sally Sedgwick, 232–252. Cambridge: Cambridge University Press.

Houlgate, Stephen. 2006. *The Opening of Hegel's Logic: From Being to Infinity*. West Lafayette, IN: Purdue University Press.

Iber, Christian. 2003. "Übergang zum Begriff. Rekonstruktion der Überführung von Substantialität, Kausalität und Wechselwirkung in die Verhältnisweise des Begriffs." In *Der Begriff als die Wahrheit: Zum Anspruch der Hegelschen "Subjectiven Logik"*, edited by Anton Friedrich Koch, Alexander Oberauer, and Konrad Utz, 49–66. Paderborn: Ferdinand Schöningh.

Ikäheimo, Heikki. 2012. "Nature in Spirit: A New Direction for Hegel-Studies and Hegelian Philosophy." *Critical Horizons* 13 (2): 149–153.

Kant, Immanuel. 1987. *Critique of Judgment*. Translated by Werner S. Pluhar. Indianapolis, IN: Hackett.

Kern, Andrea, and Christian Kietzmann, eds. 2017. *Selbstbewusstes Leben. Texte zu einer transformativen Theorie der menschlichen Subjektivität*. Berlin: Suhrkamp.

Khurana, Thomas, ed. 2013a. *The Freedom of Life*. Berlin: August Verlag.

Khurana, Thomas. 2013b. "Life and Autonomy: Forms of Self-Determination in Kant and Hegel." In *The Freedom of Life: Hegelian Perspectives*, edited by Thomas Khurana, 155–194. Berlin: August Verlag.

Khurana, Thomas. 2017. *Das Leben der Freiheit: Form und Wirklichkeit der Autonomie*. Berlin: Suhrkamp.

Knappik, Franz. 2015. "Hegel's Modal Argument against Spinozism: An Interpretation of the Chapter 'Actuality' in the *Science of Logic*." *Hegel Bulletin* 36 (1): 53–79.

Knappik, Franz. 2016. "Hegel's Essentialism: Natural Kinds and the Metaphysics of Explanation in Hegel's Theory of 'the Concept.'" *European Journal of Philosophy* 24 (4): 760–787.

Kreines, James. 2004. "Hegel's Critique of Pure Mechanism and the Philosophical Appeal of the *Logic* Project." *European Journal of Philosophy* 12 (1): 38–74.

Kreines, James. 2006. "Hegel's Metaphysics: Changing the Debate." *Philosophy Compass* 1 (5): 466–480.

Kreines, James. 2008a. "The Logic of Life: Hegel's Philosophical Defense of Teleological Explanation of Living Beings." In *The Cambridge Companion to Hegel and Nineteenth-Century Philosophy*, edited by Frederick C. Beiser, 344–377. Cambridge: Cambridge University Press.

Kreines, James. 2008b. "Metaphysics without Pre-Critical Monism: Hegel on Lower-Level Natural Kinds and the Structure of Reality," *Hegel Bulletin* 57/58: 48–70.

Kreines, James. 2015. *Reason in the World: Hegel's Metaphysics and Its Philosophical Appeal*. Oxford: Oxford University Press.

Lampert, Jay. 2005. "Hegel on Contingency, or, Fluidity and Multiplicity." *Hegel Bulletin* 26 (1–2): 74–82.

Larson, James. 1979. "Vital Forces: Regulative Principles or Constitutive Agents? A Strategy in German Physiology, 1786–1802." *Isis* 70 (2): 235–249.

Lauer, Quentin. 1982. *Hegel's Concept of God*. Albany: SUNY Press.

Lécrivain, André. 2000. "Actuality and Objectivity in Hegel's Philosophy." *The Philosophical Forum* 31 (3/4): 328–348.

Lenoir, Timothy. 1980. "Kant, Blumenbach, and Vital Materialism in German Biology." *Isis* 71 (1): 77–108.

Lenoir, Timothy. 1982. *The Strategy of Life: Teleology and Mechanics in Nineteenth-Century German Biology*. Chicago: University of Chicago Press.

Longuenesse, Béatrice. 1998. *Kant and the Capacity to Judge: Sensibility and Discursivity in the Transcendental Analytic of the "Critique of Pure Reason."* Princeton, NJ: Princeton University Press.

Longuenesse, Béatrice. 2007. *Hegel's Critique of Metaphysics*. Cambridge: Cambridge University Press.

Machery, Pierre. 2011. *Hegel or Spinoza*. Translated by Susan M. Ruddick. Minneapolis: University of Minnesota Press.

Makkreel, Rudolph. 1991. "Regulative and Reflective Uses of Purposiveness in Kant." *The Southern Journal of Philosophy* 30 (Suppl.): 49–63.

Malabou, Catherine. 2005. *The Future of Hegel: Plasticity, Temporality, and Dialectic*. Translated by Lisabeth During. New York: Routledge.

Marcuse, Herbert. 1987. *Hegel's Ontology and the Theory of Historicity*. Translated by Seyla Benhabib. Cambridge, MA: MIT Press.

Martin, Christian. 2016. "Hegel on Judgments and Posits." *Hegel Bulletin* 37 (1): 53–80.

Martin, Wayne. 1997. *Idealism and Objectivity: Understanding Fichte's Jena Project*. Stanford, CA: Stanford University Press.

Martin, Wayne. 2007. "In Defense of Bad Infinity: A Fichtean Response to Hegel's *Differenzschrift*." *Bulletin of the Hegel Society of Great Britain* 55: 168–187.

Matherne, Samantha. 2014. "Kant and the Art of Schematism." *Kantian Review* 19 (2): 181–205.

McDowell, John. 1996. *Mind and World*. Cambridge, MA: Harvard University Press.

McDowell, John. 1998a. "Some Issues in Aristotle's Moral Psychology." In *Mind, Value, and Reality*, 23–49. Cambridge, MA: Harvard University Press.

McDowell, John. 1998b. "Two Sorts of Naturalism." In *Mind, Value, and Reality*, 167–197. Cambridge, MA: Harvard University Press.

McDowell, John. 1998c. "Virtue and Reason." In *Mind, Value, and Reality*, 50–73. Cambridge, MA: Harvard University Press.

McDowell, John. 2009. "The Logical Form of an Intuition." In *Having the World in View*, 23–43. Cambridge, MA: Harvard University Press.

McLaughlin, Peter. 1990. *Kant's Critique of Teleology in Biological Explanation: Antinomy and Teleology*. Lewiston, NY: Edwin Mellon Press.

McLaughlin, Peter. 2014. "Mechanical Explanation in the 'Critique of the Teleological Power of Judgment.'" In *Kant's Theory of Biology*, edited by Ina Goy and Eric Watkins, 149–166. Berlin: De Gruyter.

Melamed, Yitzhak. 2010. "Acosmism or Weak Individuals? Hegel, Spinoza, and the Reality of the Finite." *Journal of the History of Philosophy* 48 (1): 77–92.

Menke, Christoph. 2006. "Spirit and Life: Towards a Genealogical Critique of Phenomenology." *Graduate Faculty Philosophy Journal* 27 (2): 159–186.

Mensch, Jennifer. 2013. *Kant's Organicism: Epigenesis and the Development of Critical Philosophy*. Chicago: University of Chicago Press.

Moyar, Dean. 2011. *Hegel's Conscience*. Oxford: Oxford University Press.

Moyar, Dean. 2018. "Die Lehre vom Begriff. Zweiter Abschnitt. Die Objektivität." In *Kommentar zu Hegels Wissenschaft der Logik*, edited by Michael Quante and Nadine Mooren, 559–650. Hamburg: Felix Meiner Verlag.

Nachtomy, Ohad, and Justin E. H. Smith. 2014. "Introduction." In *The Life Sciences in Early Modern Philosophy*, edited by Ohad Nachtomy and Justin E. H. Smith, 1–7. Oxford: Oxford University Press.

Neiman, Susan. 1994. *The Unity of Reason: Rereading Kant*. Oxford: Oxford University Press.

Neuhouser, Frederick. 1990. *Fichte's Theory of Subjectivity*. Cambridge: Cambridge University Press.

Neuhouser, Frederick. 2000. *Foundations of Hegel's Social Theory: Actualizing Freedom*. Cambridge, MA: Harvard University Press.

Neuhouser, Frederick. 2013. "Hegel on Life, Freedom, and Social Pathology." In *Freiheit: Stuttgarter Hegel-Kongress 2011*, edited by Gunnar Hindrichs and Axel Honneth, 681–700. Frankfurt am Main: Klostermann.

Newlands, Samuel. 2011. "Hegel's Idealist Reading of Spinoza," *Philosophy Compass* 6 (2): 100–108.

Ng, Karen. 2009. "Hegel's Logic of Actuality." *Review of Metaphysics* 63 (1): 139–172.

Ng, Karen. 2013. "Life, Self-Consciousness, Negativity: Understanding Hegel's Speculative Identity Thesis." In *The Freedom of Life: Hegelian Perspectives*, edited by Thomas Khurana, 33–67. Berlin: August Verlag.

Ng, Karen. 2017. "From Actuality to Concept in Hegel's Logic." In *The Oxford Handbook of Hegel*, edited by Dean Moyar, 269–290. Oxford: Oxford University Press.

Ng, Karen. 2018a. "Life and Mind in Hegel's *Logic* and Subjective Spirit." *Hegel Bulletin* 39 (1): 22–44.

Ng, Karen. 2018b. Review of *Reason in the World: Hegel's Metaphysics and Its Philosophical Appeal*, by James Kreines. *The Philosophical Review* 127 (3): 403–408.

Ng, Karen. 2019. "Life and the Space of Reasons: On Hegel's Subjective Logic." *Hegel Bulletin* 40 (1): 121–142.

Ng, Karen. Forthcoming. "Life (Leben)." In *The Cambridge Kant Lexicon*, edited by Julian Wuerth. Cambridge: Cambridge University Press.

Novakovic, Andreja. 2017. *Hegel on Second Nature in Ethical Life*. Cambridge: Cambridge University Press.

Nuzzo, Angelica. 1995. "Zur logischen Bestimmung des ontologischen Gottesbeweises: Bemerkungen zum Begriff der Existenz im Anschluß an Hegel." *Hegel-Studien* 30: 105–120.

Nuzzo, Angelica. 1999. "The Idea of 'Method' in Hegel's *Science of Logic*: A Method for Finite Thinking and Absolute Reason." *Hegel Bulletin* 39/40: 1–18.

Nuzzo, Angelica. 2003. "The Truth of *Absolutes Wissen* in Hegel's *Phenomenology of Spirit*." In *Hegel's "Phenomenology of Spirit": New Critical Essays*, edited by Alfred Denker and Michael Vater, 265–294. Amherst, NY: Humanity Books.

Nuzzo, Angelica. 2005. "The End of Hegel's Logic: Absolute Idea as Absolute Method." In *Hegel's Theory of the Subject*, edited by David G. Carlson, 187–205. London: Palgrave Macmillan.

Nuzzo, Angelica. 2008. *Ideal Embodiment: Kant's Theory of Sensibility*. Bloomington: Indiana University Press.

Nuzzo, Angelica. 2011. "Thinking Being: Method in Hegel's Logic of Being." In *A Companion to Hegel*, edited by Stephen Houlgate and Michael Baur, 111–138. Oxford: Blackwell.

Papazoglou, Alexis. 2012. "Hegel and Naturalism." *Hegel Bulletin* 33 (2): 74–90.

Parkinson, G. H. R. 1977. "Hegel, Pantheism, and Spinoza." *Journal of the History of Ideas* 38 (3): 449–459.

Pendlebury, Michael. 1995. "Making Sense of Kant's Schematism." *Philosophy and Phenomenological Research* 55 (4): 777–797.

Peters, Julia. 2016. "On Naturalism in Hegel's Philosophy of Spirit." *British Journal for the History of Philosophy* 24 (1): 111–131.

Petry, Michael John, ed. 1987. *Hegel und die Naturwissenschaften*. Stuttgart: Frommann-Hozboog.

Petry, Michael John, ed. 1993. *Hegel and Newtonianism*. Dordrecht: Springer.

Pinkard, Terry. 2000. *Hegel: A Biography*. Cambridge: Cambridge University Press.

Pinkard, Terry. 2002. *German Philosophy 1760–1860: The Legacy of Idealism*. Cambridge: Cambridge University Press.

Pinkard, Terry. 2005. "Speculative Naturphilosophie and the Development of the Empirical Sciences: Hegel's Perspective." In *Continental Philosophy of Science*, edited by Gary Gutting, 19–34. London: Blackwell.

Pinkard, Terry. 2012. *Hegel's Naturalism: Mind, Nature, and the Final Ends of Life*. Oxford: Oxford University Press.

Pippin, Robert. 1976. "The Schematism and Empirical Concepts." *Kant-Studien* 67 (2): 156–171.

Pippin, Robert. 1978. "Hegel's Metaphysics and the Problem of Contradiction." *Journal of the History of Philosophy* 16 (3): 301–312.

Pippin, Robert. 1979. "Kant on Empirical Concepts." *Studies in History and Philosophy of Science* 10 (1): 1–19.

Pippin, Robert. 1989. *Hegel's Idealism: The Satisfactions of Self-Consciousness*. Cambridge: Cambridge University Press.

Pippin, Robert. 1997. "Avoiding German Idealism: Kant, Hegel, and the Reflective Judgment Problem." In *Idealism as Modernism: Hegelian Variations*, 129–153. Cambridge: Cambridge University Press.

Pippin, Robert. 2000. "Fichte's Alleged Subjective, Psychological, One-Sided Idealism." In *The Reception of Kant's Critical Philosophy: Fichte, Schelling, and Hegel*, edited by Sally Sedgwick, 147–170. Cambridge: Cambridge University Press.

Pippin, Robert. 2002. "Leaving Nature Behind: Or Two Cheers for 'Subjectivism.'" In *Reading McDowell: On Mind and World*, edited by Nicholas H. Smith, 58–75. London: Routledge.

Pippin, Robert. 2005. "Concept and Intuition: On Distinguishability and Separability." *Hegel-Studien* 39: 25–39.

Pippin, Robert. 2011. *Hegel on Self-Consciousness: Desire and Death in the "Phenomenology of Spirit."* Princeton, NJ: Princeton University Press.

Pippin, Robert. 2019. *Hegel's Realm of Shadows: Logic as Metaphysics in "The Science of Logic."* Chicago: University of Chicago Press.

Popper, Karl. 1940. "What Is Dialectic?" *Mind* 49 (196): 403–426.

Rand, Sebastian. 2007. "The Importance and Relevance of Hegel's Philosophy of Nature." *Review of Metaphysics* 60 (2): 379–400.

Rand, Sebastian. 2015. "What's Wrong with Rex? Hegel on Animal Defect and Individuality." *European Journal of Philosophy* 23 (1): 68–86.

Ravven, Heidi M. 2003. "Hegel's Epistemic Turn—or Spinoza's?" *Idealistic Studies* 33 (2–3): 95–202.

Redding, Paul. 1996. *Hegel's Hermeneutics*. Ithaca, NY: Cornell University Press.

Redding, Paul. 2007. *Analytic Philosophy and the Return of Hegelian Thought.* Cambridge: Cambridge University Press.

Redding, Paul. 2014. "The Role of Logic 'Commonly So Called' in Hegel's *Science of Logic.*" *British Journal for the History of Philosophy* 22 (2): 281–301.

Redding, Paul. 2015. "An Hegelian Solution to a Tangle of Problems Facing Brandom's Analytic Pragmatism." *British Journal for the History of Philosophy* 23 (4): 657–680.

Redding, Paul. 2017. "Findlay's Hegel: Idealism as Modal Actualism." *Critical Horizons* 18 (4): 359–377.

Redding, Paul. 2019a. "Hegel's Treatment of Predication Considered in the Light of a Logic for the Actual World." *Hegel Bulletin* 40 (1): 51–73.

Redding, Paul. 2019b. "Time and Modality in Hegel's Account of Judgment." In *The Act and Object of Judgment: Historical and Philosophical Perspectives*, edited by Brian Ball and Christoph Schuringa, 91–109. New York: Routledge.

Redding, Paul. 2020. "The Objectivity of the Actual: Hegelianism as a Metaphysics of Modal Actualism." In *Idealism, Relativism and Realism: New Essays on Objectivity Beyond the Analytic-Continental Divide*, edited by Dominik Finkelde and Paul Livingston. Berlin: De Gruyter.

Redding, Paul, and Paolo Diego Bubbio. 2014. "Hegel and the Ontological Argument for the Existence of God." *Religious Studies* 50: 465–486.

Reill, Peter Hanns. 2005. *Vitalizing Nature in the Enlightenment.* Berkeley: University of California Press.

Reinhold, Karl. 1985. "The Foundation of Philosophical Knowledge." In *Between Kant and Hegel: Texts in the Development of Post-Kantian Idealism*, translated by George di Giovanni and H. S. Harris, 51–103. Indianapolis, IN: Hackett.

Richards, Robert J. 2000. "Kant and Blumenbach on the *Bildungstrieb*: A Historical Misunderstanding." *Studies in History and Philosophy of Biological and Biomedical Sciences* 31 (1): 11–32.

Richards, Robert J. 2002. *The Romantic Conception of Life: Science and Philosophy in the Age of Goethe.* Chicago: University of Chicago Press.

Rometsch, Jens. 2013. "What Does Life Mean for Knowledge? A Reflection on Hegel's *Science of Logic.*" *Revue Philosophique de Louvain* 111 (2): 335–359.

Schelling, F. W. J. 1980. "New Deduction of Natural Right." In *The Unconditional in Human Knowledge: Four Early Essays (1794–1796)*, translated by Fritz Marti, 221–247. Lewisburg, PA: Bucknell University Press.

Schelling, F. W. J. 1994. *On the History of Modern Philosophy.* Translated by Andrew Bowie. Cambridge: Cambridge University Press.

Schelling, F. W. J. 2010. "On the World Soul." Translated by Iain Hamilton Grant. *Collapse* 6: 58–95.

Schick, Friedrike. 2003. "Begriff und Mangel des formellen Schliessens: Hegels Kritik des Verstandesschlusses." In *Der Begriff als die Wahrheit: Zum Anspruch der Hegelschen "Subjektiven Logik,"* edited by Anton Friedrich Koch, Alexander Oberauer, and Konrad Utz, 85–100. Paderborn: Ferdinand Schöningh.

Schmusli, Efraim. 1970. "Hegel's Interpretation of Spinoza's Concept of Substance." *International Journal for Philosophy of Religion* 1 (3): 176–191.

Schrader, George. 1957/1958. "Kant's Theory of Concepts." *Kant-Studien* 49: 264–278.

Schulting, Dennis, ed. 2016. *Kantian Nonconceptualism.* New York: Palgrave Macmillan.

Sedgwick, Sally. 2012. *Hegel's Critique of Kant: From Dichotomy to Identity.* Oxford: Oxford University Press.

Sell, Annette. 2006. "Leben." In *Hegel-Lexicon*, edited by Paul Cobben, Paul Cruysberghs, Peter Jonkers, and Lu De Vos, 301–305. Darmstadt: Wissenschaftliche Buchgesellschaft.

Sell, Annette. 2013. *Der lebendige Begriff. Leben und Logik bei G.W.F. Hegel.* Freiburg: Verlag Karl Alber.

Sellars, Wilfrid. 1997. *Empiricism and the Philosophy of Mind.* Cambridge, MA: Harvard University Press.

Siep, Ludwig. 2014. *Hegel's Phenomenology of Spirit.* Translated by Daniel Smyth. Cambridge: Cambridge University Press.

Sloan, Phillip R. 2002. "Preforming the Categories: Eighteenth-Century Generation Theory and the Biological Roots of Kant's A Priori." *Journal of the History of Philosophy* 40 (2): 229–253.

Smith, Justin E. 2011. *Divine Machines: Leibniz and the Sciences of Life.* Princeton, NJ: Princeton University Press.

Spinoza, Benedict de. 1996. *Ethics.* Edited and Translated by Edwin Curley. London: Penguin Books.

Stern, Robert. 1990. *Hegel, Kant and the Structure of the Object.* New York: Routledge.

Stern, Robert. 2008. "Hegel's Idealism." In *The Cambridge Companion to Hegel and Nineteenth-Century Philosophy*, edited by Frederick C. Beiser, 135–174. Cambridge: Cambridge University Press.

Stern, Robert. 2009. *Hegelian Metaphysics.* Oxford: Oxford University Press.

Stone, Alison. 2005. *Petrified Intelligence: Nature in Hegel's Philosophy.* Albany: SUNY Press.

Stone, Alison. 2013. "Hegel, Naturalism, and the Philosophy of Nature." *Hegel Bulletin* 34 (1): 59–78.

Strawson, P. F. 1996. *The Bounds of Sense: An Essay on Kant's "Critique of Pure Reason."* London: Routledge.

Testa, Italo. 2013. "Hegel's Naturalism or Soul and Body in the Encyclopaedia." In *Essays on Hegel's "Philosophy of Subjective Spirit,"* edited by David S. Stern, 19–36. Albany: SUNY Press.

Thompson, Evan. 2007. *Mind in Life: Biology, Phenomenology, and the Sciences of Mind.* Cambridge, MA: Harvard University Press.

Thompson, Michael. 2004. "Apprehending Human Form." In *Modern Moral Philosophy*, edited by A. O'Hear, 47–74. Cambridge: Cambridge University Press.

Thompson, Michael. 2008. *Life and Action: Elementary Structures of Practice and Practical Thought.* Cambridge, MA: Harvard University Press.

Walsh. W. H. 1957. "Schematism." *Kant-Studien* 49: 95–106.

Watkins, Eric. 2001. *Kant and the Sciences.* Oxford: Oxford University Press.

Watkins, Eric. 2005. *Kant and the Metaphysics of Causality.* Cambridge: Cambridge University Press.

Westphal, Kenneth. 1989. *Hegel's Epistemological Realism.* Dordrecht: Kluwer.

Westphal, Kenneth. 2003. *Hegel's Epistemology.* Indianapolis, IN: Hackett.

Williams, Robert. 2017. *Hegel on the Proofs and the Personhood of God.* Oxford: Oxford University Press.

Wolff, Michael. 1999. "On Hegel's Doctrine of Contradiction." *Owl of Minerva* 31 (1): 1–22.

Wood, Allen W. 1990. *Hegel's Ethical Thought.* Cambridge: Cambridge University Press.

Wood, Allen W. 2006. "Fichte's Intersubjective I." *Inquiry* 49 (1): 62–79.

Wood, Allen W. 2016. *Fichte's Ethical Thought.* Oxford: Oxford University Press.

Wretzel, Joshua. 2018. "Organic Imagination as Intuitive Intellect: Self-Knowledge and Self-Constitution in Hegel's Early Critique of Kant." *European Journal of Philosophy*. Online Preview. doi: 10.1111/ejop.12328.

Yeomans, Christopher. 2012. *Freedom and Reflection: Hegel and the Logic of Agency*. Oxford: Oxford University Press.

Zambrana, Rocío. 2015. *Hegel's Theory of Intelligibility*. Chicago: University of Chicago Press.

Zammito, John H. 1992. *The Genesis of Kant's "Critique of Judgment."* Chicago: University of Chicago Press.

Zammito, John H. 2006. "Teleology Then and Now: The Question of Kant's Relevance for Contemporary Controversies over Function in Biology." *Studies in History and Philosophy of Science* 37 (4): 748–770.

Zammito, John H. 2012. "The Lenoir Thesis Revisited: Blumenbach and Kant." *Studies in History and Philosophy of Biological and Biomedical Sciences* 43 (1): 120–132.

Zuckert, Rachel. 2007. *Kant on Beauty and Biology: An Interpretation of the Critique of Judgment*. Cambridge: Cambridge University Press.

Index

For the benefit of digital users, indexed terms that span two pages (e.g., 52–53) may, on occasion, appear on only one of those pages.

9 780190 94767